THE ZONDERVAN 2020
PASTOR'S
ANNUAL

For a *FREE* downloadable copy of the book, please
visit: https://www.zondervan.com/zpa2020.

THE ZONDERVAN 2020
PASTOR'S ANNUAL

An Idea and Resource Book

T. T. Crabtree

ZONDERVAN
REFLECTIVE

ZONDERVAN REFLECTIVE

The Zondervan 2020 Pastor's Annual
Copyright © 1979, 1999, 2019 by Zondervan

ISBN 978-0-310-53665-9 (softcover)

ISBN 978-0-310-09963-5 (ebook)

Requests for information should be addressed to:
Zondervan, *3900 Sparks Dr. SE, Grand Rapids, Michigan 49546*

Much of the contents of this book was previously published in *The Zondervan 2000 Pastor's Annual.*

Cover design: Angela Grit
Cover photo: © Chaleow Ngamdee/Shutterstock
Interior design: Sue Vandenberg Koppenol

Printed in the United States of America

19 20 21 22 23 24 25 26 27 28 29 /LSC/ 15 14 13 12 11 10 9 8 7 6 5 4 3 2 1

CONTENTS

Mar 25 Wed   The Gift of Performing Miracles *(1 Cor. 12:10)*
Mar 29 Sun AM   The Cross and Discipleship *(Matt. 16:24–25)*
Mar 29 Sun PM   Hindrances to Spiritual Growth *(1 Peter 2:2)*
Apr 1   Wed   The Gift of Healing *(1 Cor. 12:9)*
Apr 5   Sun AM   When Death Brings Life *(John 12:32–33)*
Apr 5   Sun PM   Understanding the Cross *(Matt. 16:21)*
Apr 8   Wed   The Gift of Helping *(1 Cor. 12:28)*
Apr 12 Sun AM   The Resurrection of Christ and Our Great
                   Salvation *(Heb. 7:24–25)*
Apr 12 Sun PM   Understanding Our Mission *(John 20:21)*
Apr 15 Wed   The Gift of Administration *(1 Cor. 12:28)*
Apr 19 Sun AM   The Church—The Family of God *(Eph. 2:19)*
Apr 19 Sun PM   Recognizing His Identity *(Matt. 21:10)*
Apr 22 Wed   The Gift of Encouraging *(Rom. 12:8)*
Apr 26 Sun AM   The Church—The Body of Christ *(Rom. 12:4–5)*
Apr 26 Sun PM   Realizing the Resurrection *(Luke 24:15–16, 30–31)*
Apr 29 Wed   The Gift of Giving *(Rom. 12:8)*
May 3   Sun AM   The Church—The Community of the Holy
                   Spirit *(John 14:26)*
May 3   Sun PM   Christ—God's Messenger *(Heb. 1:1–2)*
May 6   Wed   The Gift of Mercy *(Rom. 12:8)*
May 10 Sun AM   Mary: A Model for Modern Mothers *(Luke 1:28)*
May 10 Sun PM   Christ—The Humiliated One *(Heb. 2:9)*
May 13 Wed   The Gift of Evangelism *(Eph. 4:11)*
May 17 Sun AM   What Is a Born-Again Christian? *(John 3:3)*
May 17 Sun PM   Christ—The Apostle and High Priest *(Heb. 3:6)*
May 20 Wed   The Gift of Preaching *(Eph. 4:11)*
May 24 Sun AM   The Great Salvation That Creates Fellowship
                   (Mark 6:1–3)
May 24 Sun PM   Christ—The Believer's Rest *(Heb. 4:16)*
May 27 Wed   The Gift of Wisdom *(1 Cor. 12:8)*
May 31 Sun AM   Guess Who's Coming to Dinner *(Rev. 3:20)*
May 31 Sun PM   Spiritual Discernment Offered *(Heb. 5:8–9)*
Jun 3   Wed   The Gift of Knowledge *(1 Cor. 12:8)*
Jun 7   Sun AM   Let Us Encourage One Another *(Heb. 10:24)*
Jun 7   Sun PM   Christ's Challenge—Perfection *(Heb. 6:1–3)*
Jun 10 Wed   The Gift of Faith *(1 Cor. 12:9)*
Jun 14 Sun AM   The Church in Your House *(Philem. 1–3)*
Jun 14 Sun PM   Christ—The Superior High Priest *(Heb. 7:24–25)*
Jun 17 Wed   The Gift of Tongues *(1 Cor. 12:10)*
Jun 21 Sun AM   The Forgotten Father *(Matt. 1:24)*
Jun 21 Sun PM   Christ—Mediator of a Better Covenant *(Heb. 8:1–2)*
Jun 24 Wed   The Gift of Tongues (continued) *(1 Cor. 12:10)*
Jun 28 Sun AM   Forms of Freedom *(Gal. 5:1, 13)*

Oct 11 Sun AM God's Spirit Makes the Difference (*Zech. 4:6*)
Oct 11 Sun PM Peter on the Mount of Transfiguration (*Matt. 17:5*)
Oct 14 Wed   The God Who Introduces Himself (*Ex. 3:14*)
Oct 18 Sun AM Obey God Because You Love Him (*Mal. 2:10*)
Oct 18 Sun PM Peter's Lesson on Humility (*Matt. 18:4*)
Oct 21 Wed   The Possibility of Positive Thinking (*Ex. 3:11*)
Oct 25 Sun AM Doing God's Will, Not Ours (*Jonah 1:3*)
Oct 25 Sun PM Peter's Lesson on Forgiveness (*Matt. 18:21–22*)
Oct 28 Wed   When Discouragement Comes (*Ex. 5:22–23*)
Nov 1   Sun AM The Stewardship of Time (*Eph. 5:15–16*)
Nov 1   Sun PM Peter in the Upper Room (*John 13:16–17*)
Nov 4   Wed   When God Brings Reassurance (*Ex. 6:2*)
Nov 8   Sun AM The Stewardship of Talents (*Matt. 25:15*)
Nov 8   Sun PM Peter in Gethsemane (*Matt. 26:40–41*)
Nov 11 Wed   The Power to Say No (*Ex. 8:25*)
Nov 15 Sun AM The Stewardship of the Body (*1 Cor. 6:19–20*)
Nov 15 Sun PM Peter Denies His Lord (*John 18:27*)
Nov 18 Wed   A Night to Be Remembered (*Ex. 12:26–27*)
Nov 22 Sun AM The Stewardship of Thanksgiving (*Ps. 118:1*)
Nov 22 Sun PM Peter's Restoration (*Luke 22:31–32*)
Nov 25 Wed   He Leadeth Me—O Blessed Thought! (*Ex. 13:18, 21*)
Nov 29 Sun AM The Stewardship of Money (*1 Tim. 6:10*)
Nov 29 Sun PM Misplaced Concern (*John 21:20–22*)
Dec 2   Wed   The Helper for Human Situations (*Ex. 15:26*)
Dec 6   Sun AM Glory to God in the Highest (*Luke 2:9, 13*)
Dec 6   Sun PM Reverence for God (*Ex. 3:4–5*)
Dec 9   Wed   Sign Your Contract with God (*Ex. 19:5–6*)
Dec 13 Sun AM And on Earth Peace (*Luke 2:13–14*)
Dec 13 Sun PM A Hymn of Praise (*Ex. 15:2*)
Dec 16 Wed   God of Grace and God of Glory (*Ex. 33:18*)
Dec 20 Sun AM Good News of Great Joy (*Luke 2:10*)
Dec 20 Sun PM The Ten Commandments for Today (*Ex. 34:28*)
Dec 23 Wed   A Significant Symbol—The Tabernacle (*Ex. 29:43–46*)
Dec 27 Sun AM Let Us Thank God and Take Courage (*Acts 28:15*)
Dec 27 Sun PM The Joy of Restored Relationships (*Ex. 34:10*)
Dec 30 Wed   Looking Backward and Looking Forward (*2 Peter 1:2*)

MISCELLANEOUS HELPS

Messages on the Lord's Supper

The Savior, Our Daily Bread (*John 6:32–35*)
The Tableau of the Table (*John 13:21*)
A Time for Beginning (*Luke 22:17–20*)

CONTRIBUTING AUTHORS

Morris Ashcraft	AM	April 19, 26
		May 3
Harold T. Bryson	PM	September 30
		October 7, 14, 21, 28
		November 4, 11, 18, 25
		December 2, 9, 13, 16, 20, 23, 27
Hiram Campbell	PM	May 3, 10, 17, 24, 31
		June 7, 14, 21, 28
		July 5, 12, 19, 26
James E. Carter	PM	January 1, 8, 15, 22, 29
T. T. Crabtree		All messages besides those attributed
		to others
David R. Grant	PM	February 5, 12, 19, 26
		March 4, 11, 18, 25
		April 1, 8, 15, 22, 29
		May 6, 13, 20, 27
		June 3, 10, 17, 24
James G. Harris	AM	June 21
James F. Heaton	PM	August 2, 9, 16, 23, 30
		September 6, 13, 20, 27
		October 4, 11, 18, 25
		November 1, 8, 15, 22, 29
W. T. Holland	AM	November 1, 8, 15, 22, 29
	PM	April 5, 12, 19, 26
Joe L. Ingram	AM	July 5, 12, 19, 26
David L. Jenkins	AM	March 1, 15, 22, 29
		April 5
	PM	July 1, 8, 15, 22, 29
		August 5, 12, 19, 26
		September 2, 9, 16, 23
Howard S. Kalb	PM	December 6
Jerold McBride	AM	January 5, 12, 19, 26
		February 2, 9, 16, 23
G. Hugh Wamble	AM	June 28
Fred M. Wood	AM	August 2, 9, 16, 23, 30
		September 6, 13, 20, 27
		October 4, 11, 18, 25

PREFACE

Favorable comments from ministers who serve in many different types of churches suggest that the *Pastor's Annual* provides valuable assistance to many busy pastors as they seek to improve the quality, freshness, and variety of their pulpit ministry. To be of service to fellow pastors in their continuing quest to obey our Lord's command to Peter, "Feed my sheep," is a calling to which I respond with gratitude.

I pray that this issue of the *Pastor's Annual* will be blessed by our Lord in helping each pastor to plan and produce a preaching program that will better meet the spiritual needs of his or her congregation.

This issue contains series of sermons by several contributing authors who have been effective contemporary preachers and successful pastors. Each author is listed with his sermons by date in the section titled "Contributing Authors." I accept responsibility for those sermons not listed there.

This issue of the *Pastor's Annual* is dedicated to the Lord with a prayer that he will bless these efforts to let the Holy Spirit lead us in preparing a planned preaching program for the year.

JANUARY

■ Sunday Mornings

"The Way to Happiness" is an excellent theme with which to launch the new year. Everyone wants to be happy, and the New Testament is our greatest authority on the subject. Jesus Christ gives us the key that will unlock the door to happiness. This key is found in the eight Beatitudes. The word translated "blessed" is sometimes translated "happy."

■ Sunday Evenings

"Experiencing the Great Salvation of God" is the suggested theme for a series of messages designed to enlarge our concepts of what God has provided for us in and through Jesus Christ. He came to do something more than give us a ticket to heaven.

■ Wednesday Evenings

We begin the new year with a series of five lessons from the fourth chapter of Paul's letter to the Philippians. The series title is "Pathway to Praise."

WEDNESDAY EVENING, JANUARY 1

Title: A Bit of Personal Advice

Text: "Whatever you have learned or received or heard from me, or seen in me—put it into practice. And the God of peace will be with you" **(Phil. 4:9 NIV).**

Scripture Reading: Philippians 4:8–9

Introduction

Advice is cheap, we have always heard. And generally we find that saying to be true. But of all the advice we receive, we usually do not expect someone to say to us, "You should try to be just like me." That, however, is the bit of personal advice Paul gave to the Philippian Christians. In his letter to the Philippians, Paul described the elements of noble living that should mark each Christian's life. Then he ended by saying that they should do the things they had seen him do. It may have been unusual advice, but it was certainly good advice.

I. A model is provided in this bit of personal advice.

Paul presented himself as a model for the Philippians to follow.

We each model our lives after someone else. In Miami, Florida, a fifteen-year-old boy was tried for the murder of an eighty-three-year-old neighbor woman. In his defense, the plea of insanity due to intoxication by television violence was entered. His defense lawyers pointed out that he was captivated by crime mystery shows on television. Obviously the boy had some problems, one of which was the television characters after whom he had chosen to pattern his life. Over the years, we have seen others imitate the lives of fictional characters.

Note the things Paul indicated we are to model after him:

A. *Things we have learned.* Among the things that people had learned from Paul were Jesus' teachings. An instructor was needed to teach Christian living, so Paul supplied this instruction.

B. *Things we have received.* The new Christians at Philippi also received a body of Christian belief, or doctrine, through Paul. Many times Paul defended what he called "his gospel," which was the gospel of God's grace. We, too, have received the common doctrines of Christian grace.

 Paul's epistles normally contain both a doctrinal and a practical section. These two areas are outlined by the verbs "learn" and "receive." Instruction in the doctrines of grace and in Christian living are two things we should model.

C. *Things we have heard and seen.* The second pair of verbs concerns things that we have heard and seen in Paul's life—characteristics we have observed.

One prominent pastor was irate when his airplane was late and he missed an important meeting at his church. He strongly expressed his anger to the flight attendants. One of them went to his church the next Sunday to see how anyone who could become so angry could also preach Christ. Fortunately, she found Christ in that service, but she easily could have been turned away by what she observed in a Christian.

II. Motivation is provided in this bit of personal advice.

Paul said that "the God of peace will be with you." If we pattern our lives after things we have learned, received, heard, and seen, we will know that the God of peace is part of our lives. This is not just a theory; it is a fact. Paul could cite particular instances when the God of peace had been with him.

A. *The God of peace provides for our needs.*

B. *The God of peace protects us in danger.*

Conclusion

Paul passed on to us this bit of personal advice, which grew out of personal experience. As we follow this advice, we will become stronger Christians.

SUNDAY MORNING, JANUARY 5

Title: Humility—The Way to Happiness

Text: "Blessed [happy] are the poor in spirit: for theirs is the kingdom of heaven" **(Matt. 5:3)**.

Scripture Reading: Matthew 5:1–12

Hymns: "Beneath the Cross of Jesus," Clephane
"Whiter Than Snow," Nicholson
"How Great Thou Art," Boberg

Offertory Prayer: On this first Sunday of the new year, we thank you, our heavenly Father, for life, health, family, and friends, but most of all for the gift of your Son, Jesus Christ. As we give of our increase, we also give ourselves. Our tithes and offerings are only a symbol of laying our all on the altar of our commitment to you. Open our hearts and minds to the blessed teachings of your Son. In his name we pray. Amen.

Introduction

Name eight things that would make you happy. If God said to you on this first Sunday of 2020, "Choose eight things that you feel would make your new year a happy one and I will give them to you," what would you choose?

Would you choose to be "poor in spirit"? Would you choose things such as mourning, meekness, hunger and thirst, being merciful, being pure in heart, being a peacemaker, or experiencing persecution? Do you think these eight things would make you happy? Jesus seems to think so.

Before you conclude that Jesus is wrong, consider the antithesis of these qualities: characteristics such as pride, pleasure-seeking, aggressiveness, compromising, impurity, cruelty, and hatred. You could not be happy with these characteristics, could you? Of course not! Therefore consider the eight Beatitudes as eight steps to happiness.

Humility is the way to happiness. In Matthew 5:3 when Jesus spoke of being "poor in spirit," he was referring to our recognition of both our spiritual neediness and the means that can supply our need. This poverty of spirit results in our discovery of God's kingdom. People who are "poor in spirit" do not boast of their attainments or talents because they know they have nothing that has not been given to them.

Why is humility the way to happiness?

I. Humility enables you to be honest about yourself.

When Jesus spoke of being "poor in spirit," he did not imply that being wealthy is wrong. Money can be handled in a Christian manner or in a non-Christian manner. Success and prosperity can lead a person to be self-satisfied and proud. Yet poverty can drive a person to dishonesty. Jesus did not teach that the poor are spiritually superior. Not money but "the love of money is the root of all evil" (1 Tim. 6:10).

Jesus declared that if you want to be happy, you must be aware of your spiritual poverty. No picture is more pathetic than that of a person who has a great need and is unaware of it. Do you remember Samson standing in the valley of Sorek? He was surrounded by Philistines: "But he did not know that the LORD had left him" (Judg. 16:20 NIV).

Poverty in spirit is the beginning of happiness. It is the admission that you are nothing without Christ. This admission is always followed by the Lord flooding one's life with the riches of his mercy and grace. To be "poor in spirit" is to be honest about yourself, and this is the way to happiness!

II. Humility impels you to commit your full potential to God.

William Barclay concluded that "Blessed are the poor in spirit" means blessed are those who have realized their own helplessness and who have placed their complete trust in the Lord. After you have done this, you will become detached from things and attached to God. You will commit your full potential to God's will. The boy who came to hear Jesus teach illustrates this commitment. He took all the food he had and turned it over to Jesus (John 6:9).

Once you are willing to do this, you will be amazed at what Christ can do with what you have to offer. Andrew asked what we are so often tempted to ask, "But what are they among so many?" In his own hands, the boy's lunch was hardly enough to satisfy one lad's hunger. But in Jesus' hands, the small meal became enough to feed more than five thousand people! Never underestimate what God can do with your five loaves and two fish. The moment you commit all that you have to Christ, the impossible begins to happen!

Poverty that produces happiness is poverty of spirit. Total submission to God's will is always best, and humility is the way to happiness because it impels you to commit your full potential to God's will.

III. Humility prepares you to be filled with the Holy Spirit.

No proud soul can be filled with and controlled by the Holy Spirit, for a life filled with pride has no room for him. Those who are unwilling to be controlled by the Holy Spirit are controlled by selfish ambition. Therefore the Lord said that we must become like little children before we enter the kingdom of heaven. Children depend on their parents. Because they are their parents' children, they are not really poor. As God's children, we are dependent on him. Children spend little time worrying about what they will eat, what they will wear, or where they will sleep. They simply assume that their needs will be met by their parents.

Our heavenly Father is responsible for our care. We are told to cast our cares on him because he cares for us. Jesus also said to his disciples, "Which of you fathers, if your son asks for a fish, will give him a snake instead? . . .

If you then, though you are evil, know how to give good gifts to your children, how much more will your Father in heaven give the Holy Spirit to those who ask him!" (Luke 11:11–13 NIV). The "poor in spirit" know they are poor in spirit. They know they can do and can be nothing apart from the indwelling Spirit of God. Those who find happiness through humility allow the Holy Spirit to fill them.

Humility that enables you to be honest with yourself, that impels you to commit your full potential to God, and that prepares you to be filled with the Holy Spirit is the way to happiness.

Conclusion

The first beacon of the Eddystone lighthouse off the coast of Plymouth, England, was placed there over two hundred years ago to warn ships of the dangerous reefs. Henry Winstanley, the architect who built it, was so confident of its strength that he had written on the cornerstone, "Blow, O Ye Winds! Rise, O Ocean! Break Forth, Ye Elements, and Try My Work!" Those were foolish words, for less than three years later a raging storm destroyed the lighthouse, along with Winstanley and others who were making repairs on it at the time.

Years later John Smeaton, an early leader in civil engineering, rebuilt it. He found a new site and dug deep to the solid rock. He was a sincere Christian, as the new cornerstone revealed: "Except the Lord Build the House, They Labor in Vain That Build It." For over ninety years it has stood every test—it was founded on rock!

Do you want the kingdom of heaven now? Then dig deeply and build your life on the foundation of humility, because it is the way to happiness!

SUNDAY EVENING, JANUARY 5

Title: One Day at a Time

Text: "Therefore do not worry about tomorrow, for tomorrow will worry about itself. Each day has enough trouble of its own" **(Matt. 6:34 NIV)**.

Scripture Reading: Matthew 6:31–34

Introduction

We must avoid the peril of living either in the past or in the future and totally missing the present. Instead, we must seize the potential of each present moment and each contemporary experience if we want to live life to the full and make a significant contribution with our lives. Many of us live under the crushing burden of accumulated yesterdays and fearful tomorrows. Doing so robs us of the opportunity to live fully in the present. Someone has said that there are two days that we should eliminate from our calendar: yesterday and tomorrow. We must beware lest we let yesterday or tomorrow hinder us from doing our best today.

Sir William Osler, a world-renowned doctor in the late nineteenth and early twentieth centuries, suggested that we should "live in day-tight compartments." The famous doctor made this suggestion because of the truth he found in the following statement: "Our main business is not to see what lies dimly at a distance, but to do what lies clearly at hand." These words from the pen of Thomas Carlyle helped the great doctor concentrate on the present and the temporary rather than living in the past or in the future.

In line with this thought, is a poem by the famous Indian dramatist, Kālidāsa:

> Look to this day!
> For it is life, the very life of life.
> In its brief course
> Lie all the verities and realities of your existence:
>> The bliss of growth,
>> The glory of action,
>> The splendor of achievement.
> For yesterday is but a dream
> And tomorrow is only a vision,
> But today well lived makes every yesterday a dream of happiness
> And every tomorrow a vision of hope.
> Look well, therefore, to this day!
> Such is the salutation to the dawn.
>> *(Quoted in Dale Carnegie, How to Stop Worrying and Start Living [New York: Pocket, 1948], 1.)*

Many of us put off living in the present to worry about the future. All of us have been guilty at times of embittering the present by filling our minds with regrets concerning the things that have happened in the past. William Barclay wrote:

> Nearly all the great men have been haunted by the sense of the shortness of time—and of the uncertainty of time . . . as we grow older, and as time grows ever shorter, there are certain things that we should remember.
>
> 1. We should never leave things half-finished—in case they are never finished.
> 2. We should carefully choose what we are going to do—for there is no longer time to do everything, and we should do the things which really matter.
> 3. We should never come to the end of a day with a quarrel or a breach between us and any fellow-man—for it may be that the quarrel will never be mended and the breach will never be closed.

4. We only get so much time, and when that is finished we cannot get any more.
5. None of us knows how much we are going to get.
6. If there is something to be learned, we must learn it now; for the longer we put it off, the harder it will be to learn it. (William Barclay, *Daily Celebration* [Waco, TX: Word, 1971], 14–16.)

W. Clement Stone said that "Do it now" is one of the great self-motivators. Those who have achieved success in life have learned to do it now rather than surrendering to procrastination.

I. The stewardship of time.

Time is loaned to us to be used in God's service. We cannot be too diligent in the proper use of time.

A. *Time is precious.* We cannot kill time without injuring eternity. We should snatch it, use it, and enjoy every minute of it.
B. *Time is short.*
C. *Time is passing swiftly.*
D. *Time is uncertain.* The most certain thing is the uncertainty of time.
E. *Time is irrevocable when gone.* All of our prayers cannot entreat one hour to return.
F. *Time is that for which we must give an account to our Savior.*

Aristotle Onassis had ten secrets of success, and one of these was related to time. He said, "Don't sleep too much or you'll wake up a failure. If you sleep three hours less each night for a year, you will have an extra month and a half to succeed in." If this multimillionaire would deprive himself of sleep to make money, in like manner God's children could make better use of their waking hours by rendering services of eternal significance.

II. The management of time.

We are responsible for the way we use the gift of time. Following are some suggestions for improving our stewardship of time.

A. *Begin each day with a prayer of thanksgiving.* The psalmist said, "This is the day the LORD has made; let us rejoice and be glad in it" (Ps. 118:24 NIV). If we face every new day with the psalmist's attitude, the first words from our lips likely will be a prayer of thanksgiving.
1. Thank God for the gift of life and for another day.
2. Thank God for the gift of faith that has let God come into your life.
3. Thank God for the members of your family.
4. If you are able to work, thank God for this privilege.
5. Thank God for friends.

    6. Thank God for what he is going to do in your heart and life during the day. Beginning each day with an attitude and prayer of thanksgiving will set the tone for the day. It will help you face every situation with a positive mental attitude and with the assurance that God will bring good to those who love and trust him (Rom. 8:28).

B. *Accept each day as an opportunity to be a helper.*

    1. Do something today that will enrich your life spiritually and in every other way. You help others to the degree that you help yourself into a harmonious relationship with God. Feed your soul with God's Word. Encourage yourself in the closet of prayer. Let God help you.

    2. Be a helper to your family. Courtship is a process that should be continued in marriage. Parents should seek to minister in a creative and positive manner to their children. When families earnestly seek to help one another, home life becomes better.

    3. Be a helper to others in your immediate circle. Do the best job you can for your employer. Help those with whom you have contacts and responsibilities during the day. Be something other than a parasite; become a contributor.

    4. Be a helper to those you meet on your daily journey. We can render services to strangers, be courteous while driving, be cheerful in our conversations, and compliment those who do a good job.

C. *Plan each day with your priorities in order.*

    1. In the morning, make a list of things that need to be done.

    2. Number these items in the rank of their importance.

    3. Focus on accomplishing the most important items first.

    4. Concentrate on doing one thing at a time.

D. *Schedule each day and allow for interruptions.*

    1. Some interruptions are nothing but time killers. We must pray for wisdom to deal with these.

    2. Some interruptions are divine appointments. We must recognize and seize these. Some interruptions that come to us throughout the day may provide us with the greatest opportunities of the day.

Conclusion

Jesus recognized and responded to the urgency of the present. He avoided the peril of living in yesterday or tomorrow. He said, "As long as it is day, we must do the works of him who sent me. Night is coming, when no one can work" (John 9:4 NIV). An anonymous author has said it powerfully:

> Now
> If you have hard work to do,
>   Do it now.

Today the skies are clear and blue,
Tomorrow clouds may come in view,
Yesterday is not for you;
    Do it now.

If you have a song to sing,
    Sing it now.
Let the notes of gladness ring,
Clear as song of bird in spring,
Let every day some music bring;
    Sing it now.

If you have kind words to say,
    Say them now.
Tomorrow may not come your way,
Do a kindness while you may,
Loved ones will not always stay;
    Say them now.

    If you have a smile to show,
    Show it now.
Make hearts happy, roses grow,
Let the friends around you know
The love you have before they go;
    Show it now.

If you need to make a decision to respond to the lordship of Jesus Christ, do it now. If you need to make a decision about the full consecration of your life to God's service, do it now. Procrastination is not only the thief of time; it is the thief of souls. The road of "later" leads to the city of "never." Do it now, for now is the acceptable time.

WEDNESDAY EVENING, JANUARY 8

Title: The Secret of Happiness

Text: "I rejoiced greatly in the Lord that at last you have renewed your concern for me. Indeed, you were concerned, but you had no opportunity to show it. I am not saying this because I am in need, for I have learned to be content whatever the circumstances. I know what it is to be in need, and I know what it is to have plenty. I have learned the secret of being content in any and every situation, whether well fed or hungry, whether living in plenty or in want. I can do all this through him who gives me strength" **(Phil. 4:10–13 NIV)**.

Scripture Reading: Philippians 4:10–13

Introduction

Paul assured those who were concerned about him and active in his care that he had learned the secret of happiness. In our day, many people are desperately searching for happiness. All kinds of contrived pleasures and activities are followed in an effort to find the secret of happiness. But Paul said that happiness is found in Christ.

In today's Scripture text, Paul reiterated the purpose of his letter to the Philippians. He thanked the people for the gift they had sent him. When he said, "You have renewed your concern for me," he was using a word for a tree that puts out shoots and branches in the spring. Paul wanted them to know that he was not complaining because of any want or need on his part; rather, he was appreciative of help when they could give it.

As the New International Version translates verse 12, Paul said, "I have learned the secret of being content." Having learned the secret of happiness, he passed it on to us.

I. Mastery of the extremes of life is a secret of happiness.

Paul had learned to master the extremes of life. Whether he had plenty or little, whether he was full or hungry, he had attained contentment that comes from Christ in whatever circumstances he found himself.

The word *happiness* is derived from *hap*, a three-letter Scandinavian word that means "luck" or "fortune." It refers to favorable things that happen to us. Most people think their happiness depends on what happens to them. Paul corrected this assumption by expressing that happiness does not depend on circumstances. Instead, it depends on how we learn to master the extremes of life, or how we cope with times when we have much or little.

In *The Adequate Man*, Paul S. Rees told of a Chicago lawyer named Horatio Spafford who, after the great Chicago fire in 1871, made arrangements for his family to travel to Europe. Mrs. Spafford and their four daughters were to go on ahead, and Mr. Spafford would join them later.

The *Ville du Havre*, the ship on which the wife and four daughters sailed, was rammed by another vessel halfway across the Atlantic and was cut in two. In the confusion that followed, Mrs. Spafford saw all four of her girls swept away to their deaths. A falling mast knocked her unconscious, and a wave deposited her body on a piece of wreckage where she later regained consciousness.

When she and the other survivors arrived in Cardiff, Wales, Mrs. Spafford cabled two words to her husband: "Saved alone." Taking the earliest ship he could find, Mr. Spafford went to his wife. It was when his ship reached the approximate spot where the *Ville du Havre* sank that God gave him the inspiration, insight, and courage to write:

> *When peace like a river attendeth my way,*
> *When sorrows like sea billows roll,*

Whatever my lot, Thou hast taught me to say,
"It is well, it is well with my soul."

II. Measurement of the source of power is a secret of happiness.

When Paul wrote Philippians 4:13, he actually revealed his secret of happiness. He had the source of power that enabled him to meet and master any situation. Often when the electricity has gone off, people realize that they have everything they need for power—the wiring, transformers, bulbs, appliances, and electronics—everything except the source of power itself. Paul shared with us the source of power: Jesus Christ. Jesus' power is inexhaustible. He constantly pours strength into those who trust him.

Conclusion

The secret of happiness is not found in what happens *to* us. It is found in what has happened *in* us—the renewal of our lives through faith in Christ. When we allow Jesus to daily replenish us, we have endless power pumping into our lives.

SUNDAY MORNING, JANUARY 12

Title: Sorrow—The Way to Happiness

Text: "Blessed are they that mourn: for they shall be comforted" **(Matt. 5:4)**.

Scripture Reading: Matthew 5:1–4; 2 Corinthians 7:10

Hymns: "God Will Take Care of You," Martin
      "Moment by Moment," Whittle
      "Surely Goodness and Mercy," Peterson

Offertory Prayer: It is good to be alive and in your house, dear Lord. These gifts we offer are a token of our love for you. Were the whole realm of nature ours, even that would be a present far too small. So we offer what we have and thank you for accepting our gifts and ourselves. In Christ's name we pray. Amen.

Introduction

The way to happiness is outlined in the first twelve verses of Matthew 5. Last Sunday we noted that the word translated "blessed" in the Beatitudes may also be translated "happy." In the first beatitude, Jesus said the initial step toward happiness is humility—being "poor in spirit."

We find a very strange statement in the second beatitude: "Blessed are they that mourn: for they shall be comforted."

What would you think of a person who said to a crying child, "Why are you so happy?" You probably would conclude that the person was either crazy or cruel! The response to Christ's remark that a mourning person is happy has been similar. The statement does not seem to add up.

23

It is here that we need to remind ourselves that the Beatitudes were not spoken to unbelievers but to the disciples. Remember verse 1? "And seeing the multitudes, he went up into a mountain: and when he was set, his disciples came unto him." What Jesus said regarding the way to happiness is directed to Christians alone, those who are capable of experiencing life at its highest level of happiness.

"Blessed [happy] are they that mourn." Does this refer to persons who wander around with a dismal countenance, downcast persons whom you dread to see because they are always bearers of some woeful news? Not at all! As J. B. Phillips translates this verse, Jesus said, "How happy are those who know what sorrow means, for they will be given courage and comfort!"

There are two kinds of sorrow, however. One leads to happiness and the other to misery. One carries with it a blessing and the other none at all. One leads to life and the other to death. Paul distinguished between the two in 2 Corinthians 7:8–10. One he called "godly sorrow" and the other he called "worldly sorrow." He explained, "Godly sorrow brings repentance that leads to salvation and leaves no regret, but worldly sorrow brings death" (v. 10 NIV). To understand this beatitude and experience the happiness it promises, we need to recognize sorrow that leads to misery and sorrow that leads to happiness.

I. Sorrow that leads to misery.

When Jesus said, "Blessed are they that mourn," he meant a different sort of mourning than what most people experience. Too often our sorrow is the wrong kind. It is what Paul called "worldly sorrow [that] brings death" (2 Cor. 7:10 NIV).

But exactly what type of sorrow leads to misery?

A. *Sorrow because of getting caught.* Remember, "many sorrows shall be to the wicked" (Ps. 32:10). And one of their many sorrows is that of getting caught. The thief who is arrested, the drug pusher who is apprehended, the student who cheats, or the husband or wife who is unfaithful may be sorry to have been caught, but this sorrow has no blessing because it is void of repentance. Our prisons house many who are sorry they were caught but who are not sorry for their sin. If given another chance, they would do the same thing again, as is evidenced by the alarming number of repeat offenders. Theirs is a sorrow that leads not to happiness but to misery.

B. *Sorrow because of failing in a sinful scheme.* The Bible warns us that "whoever digs a hole and scoops it out falls into the pit they have made" (Ps. 7:15 NIV), and that "[God] catches the wise in their craftiness" (1 Cor. 3:19 NIV). For example, a man crashed his car and its frame is bent. He has the body repaired and painted, and then attempts to sell it without telling the prospective buyer the whole truth. Liking the car, the buyer takes it for a test drive and has a mechanic friend

24

look it over. To the mechanic's trained eye, the bent frame is obvious. The buyer returns the damaged vehicle, and the sale falls through. The owner is sorry but only because he failed in his scheme to deceive another. This same type of sorrow may result from failure to destroy another's reputation or failure to be accepted as more than we know ourselves to be.

C. *Sorrow because of the consequences suffered.* Sorrow for consequences rather than for sin leads to misery. Simon the sorcerer thought Peter and John had magic more powerful than any he knew about, so he offered them money and said, "'Give me also this ability so that everyone on whom I lay my hands may receive the Holy Spirit.' Peter answered: 'May your money perish with you, because you thought you could buy the gift of God with money! You have no part or share in this ministry, because your heart is not right before God. Repent of this wickedness and pray to the Lord in the hope that he may forgive you for having such a thought in your heart. For I see that you are full of bitterness and captive to sin.' Then Simon answered, 'Pray to the Lord for me so that nothing you have said may happen to me'" (Acts 8:19–24 NIV). Simon did not seem to be sorry for his sin but rather asked Peter to pray so its consequences might be removed.

There is sorrow that leads to misery because of the consequence suffered. But the sorrow of which Jesus spoke in the second beatitude is quite different, for it is sorrow that leads to happiness.

II. Sorrow that leads to happiness.

In contrast to the world's sorrow that brings death, Paul recommended "godly sorrow [that] brings repentance that leads to salvation" (2 Cor. 7:10).

A. *Sorrow that is born of conviction.* J. B. Phillips's translation of 2 Corinthians 7:8 stresses the right kind of sorrow: "I can see that the letter did upset you, though only for a time, and now I am glad I sent it, not because I want to hurt you but because it made you grieve for things that were wrong." The Corinthians' sorrow eventually led to happiness because it was born of conviction. Edward Hastings interprets the beatitude, "Blessed are they who are ashamed of themselves, of their shabbiness in character, their meanness of conduct."

Sorrow for sin is not a symptom of a sick soul; it is evidence of returning health. People who are deeply convicted of their sin will come to the Savior as instinctively as sick people will go to a doctor. This type of sorrow leads to happiness.

B. *Sorrow that is expressed.* Sorrow that leads to happiness inevitably expresses itself. It cannot be contained! The word used for "to mourn" is the strongest such word in the Greek language. Often it is used for mourning for the dead. It is the sort of grief that so intensely grips a person that it cannot be concealed. It brings not only heartache and tears but also confession and a changed life.

1. Through confession. David's return to purity and thus happiness began with his confession: "For I know my transgressions, and my sin is always before me. Against you, you only, have I sinned and done what is evil in your sight" (Ps. 51:3–4 NIV).

2. Through a changed life. "The sorrow which God uses means a change of heart and leads to salvation" (2 Cor. 7:10 PHILLIPS). People are really changed when they suddenly come up against something that opens their eyes to what sin is and to what sin does. A boy may go his own way and never think of effects or consequences. Then one day he may see a friend destroyed by drugs, alcohol, or immorality. Suddenly he sees sin for what it is and experiences cutting sorrow for his own sin, which is expressed through a changed life.

C. *Sorrow that is blessed.* Jesus said, "Blessed are they that mourn." Here "blessed" has a dual meaning. It means "blessed" and "happy."
Four blessings result from sorrow that leads to happiness.

1. Forgiveness of sin. First John 1:9 promises, "If we confess our sins, he is faithful and just to forgive us our sins, and to cleanse us from all unrighteousness." No people who mourn over their sins can know the comfort that is promised until their sins are forgiven. So long as the burden and guilt of sin rests heavily on them, they cannot be comforted. It is when they experience the loving forgiveness of Christ that comfort and the "peace that passes all understanding" become theirs.

2. Restoration of fellowship. First John 1:7 says, "But if we walk in the light, as he is in the light, we have fellowship one with another, and the blood of Jesus Christ his Son cleanseth us from all sin."

   David's lust led to murder, which in turn led to falsehood and estrangement from God. Following Nathan's accusation, David became deeply convicted of his sin. His personal anguish is recorded in Psalm 51. Then he prayed for the restoration of fellowship: "Restore to me the joy of your salvation and grant me a willing spirit, to sustain me" (v. 12 NIV). His sorrow led to confession, which led to forgiveness, which led to restoration of fellowship with God.

3. Strengthening of character. "How happy are those who know what sorrow means, for they will be given courage and comfort" (Matt. 5:4 PHILLIPS). Sorrow can have a godly reference. God can turn sickness and sorrow into good. "We know that in all things God works for the good of those who love him, who have been called according to his purpose" (Rom. 8:28 NIV).

26

God uses sorrow to build character and thus to bring happiness. You cannot reverse the beatitude to say, "Blessed are they who never mourn. Blessed are they who are always lighthearted and never serious." If there were no suffering or sorrow, there would be no sympathy.

4. God's comfort. Jesus said that those who mourn "shall be comforted." Hastings said the word *comfort* is suggestive of bracing rather than soothing. It speaks of strength that comes from companionship with God. Jesus assured us here, out of his knowledge of life and his rich experience of the human heart, that only those who enter fully into the depths of life—their own and others—are truly blessed. Only those who enter into the abundance of God's life receive the blessing of divine comfort.

Conclusion

On the Pennsylvania Railroad during the early 1900s, two trains collided, killing several people. It was determined that the surviving engineer was responsible for the accident. He was questioned repeatedly, and the entire experience became too much for him to handle. Eventually he was driven into a psychotic state and could hardly carry on an intelligent conversation.

The president of the railroad, Mr. Atterbury, asked to meet with the engineer, who apprehensively came to the president's office.

Mr. Atterbury placed his arm around the engineer's shoulders and said, "Old man, we have had a streak of bad luck, haven't we?" For some time the president and the engineer stood together weeping.

Then Mr. Atterbury said, "One thing I want you to remember as long as you work for us is that whenever any employee of the Pennsylvania Railroad is troubled, I am troubled too."

Soon the old engineer began to speak and think clearly. Because his boss cared enough to grieve with him, he was healed.

All around us are faultfinders on the prowl to heap guilt and blame on others. But you and I can join the blessed minority who care and are willing to mourn even with those who are to blame. When we become such mourners, we will both comfort and be comforted.

SUNDAY EVENING, JANUARY 12

Title: The Only Way of Salvation

Text: "Jesus saith unto him, I am the way, the truth, and the life: no man cometh unto the Father, but by me" **(John 14:6)**.

Scripture Reading: John 14:6

Introduction

As the time of Jesus' crucifixion approached and he told his disciples that he must die on a cross, their hearts were distressed. They could not understand many of the things he told them; understanding came only as they looked back and, by the Holy Spirit's aid, recalled what he had said. As Jesus revealed the necessity for his death and departure from them, he also gave them some wonderful promises concerning the heavenly Father's home and the possibility of a continuing and unending fellowship with God and one another (John 13:33, 36).

In a way, Jesus knew that his disciples could not understand that his death on a cross was the only way to provide salvation for humankind. Today we can understand what Jesus meant when he said, "I am the way, the truth, and the life: no man cometh unto the Father, but by me" (John 14:6).

I. Jesus Christ is the way out.

A. *Jesus is the way out of slavery and sin.* Without being aware of it, people are slaves to sin. Sin may manifest itself in attitudes, actions, or ambitions. Those who have not made Jesus Christ the Master of their lives are servants of something much lower.

Sin not only enslaves; it also separates people from God, others, and their better selves. Jesus alone can deliver a person from slavery to sin. Each of us needs pardon from past guilt and deliverance from the power and practice of evil.

B. *Jesus is the way out of failure and the waste of sin.* "What shall it profit a man, if he shall gain the whole world, and lose his own soul?" (Mark 8:36). Without salvation people are failures throughout eternity even if they ruled an empire or possessed millions of dollars while living on earth. Only Jesus can pay the wages of our sin and deliver us from spiritual death and eternal torment.

C. *Jesus is the way out of the disappointment of sin.* Faithless living always disappoints. No one can play on Satan's team and be a winner. No one would want to go bankrupt, yet every person who goes through life without God follows a way that brings vast disappointment in the end.

II. Jesus Christ is the way through.

A. *Jesus is the way through an uncertain tomorrow.* No one knows what tomorrow has in store. The only thing certain about the future is its uncertainty. Only Jesus, who holds the future, can make us adequate for what the future holds.

B. *Jesus is the way through a desert of difficulties.* Just as the children of Israel journeyed through the wilderness facing one difficulty after another and following the cloud by day and the light by night, so we can endure hardship as we follow Jesus closely. Nowhere are we promised that life will be easy and comfortable if we simply trust Christ and do what is right. God does not usually reward us by making life easy. However, he does promise to be with us, and he assures us that no trial or trouble will be too much for us to bear if we trust him for help (1 Cor. 10:13).

III. Jesus Christ is the way in.

A. *Jesus is the way into an abundant life.* Everyone wants an abundant life. Unfortunately, many confused people think the abundant life of which Jesus spoke is an affluent life. It does not take much study to discover that an abundant life and an affluent life cannot be equated.

Jesus is the way into forgiveness of sin. His forgiveness is full, free, and forever. Part of an abundant life is awareness of being pure and right with God.

Assurance of eternal life is also part of the abundant life that Jesus came to provide (John 3:16). Eternal life is given to those who receive Jesus and permit him to occupy the throne of their lives.

B. *Jesus is the way into joy unspeakable.* Jesus was eager for his disciples to experience fullness of joy (John 15:11). Joy is a condition of the heart that is much deeper and more permanent than happiness. Happiness is the result of circumstances, while joy is holy happiness from God that can fill a person's heart even in the most adverse circumstances.

C. *Jesus is the way into triumphant, true success.* No one wants to be a failure. No one rejoices in losing. Everyone likes to be a winner. By faith in and obedience to the Savior, children of God are able to experience wonderful success in matters that really count, both now and throughout eternity.

IV. Jesus Christ is the way up.

A. *Jesus is the way up to our very best.* Humans were made to walk and talk with God. They were made to worship and serve God and live by the law of heaven, which is love, rather than by the law of the world, which is greed and hate. Jesus makes life complete. Until one comes to know him, life at its best is but a fraction. If you want to find the best way of living, you must go to Jesus Christ.

B. *Jesus is the way up to God (John 14:6; Acts 4:12).* Through Jesus Christ, God came down to dwell among people. He came to die on a cross to take away our sins. By his death he removed everything that separates sinners from God. Through faith in Jesus, we are forgiven and received by God as his own dear children.

C. *Jesus is the way up to heaven.* Only Jesus can take a person to heaven when this life is over, because only Jesus was both competent and willing to bear the penalty of our sin on the cross. Because he has paid the wages of our sin, he is able to offer us the gift of eternal life.

Conclusion

Jesus reveals the only way to God, the truth about God, and the kind of life that is received from God. Accept him by faith, and you can rejoice in being spiritually alive.

WEDNESDAY EVENING, JANUARY 15

Title: The Seven First Words of the Church

Text: "I can do all things through Christ which strengtheneth me" **(Phil. 4:13)**.

Scripture Reading: Philippians 4:13

Introduction

We are always interested in a baby's first words. It usually takes a great deal of imagination and a bit of interpretation, but we try to determine those first words a baby speaks. They are even often recorded in a baby book.

We are also interested in a person's last words. Supposedly they give some kind of insight into that person and his or her personality. So we hold those last words close.

The seven last words of Christ have been taken from the gospel accounts of Jesus' crucifixion and made the subject of music and countless sermons.

Somewhere sometime someone identified the seven last words of the church as "We never did it that way before." If those are the seven last words of the church, let me share with you the seven first words of the church: "I can do all things through Christ." These memorable words are found near the end of Paul's letter to the Philippians. Not only are they a good summary of Paul's life, but they are also an adequate statement of the first words of the church—the words on which the church bases its life and ministry.

I. These seven first words are positive.

Notice that Paul said, "I can."

How often and how easy it is to say, "I can't." People may say that they can't control their temper, cope with jealous thoughts, stand their job, tithe, teach a Sunday school class, pray in public, live a good life, and so on. Yet these are things that some people obviously can do.

Instead of the negative "I can't," consider the positive "I can." Many churches emphasize what they do not have in the way of budget or buildings. Instead, they should focus on what they do have in the way of people, possibilities, and the power of the Holy Spirit.

II. These seven first words suggest a pattern.

Paul said, "I can do all things." Against public opinion or endorsement of the "right" people and established patterns, Paul set out to do *all* things. The list of his accomplishments is impressive.

When we think of everything we should achieve as Christians, the list seems overwhelming: world evangelization, world missions, world hunger, world peace. . . . We can't do all that!

But look at Paul's pattern. He traveled to one place and completed one mission. Then he moved on to the next place. We should follow this pattern. In fact, even Jesus came to one place, at one time, to one people. We cannot do it all, but we must do something.

In his book *The Reluctant Witness*, Kenneth Chafin told of a seminary student who was very sensitive to other people's needs. When he finished school, he went to serve as pastor of a mission in a deprived community. He discovered people in need all around him and began to help them.

When the young minister and Chafin discussed the people he was trying to assist, Chafin asked if the sheer number of those who had problems and needed help was discouraging to his efforts. He seemed surprised by the question and answered, "I'm so busy trying to help the people around me who need help that I don't think too much about all the others. But I have the feeling that when I reach out to the persons in front of me and embrace their need, I have within my arms the whole world."

III. These seven first words affirm a presence.

Jesus working through individuals is what makes possible victorious Christian living and effective Christian ministry. Paul's entire life and ministry were explained by Christ. It can be the only explanation for your life too, if it is lived for Christ. An old French peasant visited the church in his village for an hour every morning before laboring in the fields and for an hour every night. When the man's priest asked him what he did in those two hours each day, he said, "I just look at Christ, and he looks at me."

IV. These seven first words show power.

Christ alone is our strength. He daily gives us power to face all obstacles.

Conclusion

The seven first words of the church, "I can do all things through Christ," send the church and its people into the world to minister with power.

SUNDAY MORNING, JANUARY 19

Title: Meekness—The Way to Happiness

Text: "Blessed are the meek: for they shall inherit the earth" (**Matt. 5:5**).

Scripture Reading: Matthew 5:1–5

Hymns: "Reach Out and Touch," Brown
            "Rescue the Perishing," Crosby
            "Am I a Soldier of the Cross?" Watts

Offertory Prayer: We come to you, our heavenly Father, knowing that apart from you all is vanity, that all other cisterns are broken and empty and that in you alone is the water of life. From the anxiety of our petty problems, we seek refuge in your presence this hour. We bring to you ourselves and our gifts. Accept and use both, we pray in Jesus' name. Amen.

Introduction

Can you truly be meek and happy at the same time? Can you picture a meek person who is also a happy person? You probably find it rather challenging.

Our misunderstanding of meekness creates this difficulty. In a world that thinks only an aggressive and ambitious person can get ahead in life, it is hard to believe that those who are meek will inherit anything, much less the earth!

Yet Jesus upheld meekness as the way to happiness. "Blessed [happy] are the meek" (Matt. 5:5). If anyone knows human nature and what it takes to make a person happy, Jesus Christ is that person. He did not imply that being fearful or weak brings happiness. Instead, Jesus referred to attitude or outlook. The meekness he described requires us to be strong people who are grounded in Christ. It demands us to have a personal relationship with God. This kind of meekness inevitably brings happiness. Meekness is the way to happiness for several reasons.

I. Meekness maintains an even temperament.

Aristotle defined meekness as the mean between two extremes—intense anger and excessive indifference. It is the happy medium between too much anger and too little passion.

William Barclay suggested that the beatitude be translated, "Blessed is the man who is always angry at the right time and never angry at the wrong time."

When is the right time to be angry? When insult or injury is suffered by others, not ourselves. But how can we develop this even temperament? How can we avoid the extremes of severe anger or apathy? We can't! But God can do for us what we cannot do for ourselves. So how does God give us an even temperament? First, through salvation; before all else we must be born again. Second, through the Holy Spirit's work in our lives. "But the fruit of the Spirit is love, joy, peace, longsuffering, gentleness, goodness, faith, meekness, temperance: against such there is no law" (Gal. 5:22–23).

II. Meekness develops self-control.

The word translated "meekness" has a second meaning. Often it was used to express the idea of "self-control." For instance, an animal that otherwise would have been wild but had been made a house pet was called meek. The animal had learned to respond favorably to commands and to behave properly. Therefore the beatitude could be translated, "Blessed are they who are entirely self-controlled." Weakness is giving in to the worst that is in you. Meekness is mastery over it.

To be meek does not mean that you are cowardly, but it does mean that you are strong enough not to retaliate when wrongly treated. Having their rights, those who are meek do not insist on them. Possessing great ability, those who are meek do not flaunt it. They would rather forgive than accuse.

Such self-control results in peace with oneself. Those who cannot control their anger, greed, lust, tongue, or ambition will never be at peace within. They will constantly be at war with themselves.

III. Meekness expresses itself through gentleness.

A third meaning of the Greek word for meekness tells us something else about this quality of a happy life. Meekness may be translated "kindness" or "gentleness." The concept of a man being a gentleman was born in the Christian faith. He is a man who is gentle, courteous, and considerate. Meekness and gentleness are characteristics of a strong, not weak, person.

A. *Gentleness is considerate of others.* "Brothers and sisters, if someone is caught in a sin, you who live by the Spirit should restore that person gently. But watch yourself, or you also may be tempted" (Gal. 6:1 NIV). A gentle person is considerate of others even when they have done wrong.

B. *Gentleness admits faults to others.* James advised, "Confess your faults one to another" (James 5:16). Proud, arrogant, or insecure people can never bring themselves to do this. However, meek, gentle, and secure individuals have courage to admit their mistakes to others. Benjamin Franklin asserted, "None but the well-bred man knows how to confess a fault or acknowledge himself in error." Humble people bravely admit their shortcomings, which leads to happiness for all involved.

C. *Gentleness encourages others.* Paul encouraged us "to slander no one, to be peaceable and considerate, and always to be gentle toward everyone" (Titus 3:2 NIV). As long as you maximize others' faults while minimizing your own, you can never be happy.

D. *Gentleness learns from others.* Gentle people are apt to learn. They accept criticism and are always eager to listen both to God and others; as a result, they learn much. Those who demonstrate meekness are happy.

IV. Meekness is assured of victory.

Jesus said of those who are meek, "They shall inherit the earth" (Matt. 5:5). This truth is affirmed many times throughout the Bible. Listen to these four passages from Psalms.

Psalm 37:9–11: "Those that wait upon the LORD, they shall inherit the earth. For yet a little while, and the wicked shall not be: yea, thou shalt diligently consider his place, and it shall not be. But the meek shall inherit the earth."

Psalm 22:26: "The meek shall eat and be satisfied."

Psalm 25:9: "The meek will he guide in judgment: and the meek will he teach his way."

Psalm 147:6: "The LORD lifteth up the meek."

It is significant that Jesus said the meek shall "inherit," not "capture," the earth. An inheritor is a receiver, not an aggressor. God in his providence has structured the world so that the meek are certain to inherit it.

Conclusion

"Meekness is so hard to develop," you say. You are right. I cannot tell myself to be meek and thus become meek. God never intended for us to be able to make ourselves meek. That is not our nature. But what we cannot do for ourselves God does for us—first through salvation and then continuing his work through the daily infilling of the Holy Spirit.

Have you been born again? Have you allowed the Holy Spirit to fill you? When you do, the wonderful quality of meekness will be yours, and you will enter the way to happiness!

SUNDAY EVENING, JANUARY 19

Title: Partial or Complete Salvation

Text: "How shall we escape if we ignore such a great salvation?" **(Heb. 2:3 NIV)**.

Scripture Reading: Hebrews 2:1–4

Introduction

The Bible is a book that reveals the way of salvation. Jesus Christ came to be our Savior. He lived a sinless life and died in our place for our sin. He rose from the dead, triumphant and victorious, to bring us salvation. Now he lives at his Father's side, making intercession for those who trust him.

Our text speaks about salvation as being a great salvation. Unfortunately, many have made only a halfhearted response and have only a fractional understanding of the great salvation available through Jesus Christ.

Our text also speaks about the tragic possibility of believers ignoring their great salvation. This verse has often been used as the text for an evangelistic sermon, emphasizing that unbelievers should no longer neglect to respond to Jesus Christ as Savior. In reality, the text is addressed to those who have already entered the gateway of salvation but who face the peril of ignoring certain phases of it, resulting in their own hurt and the injury of others. Have you made a halfhearted response to the great salvation that God offers to you through Jesus Christ?

Only Jesus can save us from the death that sin brings. Salvation from death, however, is only part of the great salvation that is offered to us. Christ alone can save us from the downward drag of our inherited evil nature. And he alone can save us from the hopeless destiny to which sin leads. We should make a complete response to our great salvation rather than ignoring some aspect of it.

For many people, salvation from the penalty of sin is a past experience. We are justified in God's sight through faith in Jesus Christ. Those who have already experienced salvation from the punishment of sin should now be in the process of being saved from the power and practice of sin. This is salvation and sanctification in the present tense. Further, all who have trusted Jesus as Savior in the past and who are presently experiencing the Holy Spirit's work in their lives look forward to salvation from sin in the future. This is salvation in the future tense; the Bible calls it glorification.

As you take inventory of your own heart and your own faith, have you become satisfied with partial salvation, or are you hungry for and seeking the complete salvation that God offers to you through Jesus Christ? If you have trusted him as Savior, you should desire his full salvation in the present. To experience complete salvation in the present, you must do a number of things.

I. Respond to Jesus as the Teacher who came from God.

A. *Jesus was more a teacher than a preacher.* His disciples and others addressed him as Master. This was the title of an authoritative teacher.

B. *Jesus came bringing God's truth from heaven to the hearts and lives of people.* We must accept him as an authoritative teacher who came to reveal the way to live if we are to experience his full salvation in the present.

C. *His followers were called disciples and learners.* This meant they had "enrolled in his school" and were seeking to receive new truth about God, life, and the issues of life in the future.

The Sermon on the Mount closes with an exhortation not only to hear but also to do the things Jesus taught. Are you seriously committed to the practice of Jesus' teachings? To be halfheartedly committed is to fail to experience the great salvation God has for you in the present.

II. Let the Holy Spirit work within you in the present (I Cor. 3:16; 6:19–20).

Some people in the church at Corinth were uninformed of the glorious truth that the Holy Spirit had filled them the moment they trusted Jesus as Savior. To be uninformed about the personality, presence, and purpose of the Holy Spirit is to live on crumbs rather than feast at the Lord's table.

A. *The Holy Spirit convicted us of our need for Christ.*

B. *The Holy Spirit effected the miracle of the new birth.*

C. *The Holy Spirit assured us of our relationship with God.*

D. *The Holy Spirit came into our hearts to change us.* He resides within us to transform our lives and cause us to be in harmony with the mind of Jesus Christ.

E. *The Holy Spirit wants to correct and instruct us.* He desires us to live in the ways of our Lord, and he recalls to our memory things that Jesus taught.

To ignore the Holy Spirit or to respond negatively to him is to deprive yourself of the fruit of the Spirit in your heart and life. There is no escape from living an unproductive and unhappy "Christian" life if you ignore the Holy Spirit's influence.

III. Let the church be your spiritual family.

The church is often called the household of faith. God meant for each of his children to be a vital functioning part of a local congregation of believers. As a baby needs a father and mother and the security of a home, the children of God need a spiritual family to give them care and shelter if they are to grow to maturity.

A. *The church is responsible for teaching you what Jesus taught.*
B. *The church, as your spiritual family, should encourage you in your walk with Christ.*
C. *The church should show you how to live a Christian life and how to serve Christ.*
D. *The church can assist you in many ways as you seek to be a loyal servant of Christ.*

Without a positive and constant response and participation in the family of God, the church, it is impossible for you to experience the full and great salvation that God offers through Jesus Christ.

IV. Let the Bible become a recording of God's messages to your heart.

Have you ever stopped to think of the Bible as a spiritual recording that contains the voice and messages of God to your heart?

A. *God's Word should be your spiritual nourishment (1 Peter 2:1–2).* You will always remain in spiritual infancy if you ignore God's Word.
B. *Daily study of God's Word can be your spiritual road map.* To ignore the Bible as a daily companion will cause many detours and wrong turns in your life.
C. *Devotional Bible reading is the listening side of prayer.* It is more important to hear what God says to us than to offer our requests to God.

Have you thought of our text as merely for unbelievers? Think again. You will note that it warns believers against ignoring the full salvation that God offers us.

Conclusion

If you are a nonbeliever, you should recognize the peril of ignorance and neglect. You should realize that every day you postpone committing your life to Jesus as Lord and Savior increases your risk of never giving your life to him. To ignore Jesus is to deprive yourself of a full spiritual life, of a loving relationship with God, of the privilege of going to heaven when you die, and of the finest and best of both this life and the life to come.

If you are a believer, you need to recognize the tragic possibility of ignoring God's great salvation. You should decide several things today in order to experience this full salvation.

A. *Determine to listen intently to the Holy Spirit's voice and God's precious Word.*
B. *Determine to obey lovingly, instantly, and completely.*
C. *Determine to trust Jesus always in all ways.*

Determine now to consult your great Savior about every issue in your life. Resolve to consent to his will so as to experience fully the great salvation he offers you.

WEDNESDAY EVENING, JANUARY 22

Title: If You Really Care, Share

Text: "It was good of you to share in my troubles. Moreover, as you Philippians know, in the early days of your acquaintance with the gospel, when I set out from Macedonia, not one church shared with me in the matter of giving and receiving, except you only; for even when I was in Thessalonica, you sent me aid more than once when I was in need. Not that I desire your gifts; what I desire is that more be credited to your account. I have received full payment and have more than enough. I am amply supplied, now that I have received from Epaphroditus the gifts you sent. They are a fragrant offering, an acceptable sacrifice, pleasing to God. And my God will meet all your needs according to the riches of his glory in Christ Jesus" (**Phil. 4:14–19 NIV**).

Scripture Reading: Philippians 4:14–19

Introduction

In his autobiography, Booker T. Washington told of some experiences he had while raising over a million dollars for Tuskegee Institute. He closed the chapter on raising money with an account of an elderly African American woman, clothed in rags and hobbling with the help of a cane, who came to him one day and said that she had spent much of her life in slavery. She knew that he was helping to educate black men and women and wanted to help. But since she had no money, she asked him to take six eggs that she had been saving and put them into the education of boys and girls. Booker T. Washington observed that of all the gifts he received for Tuskegee Institute, none touched him so deeply as that one. The woman who gave those six eggs had discovered the secret of effective giving. She cared, so she shared.

The church at Philippi cared for Paul, so they shared with him. Their generosity warmed Paul's heart, and he thanked them graciously. Paul appreciated their gifts not just for his own sake but because of what the gifts meant to the Philippians themselves. He implicitly believed that money given for the work of Christ blesses those who give as much as those who receive. Remember, it was Paul who passed on the familiar words of Jesus, "It is more blessed to give than to receive" (Acts 20:35). Paul made a similar remark to his generous friends in Philippi.

Usually we start at the point of a church's needs when we talk about giving. Paul started at a different point: the relationship of a believer to Christ. Because a person is "in Christ," he or she will give, and the results will help both the one who receives and the one who gives.

I. The basis of sharing: caring.

Evidence shows that the Philippian church cared deeply for Paul. Because of this care, they shared. Caring is always the basis of effective sharing: we care for missions, so we share; we care about evangelism, so we share; we care about the Christian education of young people, so we share. Caring, or love, is the highest motive in Christian giving. Our whole basis of caring is that Someone cared enough for us to die on a cross for us.

II. The results of sharing.

Notice the intriguing statement in verse 17. Paul suggested that money given to the work of Christ builds up a credit account that yields dividends far more than the amount we invest. Since we all want our money to yield the best possible return, here is a way that our money can bear returns for eternity.

A. *What money enables people to do together.* In verse 15 Paul indicated that the church had entered into a partnership with him. Giving as a church allows us to enter into a partnership with one another that strengthens our Christian witness and ministry.

B. *What money does for those who receive it.* Money given in Christ's name creates gratitude in the hearts of those who receive it.

C. *What money does for those who give it.* Money becomes for those who give it an acceptable sacrifice to God. We are no longer obligated to offer animal sacrifices to God, because his Son paid the price for our sin. We know that what God wants is the sacrifice of ourselves, the giving of our lives to him. This is what we do in Christian giving. Our money represents ourselves.

D. *What money allows God to do for us.* Paul asserted that God will meet all our needs. In Paul's case, he did this through the gifts donated by the Philippian church. No gift that is shared in Christ's name will make the giver poorer. We draw our entire sustenance from God anyway.

Conclusion

Sharing because of caring becomes a way of life. It brings tremendously rich dividends to those who practice it.

SUNDAY MORNING, JANUARY 26

Title: Hunger and Thirst—The Way to Happiness

Text: "Blessed are they which do hunger and thirst after righteousness: for they shall be filled" **(Matt. 5:6)**.

Scripture Reading: Matthew 5:1–6

Hymns: "Teach Me to Pray," Reitz
         "Make Me a Channel of Blessing," Smyth
         "Something for Thee," Phelps

Offertory Prayer: Our Father God, provide us with a holy hunger and thirst for righteousness. Remove our lust for lesser things and create within us pure hearts. Receive our gifts and our love. In the name of our Savior, we pray. Amen.

Introduction

No two people are exactly alike. Nor have they ever been or will they be. We are different from one another in so many ways. We have different fingerprints; eye, hair, and skin colors; heritage; intelligence levels; and personalities, not to mention height and weight. But we all are alike in that we hunger and thirst. Jesus, in his usual manner of simplifying that which is complicated, used this common demonstration to express the truth of the fourth way to happiness.

"Blessed [happy] are they which do hunger and thirst after righteousness: for they shall be filled." That is certainly a strange statement. How could hunger or thirst make a person happy? Jesus explained that the right kind of hunger and thirst leads to happiness.

Jesus was actually asking, "How much do you want righteousness? As much as a hungry person wants food? As much as a thirsty person wants water?" Then he asserted that if you truly hunger and thirst after righteousness, you will be blessed, or happy. But why?

Hunger and thirst are the way to happiness:

I. Because of the things they suggest.

Just what do the words *hunger* and *thirst* suggest? From one viewpoint, they suggest agony and pain. But Jesus looks on the bright side of hunger and thirst. These words suggest four positive things—life, health, growth, and enjoyment.

A. *Life.* As soon as all babies enter this world, they hunger and thirst for one reason: they are alive! And as soon as you are born into God's kingdom, you begin to hunger and thirst for righteousness. Peter said, "As newborn babies, desire the sincere milk of the word, that ye may grow thereby" (1 Peter 2:2).

   In west Texas a normal mesquite tree uses fifty-five gallons of water per day in the summertime. That is why so many of them are destroyed; the water is better used for grass. Nevertheless, the moment a mesquite tree stops drinking, it is dead. Similarly, if you do not hunger or thirst for righteousness, perhaps you have no life! But where there is hunger, an inner yearning for more, you can know that you have the life Christ came to give. And this life always brings happiness!

B. *Health.* A Christian who insists on attending church every week, who looks forward to Bible study, and who always offers a helping hand to those in need has good spiritual health. A Christian who loves to worship with fellow believers, who has an appetite for Bible reading and study, and who just can't get enough of God will always receive a good report from the Great Physician on his or her spiritual checkup. Those who are spiritually healthy are happy.

C. *Growth.* To hunger and thirst for righteousness means to eat well spiritually. When we regularly feast on nourishment from God, we grow. As we grow, we hunger and thirst for the deeper, or meatier, things of God. The church at Corinth experienced delayed spiritual growth because they remained satisfied with the milk of God's Word and developed no appetite for the meat of his Word. Therefore Paul wrote to them, "Brothers and sisters, I could not address you as people who live by the Spirit but as people who are still worldly—mere infants in Christ. I gave you milk, not solid food, for you were not yet ready for it. Indeed, you are still not ready" (1 Cor. 3:1–2 NIV).

D. *Enjoyment.* Maybe I had a better appetite as a boy, but it seems like no one makes pecan pies or chocolate cakes as good as my mother's. Eating was, and still is, something to be enjoyed. But a healthy appetite is essential to enjoying a meal. Those who hunger for righteousness enjoy feasting on God's Word. They enjoy Christian worship, prayer, and fellowship. As they satisfy their appetites, they will experience happiness.

II. Because of the lessons they teach.

When you are hungry or thirsty, you can learn a number of things that you might never learn otherwise. If lost in a desert, you might learn to retrieve water from a cactus plant or find wild berries. Likewise, hunger and thirst for righteousness can teach us many lessons.

A. *Things cannot fully satisfy.* Jesus said, "It is written: 'Man shall not live on bread alone, but on every word that comes from the mouth of God'" (Matt. 4:4 NIV).

Do you remember old King Midas who had such a hunger for gold that he wished all he touched would turn into gold? One day his wish was granted. All he touched turned into gold—his furniture, dinnerware, clothing, everything! And it was all so wonderful until his little girl came running home. When he reached out to touch her, she also turned to gold. It was then that King Midas realized that things alone cannot fully satisfy. As Jesus said, "Life does not consist in an abundance of possessions" (Luke 12:15 NIV).

B. *God alone meets our total needs.* "As the deer pants for streams of water, so my soul pants for you, O God. My soul thirsts for God, for the living God. When can I go and meet with God?" (Ps. 42:1–2 NIV). God has placed an insatiable hunger and thirst for him inside each of us. When Philip said, "Lord, show us the Father and that will be enough for us" (John 14:8 NIV), he voiced a longing that is as old as humankind.

III. Because of the desires they create.

Just what is this "righteousness" for which we are to hunger and thirst? It is more than judicial justice or a rigid code of conduct. It is nothing less than goodness.

A. *The desire for personal goodness.* Paul said that he desired to do what is good, but he could not carry it out (Rom. 7:18). He realized that he was not all he wanted to be. But we can know that if we desire personal goodness, our heavenly Father will give us power to do what is right.

I am glad Jesus did not say that only those who are righteous would be blessed. Instead, he said that those who hunger and thirst (desire) to be righteous are blessed. When the desire for personal goodness saturates us, happiness becomes a reality!

B. *The desire to do good to others.* "What does the LORD require of you? To act justly and to love mercy and to walk humbly with your God" (Mic. 6:8 NIV). When we have a sincere desire to do good to others, we become generous in our remarks about and to others. We go the second mile for others. Soon we begin to question our motive: "Are we doing good to others simply because it brings happiness to us, or because we want to benefit others?" Either way, doing good to others is a very happy way to live.

C. *The desire to know God.* Who alone is really good? Jesus questioned, "Why do you call me good? . . . No one is good—except God alone" (Luke 18:19 NIV).

Some desires degrade or, when satisfied, destroy. But the desire to know God edifies and instills happiness. No one is happier than those who hunger and thirst to know God more and who satisfy that hunger daily by reading God's Word, praying, and serving him.

IV. Because of the satisfaction they obtain.

Jesus promised that those who hunger and thirst after righteousness "shall be filled," or satisfied. But what satisfaction does this hunger and thirst bring?

A. *The satisfaction of experiencing goodness in this life.* "The LORD is my shepherd, I lack nothing. He makes me lie down in green pastures, he leads me beside quiet waters. . . . You prepare a table before me in the presence of my enemies. You anoint my head with oil; my cup overflows. Surely your goodness and love will follow me all the days of my life" (Ps. 23:1–2, 5–6 NIV).

B. *The satisfaction of entering into complete goodness in the life to come.* Those who hunger will eat, and those who thirst will drink. Both will be satisfied. This promise is without qualification.

Conclusion

Do you hunger and thirst for more than this world offers? Jesus said, "Let anyone who is thirsty come to me and drink. Whoever believes in me, as Scripture has said, rivers of living water will flow from within them" (John 7:37–38 NIV). Are you hungry and thirsty? There is room for you at his banquet table today.

SUNDAY EVENING, JANUARY 26

Title: The Salvation of Your Life

Text: "Therefore, my dear friends, as you have always obeyed—not only in my presence, but now much more in my absence—continue to work out your salvation with fear and trembling, for it is God who works in you to will and to act in order to fulfill his good purpose" **(Phil. 2:12–13 NIV)**.

Scripture Reading: Titus 2:11–14

Introduction

Today we consider the great salvation that God provides for us in the present.

Dale Moody said, "There is one way of salvation; there are two sides to the salvation experience; and there are three phases of the great salvation that God offers." The one way is by grace through faith in Jesus Christ. The two sides of the salvation experience are the divine side and the human side. The three phases of our great salvation are the past, present, and future. Salvation in the past includes our conviction of sin by the Holy Spirit that leads us to trust Jesus Christ and turn from sin. The Holy Spirit effected the miracle of the new birth, and we were justified in God's sight by our faith in Jesus Christ. That is the first phase of our salvation. For those who are Christians, it is salvation in the past tense.

Salvation in the present tense began at the moment of our conversion and will continue until our death or the Lord's return, whichever is first. Salvation in the present is a process in which the Holy Spirit works within our hearts and reveals to us and through us the nature and character of a true follower of Christ.

Salvation in the future occurs after the Lord's triumphant return. It is salvation from the very presence of evil and sin.

Today we will focus on our salvation in the present. Listen to how J. B. Phillips paraphrases our text: "So then, my dear friends, as you have always obeyed me—and that not only when I was with you—now, even more in my absence, complete the salvation that God has given you with a proper sense of awe and responsibility. For it is God who is at work within you, giving you the will and power to achieve his purpose" (Phil. 2:12–13).

I. Salvation in the present tense.

A close study of the text in its context reveals that Paul was addressing those who were already his brothers and sisters in the faith. They had experienced the miracle of the new birth, turned from sin, and received Jesus as Lord and Savior. Paul understood the conversion experience as being just the beginning of God's good work within them (Phil. 1:6).

II. Salvation in the present tense is available to each of us.

    A. *By his death on the cross, Jesus made possible for us salvation from death that results from sin.*

    B. *By his victory over death, Jesus rescued us from the power and practice of sin. He saves all who are willing to obey him and his instruction.*

The words of our text introduce God into our present salvation. He is the God of love and power who has come to dwell within us through faith in his Son, Jesus Christ. Our God is not some deceased ruler whose power and presence were limited to the work of creation. He is an active God who dwells within the heart of every believer to deliver from the tyranny of evil in the present.

God lives within us through his Holy Spirit to give us a feeling of holy dissatisfaction with sin (Matt. 5:3–5). He creates within us a hunger and thirst for righteousness (Matt. 5:6). As God works within our hearts, he imparts to us the desire and ability to live according to our higher nature.

To fully experience our great salvation, we must respond to Jesus as the authoritative Teacher sent from God to impart the wisdom of heaven to those living in the present. Jesus affirmed that all who hear and practice his teachings will have strength and stability when the storms of life threaten to destroy them (Matt. 7:24–27). We cannot escape collapse or catastrophe when the pressures of life beat against us if we have neglected to respond to our Savior.

As Christians, as disciples, we must move beyond the initial experience of trusting Jesus Christ as Savior. We must let him be the master Teacher who has come to deliver us from sin.

III. Present-day salvation illustrated.

Jesus wants to do more than save your soul from the penalty of sin and ultimately your body from the presence of sin. He wants to save your life today from the destructive power of sin. This redemption can be illustrated by his teachings in the Sermon on the Mount about overcoming anxiety (Matt. 6:25–34). To experience salvation from anxiety we must do several things.

   A. *We must trust our loving Father (Matt. 6:30–32).*
   B. *We must evaluate our motives and properly appreciate ourselves (Matt. 6:26).*
   C. *We must accept ourselves as God's unique creation (Matt. 6:27).*
   D. *We must dedicate our lives to seeking and obeying God's will (Matt. 6:33).*
   E. *We must determine to live one day at a time (Matt. 6:34).*

If we disregard this salvation from anxiety, we will miss God's full salvation for us in the present. When we worry about yesterday's failures and fear what might happen tomorrow, there is no power under heaven that can save us from the burden of anxiety. Our only hope is to fully respond to the Lord's teachings.

Conclusion

Our great salvation includes redemption from the penalty of sin in the past. We now need to accept salvation from the practice of sin in the present, but we cannot do it on our own. Living a Christian life is a cooperative venture as we walk with God while he works within us.

God has also given us a great salvation in the future through Jesus Christ. Ours truly is a great salvation. Let us not neglect any phase of it.

WEDNESDAY EVENING, JANUARY 29

Title: God's Supply

Text: "My God shall supply all your need according to his riches in glory by Christ Jesus" **(Phil. 4:19).**

Scripture Reading: Philippians 4:14–19

Introduction

Supplies are important in every human endeavor. Before school opens in the fall, parents purchase school supplies so their children will have the necessary materials to do their work. When an army goes to war, supplies are imperative—support supplies such as food and shelter in addition to military supplies. And the logistics of transporting supplies to the troops often becomes quite a problem.

Likewise, God supplies his people with what they need to get their jobs done. Paul referred to the present when he said that God would supply our needs. He was not merely implying a future hope.

The Philippian church had supplied Paul's need. So this turned his thoughts to God, who supplied their every need. Notice the significant things Paul said about the way God supplies our needs.

I. God's supply is personal.

Paul said, "My God. . . ." God was personal and real to Paul. God directs his provisions to us personally. He also uses other people to supply our needs. The people of the Philippian church were the instruments through whom Paul's need was met.

A deacon was praying in a church prayer meeting for a family who had suffered loss and needed help. Then he mentioned in his prayer that God should not be concerned about food for the family, because the deacon himself would provide it. God met the family's need through the deacon.

II. God's supply is positive.

Paul was able to tell the Philippians that God would supply all their needs. He knew that God keeps his promises, and we can be positive that God does supply all our needs.

What prompted Paul to make such a positive statement? Paul knew from personal experience that God would do it, for throughout Paul's ministry God had provided for him.

III. God's supply is providential.

In God's providential care all our needs will be met. However, there is a difference between needs and wants. Several years ago, someone reported that at the beginning of the century the average American wanted 72 different things and considered 18 of them important. A half century later, the average American wanted 496 things and considered 96 of them necessary.

God may not supply all our wants, but he certainly will meet all our needs. Alexander McLaren said the axiom of the Christian faith is that whatever we do not obtain we do not require.

God's supply is plentiful. He gives to us "according to his riches in glory"— that is, in abundance!

A poor woman went to the beach for the first time and observed the water rolling to the shore, wave after wave. Rushing down to the water's edge, she fell on her knees and scooped up some water in her hands, exclaiming, "Thank God for something of which there is enough!"

IV. God's supply is in his presence.

Paul indicated that God's supply is "by Christ Jesus." The greatest supply he gives to us is his presence. Jesus promised that he will never leave us nor forsake us; he will be with us until the end of the age.

Christ's power will supply our needs again and again. Sir Robert Stopford was a junior officer of Lord Nelson and commanded one of the admiral's ships on a long sea chase against the enemy that took them to the West Indies. The journey was full of hardship and risk. Stopford wrote to a friend that they were half-starved and otherwise inconvenienced by being out of port for so long, but their reward was that they were with Nelson. How much greater is the reward of those who continually dwell in the presence of the Lord and receive every necessary provision from his hand.

Conclusion

God's supply is truly adequate for our every need.

FEBRUARY

- **Sunday Mornings**

    Complete the Beatitude series "The Way to Happiness."

- **Sunday Evenings**

    Continue the series "Experiencing the Great Salvation of God."

- **Wednesday Evenings**

    Begin a series of studies on spiritual gifts with the theme "Concerning the Gifts of the Holy Spirit." A positive response on the part of each believer to the Father's gift of the Holy Spirit is absolutely essential if we would truly be God's people.

SUNDAY MORNING, FEBRUARY 2

Title: Mercy—The Way to Happiness

Text: "Blessed are the merciful: for they shall obtain mercy" **(Matt. 5:7)**.

Scripture Reading: Matthew 5:1–7

Hymns: "Reach Out and Touch," Brown
"Teach Me, O Lord, to Care," Ware
"Rescue the Perishing," Crosby

Offertory Prayer: Our Father God, all of our needs lead us to you. From your mercy we draw our strength. Grant us the ability to be as merciful toward others as you have been toward us. Receive our gifts as expressions of our love and devotion. In the name of Christ our Redeemer we pray. Amen.

Introduction

John Wesley visited General Oglethorpe when he was governor of the colony of Georgia. The general mentioned an incident involving a man who had angered him, and remarked, "I shall never forgive him!" Wesley answered, "Then I hope, sir, you never sin." Evidently Wesley was reminded of Jesus' teaching that those who are not merciful and forgiving will not be treated with mercy and forgiveness.

Living without mercy is the prelude to dying without mercy. On the other hand, living with mercy results in being treated with mercy. As Jesus said it, "Blessed [happy] are the merciful: for they shall obtain mercy."

This beatitude raises three very practical questions: What is mercy? How can I become merciful? And what can I expect as a result? Finding the answer to these questions is the way to happiness.

I. What is mercy?

Of the more than 180 times in which *mercy* appears in the Old Testament, the King James Version translates it 96 times as "mercy," 38 times as "kindness," and 30 times as "lovingkindness."

A. *Mercy is not emotionalism.* To be merciful is far more than to shed tears. Of course, those who are merciful sometimes weep. Jesus did not restrain his tears as Martha and Mary grieved over their brother's death. Another time he looked at a city and wept over it. There is something startling about this strong man's weeping. "Jesus wept." But he did far more than weep—he gave himself for whom he wept.

It is easy for some to shed tears that are meaningless and unproductive. Theirs is emotion without motion—and this is *not* mercy!

B. *Mercy is not humanitarianism.* "If I give all I possess to the poor and give over my body to hardship that I may boast, but do not have love, I gain nothing" (1 Cor. 13:3 NIV).

Mercy goes beyond handing out used clothes to flood victims or food to the elderly. It is possible to give your body to be burned and not have love. Acts of mercy that are void of an attitude of mercy are invalid. The mercy of which Christ spoke is far more than the mechanics of doing good.

C. *Mercy is an attitude.* It is not something that can be "turned on and off" at will. Mercy is more than end-of-the-year giving to the church for tax purposes. Mercy, as demonstrated by Christ, involves the way a person truly feels. It is an underlying attitude of life. Mercy is to see others as Christ sees them and feel toward others as he feels toward them. In short, mercy is to have the attitude of Christ toward everyone.

D. *Mercy is action.* Mercy is equally action. If we have an attitude of mercy, we will perform deeds of mercy. When springtime comes, it cannot be kept a secret. It expresses itself through blossoming buds and singing birds. And when the springtime of mercy is in our hearts, it makes itself known in a multitude of ways.

When mercy is translated into action, we are kind and gracious in our judgment of others. We look for the best in others. We ask ourselves, "What circumstances led this person to do wrong?" rather than, "How can I expose or punish the wrongdoer?" Redemption, not condemnation, will be our concern.

Mercy that is action ministers to others. Even as calloused as the censorious lawyer was, he admitted that a "neighbor" is one who "shows" mercy, not simply feels it. Those who are merciful dare to help lighten others' loads.

Mercy that is action forgives others. Perhaps there is no greater expression of love than forgiveness. When you have every right to be resentful but choose to forgive, you experience happiness that only mercy can bring.

II. How can I become merciful?

"Blessed are the merciful"—that is good, but how can I become merciful? I find it so easy to criticize. How can I change?

A. *Remember your own need of mercy.* We often make mistakes that require God's mercy, so we should be merciful to others. Paul reminds us to watch our own actions when we become aware of another who "is caught in a sin" (Gal. 6:1 NIV).

B. *Become more acquainted with anyone you are inclined to judge.* Chances are you really do not know that person very well. The word *prejudice* means "prejudging," or making an estimate of others without knowing the facts. We frequently do this without knowing the person at all! It is easy to be unrelenting in our judgment of those we do not know, so we need to become better acquainted with others' backgrounds, the problems they face, and the reasons for the scars they bear.

C. *Allow Christ to show his mercy through you.* "Christ in you, the hope of glory" is the affirmation of Colossians 1:27. And Christ in you is your only hope of becoming a loving, merciful person. As you surrender your bitterness and resentment to Christ and allow him to live and work freely through you, mercy becomes a normal attitude of life.

III. What can I expect as a result?

"For they shall obtain mercy" is the promise attached to this beatitude (Matt. 5:7). The mercy that comes to those who are merciful includes the following:

A. *Peace within yourself.* You are well on your way to a happy life when you allow the Holy Spirit to cleanse you of stubbornness and unforgiveness.

B. *Mercy from others.* In many ways life is like a mirror. Life reflects what you put into it. If we are unkind, life becomes unkind. If we judge others, we will be judged by others. On the other hand, love produces love and mercy produces mercy.

C. *Mercy from God.* To the extent that we forgive others, we are forgiven by God (Matt. 6:14–15). Therefore the "merciful shall obtain mercy."

Conclusion

The world desperately needs to see mercy in action. Why not be merciful this week? You will be blessed and happy, and many other people will be happy also!

SUNDAY EVENING, FEBRUARY 2

Title: Salvation in the Future Tense

Text: "And do this, understanding the present time. The hour has already come for you to wake up from your slumber, because our salvation is nearer now than when we first believed. The night is nearly over; the day is almost here" **(Rom. 13:11–12 NIV).**

Scripture Reading: Philippians 3:20–21; Hebrews 9:24–28

Introduction

We truly have a great salvation. Consequently, we should understand the amazing fullness of the salvation that God gives us through faith in Jesus and cooperation with the Holy Spirit as he works within us.

The Holy Spirit led the New Testament writers to relate salvation in a variety of ways. It is commonly described in terms of justification and regeneration. The New Testament portrays salvation in the present tense as a process that started with our conversion and continues from day to day. God is presently at work in us to deliver us from the sin that surrounds us. This is not salvation from the *punishment* of sin or the very *presence* of sin. Rather, it is salvation from the *power* of sin.

If you disregard any phase of this great salvation, your spiritual life will be impoverished. If you fail to appreciate what God has done for you in the past, you will live in uncertainty in the present and with much anxiety concerning the future. Today we want to focus on our great salvation in the future.

Socialist leader Karl Marx criticized religion by declaring that "religion is the opiate of the people." We must admit that sometimes salvation in the future is overemphasized, resulting in the neglect of God's will in the present. Others have thought of Jesus only as a funeral director who comes at the time of death to carry the soul into the presence of God. This is a caricature of New Testament teachings regarding our Lord's gracious provisions for us in the present as well as the future.

Understanding what the New Testament teaches about salvation in the future can be a great source of comfort to the aged believer and a thrilling challenge to the young disciple.

1. *This knowledge can help us in our struggle against evil.*
2. *This information can support us in our sorrows.*
3. *This insight can strengthen us in our conflicts.*
4. *This revelation of truth can serve as a reliable test for our scale of values.*

Understanding our great salvation in the future can help us discover what the ultimate values of life are and what the ultimate victory will be.

50

I. A great positive concerning heaven.

We have many questions as we face life beyond death, but the Bible does not give a detailed description of what we can expect. It does, however, provide some insight and understanding.

For one thing, God will be at the very center (John 14:1–3; Rev. 21:3). Heaven is more than a residence. It is a relationship with God as he has revealed himself in his Son, Jesus Christ. Devout believers have often thought in terms of how wonderful heaven will be because they will be reunited with loved ones who have preceded them in death. As comforting as this thought is, our primary focus will be on God rather than on our fellow believers.

Do you love God in the present? Do you hunger for an abiding sense of his loving presence at this very moment? Do you love him with all of your heart and soul and mind and strength? If so, heaven will be wonderful for you. If, however, you find in your heart an absence of love for God, and if you feel that you are ignoring him, you should be concerned about whether you have truly been born into his family.

II. Some great negatives concerning heaven.

A. *There will be no sin (Rev. 21:27).* Does sin in the present disturb you like a painful rock in your shoe as you walk the road of life? If so, rejoice because sin will be absent in heaven.

B. *There will be no tears of sorrow (Rev. 21:4).* Tears of sadness that we experience in the present are due to hardships that result from sin in our lives or in the lives of others. God will wipe away our tears not with a lace handkerchief but by removing the cause for those tears.

C. *There will be no pain.* Physicians will no longer be needed because sickness will be a thing of the past.

D. *There will be no death.* There will be no cemeteries on the hillsides of our heavenly home. Many people living in the present fear death, but for those who have trusted Christ, there will come a time when death will be no more.

E. *There will be no separation from those we love.* "And there was no longer any sea" (Rev. 21:1 NIV). In this context, the sea was what separated John from those who were dear to him in the city of Ephesus. He saw the sea as a barrier that divided people who loved each other. All barriers will be absent in heaven, and we will love each other sincerely and steadfastly.

F. *There will be no boredom or idleness.* "His servants will serve him" (Rev. 22:3 NIV). Heaven is not a place where we will rest and rust; it will be a place where we grow and minister to one another.

G. *There will be no temple in heaven (Rev. 21:22).* All of heaven will be a holy place of worship, and we will constantly be aware of God's presence.

H. *There will be no night (Rev. 21:25).* Darkness conceals and often creates fear and uncertainty. In heaven we will enjoy the perfect security that comes from God's loving presence.

I. *There will be no limitations to goodness (1 John 3:1–2).* We will be like God and no longer be hindered by a nature tainted with sin.

Conclusion

Salvation in the past, present, and future is made possible for us by God's grace. It is by his undeserved mercy that we are provided a Savior in Jesus Christ. Jesus alone is the agent through whom we obtain this great salvation. Surrender yourself to him that he might forgive your past and give you the gift of eternal life. Commit your life to him so you may experience a rich salvation in the present and look forward to the completion of that salvation in the future. Welcome him into your heart today, for he stands at the door waiting to come into your life (Rev. 3:20).

WEDNESDAY EVENING, FEBRUARY 5

Title: Gifts of the Spirit

Text: "To each one the manifestation of the Spirit is given for the common good" (**1 Cor. 12:7 NIV**).

Scripture Reading: 1 Corinthians 12:1–7

Introduction

This is an introductory message to a series of studies on the gifts of the Spirit. Even though the Lord gives each of his children one or more gifts, there are some basic facts that relate to all of them. Keep these in mind as we consider the Spirit's gifts.

I. All gifts are to honor Jesus (I Cor. 12:3).

A. *Jesus is at the very center of all Christendom.* "In him we live, and move, and have our being" (Acts 17:28). All that Christians have and all that they do are to honor Jesus.

B. *Jesus is the central message of the New Testament.* All the messages and promises in the New Testament point either directly or indirectly to him.

C. *Jesus is to be honored by all the gifts.* The only purpose of the gifts is to honor Jesus. Any gift that does not honor him is not of the Spirit. If a gift of the Spirit is not used to honor God, the person using the gift sins against God.

II. All gifts are to build up the church (I Cor. 12:7).

A. *The church is the body of Christ (1 Cor. 12:7, 12–13).* For the body to be strong and to function as it should, it needs to be built up. The gifts of the Spirit are for this purpose.

B. *The church is a divinely established institution (Matt. 16:18).* The Lord placed the church on his earth for the propagation of the gospel. The gifts of the Spirit enable the church to accomplish their mission.

III. All gifts are for a common cause.

A. *Each gift is to supplement and complement all the others.* No gift of the Spirit works independently of the others. Instead, each gift is to function in relation to all the others.

B. *Each Christian is to use his or her gifts to supplement and complement other Christians' gifts.* This cooperation is what enables the Lord's work to progress. He endows some of his children with one ability and others with another gift; they are to use these gifts together for the Lord's work. The church is to work somewhat like a football team, for example. On a football team, some members are assigned to block and some to run with the ball. It takes both to be a successful team.

IV. All gifts are important.

A. *This is a fact that each Christian needs to thoroughly fix in his or her mind.* The gifts of the Holy Spirit are the gifts of a sovereign God. Anything that anyone does for the Lord is important. Each person is to take inventory of his or her abilities, thank God for them, and use them according to God's plan.

B. *This is a fact that will make the world take notice.* The gifts of the Spirit make each individual important. No one is ignored, and no one is more important than another in God's sight. When others see the personal interest God takes in each person, they will be attracted to God.

V. All gifts are according to the Bible.

A. *The Bible is the inspired Word of God.* "All scripture is given by inspiration of God, and is profitable for doctrine, for reproof, for correction, for instruction in righteousness" (2 Tim. 3:16). There is no way the Spirit could inspire the writing of the Bible and then contradict himself in bestowing gifts.

B. *The Bible is the recorded revelation of God.* The Holy Spirit uses the Scriptures to inspire and inform. He also gives the human mind the ability to understand the revelation found in the Bible.

Conclusion

As a Christian, you have one or more gifts of the Holy Spirit. It is your privilege to discover them and use them for God's glory.

SUNDAY MORNING, FEBRUARY 9

Title: Purity—The Way to Happiness

Text: "Blessed are the pure in heart: for they shall see God" **(Matt. 5:8).**

Scripture Reading: Matthew 5:1–8

Hymns: "I Would Be True," Walter
"Fairest Lord Jesus," Anonymous
"O Love That Wilt Not Let Me Go," Matheson

Offertory Prayer: Our heavenly Father, we ask your forgiveness for the impurities that so often pollute our lives. As we continue to study the Beatitudes that point the way to happiness, may we carry them with us into every aspect of our lives. We bring to you our offerings in this moment of worship. May they truly express a commitment to surrender our own desires. In the name of Christ our Lord we pray. Amen.

Introduction

Nearly a million Americans will die of heart diseases this year, so we should be concerned about heart failure. But we should be equally concerned about heart impurity. This type of heart disease, if not "cured," may render a person spiritually dead for eternity. Many people who go through the motions of living are in reality dead. They are unresponsive to God's will, deaf to his call. Such individuals are in touch only with the world. They may attend church, sing on the worship team, teach a Sunday school class, or even help conduct a worship service, but they lack the spiritual dimension that only God can create in their lives.

In the beatitude we will study today, "Blessed are the pure in heart: for they shall see God," Jesus explains that heart disease can be avoided by keeping a pure heart. Three practical questions this beatitude raises are: Who are the pure in heart? How will they see God? And why are they happy?

I. Who are the pure in heart?

The word *pure* is used twenty-eight times in the New Testament alone. But what does it really mean? Are the pure in heart half-divine, half-human beings? Do they have no normal desires, no healthy drives, no emotional feelings? Are they saints who have lost all contact with the real world? Are the pure in heart perfect individuals who have never sinned?

Of course not. Jesus addresses ordinary people who have ordinary problems, and he gives them an extraordinary way to experience happiness. He offers them sound advice, which if followed, will always lead to a better life.

A. *The pure in heart are those who are cleansed.* An initial cleansing happens when a person commits his or her life to Jesus Christ. Purity cannot be produced by any human will. In fact, God said, "A new heart also will I give you, and a new spirit will I put within you: and I will take away the stony heart out of your flesh" (Ezek. 36:26). Such purity is produced only by becoming a new creature, experiencing a new birth.

To be saved, however, is not enough. A pure heart is not the result of a once-in-a-lifetime experience. It is produced from daily confession of our sins, which results in continual cleansing from them. Failure to realize this explains the unhappiness in some Christians' lives. They become cluttered with sin, and happiness becomes a matter of the past. We must remember John's promise, "If we confess our sins, he is faithful and just to forgive us our sins, and to cleanse us from all unrighteousness" (1 John 1:9).

B. *The pure in heart are those who have one goal in life.* Purity actually means singleness of mind, to be guided by one purpose.

The farther you expect to go in life, the more important is your aim. If you are not planning to go very far, then you may aim haphazardly. For example, imagine that you will shoot directly to the moon. There is no opportunity for a mid-course correction. If, in the launching of your rocket, the calculations are off by just one degree, you would miss the moon by more than one million miles!

Our aim in life must be extremely accurate. If our heart is out of line, if impurities have pushed us off course, we will surely miss the highest goal God has in mind for us. The pure in heart are those who have one aim in life: to glorify God.

C. *The pure in heart are those who have clean thoughts.* The 2,350-mile-long Mississippi River is the largest river in the United States. As it nears the Gulf of Mexico, it stretches to more than one mile in width. But to understand the river, you must also view it as it begins as a tiny, clear stream less than two feet deep, rushing out of the northern end of Lake Itasca in north-central Minnesota.

Just as we must visit the beginnings of a mighty river to understand its majestic flow, so we must look deeply into the source of morality to unlock the secret of a pure heart. That small brook that feeds the noble life bubbles forth from the hidden thoughts of one's heart.

Proverbs 23:7 reminds us that as a person "thinketh in his heart, so is he." It is what we think, not what we profess, that creates purity within. The pure in heart are those who have clean thoughts and, consequently, a clean life that produces happiness.

II. How will they see God?

This beatitude clearly states that those who are pure in heart will see God. But how? The pure in heart will "see" God by experiencing his reality, not by beholding him with physical eyes. During our Lord's earthly ministry, multitudes looked at him but saw nothing, unaware that they had viewed God in the flesh. To see God is to experience God and become sure of him. Purity removes obstacles that blur and distort his true image. That is why the pure in heart will see God.

A. *The pure in heart will see God by meeting the requirements.* This beatitude seems to teach that to see God, you must be pure in heart—that is, be cleansed from sin, have God's glorification as your aim, and think clean thoughts. All of this is possible only as we daily commit ourselves to God's will.

B. *The pure in heart will see God by believing that this experience is available to all.* A vision of God is a possibility within the grasp of each of his children. It is not simply for some great saint who is nearing the sunset of life. It is not simply for a remarkably devoted person who has committed his or her life to some area of Christian service. It is for all Christians of all times.

The pure in heart will see God by claiming this experience today. Too often we stress the future tense used in this beatitude. We say, "Yes, they *shall* see God." Of course it is true that later we will see him face-to-face. But it is equally true that God becomes a living reality and a friend closer than a brother in the present. To see God is to be certain of God, to experience him in the midst of life.

III. Why are they happy?

The beatitude promises, "Blessed [happy] are the pure in heart." And the answer to why they are happy is given in that same statement: "for they shall see God." The pure in heart are happy because they see God. And when they see God, the following things happen:

A. *They see themselves.* When Job saw God, he was able to see himself. Job said, "My ears had heard of you but now my eyes have seen you. Therefore I despise myself and repent in dust and ashes" (Job 42:5–6 NIV). When we see God, we are made painfully aware of our sins. And when we see our sins, we commit them to the Lord and purity becomes a reality.

B. *They are transformed.* A view of God does more than reveal our own sinfulness; it transforms us into the kind of people God wants us to be.

C. *They gain courage.* It is said of Moses that he endured as though he saw God. There is something about having this inner vision of God that provides courage and determination. When we take our eyes off God and focus on the oppositions and trials we face, we are apt to quit too soon and thus not win the crown.

D. *They become useful.* The person who has seen God is the most eager to serve him. A vision of God always imparts a burning desire to serve him. No sooner does God call for volunteers than Isaiah replies eagerly, "Here am I; send me" (Isa. 6:8). And Paul, having met Christ on the Damascus road, asked, "Lord, what wilt thou have me to do?"(Acts 9:6).

E. *They impart a sense of God's presence.* Those who had seen the disciples close to Jesus "took knowledge of them, that they had been with Jesus" (Acts 4:13). It is impossible to see God and to spend time with him without emanating a sense of his presence. A little boy was asked, "What is a saint?" He replied, "A saint is a person who lets the light shine through." Evidently he got this idea by watching the sun shine through the prophets and other great people of God in the stained-glass windows of his church. But he was certainly not far off base. A saint, or a person who is pure in heart, will let the light of God's grace and mercy shine through. As that person's heart remains pure, it remains transparent to God's light.

Conclusion

On one occasion, Alfred Lord Tennyson was asked, "What is your greatest desire?" He answered, "A clearer vision of God." Perhaps it was this single desire that prompted his final instructions to his son. He asked his son as the executor of his estate to place his poem "Crossing the Bar" at the end of his collection of poems when they were published. He seemed to mean that his final wish was to see his pilot. He captured the truth of Christ's beatitude, "Blessed are the pure in heart: for they shall see God."

SUNDAY EVENING, FEBRUARY 9

Title: The Scriptures and Our Great Salvation

Text: "But as for you, continue in what you have learned and have become convinced of, because you know those from whom you learned it, and how from infancy you have known the Holy Scriptures, which are able to make you wise for salvation through faith in Christ Jesus" **(2 Tim. 3:14–15 NIV).**

Scripture Reading: 2 Timothy 3:14–17

Introduction

Our text speaks of salvation as comprehensive and exhaustive, rather than being limited to the initial experience that occurs when a person receives Jesus Christ as Lord and Savior.

Ours is truly a great salvation. It includes salvation from the penalty of sin, which, for believers, is a past work of God in their lives. It includes salvation from the presence of sin, which is a future experience for all Christians. Salvation from the presence of sin comes at the consummation of the ages when Jesus Christ returns to fully redeem believers from their human sinful state (Phil. 3:19–20; Heb. 9:27–28).

Our text speaks of our great salvation as a present experience and the Bible's role in helping each believer experience this great salvation. We first come to know Jesus through the good news of God's Word. Through this same Word, we learn about our heavenly home beyond this life. But God has given us the Bible so we can experience deliverance from the tyranny and destructiveness of sin in the present.

There is absolutely no way by which believers can experience the fullness of God's salvation in the present if they ignore God's Word. The writer of Hebrews addressed himself to believers. He warned them against the peril of ignoring the messages that teach us how to experience redemption in every area of life (cf. Heb. 2:1–3). Paul was speaking in this direction and with this emphasis when he said to the believers in Rome, "Everything that was written in the past was written to teach us, so that through the endurance taught in the Scriptures and the encouragement they provide we might have hope" (Rom. 15:4 NIV). Giving careful attention to the teachings in the Bible makes it possible for us to live a life that will glorify God (Rom. 15:5–6).

It is both interesting and profitable for Christians to discover how Jesus used the Scriptures during the great crises of his life (Matt. 4:1–11). Jesus was guided by the great truths in the Bible and used them to gain strength when pressured to swerve from God's will. He also used the Scriptures when defining his purpose for being (Luke 4:16–21). If our Lord found it necessary to rely on the great truths of God's Word, we should do likewise.

The rest of this message deals with some practical suggestions regarding our use of the Bible.

I. The function of the Bible.
    A. *The Bible reveals God's nature and the way of salvation (2 Tim. 3:14–16).*
    B. *The good news about God recorded in the Bible is used by the Holy Spirit to effect the new birth when one receives Jesus Christ as Lord and Savior (Rom. 1:16; James 1:21; 1 Peter 1:23).*
    C. *The Bible serves as milk that nourishes God's infants following their conversion experience (1 Peter 2:1–3).*
    D. *The Bible provides authoritative guidance for conduct that both pleases God and brings satisfaction to the believer (2 Tim. 3:16). Scripture is:*
        1. Profitable for teaching.
        2. Profitable for reproof.
        3. Profitable for correction.
        4. Profitable for instruction in righteousness.
    E. *The Bible is intended to equip receptive and responsive believers for fruitful service to God and others (2 Tim. 3:17).*

II. How to read the Bible.
Everyone needs practical suggestions regarding how to read and study the Bible effectively.

A. *Read the Bible regularly (Ps. 1:1–2).* As we feed our body daily, so we should feed our spirit daily.
B. *Read the Bible personally and subjectively.* Put yourself into every situation. Put yourself right in the middle of each verse and let God speak to you.
C. *Read the Bible intelligently.*
  1. Try to discover the historical situation behind the passage of Scripture you are reading. You need to know what the writer meant at the time the Scriptures were written to understand it to the fullest.
  2. Discover the meaning of the words used in the passage. A good Bible dictionary can be very helpful at this point.
  3. Be logical in your study of the Bible—that is, read it according to the correct interpretation of the language and the writer's purpose. Do not treat the Bible in a magical or superstitious way. Is the writer speaking literally or poetically? Is he speaking in terms of a legalistic precept, or is he dealing with a great principle? You cannot interpret figurative language in a literal way and come to the right conclusion and vice versa.
  4. Always remember that the Bible is a spiritual book. It is an inspired book produced by the Holy Spirit as he worked in and through holy men. Only with the Holy Spirit's help can you fully grasp God's Word for your life.
D. *Read the Bible systematically.* Read a book of the Bible straight through. Don't just skip around.
E. *Read the Bible prayerfully.* Consider Bible study as the listening side of the prayer experience.
F. *Read the Bible obediently.* As God reveals his good and loving will for you, be obedient to him.

Conclusion

Here are several practical suggestions as you decide to study the Bible with more diligence and spiritual hunger.

1. Look for promises to claim.
2. Look for commands to obey.
3. Look for sins to avoid.
4. Look for failures to avoid.
5. Look for examples to follow.
6. Always look to the Savior for guidance and help.

The Bible speaks of the great Savior who wants to save you from the penalty of sin. He is willing to redeem you today if you will come to him in faith, committing your life to him.

By using the Scriptures to teach and instruct you, this precious Savior wants to save you from the faults and flaws to which human nature is so inclined. He will speak to your heart through the Scriptures if you will let him. Don't neglect your great salvation by ignoring God's Word.

WEDNESDAY EVENING, FEBRUARY 12

Title: Calling Jesus Lord

Text: "I want you to know that no one who is speaking by the Spirit of God says, 'Jesus be cursed,' and no one can say, 'Jesus is Lord,' except by the Holy Spirit" (**1 Cor. 12:3 NIV**).

Scripture Reading: 1 Corinthians 12:1–7

Introduction

The most profound thought that crosses a human mind is the love of God as it is revealed in Jesus Christ. It is beyond our understanding that Jesus would come to earth and live and die for humankind's sin, providing salvation for those who have faith in him. How that faith comes about is the theme of this message. The basic work of the Holy Spirit is to lead those who are lost to an intelligent and yet simple confession of Jesus as Lord. No one can make this confession apart from the gift of the Holy Spirit.

I. First, consider some general comments about this confession.

A. *There are two observations regarding the true test of the inspiration of the Spirit of God.* First, its nature is always intelligible. Second, the Holy Spirit always focuses attention on Jesus Christ.

B. *The Holy Spirit's main goal is to glorify Christ and secure Christ's lordship in people's lives.* In other words, the ministry of the Holy Spirit is Christ-centered. The true test of any work of the Spirit is the place it gives to Jesus Christ. The Holy Spirit directs all his powers toward Jesus' glorification.

C. *The confession of Jesus as Lord distinguishes believers from unbelievers.* This confession becomes the basis of all the other gifts that will be considered in later messages. Unless a person has accepted Jesus as Savior and made him Lord, there is no way the Spirit can give additional gifts.

II. Second, consider how the Holy Spirit enables people to acknowledge Jesus as Lord.

A. *He reveals the sinfulness of sin (John 16:8).* Conviction of sin is a prerequisite to repentance and receiving the divine nature. The sin referred to in John 16:8 is failure to believe in Jesus as Savior. *Reprove* is a legal term implying the presentation of evidence or proof. It brings to light true character.

60

B. *He reveals the certainty of truth about righteousness (John 15:26).* In revealing the truth, the Word takes prominence. The Word is both incarnate (John 1:14), Jesus Christ, and written, the Bible.

C. *He reveals Christ's sufficiency (John 16:14–15).* For people to be saved from their sinful nature, they must realize that they are sinners. The Holy Spirit makes them aware of this fact. After they come to realize their sinful condition, they must see Jesus as sufficient to save from any sin. This is also the Holy Spirit's work.

Conclusion

At this time, it is fitting to do some soul searching. Is Jesus your Savior? Are you aware of your sinful condition, and do you now see Jesus as Lord? The Holy Spirit is at work. He wants you to be saved. Listen to him speaking to your heart, and commit your life to Jesus as your Savior.

SUNDAY MORNING, FEBRUARY 16

Title: Peacemaking—The Way to Happiness

Text: "Blessed are the peacemakers: for they shall be called the children of God" **(Matt. 5:9)**.

Scripture Reading: Matthew 5:1–9

Hymns: "Pass It On," Kaiser
"Christian Hearts in Love United," Zinzendorf
"Let Us Break Bread Together," Spiritual

Offertory Prayer: Our Father God, in a world filled with corruption and violence, help us to be instruments of peace. Let us face each new day by meeting its choices with gratitude, its difficulties with fortitude, and its conflicts with courage.

Accept the gifts we lay on your altar as an expression of our devotion to Jesus Christ, the Prince of Peace, in whose name we pray. Amen.

Introduction

Disagreements, feuds, and suspicion seem to be the rule of the day rather than the exception. Even the routine of daily life can lead a person to explode emotionally and spiritually. To those who calm the troubled waters of humankind's discord, Jesus promises joy and blessings. In fact, Jesus said that peacemakers would be known as the children of God.

In each of the twenty-seven books of the New Testament, the word *peace* is found. It appears eighty-eight times. The story of the good news of Jesus Christ begins with the words, "Glory to God in the highest, and on earth peace, good will toward men" (Luke 2:14). Near the conclusion of our Lord's ministry, his loving benediction is, "Peace I leave with you, my peace I give unto you" (John 14:27). And the apostle Paul introduced each of his epistles with that familiar greeting, "Grace to you and peace." God needs human instruments through whom this peace may be shared. And in this beatitude, Christ challenges each of us to become a peacemaker. A person must qualify for the privilege of peacemaking. It is a right reserved only for those who meet three requirements.

I. The privilege of peacemaking.

A. *The privilege of peacemaking is the privilege of those who are at peace with God.* This beatitude is constructed on the six preceding beatitudes. We are not privileged to become peacemakers until we admit our spiritual poverty, mourn over sin, practice the self-control that results from meekness, hunger and thirst for righteousness, show mercy, and become pure in heart.

   The fact that we need to make peace with God does not mean that God is angry with us or that he is standing to one side unwilling to communicate with us. The only cause of alienation between us and God is our sin and disobedience. Henry David Thoreau, although a transcendentalist rather than an evangelical, sought to fellowship with God by Walden Pond. He claimed to maintain an intimate communion with God that was perhaps more intimate than relationships between many believers. As he neared the end of his life, someone asked if he had made his peace with God. Thoreau replied, "We never quarreled." In feeling at peace with God, he was at peace with others and thus a peacemaker with humankind.

B. *The privilege of peacemaking is the privilege of those who are at peace with others.* "If you are offering your gift at the altar and there remember that your brother or sister has something against you, leave your gift there in front of the altar. First go and be reconciled to them; then come and offer your gift" (Matt. 5:23–24 NIV). The ending of hostilities and the refusal to have conflict is not necessarily peace. For instance, two people may stop entering into violent dialogue but retreat into days of stony silence instead. They are not friends; they have simply refused to speak with one another. Two countries may declare a cease fire, but that does not guarantee a lasting peace.

   Peace is a positive attribute. It is actually a matter of the right kind of relationships. Constant goodwill results when individuals are at peace with one another. To be at peace with others, we must not insist that they meet us halfway. Peacemakers reach out, take the initiative. Their concern is not who is to blame but rather how reconciliation and peace can be attained. Peacemakers are not fault-finders; they are healers.

C. *The privilege of peacemaking is the privilege of those who are at peace with themselves.* Those who try to calm the troubled waters of others' oceans without first smoothing the ripples of their own pond find their efforts in vain. People who are always at war with fellow workers, family, and friends are at war with themselves.

We may speak a word that unintentionally causes friends to hurt within, or we may share a story that, whether true or false, injures another. When this becomes a pattern in our lives, it is obvious to everyone around us that we are not at peace with ourselves. Peacemakers begin with themselves.

II. The purpose of peacemaking.

Peacemaking is not peace at any price. It is not appeasement or cowardice. Some individuals pride themselves in never becoming involved in a feud, when the truth is they lack courage to stand up for what is right. If decency and justice are to be defended, they let others do the work. Those who live by this cowardly code of conduct are really enemies of peace.

The apostle Paul saw reconciliation as the purpose of the ministry of both Christ and Christians. "All this is from God, who reconciled us to himself through Christ and gave us the ministry of reconciliation: that God was reconciling the world to himself in Christ, not counting people's sins against them. And he has committed to us the message of reconciliation" (2 Cor. 5:18–19 NIV).

A. *The purpose of peacemaking is to bring reconciliation between us and God.* "We are therefore Christ's ambassadors, as though God were making his appeal through us. We implore you on Christ's behalf: Be reconciled to God" (2 Cor. 5:20 NIV). Jesus reminds us that peace between God and humankind is not peace at any price. God is not an appeaser. He does not compromise. He offers peace on the terms of absolute surrender. "Unless you repent, you too will all perish" (Luke 13:3 NIV).

B. *The purpose of peacemaking is to bring reconciliation between us and others.* Perhaps the most well-known prayer offered by St. Francis of Assisi begins with these words: "Lord, make me an instrument of Thy peace." The singing evangelist then went on to pray, "Where there is hate, may I bring love. Where there is offense, may I bring pardon." This is the ultimate purpose of peacemakers.

III. The promise of peacemaking.

"Blessed are the peacemakers: for they shall be called the children of God" (Matt. 5:9).

A. *The promise of peacemaking is made to those who work for peace.* Jesus said in the beatitude, "Blessed are the peacemakers." The kind of peace of which he was speaking does not just happen. A nation may drift into war, but if peace is to be maintained, it is the result of deliberate effort. Peacemakers do more than dream of peace; they roll up their sleeves, get involved in the difficulties of life, and make peace happen.

There are many things we cannot do. We may not all be able to accumulate great fortunes, or write musical masterpieces, or capture beautiful scenes on canvas. But we can all be peacemakers. Each of us can overcome evil with good.

B. *The promise of peacemaking is the promise of happiness.* Jesus promised, "Blessed [happy] are the peacemakers." Happiness is the inevitable result of knowing that you have had an important part in salvaging good from an otherwise hopeless situation. All of us can think of people who have interceded on our behalf as peacemakers. We will always be indebted to them for saving us from disaster. The promise of happiness is fulfilled both in the lives of peacemakers and in the lives of those for whom peace was made.

The promise of peacemaking is the promise of being known as "the children of God" (Matt. 5:9). This is a unique beatitude, for not one of the other beatitudes has an ending like this one. The old statement, "Like father, like son," is true in this case. Likely the reason Jesus said peacemakers would be called children of God is because as they make peace they resemble their heavenly Father. What better compliment could be paid to anyone?

Conclusion

Peacemaking is the way to happiness. This privilege is yours only when you are at peace with God, with others, and with yourself. The promise made to those who work for peace is the promise of happiness and the promise of being known as God's children. "Blessed are the peacemakers: for they shall be called the children of God!"

Sunday Evening, February 16

Title: Prayer and Our Great Salvation

Text: "Jesus told his disciples a parable to show them that they should always pray and not give up" (**Luke 18:1 NIV**).

Scripture Reading: Luke 18:1–8; Matthew 7:7–11

Introduction

Our salvation is so great that most of us never enter into an understanding of its full significance. The word *salvation* is a word that refers to many of God's activities on our behalf. For example, it is used to refer to our initial experience with God when we receive Jesus Christ as Lord and Savior and also to describe the ultimate consummation of God's gracious work in us and for us when Jesus Christ comes again. *Salvation* is also used to describe the total process by which the Holy Spirit seeks to reproduce within each believer the character of Jesus Christ and in which the believer cooperates with the Holy Spirit to become truly Christian in every area of life.

Today we focus our attention on another of the great gifts that God uses to bring about our full redemption from sin as a present experience. Last Sunday we looked at how God has provided the Scriptures so that his children can be delivered from sin's destructive power. Today we look at God's gift of prayer as part of the divine means made available to those who experience salvation. Ignoring this means by which it is possible for us to experience full salvation is to impoverish our lives today and deprive us of spiritual rewards beyond Christ's second coming and the resurrection of the dead.

I. The experience of salvation begins with a prayer (Luke 18:13–14).

That the Christian life begins with prayer can be illustrated by the account of the tax collector who cried out to God for mercy, was heard, and experienced justification. To have Jesus Christ in your heart, you must invite him to come in, for he will not be an intruder or an unwelcome guest (Rom. 10:10–13).

II. The experience of full salvation is made possible by prayer.

Salvation of the soul from the penalty of sin is just the beginning of God's great salvation for us. He wants to save us from the power and practice of sin. We know that God has given us the Scriptures to deliver us from evil and to make possible a fruitful life (Ps. 1:1–3). God declared to Joshua that attention to his Word would provide him with the key to success (Josh. 1:8). Peter said that the Holy Scriptures provide food for the nourishment of believers' souls (1 Peter 2:1–2).

Today let us focus our hearts and minds on the exciting truth that our heavenly Father has designed prayer to help his children experience salvation in the present. After the gift of faith and a personal relationship with him, there is no greater gift that our Father God has given us than the gift of prayer.

Some people see prayer as a duty, and it is. Some see prayer only as one of God's commandments to us; if you think of it as a commandment, be assured that it was motivated by God's love for us. Others see prayer as a necessity like food and air.

Let us recognize and respond to prayer as a divine invitation to come into our heavenly Father's throne room so we may receive the blessings he has for us. Prayer will equip us to live on the highest possible plane and to experience life in its richest quality.

Prayer should be recognized as an opportunity for communication with God in the form of dialogue rather than a monologue. Hearing what our Father has to say is much more important than merely voicing our petitions.

A. *Prayer brings an awareness of God's nearness (James 4:8)*. This can bring great comfort and inspire confidence as we realize that God waits like the father of the prodigal son for us to come home.

B. *The prayer of confession brings the assurance of forgiveness (1 John 1:9)*. To confess means to agree with God. Sin is a present reality because all of us are less than perfect. God wants to forgive us, cleanse us, and make wonderful fellowship possible.

C. *The prayer of humility brings mercy and grace for every time of need (Heb. 4:16)*. Our Savior is compassionate because he has suffered as we have; he is able to minister to our deepest personal needs.

D. *The prayer of petition and thanksgiving brings peace that passes understanding (Phil. 4:6–7)*. Children of God are encouraged to make every need and every problem a matter of earnest prayer to the loving Father.

Conclusion

The prayer for pardon brings conversion, cleansing, and acceptance. Call on God now, for he has promised to hear you and bless you. He will not turn you away. God is waiting to show you grace and mercy.

WEDNESDAY EVENING, FEBRUARY 19

Title: Concerning Spiritual Gifts

Text: "Now about the gifts of the Spirit, brothers and sisters, I do not want you to be uninformed" (**1 Cor. 12:1 NIV**).

Scripture Reading: 1 Corinthians 12:1–7

Introduction

Augustine related of a certain heathen, who showed him his idols, saying, "Here is my god: where is thine?" then, pointing up at the sun, he said, "Lo! here is my God: where is thine?" so, showing him divers creatures, still upbraided him with, "Here are my gods: where are thine?" Augustine answered him, "I showed him not my God, not because I had not one to show him, but because he had not eyes to see him" (Elon Foster, *6000 Sermon Illustrations* [Grand Rapids: Baker, 1972], 60).

The Holy Spirit has many wonderful gifts for believers, but many do not recognize them because of spiritual blindness. The word *gifts* will be emphasized in this message.

I. First, consider the subject itself, "gifts."

A. *Two words are interpreted "gift."* The first is *charis*, usually interpreted "grace." The Holy Spirit's gifts are of grace; they cannot be bought or earned. The other is *charisma*, from which we get our word *charismatic*. This word has a wide range of uses—from the gift of salvation

(Rom. 6:23) to the gift of providential care (2 Cor. 1:11). It is usually used for special abilities given to individuals by God. Thus a spiritual gift may be defined as a God-given ability for service.

B. *The gifts are to be distinguished from other words that relate to the Holy Spirit.*

   1. The *gift* of the Spirit and the *gifts* of the Spirit are separate. All believers have the *gift* of the Spirit—that is, he is in every believer (Acts 2:38). The *gifts*, however, are special abilities given according to God's will to those who are indwelt with the Holy Spirit.

   2. The gifts are separate from talents. Talents are associated with aptitudes and skills. Gifts are spiritual abilities. Talents depend on natural power, gifts on spiritual power. Talents instruct or inspire on a natural level. The gifts of the Holy Spirit empower believers.

   3. The gifts are separate from offices. A person may have a gift belonging to an office without holding that position. But a believer may not hold a divinely appointed office without the corresponding gift to perform it.

   4. The gifts are separate from fruit. Gifts deal with service, but fruit with character. Gifts are means to an end; fruit is the end. Gifts are what a person has, and fruit is what a person is. Gifts are from without, fruit from within. All gifts are not for all believers, but all believers have a gift. Gifts will cease, but fruit will not cease.

   5. The gifts are separate from goodness. It is better to be good than gifted. Love is the theme of the chapter that stands in the middle of a discussion of gifts.

II. Second, consider the purpose of the gifts (1 Cor. 12:7).

   A. *The purpose of the gifts of the Holy Spirit is to bring together, to be helpful or useful.* The church is to be built up by continuous use of the gifts (Eph. 4:12).

   B. *The word "gifts" is plural—there are many.* Paul used the parts of the human body working together as an analogy to illustrate how every spiritual gift is of vital importance. Every person using the gifts he or she has been given supplements and complements the gifts given to fellow believers.

Conclusion

Each child of God has the gift of the Spirit, for the Holy Spirit dwells within all believers. Each child of God also has some spiritual gift (Eph. 4:7) to be used for the glory and honor of God.

SUNDAY MORNING, FEBRUARY 23

Title: Persecution—The Way to Happiness

Text: "Blessed are those who are persecuted because of righteousness, for theirs is the kingdom of heaven. Blessed are you when people insult you, persecute you and falsely say all kinds of evil against you because of me. Rejoice and be glad, because great is your reward in heaven, for in the same way they persecuted the prophets who were before you" **(Matt. 5:10–12 NIV)**.

Scripture Reading: Matthew 5:10–12

Hymns: "Stand Up, Stand Up for Jesus," Duffield
"Lead On, O King Eternal," Shurtleff
"Onward, Christian Soldiers," Baring-Gould

Offertory Prayer: Our heavenly Father, in a violent world filled with disturbing problems and saddening sights, may our hearts be strengthened even in the face of personal persecution. Save us from pitying ourselves on those rare occasions when we must bear the cross of Christ.

We offer our thanks with humble hearts. Receive from our hands the gifts that express our devotion to you. May these gifts be used as a means to further your kingdom. In Jesus' name we pray. Amen.

Introduction

We are made to love and to be loved. We like to be liked. Friendship is the atmosphere in which we breathe most freely. To be ridiculed as a child is a heartbreaking experience, but the pain is not lessened as one becomes an adult. Persecution in the form of harassment and unfair accusations may destroy our private castles of security. Of all the injuries that can be afflicted on a human being, persecution possibly comes the closest to making life hell on earth.

Therefore the Lord's final beatitude seems almost paradoxical. "Blessed are those who are persecuted because of righteousness, for theirs is the kingdom of heaven." This is probably the most difficult of the Beatitudes to believe. The reason for this difficulty is that persecution seems to be the antithesis of happiness. Furthermore, it seems like a strange statement to come from the lips of such a compassionate Savior. How can we understand our Lord when he congratulated those who were persecuted and encouraged them to rejoice in their persecution? Obviously there is a paradox to be explained.

I. A paradox to be explained.

"Blessed [happy] are those who are persecuted." It seems incredible that our Lord would say something so contradictory, and it is probably the most confusing declaration he ever made.

68

A. *It is a paradox that a person can be "happy" when suffering.* How can anyone be happy when being persecuted or lied about? We enjoy the sense of security that comes from occasional words of approval, but persecution destroys everything that brings enjoyment and security.

Persecution encourages self-examination, which always makes a person happier. We must be careful to avoid coming to the conclusion that we are suffering for righteousness' sake each time we are persecuted. More often we suffer for something we have done wrong rather than right. When a newly enlisted soldier discovers that he is out of step with the rest of his troop, his first action should be to listen to see if he is in error. One value of persecution is that it promotes self-examination so we can understand why others do not like us. Perhaps we should ask ourselves whether we measure up to the preceding beatitudes.

Persecution affords an opportunity to demonstrate our loyalty to Christ. Many of us deny him by our silence when we have a chance to stand up and be counted. We are afraid that open loyalty to Jesus may bring persecution. To stand faithfully by our Savior's side does bring persecution, but it also brings happiness.

B. *It is a paradox that a person can be persecuted for doing good.* The Living Bible says, "Happy are those who are persecuted because they are good" (Matt. 5:10), and the *Good News* translation reads, "Happy are those who are persecuted because they do what God requires" (GNT).

Sometimes a person is persecuted for doing good because doing good disturbs others. No one embodied the Beatitudes more perfectly than Jesus Christ himself. Yet he was the most hated advocate of the Christian faith. Even though he advised his disciples against needlessly antagonizing their enemies, their Christlike goodness upset others.

The church and individual Christians who dare to stand by the principles of Christ must be prepared for persecution. Whenever the church ceases to be the moral conscience of its community, it also ceases to be the yeast in the bread, the salt of the earth, and the light set on the hill.

Sometimes doing good interferes with those who want to do bad. For example, the pure in heart insist on truth. This interferes with those who want to follow their passions or prejudices. People who are merciful advocate forgiveness while others demand vengeance. Peacemakers quietly seek to stop hostility while warmongers insist that the only solution to a world problem is open warfare.

II. A pattern to be avoided.

Nero's persecution that slaughtered Christians by the hundreds may not be the pattern in America, but persecution continues to be real and tends to follow the pattern Christ mentioned in verse 11. This pattern of persecuting others should be avoided. Jesus said, "Blessed are you when people insult you, persecute you and falsely say all kinds of evil against you because of me" (NIV).

A. *The pattern of slander.* Jesus mentioned those who "insult you." This expression speaks of misrepresentations that degrade another person's reputation. The early church was not immune to such slander. They were accused of cannibalism as they gathered to observe the Lord's Supper. They were charged with immoral practices as they gathered for their love feast. The people of the early church were even accused of being fanatical doomsayers as they spoke of the ultimate end of the world. Some people today continue to use slander as an effective tool for persecution. But Christ reminds us that this pattern should be avoided.

B. *The pattern of harassment.* In verse 11 Jesus spoke of those who "persecute you." Persecution may be defined as repeatedly raiding another or as continually annoying another. For instance, the only crime of first-century believers was that they put Christ before Caesar. They were harassed for this dedication and were killed by the thousands.

However subtly the pattern of harassment may be followed, Jesus clearly commanded us to avoid it. We may not understand or appreciate another person, but persecution through harassment in any form is forbidden.

C. *The pattern of falsehoods.* Continuing in verse 11, Jesus spoke of those who "falsely say all kinds of evil" about believers. Slander usually has some element of truth in it, however small. But falsehood has no truth in it whatsoever. Jesus became the object of many wicked accusations. His enemies tried to destroy his good name and discount his miracles and ministry. Inevitably, this type of persecution will come to any Christian whose lifestyle clearly shows that Jesus Christ makes a difference. It is never easy to suffer this form of persecution, but every Christian must be ready to face it. Obviously, telling falsehoods is a pattern to be avoided by those who want to experience the blessings of this beatitude.

III. The promise to be enjoyed.

In verses 10–12 Jesus mentioned that all who endure persecution will be rewarded. It is a promise made only to those who suffer for righteousness' sake and who are spoken against falsely for Christ's sake. This is a threefold promise.

A. *It is a present promise.* In verse 10 Jesus said, "For theirs is the kingdom of heaven." Even in the midst of persecution you can enjoy this promise. It is for the here and now. When believers must suffer because of their faith, they have discovered the way to experience the closest possible companionship with their Lord. The promise that "theirs is the kingdom of heaven" becomes a reality.

B. *It is a future promise.* "Rejoice and be glad, because great is your reward in heaven" (v. 12 NIV). The apostle Paul must have been aware of this promise when he wrote, "As it is written: 'What no eye has seen, what no ear has heard, and what no human mind has conceived'— the things God has prepared for those who love him—these are the things God has revealed to us by his Spirit" (1 Cor. 2:9–10 NIV).

C. *It is a perennial promise.* Jesus continued, "For in the same way they persecuted the prophets who were before you" (Matt. 5:12 NIV). This is a promise of being identified with God's chosen people, a promise that is realized both in the present and in the future. To suffer persecution is to walk the same road as the prophets and martyrs. To suffer for what is right is to be part of a great succession.

George Bernard Shaw said that the finest compliment the world can pay any author is to burn his books, thus showing that his books are so dynamic and explosive as to be considered intolerable. And the finest compliment that can be paid to Christians is persecution because of righteousness, for then they have been identified with God's choicest people.

Conclusion

In America, where it is so easy for Christians to live comfortable and safe lives, we often forget that persecution of Christians is rampant in many parts of the world. Whether persecution comes in the open threat on one's life or in the insidious words spoken by a fellow Christian, you must be willing to suffer persecution for righteousness' sake if you want to experience the happiness that Jesus promised. The promise "Theirs is the kingdom of heaven" continues to bless those who endure through severe persecution.

SUNDAY EVENING, FEBRUARY 23

Title: The Holy Spirit and Our Great Salvation

Text: "Do you not know that your bodies are temples of the Holy Spirit, who is in you, whom you have received from God? You are not your own; you were bought at a price. Therefore honor God with your bodies" (**1 Cor. 6:19–20 NIV**).

Scripture Reading: 1 Corinthians 6:9–20

Introduction

Paul was a great missionary who preached the gospel in Corinth, a famous city that stood at the gateway between two worlds. It was cosmopolitan, sophisticated, and wicked. The people who responded to the gospel experienced forgiving grace and accepted Jesus Christ as their Lord and Savior. They became children of God through faith in Jesus Christ.

The apostle Paul, as God's servant and as the instrument of his love, instructed the Corinthian believers in the heritage they received as God's children. Through example and teaching, he communicated to them that salvation through Jesus Christ is more than a mere introduction into the family of God and a relationship with him. Paul stressed that their great salvation was more than the salvation of their souls and a ticket to heaven at the end of the way. Paul explained that salvation not only involves the soul, but it also provides deliverance and freedom from self-destructive attitudes and actions that prevent a person from reflecting God's goodness. Paul noted that these believers previously had been part of a corrupt society. He reminded them of a dramatic change in their relationship with God—a relationship that had now become real through faith in Jesus Christ and the Holy Spirit's presence within (1 Cor. 6:11).

The point of this section of Corinthians is to emphasize that salvation through Jesus Christ includes redemption of the body from evil just as it includes salvation of the soul. Paul affirmed that we are to serve God and introduce him to others while we are in the body. He was saying to new believers, "Honor God in your body. Demonstrate his grace through your body. Introduce others to God by means of the Holy Spirit's presence within your innermost being. Become the kind of people who will serve as temples where God can come and meet unbelievers and where unbelievers can come and experience God's presence and learn about his great love."

Paul had stood in Corinth among pagan temples that were supposedly the dwelling places of the gods. He now declared that the church was the shrine of the Holy Spirit. He said that to live an immoral life was to defile the temple in which God wanted to work to meet the needs of an unsaved world.

We have seen how God uses Scripture to help us fully comprehend our great salvation in the present. We know that he has given us the privilege of prayer so that we can achieve this goal. Today let us respond to the Holy Spirit as a way to enable us to experience our complete salvation.

I. The Holy Spirit came into the world on the day of Pentecost to continue the work of Jesus Christ.

II. The Holy Spirit convinced us of our need for salvation (John 16:8–11).

The Holy Spirit convicts people of their sin. This conviction serves the same function for the soul that fever does for the body. Fever is not the illness; it is just a symptom of the illness. Fever is the body's cry for a cure. The guilt we feel about our sin is God's way of telling us that we have a problem that needs to be solved. Only Jesus Christ can solve it.

III. The Holy Spirit effected the new birth when we received Christ as Savior (John 3:7–8; Titus 3:5).

IV. The Holy Spirit gave us assurance of kinship (Rom. 8:11–16).

God desires that we have assurance of our relationship with him, that we know him as our loving Father (1 John 3:1–2). The joy of this assurance belongs to all believers who trust and obey the Spirit as he leads us in understanding God's Word and in bringing our lives into harmony with God's will.

V. The gift of the Spirit is God's seal of ownership and his guarantee of our ultimate salvation from death and the grave (Eph. 1:13–14).

The gift of the Holy Spirit is how God puts the official seal of his ownership on each believer. The presence of the Holy Spirit is the guarantee that he will rescue us from death and the grave and return us to the home of our heavenly Father. This is salvation in the future tense.

VI. The Holy Spirit creates conflict with our sinful nature (Gal. 5:16–21).

The new birth and the infilling of the Holy Spirit do not instantly set us free from the tyranny of our sinful nature. Conversion is a significant experience of turning from all self-destructive attitudes and actions that are contrary to God's will. The Holy Spirit comes in to purge out these enemies of the soul and to establish God's will. His activity is in some ways similar to that of a friendly army that comes in to assist a country in driving off invaders. The work of the Holy Spirit has some parallels to the work of a powerful antibiotic drug that is injected into the body of a sick person to defeat an infection.

VII. The Holy Spirit leads us in cultivation of the fruit of the Spirit (Gal. 5:22–23).

The Holy Spirit is interested in doing more than destroying evil. He wants to nourish the growth of our inner being so we will reflect the grace and beauty of Jesus Christ. The words of Galatians 5:22–23 present a verbal portrait of Jesus Christ. This fruit is the heritage of every believer who makes a proper response to God's gift of the Holy Spirit.

Conclusion

What will your response be to God's gift of the Holy Spirit? It is possible for you to reply negatively to the Holy Spirit. You may remain in ignorance concerning his gracious work, or you may neglect to make a positive and constant response to his work. Some people are afraid to let the Holy Spirit do his work because they mistakenly feel that they would become some kind of religious nut.

Instead of a negative response, let us each make a positive response.

1. *Recognize the presence of the Holy Spirit who has come to dwell within us.*
2. *Rejoice in what the Holy Spirit has done for us in the past.*
3. *Release yourself to the Holy Spirit's control with trust (Acts 5:32).*
4. *Respond fully to the Holy Spirit as you come to understand his work.*

Let us walk in the Spirit (Gal. 5:16) and be led by the Spirit (v. 18). Let us daily be under the control of the Holy Spirit (Eph. 5:18) and listen to him as he speaks to our hearts through Scripture and through life experiences (Heb. 3:7–8).

WEDNESDAY EVENING, FEBRUARY 26

Title: The Filling of the Holy Spirit

Text: "Do not get drunk on wine, which leads to debauchery. Instead, be filled with the Spirit" **(Eph. 5:18 NIV)**.

Scripture Reading: Ephesians 5:18–21

Introduction

Not everyone agrees on what is meant by the "filling of the Holy Spirit." This message is not meant to be controversial. It is hoped that agreement will be reached on the use of terms and that all will benefit from the discussion.

I. First, consider the character of being filled.

What is the meaning of being filled?

A. *To be filled by the Spirit is to be controlled by him.* In Ephesians 5:18 Paul spoke of not being drunk with wine. When a person is drunk, he or she is under the control of alcohol. Then the contrast is made—"Be filled with [controlled by] the Spirit."

B. *We are commanded to be controlled (Eph. 5:18).* Believers are automatically indwelt by the Spirit but not controlled. They are commanded to be controlled by yielding to the Holy Spirit. If they don't do so, they are disobedient and sinful. The verb translated "be filled" is ongoing action. Thus being filled with the Spirit is a continual process.

II. Second, consider the conditions of being filled.

A. *Two general concepts are associated with being filled: desire (Matt. 5:6) and obedience.* The Holy Spirit will not violate a believer's will, nor will a believer be used in a way contrary to God's will.

B. *Obedience is key to being Spirit-filled.*

    1. Dedication is the foundation of a Spirit-filled life. Christians are exhorted not to quench the Spirit (1 Thess. 5:19), and dedication is the opposite of quenching. It involves the initial commitment

found in Romans 12:1–2: presentation of the whole self, separation from the world, and transformation of the mind.

2. Direction is a continuous part of being filled. Every Christian who desires to be controlled by the Spirit needs and must be willing to be directed by him in any of the variety of ways he chooses. The Lord recognizes sin in his children's lives and has made provision for it. He wants each of his children to respond to him favorably and be cleansed and victorious.

3. Dependence is vital to being Spirit-filled. Christians have high standards that cannot be attained by human strength. Only when believers walk with God in total dependence can they be Spirit-filled. Physical walking is an illustration. When we lift one foot to take a step, we depend on the other foot to hold us up.

III. Third, consider the consequence of being Spirit-filled.

A. *It results in Christlike character (Gal. 5:22–23).* Love has as its object the glory of God. Joy is seeing other Christians advance in their knowledge of truth. Peace is tranquility that comes from a right relationship with God. Longsuffering is the quality of never desiring revenge. Gentleness is beneficent thoughts. Goodness is kindness in action. Faithfulness is using all opportunities of service. Meekness is humility and servitude. Self-control is discipline.

B. *It results in worship and praise (Eph. 5:18–20).* Worship is the outward expression of praise and the inner expression of melody-making in the heart. It is having a thankful heart.

C. *It results in submissiveness.* When we are Spirit-filled, we will put the needs of others ahead of our own.

D. *It results in service (John 7:37–39).* The Lord only bestows gifts for usefulness. Christians do not receive from the Lord something they do not use.

Conclusion

One of the most vital needs of the world today is for God's servants to be controlled by the Holy Spirit. This will make for a dynamic church, useful Christians, and God's glory. I hope each of you will meet all the conditions and from now on live a life under his control.

MARCH

- **Sunday Mornings**

    As a prelude to Easter, begin the series "The Centrality of the Cross."

- **Sunday Evenings**

    Continue biblical studies based on the great salvation available to us through Jesus Christ in the series "Experiencing the Great Salvation of God."

- **Wednesday Evenings**

    Continue the series "Concerning the Gifts of the Holy Spirit."

SUNDAY MORNING, MARCH 1

Title: Behold the Lamb of God

Text: "The next day John saw Jesus coming toward him and said, 'Look, the Lamb of God, who takes away the sin of the world!'" **(John 1:29 NIV)**.

Scripture Reading: John 1:15–34

Hymns: "Alas! and Did My Savior Bleed," Watts
          "There's a Wideness in God's Mercy," Faber
          "Love Divine, All Loves Excelling," Wesley

Offertory Prayer: Our heavenly Father, the finest and noblest gifts we could offer you could never approach the magnitude of your gift to us—your Son and our Savior, the Lord Jesus Christ. Therefore, Father, our giving is merely an expression of our love for you. Our material gifts we bring as a token of that which you want from us most of all—ourselves. Bless these gifts, Father, and use them to bring honor and glory to your name. Through Jesus Christ we pray. Amen.

Introduction

Throughout the two thousand years of Christian history, the cross has been the focal point of our faith. Every other aspect of Christianity is given validity and power because of the cross and that for which it stands.

Without the cross, Christianity would be nothing but a religion. Because of the cross, Christianity is a way of life. Every one of Satan's efforts to tempt Jesus was aimed at getting him to bypass the cross. Never did Satan try to convince Jesus that he was not the Son of God or that he did not have "all power in heaven and in earth." But he did try to persuade him to choose some route besides the cross in his mission to save humanity.

But the cross was central in Jesus' mind. Time and again, in his words and in his actions, the cross and its redemptive message surfaced and confronted the people to whom he ministered. It was consistently a troubling thing to those who listened to him. It was offensive to the disciples and to the Jews.

I. The witness of John (John 1:19–28).

A. *John, a recluse who lived in the Jordan River Valley, was an unusual man in many respects.* He dressed strangely, wearing a coat of coarse camel hair. His diet was locusts and wild honey. Furthermore, he was not a social person. Yet John was a man with a mission—a mission to prepare the way for the coming Messiah. He was the herald who came before the King.

B. *It was John's unpopular task to shock people into awareness of their sin and of their need to repent and forsake their sins.* His was the first prophetic voice to be heard among God's people since the days of Malachi four hundred years earlier. No one living had ever heard a true prophet of God, nor had anyone seen the fiery eyes of a person who had been filled by the Spirit of God and used as a voice through which God himself spoke. John's word contained a piercing authority that disturbed consciences, confronted minds, and smote hearts.

C. *The priests and Levites sought out John in the wilderness of the Jordan and asked his identity.* They suggested three persons whom John might claim to be: the Messiah, Elijah, or "that prophet who is to come." John answered that he was nothing but a voice crying in the wilderness, pleading with humanity to prepare the way for the King, and to that end he was born. John's witness was to fade away so that Jesus Christ could be seen. He saw himself only as a finger pointing to Christ.

II. The witness of Jesus (John 1:29–31).

A. *Here appears the title of Jesus that is woven again and again into the language of the New Testament—the Lamb of God.* What was likely in John's mind when he made this incomparable declaration concerning Jesus' identity? He may have been thinking of the Passover lamb. The story of the Passover and its thrilling events was cherished in every Jewish family. So John may have been thinking, *Every year during the Passover, thousands of lambs are slain on the temple altar. But you continue to sin, dishonor God, and break his commandments. Jesus is the Lamb of God who takes away the sins of the entire world! He is the Lamb who will provide the sacrifice to end all sacrifices for sin.*

B. *John was the son of a priest, so he was familiar with the rituals of the temple and its many sacrifices.* He knew that every morning and evening a lamb was sacrificed in the temple for the sins of the people. As long as the temple stood, this daily sacrifice was made. In giving Jesus this symbolic title, John may have been thinking, *In the temple two lambs are offered daily to make restitution for your sins, but you continue to sin because you know that tonight, tomorrow, and the next day more lambs will be slain for your sins! But there is a Lamb who will die one time, and his death will have sufficient power to atone for your sins once and for all and also to change your lives!*

C. *Two great pictures of the Lamb are recorded in the Prophets.* Jeremiah wrote, "I was like a lamb or an ox that is brought to the slaughter" (Jer. 11:19). Isaiah wrote of the One who was brought "as a lamb to the slaughter" (Isa. 53:7). Both of these prophets had the vision of One to come who would, by his persecution and sacrifice, redeem his people. Perhaps John was thinking, *Your prophets dreamed and preached about One who was to come who would suffer and die for humanity. He has come! He is in your midst!*

D. *A fourth picture may have flashed into John's mind as he spoke of Jesus as the Lamb of God.* In the time between the Old and New Testaments, there were years of great struggle for God's people in which the Maccabees fought and died and conquered. In those days, the lamb, especially the horned lamb, was the symbol of a great conqueror. Judas Maccabeus, Samuel, David, and Solomon have been so described. So the lamb, as strange as it seems, stood for the conquering champion of God, a symbol of majesty and power. In Jesus we have the champion of God who fought with sin and mastered it in a single contest—on the cross!

E. *There is sheer wonder in the name "the Lamb of God."* It appears twenty-nine times in the book of Revelation. To John, as he wrote down that apocalyptic vision, it became one of the most precious titles of Christ and sums up his love, sacrifice, and triumph (see Rev. 5:6, 11–14).

III. The witness of the Spirit (John 1:32).

A. *John, upon baptizing Jesus in the Jordan River, saw a dove descend out of heaven and alight on Jesus' head.* In a flash of divine revelation, John knew immediately that it was the Holy Spirit coming to reside in the Lord Jesus. In Palestine the dove was a sacred bird. In Genesis 1:2 we read that the Spirit of God *moved* (and the Hebrew word suggests *brooded*) upon the surface of the waters that covered the dark world. It is a word used to describe a fowl brooding over its nest in order to bring forth life. The rabbis used to say that the Spirit of God moved and fluttered like a dove over the ancient chaos, breathing order and beauty into it. So the picture of the dove was one that all Jews knew and loved.

B. *The Old Testament word for "spirit" is ruach, which means "wind."* To the Jews, three basic ideas of the Spirit existed. The Spirit was *power*—like that of a rushing, mighty wind. The Spirit was *life*—the very center and essence of life. And the Spirit was *God himself*. So, to John, this symbolic demonstration expressed to him: "This man is God! This man is the unlimited possessor of God's power! This man is the source of all true life!"

C. *After his baptism by John, Jesus went into the wilderness to be tempted by the devil.* There, with perfect timing and impeccable expertise, he fielded each of Satan's temptations with the Word of God. Then he embarked on his mission among humanity. He chose twelve disciples whom he would teach his way of life. At the same time, he would be preparing them to accept him as the Lamb of God who would die to provide atonement for the sins of the world.

Conclusion

In the very first week of Jesus' public ministry the cross was implicit. Jesus was presented to the world by his forerunner, John the Baptist, as "the Lamb of God, who takes away the sin of the world!"

An old preacher was once heard preaching on a village green in England. He had lived on the American prairies, and his illustrations were fascinating. He told of a prairie fire and described the way in which the Indians saved their wigwams from the blaze by setting fire to the dry grass immediately adjoining their settlement.

"The fire cannot come where the fire has already been!" the old preacher cried. "That is why I call you to the cross. Judgment has already fallen there and can never come again. He who takes his stand at the cross is safe forevermore. He can never come into condemnation; he is passed from death unto life. He is at perfect peace in God's safety zone!"

Eternal safety can be found only in the cross of our Lord Jesus Christ; nowhere else can we experience the cleansing redemption that makes us God's children.

SUNDAY EVENING, MARCH 1

Title: The Church and Our Great Salvation

Text: "As you come to him, the living Stone—rejected by humans but chosen by God and precious to him—you also, like living stones, are being built into a spiritual house to be a holy priesthood, offering spiritual sacrifices acceptable to God through Jesus Christ" **(1 Peter 2:4–5 NIV)**.

Scripture Reading: 1 Peter 2:1–10

Introduction

The salvation that God offers to us through Jesus Christ is truly a great salvation. There are no disappointments for those who sincerely respond to God's offer of full redemption from the penalty of sin, the practice of sin, and ultimately, the very presence of sin.

Salvation in the past tense—the new birth, or justification by God—is wonderful. Blessed indeed is the person who can look back and say, "I have been saved. I have committed my life to Jesus as Lord and Savior and experienced the joy of forgiveness and the privilege of becoming a member of God's family."

Salvation in the future tense, which includes the promise of victory over death and the grave and the privilege of fellowship with the Father and the saints for eternity, is certainly a great salvation that brings joy to each believer. The New Testament calls this glorification. The gift of the Holy Spirit is God's guarantee to each believer of the final redemption from the consequences of sin (Eph. 1:13–14). The Holy Spirit's presence within the hearts of believers is divine assurance that they will be raised from the dead (Rom. 8:11).

Salvation in the present tense—called sanctification in the New Testament—is also part of God's plan for each of his children. It is not God's will that his children live under the dominion of evil in the present. Jesus Christ came to save us from the power and practice of sin as soon as we experience the new birth; this protection continues until either death or Jesus' glorious return.

To fully experience our great salvation in the present, we must be on guard against neglecting to work with God as he unfolds his complete plan for us (Heb. 2:1–4). God has provided at least four great ways to stimulate the growth of those who have experienced the new birth. If we postpone making a proper response to God's Word, we face the danger of spiritual illiteracy and an aimless, self-destructive life (Ps. 119:9–11, 105; Heb. 2:1). Any believer who ignores the Bible will suffer from spiritual malnutrition (1 Peter 2:2).

When we neglect the privilege of prayer, we impoverish our spiritual lives and deprive ourselves of God's loving counsel. "You do not have because you do not ask God" (James 4:2 NIV). Through prayer God communicates to us his love and guidance.

To neglect the Holy Spirit is to experience the agony and frustration of living only in the power of the flesh (Rom. 7:24). When we make a proper response to the Holy Spirit, we can live victorious lives that are pleasing to the Father and that bring joy to our hearts.

The fourth great way to experience spiritual growth in the present is to be involved with church.

I. Each believer is indebted to the church.

Had it not been for the church, we would not know about God's love and the great salvation offered to us through Jesus Christ. We owe much gratitude to the church for their role in helping us to know Jesus Christ.

    A. *The church has been commanded to be an evangelizing force in all nations until the end of the age (Matt. 28:19–20).* Believers have a responsibility to communicate the message of God's grace revealed in the life, death, and resurrection of Jesus Christ.

    B. *The church has been commanded to baptize new believers.* Baptism was to be a distinctive act of public identification with those who believed that

Jesus Christ had died for their sins, conquered death, and risen from the dead. If believers in the past had refused to become members of local congregations, the church would have died.

C. *The church has been commanded to be a school of Christian discipleship.* New believers should be instructed and led toward spiritual maturity. It is God's will that all believers enroll in this school of Christian discipleship and become learners for their entire lives.

D. *The church has been commanded to serve as witnesses.* Jesus wants the church to be communicators of God's wonderful works revealed through Jesus Christ and experienced in their own lives.

II. The church has never been flawless.

One of the devil's strategies against unbelievers is to call attention to the imperfections of the church. The church has never been perfect, nor will it ever be perfect this side of heaven.

A. *The church has always been composed of imperfect disciples (1 Peter 2:1).* The words of this verse are addressed to those who have received Jesus Christ as Lord and Savior. These believers still have many traits of the old life that must be put aside if they are to fully manifest their new relationship to God. Peter described this relationship as "a chosen race, a royal priesthood, a holy nation, God's own people" (1 Peter 2:9 RSV).

B. *The church will always include immature disciples (1 Peter 2:2).* There are many things that only growth, self-discipline, and time can solve in human families. The same is true in God's family. We must move out of childhood toward maturity.

C. *The church has always been and will always be under satanic attach.* The fact that Jesus has called us to be God's children does not immunize us against evil or build a wall over which Satan cannot come to tempt us.

III. "You also, like living stones, are being built into a spiritual house" (1 Peter 2:5 NIV).

Each believer has the privilege and responsibility to make a positive response to the presence of the church in the world today.

A. *Jesus saw the church as a spiritual temple with each believer a living stone.* The Holy Spirit seeks to help each of us be a beautiful and precious stone in the temple that Jesus Christ is building in the world today.

B. *The church is the bride of Christ; as such, it is the object of his sacrificial love (Eph. 5:25–33).* To neglect the church is to diminish your spiritual progress, vitality, and worth; and it is to disappoint him to whom the church is very precious.

C. *The church is the body of Christ through whom he continues to work in the world today (1 Cor. 12:27; Rom. 12:4–8).* The church was created by God, and through the church he is carrying on his work today.

Conclusion

If you neglect the church, you hinder your chance of fully experiencing God's great salvation. In fact, you will fail in your Christian life if you dismiss the spiritual growth that comes from being in fellowship with other believers. By giving yourself to the Lord in loving service through his church, you will enrich your life and be a blessing to others.

WEDNESDAY EVENING, MARCH 4

Title: The Gift of Apostleship

Text: "God has placed in the church first of all apostles, second prophets, third teachers, then miracles, then gifts of healing, of helping, of guidance, and of different kinds of tongues" (**1 Cor. 12:28 NIV**).

Scripture Reading: 1 Corinthians 12:27–31

Introduction

So far our weekly discussions on the gifts of the Spirit have been general. This message deals with a specific gift—apostleship.

I. Some general remarks about apostleship.

A) *Example of the word* apostleship.

> Two young seminary students spent the summer before their graduation as short-term missionaries in Taiwan. Good friends, they had often discussed whether the Lord wanted them on the mission field. Now they decided to spend three months to see how they acclimated.
>
> One enjoyed his stint to the hilt. He adapted readily to the culture. He never got sick. He learned snatches of the language. The time flew by.
>
> The second prospective missionary hated the food, learned only a few words of the language, became ill three times, and wanted to spend most of his time with the Americans rather than with the nationals. At the end, he exclaimed, "I never want to be a missionary." His companion could hardly wait to apply to the missionary board to return after his final seminary year. (Leslie B. Flynn, *19 Gifts of the Spirit* [Wheaton, IL: Victor, 1974], 38.)

This illustration is an indication of what is being talked about when apostleship is the subject, for the term is closely identified with missionaries in contemporary thinking.

B) *Use of the word* apostle. A word study of this term in the New Testament is needful to understand the gift. It is found between seventy and eighty times in the New Testament and in nineteen of the twenty-seven New Testament books. Thus the very number indicates something of the gift's significance. The distribution of the word *apostle* throughout the New Testament and its use by multiple writers places much emphasis on the missionary concept.

II. A specific examination of apostleship as found in the New Testament.

A. Apostle *always means "one who is sent."* Prior to the resurrection of Jesus, he was the one who did the sending. Since the resurrection and ascension of Jesus, the Holy Spirit does the sending but still with the same authority and purpose.

B. *Apostles stand fully under the jurisdiction of their Master.*

   1. Apostleship is according to God's sovereign will. It is not the result of a person's decision but results solely from the sender's initiative.
   2. Apostles are representatives of Jesus Christ. This means there is no reason for apostles to boast. Apostleship is a position of deep humility—never of exaltation.
   3. Apostleship is not an office or position. It is a commission. Apostles are commissioned, or sent, by the Lord Jesus. This being true, it is a privilege to go wherever the Master sends.
   4. Apostles receive their character from the One who sends them.

C. *The gift of apostleship denotes the commissioned representative of a congregation (2 Cor. 8:23).* The supreme task of apostles is to propagate the gospel of Jesus Christ. Because they act according to God's will, they have no option as to personal autonomy and should be fully committed to God's service. Jesus gives apostles the power to act; by their action they give proof of the commission.

Conclusion

There is a pressing need and call for missionaries all over the world. The Holy Spirit is ready to give the gift of apostleship to those whom he chooses. It is critical that each of us listen carefully to what he speaks to our hearts, for every believer is to be an instrument of the Holy Spirit in reaching the lost.

SUNDAY MORNING, MARCH 8

Title: Great Crowds Followed Him

Text: "When he came down from the mountain, great crowds followed him" **(Matt. 8:1 RSV).**

Scripture Reading: Matthew 5:1–2; 7:28–8:1

Hymns: "Come, Thou Almighty King," Anonymous
"Christ Receiveth Sinful Men," Neumeister
"My Savior's Love," Gabriel

Offertory Prayer: Holy Father, you have been gracious and generous to us. Today we thank you for the glad consciousness of forgiven sin and for the precious privilege of being members of your family. We rejoice in the privilege of serving you and working with you to help others come to know the great salvation that is available through Jesus Christ. Please accept our tithes and offerings. In Jesus' name. Amen.

Introduction

The passage of Scripture that falls between Matthew 5:1 and 8:1 is known as the Sermon on the Mount. It is significant that this message was delivered to the crowds that had begun to follow Jesus and that once he had completed this message, the crowds followed him down from the mountain. But the more significant thing is that crowds continue to follow Jesus Christ after two thousand years have rolled by. By the grace of God, we have been chosen to be among the crowds that follow him and listen to him.

What is the secret of this magnetism of the Teacher who spoke these remarkable words? What is it that causes this fellowship of the crowds after two thousand years? Why is it that you and I continue to follow him?

I. We follow Jesus because of who he is.

Famous celebrities attract a crowd wherever they go. To enjoy any privacy at all, they must conceal their identity and their presence.

Jesus Christ was and is the God-man, the eternal God clothed in a human body. He is the Messiah promised by the prophets, the One for whom Israel had been waiting. God revealed this truth to Peter, and Peter verbalized the conviction of his heart by declaring, "You are the Christ, the Son of the living God" (Matt. 16:16 RSV). Jesus was more than just a good man and a great teacher. He is God in human flesh. Because of who he is, we continue to follow him.

II. We follow Jesus because of what he did.

We follow Jesus Christ because of what he did during his earthly life. He ministered to the sick, comforted the grieving, gave hope to the discouraged, and fed the hungry. But his greatest achievements were on a cross and in a tomb. On the cross, he took our place, demonstrating the height and depth and breadth of his love for unworthy sinners. He paid our sin debt by dying as a substitute for each of us. In the tomb, our Lord conquered death and the grave. He demonstrated that death will have no final victory over those who trust him. By conquering death and the grave, Jesus became a living Savior, able to save unto the uttermost those who come to God by him. Because of what Jesus did, we continue to follow him two thousand years later.

III. We follow Jesus because of what he can do.

We follow Jesus because he is able to forgive our sins and make us clean and acceptable to the Father God, because he can give the gift of eternal life and cause us to love the things that are lovable in God's eyes, because he gives us a new quality of life, because he gives us victory over the evil within us and the evil that threatens us from without, because he is able to help us be productive and victorious as we live the abundant life he provides. We follow him because it is through him that we can achieve our highest possible manhood and womanhood.

IV. We follow Jesus because we need him.

Children need their parents. A husband needs his wife. A wife needs her husband. We need our friends. We need certain professionals who can provide us with services in times of need. All of us are in need of others. More than anyone else in all of existence, Jesus Christ is the One we need. Thus we follow him. With selfish motives and with the best of interests, we follow him because it pays to serve him.

V. We follow Jesus because he needs us.

We would not be presumptuous in making such a statement, for it is in the divine plan that God uses men and women to share the good news of his love with others. God could have chosen to use the angels to tell the message of his love, but he didn't. God could have chosen to use the sky as a great screen on which he could have revealed the message of his love, but he didn't. We follow him because he needs us. If we do not follow him, the work he began and wishes for us to continue will come to an end.

VI. We follow Jesus because others need him.

People have many needs. They need such things as food, clothing, shelter, education, jobs, medical care, and insurance. But humankind's greatest need is for a right relationship with God that comes through repentance toward God and faith in the Lord Jesus Christ. We can meet their greatest need when we help them receive the forgiveness of sin and the gift of new life that comes only through Jesus Christ.

Conclusion

The crowds followed Jesus during his earthly ministry, and they have continued to follow him down through the centuries. You and I can rejoice over the privilege of being among the crowds that follow him. If you have not yet begun to follow him, right now would be a good time to forsake the way of life that ends in disappointment and come to him who alone can give you life and hope and peace and joy. Become a true follower of Jesus Christ because of who he is, what he has done, and what he can do in your life.

SUNDAY EVENING, MARCH 8

Title: Salvation in This Present Day

Text: "The grace of God has appeared that offers salvation to all people" **(Titus 2:11 NIV)**.

Scripture Reading: Titus 2:11–14

Introduction

Paul rejoiced greatly over God's free salvation that he has provided for the benefit of all people of all time. Paul was so filled with gratitude that he had an inner compulsion to proclaim his faith to the ends of the earth.

In the words that follow our text, Paul described the nature of this great salvation. He declared that "it teaches us to say 'No' to ungodliness and worldly passions, and to live self-controlled, upright and godly lives in this present age" (Titus 2:12 NIV). Verses 12–15 set forth some things that our salvation teaches us. These verses contain God's plan for our great salvation from the power and practice of sin in the present.

I. "The grace of God . . . has appeared."

A. *Grace.* The Greek meaning of this word refers to favor conferred freely upon a friend by a friend.

B. *Grace in the New Testament has a distinct meaning.* Through Christ, God has freely conferred his favor, kindness, and mercy on those who have rebelled against him and fallen short of glory.

This type of grace was demonstrated by a father who offered forgiveness to a man who had driven drunk and killed his son. The father urgently requested that the man give his heart to Jesus Christ and be changed.

II. "Grace . . . that brings salvation has appeared to all men."

A. *God's gracious salvation is available to everyone without respect of persons.* It is available for the old, young, and middle-aged regardless of race or nationality.

B. *This great salvation comes from the impartial and unlimited love and grace of God.*

C. *This great salvation has appeared for the salvation of all sinners, no matter how they have sinned.*

III. God's great salvation instructs us.

A. *A disciple is a learner who needs training.*

B. *A disciple is born as an infant into God's family and needs growth and education.*

C. *Discipleship is a process of becoming what God wants us to be.* It requires self-discipline as we seek to develop into people who are more like Christ.

Paul wrote to the Philippians, "Forgetting what is behind and straining toward what is ahead, I press on toward the goal to win the prize for which God has called me heavenward in Christ Jesus" (Phil. 3:13–14 NIV).

IV. Our salvation "teaches us to say 'No' to ungodliness and worldly passions."

A. *There are some considerable negatives in the life of discipleship.* Most of us would say no to the offer of a rattlesnake for a pet. Most of us would say no to the offer of exposure to a contagious disease. Most of us would say no to the offer of a drink of poison.

B. *To what should we say no?* We should say no to the ungodly and worldly life that appeals to the flesh and to values that are significant only in this world.

We should refute those attitudes or ways that are contrary to God's will but were once considered normal. "At one time we too were foolish, disobedient, deceived and enslaved by all kinds of passions and pleasures. We lived in malice and envy, being hated and hating one another" (Titus 3:3 NIV).

V. There are some great positives in the life of discipleship.

Our great salvation teaches us to say yes to good things.

A. *In relationship to ourselves, we should live with self-control under the Holy Spirit's guidance.* Frank Sinatra is best remembered for his popular song that says, "I did it my way." True followers of Christ should be able to sing, "I did it his way."

B. *In relationship to others, we should be just, honest, helpful, and dependable.* We are to be people of genuine integrity motivated by a caring concern for the welfare of others.

C. *We should be submissive, responsive, and open to God's will.*

Conclusion

We are to live in view of the hope of our Lord's return. He gave himself for us, dying to redeem us from all iniquity. He arose to purify for himself a special people who are eager to do good. Our great salvation is not limited to something that is yet to happen. God wants our salvation to be in process at the present time.

WEDNESDAY EVENING, MARCH 11

Title: The Gift of Prophecy

Text: "And God has placed in the church first of all apostles, second prophets, third teachers, then miracles, then gifts of healing, of helping, of guidance, and of different kinds of tongues" (**1 Cor. 12:28 NIV**).

Scripture Reading: 1 Corinthians 14

Introduction

The gift of prophecy is the subject of today's message. The person who is called to preach is a prophet endowed by God with the ability to speak forth God's Word.

The noun *prophet* is found 144 times in the New Testament—37 in Matthew, 29 in Luke, 30 in Acts, 14 in John, 6 in Mark, and 10 in Paul's writings. The remainder of the 144 times are found scattered throughout the rest of the New Testament. The verb *prophesy* is found 28 times in the New Testament. Obviously, a subject found so many times in the New Testament is an important matter to consider.

I. First, consider the basic meaning, prominence, and contemporary thought about the term *prophecy.*

A. *Two general applications of the word* prophecy *exist.*
   Applied to time, it may mean foretelling, but it does not mean this exclusively. The prefix on the word can mean "advance" or "before." But the word does not necessarily mean telling what will happen in the future. A much more common application is the idea of forth-telling, or making known. When a person prophesies, he or she is interpreting God's will and proclaiming God's revelation.

B. *Paul gave preference to prophecy over all other gifts of grace (1 Cor. 14:1).* As a leader in the church, a prophet needs support from the members.

C. *The contemporary concept of the word* prophecy *would best be described as preaching, or Spirit-empowered proclamation.* A preacher is an instrument of God who is impelled by the Holy Spirit, able to transform the Holy Spirit's impulse into understandable language. Prophecy has come to mean the proclamation of the written Word of God in wisdom and power.

II. Second, consider the marks of a true prophet and the warnings of a false prophet.

A. *The Bible provides several marks of a true prophet.*
   1. First Corinthians 14:3 gives three indicators.
      a. A true prophet speaks to edify the church—specifically, to increase people's knowledge of Christian truth and to increase their ability to live effective Christian lives.

        b. A true prophet speaks to effect spiritual progress. Every prophet is to encourage others and show them a way out of sin and depression.

        c. A true prophet speaks to provide comfort. Just as people need encouragement to leave their lives of sin behind, they also need comfort. This world is characterized by hurt and pain. A true prophet brings a message of hope and comfort.

    2. First Corinthians 14:14–25 gives some additional indicators.

        a. A true prophet is used to convict people of their sin. God uses the gift of prophecy to make people realize that they are sinners who need forgiveness.

        b. A true prophet leads in worship. Worship should never be selfish. It is not according to personal preference, but for the good of all. Worship must be intelligible to those who listen.

  B. *The Bible gives some signs of a false prophet.* False prophets are God's enemies, and their prophecy is self-imposed. They are arrogant, deceitful, and shameless liars (Matt. 24:24; Mark 13:22; 1 John 4:1).

Conclusion

A prophet of God is called by God and gifted by the Holy Spirit to carry out an awesome responsibility. And those who hear a true prophet have the important responsibility of listening and doing.

SUNDAY MORNING, MARCH 15

Title: The Temple of His Body

Text: "The Jews then responded to him, 'What sign can you show us to prove your authority to do all this?' Jesus answered them, 'Destroy this temple, and I will raise it again in three days'" **(John 2:18–19 NIV)**.

Scripture Reading: John 2:13–25

Hymns: "Great Redeemer, We Adore Thee," Harris
           "Ask Ye What Great Thing I Know," Schwedler
           "O for a Thousand Tongues," Wesley

Offertory Prayer: Our Father, we thank you for the gift of your presence and for the promise that you will be with us always, even to the end of the world. We pray that our gifts to you today may come out of the overflow of our love for you and that they may express our gratitude for what you have done for us. Remove any trace of pride or self in our giving and make it truly an act of worship. In Jesus' name we pray. Amen.

Introduction

In a famous painting, an artist has depicted the boy Jesus with an armful of wood on his way to Joseph's carpenter shop. The rays of sunlight that fall across his shoulders leave a shadow of a cross on the ground beside him.

Of course the picture is nothing more than a conception that grew out of the artist's imagination, but the implications are true. The supreme objective of our Lord Jesus Christ was the cross. From his baptism in the Jordan River, when John the Baptist declared of him, "Look, the Lamb of God, who takes away the sin of the world!" (John 1:29 NIV), until his crucifixion three and a half years later, Jesus' steps were resolutely in the direction of the cross.

In today's text, John revealed three distinct facets of our Lord's personality; each relates in a unique way to his death on the cross. We see him show anger, we hear him announce his mission to die, and we observe his divine magnetism that made him appeal to the people—for not only did he work miracles on their behalf, but he also knew what was in their hearts.

I. Jesus' anger (John 2:13–17).

A. *The "gentle Jesus, meek and mild" concept has been so overworked that many preach and follow a Christ who has scant resemblance to the Christ of the New Testament.* Certainly Jesus spoke of himself as being "meek and lowly in heart" (Matt. 11:29), a description that reveals his patience with sinful people such as we are. But this does not suggest that he is indulgent, that he takes sin lightly in the lives of his people. We cannot ignore these types of statements in the Gospels. When Jesus was in the presence of the hypocritical Pharisees, "he looked around at them in anger" (Mark 3:5 NIV). There was nothing "meek and mild" about Jesus when he sent that fierce message to Herod that began, "Go tell that fox . . . !" (Luke 13:32 NIV). Nor was Jesus mild when he turned on his heel, his eyes blazing with fire, and said to Peter who had so grossly misunderstood the cross and had urged Jesus to bypass it, "Get behind me, Satan!" (Matt. 16:23 NIV). Then there were those blistering words he hurled at the Pharisees: "You snakes! You brood of vipers! How will you escape being condemned to hell?" (Matt. 23:33 NIV).

B. *At the very beginning of his public ministry, we see Jesus demonstrate righteous anger.* The incident of Jesus' anger in our text had to do with the desecration of the temple, his "Father's house." We can hardly imagine how Jesus felt, with the cross ever before him, as he walked through the outermost court of the temple. He was coming to his Father's house, which practically shouted that one final redemptive sacrifice was going to be offered. This single sacrifice would fulfill and end all of the sacrifices and rituals that had been part of the temple since the days of Solomon! So when Jesus saw the shameful

90

desecration in the actions of money changers, he expressed strong indignation.

C. *The disciples were amazed by what Jesus did.* Out of a burning passion for the true purpose of the temple to be maintained, Jesus had dared to challenge the ecclesiastical leaders. The whip he held was not for conquest but for cleansing. Jesus knew, because it had long ago been prophesied that he would one day be destroyed as the "living temple" in which the glory of God had dwelled among humanity (Ps. 69:9).

II. Jesus' announcement (John 2:18–22).

A. *Manner of cleansing the temple.*

The Jews who questioned Jesus (v. 18) in regard to his cleansing of the temple were members of the high priest's party, the Sadducees, who controlled the temple finances. Understandably they were incensed because of what Jesus had done. The practice of money changing and selling animals for temple sacrifices each year at the Passover feast was a major source of revenue for them. What did they ask of Jesus? "Give us some 'proof' that you have the authority to do what you have just done!" Yet when Jesus, this unknown Galilean, swept into the temple a few moments earlier, no one lifted a finger to stop him! Why? Because Jesus demonstrated divine authority that literally paralyzed the religious leaders who were present. The very manner in which he had cleansed the temple was sign enough.

B. *Implications of cleansing the temple.*

Jesus gave the religious leaders an answer, however, and it was one of the most profound, prophetic statements he made while he was on earth: "Destroy this temple, and I will raise it again in three days" (John 2:19 NIV). What did he mean? Jesus was actually saying two things.

First, he was prophesying his death and resurrection. Here we see the cross in his mind already, for these very people would destroy the temple of his body—yet in three days he would raise it again.

There is another implication. In the Jews' destruction of the "temple of Jesus' body" and the purposes for which God intended it, they would not succeed in stopping the onward march of God's redemptive plan for sinful humanity. For in his resurrection, Jesus would also provide power—through the coming of the Holy Spirit—for a new organism called the church, the "called out."

The Jews completely misunderstood Jesus, however, for they thought he spoke of the actual temple building. Their statement was one of contempt: "How dare you infer that you could rebuild this temple, already forty-six years in the making, in three days!"

C. *Explanation of cleansing the temple.*

John's explanation in verse 21 is profound in its simplicity: "But the temple he had spoken of was his body" (NIV). The Jews would destroy the temple in which the glory of God dwelt. But that act of destruction, permitted by God as part of his sovereign plan for our redemption, would start a new movement that all of humankind's most diabolical schemes could never stop. For when Jesus was raised from the dead, the church became "the body of Christ." By virtue of the three days of his death and resurrection, Jesus transformed a band of Jewish disciples into a universal fellowship in which all people could find God and forgiveness for their sins.

III. Jesus' appeal (John 2:23–25).

A. *What had Jesus done in this act of cleansing the temple?* First, he had challenged the religious institution of the people to a radical renewal. In their ceremony and ritual, they had lost the heart of God's purpose for his people. They were "going through religious motions," but there was no redemptive spirit in what they did; nobody was being convicted because of his or her sins, and nobody felt compassion or love from any direction.

Second, Jesus told them, by prophetic implication, how this renewal was to come about. There would be a cross, a death, but it would be followed by a resurrection, which would cause the empowerment of those who dared to believe.

Those who believed as a result of this saving power constituted a body of believers whose influence would not be vested in the four walls of a temple or building. Instead, they "went out and preached everywhere" (Mark 16:20 NIV), proclaiming the Word in the power of the Holy Spirit.

B. *"He did not need any testimony about mankind, for he knew what was in each person" (John 2:25 NIV).* Jesus knew the sin and evil that had twisted and scarred people's souls. But he also knew the potential in those who come to the cross and believe in the name of the crucified, risen Son of God. He knew that the lives of those who came to him would be transformed, and they would become radiant evangels of his gospel, his truth. And because of the number of those who believed, they would do greater works than he had been able to do in his brief time on earth. For the majority of Jesus' time was spent discipling people to carry this good news to the ends of the earth.

Conclusion

During the height of World War II, Sir Winston Churchill paid a great tribute to the young men of the Royal Air Force who had "mounted up with wings as eagles" and with their sheltering wings guarded the land they loved. Churchill said: "Never in the history of mankind have so many owed so much to so few." But when we think of Jesus, who died on the cross to take away our sins, we say this: "Never in the history of the universe has mankind owed so much to *one*—the almighty God, in the person of his Son, the Lord Jesus Christ."

"Destroy this temple, and I will raise it again in three days." That is the message of the cross. Jesus died, but he did not stay dead! Do you believe it?

SUNDAY EVENING, MARCH 15

Title: Salvation from the Power and Practice of Sin

Text: "Do not let sin reign in your mortal body so that you obey its evil desires" **(Rom. 6:12 NIV)**.

Scripture Reading: Romans 6:1–14

Introduction

The poor performance of professed disciples is the greatest stumbling block in the path of unbelievers becoming followers of Christ. And a genuine fear of spiritual failure keeps many sincere seekers from making a commitment to Christ in faith. A believer who is experiencing victory over the power of sin is the best possible testimony to the saving power of Jesus Christ.

Jesus wants to save us from the penalty of sin, which is death that separates us from God. To save us from this penalty, he needs our consent to let him come and live within our hearts (Rev. 3:20). Christ also wants to save us from the power of sin in the present. For him to accomplish this, we must give him our cooperation in addition to our consent.

For you to experience salvation from the power and practice of sin in the present, Jesus Christ needs your faith, your commitment, and your cooperation.

I. To be saved from the power of sin, proclaim your faith in believer's baptism.

    A. *In the days of the New Testament, faith in Jesus Christ was manifested by a believer submitting to believer's baptism.* In those days there were no altar calls or cards to sign.

    B. *Believer's baptism was by immersion.* The Jews had used baptism as a ceremony by which a convert from paganism to Judaism manifested death to the old way of life and new birth to a life of faith and commitment.

Baptism is a powerful symbolic way for a person to proclaim a new relationship with God.

II. To be saved from the power of sin, respond to the implications of baptism.

    A. *Baptism, properly understood, involves death to a sinful way of life.* Believers who receive baptism are proclaiming a desire to be dead to their former way of life. In the future, those persons respond to sinful stimuli as a dead person responds when spoken to.

    B. *Baptism, properly understood, involves burial of the old way of life.* Believers can be strengthened in the struggle against evil by remembering their death and burial to a sinful way of life.

    C. *Baptism, properly understood, involves resurrection to a new way of life.* When believers are baptized, they declare a desire to be alert and responsive to the Holy Spirit's guidance.

III. The negative and positive obligations of believer's baptism.

"Count yourselves dead to sin but alive to God in Christ Jesus" (Rom. 6:11 NIV).

    A. *The negative:* "Do not let sin reign in your mortal body so that you obey its evil desires. Do not offer any part of yourself to sin as an instrument of wickedness" (Rom. 6:12–13 NIV).

        1. Do not let sin reign in your mind.
        2. Do not let sin capture your eyes.
        3. Do not let sin rule your hearing.
        4. Do not let sin dictate your speech.
        5. Do not let sin dominate your sexuality.
        6. Do not let sin control your hands.
        7. Do not let sin direct your feet.

    B. *The positive:* "Offer yourselves to God as those who have been brought from death to life; and offer every part of yourself to him as an instrument of righteousness" (Rom. 6:13 NIV).

        1. God does his work through people.
        2. When God wants a word spoken, he uses someone to speak it.
        3. When God wants a deed done, he uses someone to do it.
        4. When God wants to encourage someone, he uses another person to communicate it.
        5. God is looking for people through whom he can do his work in the world today.

Conclusion

It is not God's will for sin to have dominion over us. We are not to be slaves of evil but are to be free by the liberating power of Jesus Christ.

Christ will save you from the past if you will give him your consent in faith. He will save you from the power of sin in the present if you will give him your continuous cooperation. Christ will save you ultimately from the very presence of sin if you will trust him and receive him into your heart today.

WEDNESDAY EVENING, MARCH 18

Title: The Gift of Teaching

Text: "So Christ himself gave the apostles, the prophets, the evangelists, the pastors and teachers" **(Eph. 4:11 NIV)**.

Scripture Reading: Romans 12:1–7

Introduction

The third largest fleet in the world is the famed "mothball" navy, comprised of . . . ships anchored in various U.S. harbors. In emergency these vessels could be readied for action in less than three months. To preserve them, each has been repainted and treated with a protective coating. All openings have been blocked. Steel and aluminum "igloos" have been built over exposed equipment. Inside the various compartments, dehumidifiers hum on. Outside, rust and corrosion are combated by electrodes ringing the hulls with a continuous electric current, which blocks the normal chemical reaction.

Sad to say, many believers seem to be in mothballs. Anchored in some sheltered ecclesiastical harbor, they forget that spiritual war rages. The church should not be inactively isolated up some religious river, but should be on the high seas fighting the foe.

One gift many Christians seem to have put in mothballs is that of teaching. With so many Sunday schools and other spots of service crying for competent Spirit-filled teachers, or complaining because of pedagogical misfits, every believer should examine his own life to see whether he possesses this gift. If he does, he should start using it. If he doesn't, he should quit trying. (Leslie B. Flynn, *19 Gifts of the Spirit* [Wheaton, IL: Victor, 1974], 74.)

The subject of this message is "The Gift of Teaching."

I. Some assumed facts exist concerning this gift.

A. *Teaching is the imparting of knowledge.* This definition would be applicable in any field, but when it comes to spiritual things and the work of the Spirit, teaching is imparting knowledge in regard to the Bible.

B. *Teaching is closely related to preaching.* Preaching is directed to the will. It involves persuasion and exhortation. Teaching is directed to understanding. Its method is explaining and clarifying.

C. *Teaching is a gift greatly needed in churches today.* A knowledge of God's Word is always a must, and knowledge of Jesus is of paramount importance. Therefore all churches need Spirit-controlled teachers.

II. We need to consider the definition of the gift of teaching.

A. *The gift of teaching is the supernatural ability to explain clearly and apply effectively the truth of God's Word.*

B. *The terms need to be separated and discussed.*

   1. This gift is a supernatural gift. All people who teach well do not necessarily have the gift of the Spirit; their ability may be a talent. The supernatural gift, however, will likely build on talent.

   2. To adequately grasp the meaning of this gift, we need to distinguish between talent and the spiritual gift. Talent is present from natural birth; gifts are present from spiritual birth. Talent operates through the common activities of society, spiritual gifts through the special grace of the church. Talent communicates any subject; gifts communicate biblical truths. Talent often leads only to an understanding of the subject, but gifts prepare for involvement and obedience. It is certainly possible to have the talent for teaching but not to have the spiritual gift of teaching.

   3. This is a gift enabling the teacher to explain clearly. Jesus used simple objects and words to explain his teachings—words such as *vine*, *seeds*, *sheep*, and *body*. The Spirit enables teachers to do the same.

   4. This gift is the ability to effectively apply the truth. It will lead to involvement as well as imparting knowledge.

   5. This gift holds to the body of truth. The truth is God's Word, the Bible. Those who have this gift do not originate their message but receive it from God.

III. This gift is very significant.

A. *Because of the importance and value of teaching, it would seem that the gift is bestowed on many believers.* There is a strong need for able teachers. The Lord does not let this need go unnoticed. Rather, he bestows this gift on as many teachers as he needs, but only on those who are willing to use it.

B. *Because of the importance and value of teaching, it would also seem that teaching has a variety of ministries.* The Holy Spirit knows all who need teaching, including various age groups, audience sizes, cultural and educational levels, and so on. He enables the necessary number of teachers to help reach these people.

C. *Because of the importance and value of teaching, and since it is evident that the gift has been given to many with various outlets, we can assume that Christians are to be equipped.*

Conclusion

Although the Holy Spirit is sovereign, and although he bestows gifts on those whom he chooses, it appears that the Christian church needs to pray for the proper character and will so that more Spirit-filled teachers will be available.

SUNDAY MORNING, MARCH 22

Title: The Serpent and the Savior

Text: "Just as Moses lifted up the snake in the wilderness, so the Son of Man must be lifted up, that everyone who believes may have eternal life in him" **(John 3:14–15 NIV).**

Scripture Reading: John 3:1–21

Hymns: "Majestic Sweetness Sits Enthroned," Stennett
"Blessed Redeemer," Christiansen
"There Is a Fountain," Cowper

Offertory Prayer: Our Father in heaven, we confess to you today our sin of ingratitude. Too often we forget that every moment we live is a gift of your divine grace. We recognize our total unworthiness, and we know we are undeserving recipients of your goodness. The gifts we bring to you today are expressions of our love and thanksgiving. Receive them and bless them, O Father, so the message of your love may be spread to the far ends of the earth. We pray in Jesus' name. Amen.

Introduction

In all the Gospels, no conversation is so carefully recorded in regard to content and detail as the one between our Lord and Nicodemus in John 3. The reason for this thoroughness is obvious: Jesus was relating to Nicodemus the very essence of the good news. When conveying God's truth, our words must be clear and understandable, and they must find their way into the hearts of people just as Jesus' words penetrated the heart of Nicodemus.

Jesus' words were so explicit that everyone who has read them in the generations since Nicodemus have found them to be clear signs marking the way to eternal life. Nowhere else in Scripture is there a more concise, easily understood presentation of the new birth. And, as with practically everything Jesus did, across the beauty and symbolism of these words spoken to Nicodemus, there was a shadow of the cross.

I. The visitor.

A. *First, let's examine the visitor who came calling on Jesus.* Most often in the Gospels, we find Jesus surrounded by ordinary people—the peasants. They did not have to take care lest certain people see them in the company of such a controversial person as Jesus. But Nicodemus was associated with the aristocracy of Jerusalem.

Along with Nicodemus's social rank, the timing of his visit was also surprising. He visited Jesus after Passover week, the first Passover Jesus had attended since starting his public ministry. Following his cleansing of the temple, Jesus had remained in Jerusalem for a time teaching and healing the people. His name had spread far and wide, and multitudes clamored to hear him, bringing their sick and afflicted for healing. Doubtlessly the Sanhedrin, the ruling body of the Jews, was seething with anger and hostility toward Jesus by now. But because of his popularity with the people, their hands were tied, at least for the moment. It was in this setting that Nicodemus, a member of the Sanhedrin, came to Jesus.

B. *We know certain things about Nicodemus that we have learned from this incident and two others involving him that are recorded in the Bible.* Obviously, he was wealthy. When Jesus died, John said that Nicodemus brought for Jesus' body "a mixture of myrrh and aloes, about seventy-five pounds" (John 19:39 NIV). Only a wealthy person could have afforded that much. Also, Nicodemus was a Pharisee. The Pharisees were considered by the Jews to be the best people in the land. There were never more than six thousand of them, and they had become Pharisees by taking a pledge before three witnesses that they would spend all of their lives observing every detail of the scribal law. So for Nicodemus to be a member of such an august brotherhood, and to wish to talk with Jesus at all, was bewildering.

C. *John records that Nicodemus was a ruler of the Jews.* This means, as we have already noted, that Nicodemus was a member of the Sanhedrin, the supreme court of the Jews, which had seventy members. Though its powers had been limited under Roman rule, it still played an important role in the government and lives of the people. Specifically, the Sanhedrin had religious jurisdiction over every Jew in the world, not just in Palestine. One of its duties was to examine and deal with anyone suspected of being a blasphemer, a false prophet, or a heretic. And again, it is remarkable that Nicodemus, being a member of this high ruling body, would dare to visit Jesus.

II. The encounter.

A. *John records that Nicodemus came to Jesus at night.* We do not know for certain why Nicodemus chose to come at night. It may have been a cautious move on Nicodemus's part, and he should not be condemned for this. He was a religious leader to whom many looked for spiritual guidance. Since he was an honest and straightforward man, he likely accepted his investigation of Jesus as a tremendous responsibility. He could not afford to enthusiastically endorse every prophet who came along without first investigating carefully.

B. *There may have been another reason for this nighttime visit.* Since Jesus was usually surrounded by great crowds of people during the day, Nicodemus may have come at night so they could be undisturbed. We can sense from the course of the conversation that Nicodemus was troubled. Even though he was an expert in the law of Moses, he was not satisfied with his religion. Something was missing, and something about the authority and manner of Jesus attracted him.

C. *Nicodemus's opening statement to Jesus revealed his honesty.* "Rabbi, we know that you are a teacher who has come from God. For no one could perform the signs you are doing if God were not with him" (John 3:2 NIV). No flattery was intended here; it was simply a positive statement expressing a conclusion that he had reached. There is also evidence that Nicodemus had not come to Jesus because of hearsay. It is more likely that he had heard Jesus teach and had seen him perform miracles.

D. *Jesus did not rebuke Nicodemus as a Pharisee, nor did he soften the requirements of the new birth for this respected and venerable leader of the Jews.* Jesus laid down the same requirements for Nicodemus that he would have for the most openly recognizable sinner! He did not say, "Now, Nicodemus, you are already a good man. You are sincere in what you believe and in what you are trying to do. God will honor these good works you have performed. Just keep on doing them, and God will bless you for it!" If Jesus had said that, Nicodemus would have left with the same dissatisfaction and longing in his heart that he had when he came, for his good works did not bring contentment. Therefore, plainly and to the point, Jesus said, "If you are not born again, Nicodemus, you will never see the kingdom of God!"

E. *A lesser man than Nicodemus would have been offended by Jesus' words.* He would have considered them an insult to his intelligence. Instead, Nicodemus pressed on. "How can a man be born when he is old?" Then Jesus talked to him about two births, the physical and the spiritual. Obviously, to exist, one must be "born of the flesh." But anything that is "flesh" grows old and dies. To be "born of the Spirit," that is, of God, is to have a new kind of life existing simultaneously with the physical life. Then Jesus shifted the analogy to the wind, of which one can see only the evidence.

III. The revelation.

A. *Nicodemus had listened to what Jesus said about the necessity of a new birth and about the Spirit, and he was caught up in the wonder and glory of it.* Perhaps half to himself and half to Jesus, he asked, "How can this be?" Jesus masterfully turned to the Old Testament Scriptures so familiar to Nicodemus. He told from the book of Numbers an account of God's judgment that fell on the disobedient Israelites. Fiery, poisonous serpents invaded the camp and bit the people. God told Moses to make a serpent of brass and put it on a pole in the middle of the camp. He was instructed to tell those who had been bitten to look at it, and they would be healed.

B. *The serpent was a despicable thing.* It was a reminder of Satan because he appeared in the form of a snake to Eve in the garden of Eden. Jesus explained to Nicodemus that he would be lifted up on an instrument of shame, and he would be considered an accursed thing because of the cross. But because he was willing to submit to that shame, millions of people would be able to come to God! The key to God and eternal life could not be achieved by good works or by keeping rules and abiding by regulations; it would be achieved by a hated and shameful cross on which Jesus would become a sacrifice for sin for the whole human race.

C. *In effect, Jesus said, "Nicodemus, if you will believe in me and believe that I have taken your sins on myself, you will not perish.* You will be saved and have eternal life. You will be assured of living forever with God."

Conclusion

Nicodemus basically exclaimed, "I would like to become a Christian, but I do not understand it!" Jesus said, "You can't understand the miraculous workings of the Holy Spirit. When you can see and understand the wind—where it comes from and where it is going—then you can understand the Spirit of God." But just as you can feel the wind, so you can experience the transforming presence of God in your life.

SUNDAY EVENING, MARCH 22

Title: The Necessity of Spiritual Growth

Text: "Like newborn babies, crave pure spiritual milk, so that by it you may grow up in your salvation" **(1 Peter 2:2 NIV)**.

Scripture Reading: 1 Peter 1:13–2:3

Introduction

We have a great salvation because we have a great Savior. We need to recognize and respond to his entire redemptive program for us, not just part of it.

The Philippian jailer asked, "What must I do to be saved?" This is an appropriate question for each of us. To be saved from the power of sin, we must daily live in fellowship with Jesus Christ. To be saved from the very presence of sin, we must wait in faith for the return of Jesus Christ at the end of the age.

Some people have never seriously asked, "What must I do to be saved?" Today you would be very wise to search your heart for the answer. To be saved from the penalty of sin, trust Jesus Christ as your Savior. To be saved from the tragedy of living a life of emptiness and failure, you must live in cooperation and fellowship with Jesus Christ as he seeks to work out God's great program in your life.

The Christian life should be seen as a process of becoming and being what God wants us to be. Many focus only on the beginning of this process. Others think only of its final consummation. Today we concentrate on an absolute essential for experiencing triumph in our spiritual lives: We must be in the process of growing.

I. Spiritual birth must come before salvation from the power of sin.

Some people would like to experience victory over failures and mistakes before they make a profession of faith and become identified with the church. These sincere people need to be more informed.

A. *The new birth, resulting in a new nature from God, must occur in the individual's soul.* No one can begin to live a Christian life and manifest the fruit of the Spirit until he or she experiences the new birth. Jesus said, "You must be born again" (John 3:7 NIV). He said this because we must be born before we can have life.

B. *Salvation is much more than a person sincerely making some good resolutions.*

C. *Salvation is much more than obedience to a code of laws.* In Romans 7 Paul described his attempts to please God and himself by obedience to laws through the power of human effort. Paul failed miserably and was very unhappy as he sought to find acceptance before God through obedience to the law.

D. *The new birth occurs as God creates new life in the heart of someone who believes the good news of salvation (James 1:18).* Some people want to experience salvation through human effort, but it cannot be experienced until they turn to God in repentance and faith.

II. We become infants in God's family when we experience the new birth.

Physical birth does not produce a full-grown person. At birth no one is strong, mature, or competent. There are some things that only time, growth, and experience can provide. The same is true in the spiritual realm.

A. *Spiritual infants, like human infants, are very precious to the Father.* God relates to each infant in terms of tender, loving care. The Father God desires that all infants be related to a spiritual family, the church, where they can be nurtured in their spiritual pilgrimage.

B. *Spiritual infants, like human infants, are nearly helpless.* There are many things that children of God are unable to do because of their immaturity. Time and growth can make a difference.

C. *Spiritual infants, like human infants, are very dependent.* Human babies are the most helpless of all infants. They are exceedingly dependent on their parents for nurture. In a similar manner, the infants of God are dependent on the church family for nurture and encouragement.

D. *Spiritual infants, like human infants, make mistakes.* Some mistakenly believe that conversion alone will solve the major problems and completely change the habits that were developed before they came to know Jesus Christ as Savior. This false expectancy has contributed to both spiritual defeat and depression. We need to realize that just as human infants make mistakes as they progress toward maturity, infants in the family of God also experience failure before they reach maturity.

To be an infant in God's family should cause us to have an attitude of humility concerning ourselves. At the same time, it should encourage us to have hope for a better tomorrow if we continue to grow.

III. The baby's hunger for food.

It is interesting to note that newborn babies immediately begin to seek nourishment from their mother. Likewise, one of the basic needs of a spiritual newborn is nourishment.

A. *Spiritual hunger is normal for children of God (Matt. 5:6).*
B. *We are commanded to hunger for nourishment from God's Word.* We should intensify this hunger so we can become strong and zealous children of God and effectively minister to others.

The absence of hunger indicates either illness or the absence of life. Those who are spiritually dead have no hunger for spiritual things. An intense hunger for the things of God indicates the presence of spiritual life.

IV. Spiritual growth is God's plan for us.

A. *Spiritual growth should be a normal pattern.*
B. *Spiritual growth is expected by the Father.*
C. *Spiritual growth, like physical growth, is difficult.*
D. *Spiritual growth, like physical growth, brings satisfaction.*
E. *Spiritual growth develops character and competency to serve.*

Conclusion

Spiritual birth begins the journey from where we are to where God wants us to be. Growth results after our spiritual birth as we identify with God's people.

Our spiritual growth is in proportion to the amount of Scripture we "eat." Every day we need to read, digest, and manifest the great truths found in God's Word.

WEDNESDAY EVENING, MARCH 25

Title: The Gift of Performing Miracles

Text: "To another miraculous powers, to another prophecy, to another distinguishing between spirits, to another speaking in different kinds of tongues, and to still another the interpretation of tongues" **(1 Cor. 12:10 NIV)**

Scripture Reading: Romans 15:18–19

Introduction

To adequately explain the gift of miracles in a biblical way is a true challenge. If you believe in God—a God who created the universe, sustains it, and controls it—you must also believe in the possibility of miracles. If, however, you believe in a natural world that is controlled by universal and unalterable laws, you probably have difficulty believing in miracles.

I. Numerous definitions have been given for the term *miracle.*

A. *"A miracle is any event, whether natural or supernatural, in which one sees a revelation of God.* Whether a miracle is outside the laws of nature or a violation of them is essentially irrelevant for faith" (G. A. Buttrick, ed., *The Interpreter's Dictionary of the Bible*, vol. 3 [Nashville: Abingdon, 1962], 402).

B. A miracle is *"an event or effect in the physical world deviating from the known laws of nature, or transcending our knowledge of these laws; an extraordinary, anomalous, or abnormal event brought about by superhuman agency. A wonder or wonderful thing; a marvel"* (*Webster's New Collegiate Dictionary* [Springfield, MO: G. & C. Merriam Co., 1961]).

C. *"A miracle is not the breaking of a law of nature.* It is not an interference with or suspension of the unchanging uniformity of the laws of the universe. It is simply a personal God putting His will into the laws of nature; it is God's doing with His infinite power, the same *quality* of action, though vastly greater in degree, that we do every hour when we exert our personal will amid the forces of nature." (F. N. Peloubet, ed., *Peloubet's Bible Dictionary* [Philadelphia: John C. Winston, 1925, 411–12.)

II. New Testament miracles are described in four terms.

A. *The first is signs.* This term is found seventy times in the New Testament and is used for a mark of identification. The signs point to something outside of themselves (Acts 2:3). They are a pledge or token of the presence and power of God, the truth of divine revelation, the law and heart of the Father, and the credentials of the messenger.

B. *The second is wonders.* This term is found sixteen times in the New Testament and is used to indicate the reaction of awe or terror. Wonders are the astonishing manifestations of God attracting people's attention to him, his nature, and his promises.

C. *The third is powers.* This term is found nine times in the New Testament and refers to the power that performs the act. It is outside of nature. It reveals the almighty power of God to save and to help in times of trouble. The parting of water at the Red Sea is an example.

D. *The fourth is works.* This term refers to the actual acts. Works are the demonstration of kindness and love. Healing of sickness is an example.

III. Some general statements about miracles should be discussed.

A. *Three marks test their truth.* Miracles are performed by good people. They attest to God's awesome and sovereign power. Miracles are helpful blessings, never done merely to startle or excite wonder. They are expressions of God's holy character, compassion, and love to all people.

B. *God will change his accustomed ways of doing things to meet human needs.*

C. *Miracles of the past can be compared to those of today.*

1. In the past, a miracle was calming a tumultuous sea; today it may be calming an anxious mind.
2. In the past, a miracle was feeding five thousand with a child's lunch; today it is feeding the world with the Bread of Life.
3. In the past, a miracle was giving sight to the physically blind; today it may be enabling those who are blinded by sin to see.
4. In the past, a miracle was raising a physically dead person to life; today it is raising those who are dead in sin to a new life.

Conclusion

As a whole, miracles do not usually happen as they did in biblical times. But this does not mean there are no miracles today. God is not limited by time. For the most part, miracles of current times are signs from the Bible, the church, and the history of Christianity. All Christians are responsible for praying, cooperating with God, and working. Then if the Holy Spirit chooses to perform a miracle, that is his business.

SUNDAY MORNING, MARCH 29

Title: The Cross and Discipleship

Text: "Jesus said to his disciples, 'Whoever wants to be my disciple must deny themselves and take up their cross and follow me. For whoever wants

to save their life will lose it, but whoever loses their life for me will find it'"
(**Matt. 16:24–25 NIV**).

Scripture Reading: Matthew 16:21–27

Hymns: "O Jesus, I Have Promised," Bode
         "Jesus, I My Cross Have Taken," Lyte
         "Must Jesus Bear the Cross Alone?" Shepherd

Offertory Prayer: Holy Father, your love has a characteristic that is too often missing from our love. Yours is totally a "giving love." While we were yet sinners, unable to give you anything of worth in return, you gave us your love in the person of your Son, Jesus. So Christianity, from its inception to its ultimate expression, is an unselfish giving. May we emulate your Spirit of giving as we bring our gifts to you today, expecting nothing in return except the joy of serving you. Bless these gifts we bring in the name of our Savior, Jesus Christ. Amen.

Introduction

The word *disciple* is a rather appealing word to Christians because it brings to mind those twelve men who were chosen by our Lord for a unique task—that of being the first messengers of the good news he came to give the world. Certainly the shepherds on the Judean hills and the wise men who came from afar were "heralds" of the Savior, but they did not have an opportunity to know the very essence of his gospel.

The familiar word *discipleship* also carries a certain appeal, for we interpret it to be the ideal lifestyle of a believer in the Lord Jesus Christ—a lifetime of following and learning from the Master. Yet, inherent in the word *disciple*, and hence in *discipleship*, is the word *discipline*. We do not find the same appeal in the word *discipline* because it has negative overtones. Everyone is born with a tendency toward rebellion against authority.

In other words, *discipline*, the avowed enemy of everyone's will, saturated the way of life Jesus came to reveal. Many who were confronted with the challenge to follow him could not accept this discipline. As the time for his crucifixion drew nearer, there was an unusual urgency in what Jesus said about the cross and about discipleship.

I. Jesus set forth his destiny.

A. *"From that time on Jesus began to explain to his disciples that he must go to Jerusalem and suffer many things at the hands of the elders, the chief priests and the teachers of the law, and that he must be killed and on the third day be raised to life" (Matt. 16:21 NIV).* It was as though Jesus had "turned a corner" in teaching his disciples about his approaching death and resurrection. Several times prior to this, he had spoken of the cross by implication. That is, through parables, metaphors, and other figures of speech, he had sought to prepare the disciples for the reality of the crucifixion. But they, typical of the Jewish thinking of that time, had their hearts set on establishing an earthly kingdom then. Their minds were closed to the possibility that Jesus would die and most especially to the thought that he would die on a cross, which was an accursed thing to every Jew.

B. *This was the appropriate time for Jesus to make this clear evaluation of his mission.* Peter had just made his marvelous confession of faith (no doubt speaking not only for himself, but for all of the disciples). So with that kind of openness established between Jesus and the disciples, it was time for him to be straightforward concerning what lay ahead. They could understand what Jesus said about suffering, for already they had encountered the hostility of the religious hierarchy. But when Jesus used the word *killed*, they were terrified! In fact, it was such a horrifying thought that apparently they did not even hear the rest of Jesus' statement indicating that he would be raised again the third day.

C. *"Peter took him aside and began to rebuke him. 'Never, Lord!' he said. 'This shall never happen to you!'"* (Matt. 16:22 NIV). Was this the same Peter who made that victorious declaration of faith shortly before at Caesarea Philippi? Note how graphically Matthew described what happened: "Peter took him aside. . . ." It was as if Peter stepped up beside Jesus and pulled him to the side as one would take a person who was upset or distressed, and led him away from the crowd. Peter "began to rebuke him." He admonished Jesus as a schoolteacher would attempt to set straight a student who had become confused about something.

D. *Jesus quickly and positively responded to Peter's actions.* Matthew said that he "turned," and the aorist tense of the verb used suggests that it was a fast and immediate act on Jesus' part. "Get behind me, Satan! You are a stumbling block to me; you do not have in mind the concerns of God, but merely human concerns" (Matt. 16:23 NIV). Peter was doing the same thing Satan had done when he tempted Jesus in the wilderness. He was saying, "Bypass the cross! Take another route! You don't have to die." Jesus told Peter, "You are a stumbling block to me." In other words, "Peter, you are tempting me to offend my Father by failing to do what he has purposed that I do!" Peter spoke the spirit of his age and of ours. The demand for a crossless Christ is still with us today. It is far more appealing to admire his perfect life and praise his beautiful teachings than it is to accept his bloody cross.

II. Jesus explained discipleship.

A. *"Jesus said to his disciples, 'Whoever wants to be my disciple must deny themselves and take up their cross and follow me. For whoever wants to save their life will lose it, but whoever loses their life for me will find it'"*

(Matt. 16:24–25 NIV). Literally, Jesus said, "If anyone *wishes* to follow me. . . ." There is no compulsion here. God has so limited himself that he will not force anyone to follow him. Jesus leaves people free to follow him in this intimate relationship or not to follow him at all. Their degree of love for the Lord determines their decision.

B. *Jesus also spoke of self-denial.* "Self" loves to be pampered, indulged, and coddled. But the Christian ideal is that when self comes under fire because of its selfishness and insubordination, don't help it! Let it squirm! When self is tempted to pout and become oversensitive because it considers itself slighted, don't sympathize with it! When self is withering under the searchlight of God's truth, let it suffer and let it die!

C. *Jesus drove home this revolutionary truth when he spoke of "taking up the cross."* Again we have the aorist tense, which suggests immediate, decisive action. "Let him take up his cross *at once!*" This was totally distasteful to Jews in general and even to the disciples. The cross was a Roman instrument of torture and disgrace, an accursed thing; and even to touch a cross rendered a Jew ceremonially unclean. Yet Jesus said that one must voluntarily take up a cross and bear it!

D. *The point is that Jesus was explaining how to deny self—self must be crucified, nailed to the cross.* Then he said, ". . . and follow me." Following Jesus is the inevitable result of "denying self." It is impossible for one to follow Christ and at the same time drag about a selfish and rebellious self.

III. Jesus pressed for a decision.

A. *"What good will it be for someone to gain the whole world, yet forfeit their soul? Or what can anyone give in exchange for their soul?" (Matt. 16:26 NIV).* We are told that Emperor Charlemagne was buried, not dressed in grave clothes and reclining in a casket, but in the robes of state and seated upright on a throne. An open Bible was on his knee, and one of his fingers pointed to the words that spoke for him when he could no longer speak for himself: "What good will it be for a man if he gains the whole world yet forfeits his soul?" (author's paraphrase).

B. *What is a person's soul?* It is not something hidden away inside, to be saved by attending church on Sunday while the rest of the person remains worldly and chained to material possessions. What profit is it if a person gains all the world has to offer in order to exalt and pamper self? When self is lost, what can a person give to recover it?

C. *The world offered its rewards to Jesus, but he refused them to do the will of his heavenly Father.* The world makes the same offer to us—to appease self and to say, in the words of the popular Sinatra ballad, "I did it my way." But if we choose to follow Jesus, we must make the same choice Jesus made. We must accept the cross—not for the same reason that he did, but that we might nail self to the cross so we can follow Jesus wherever he leads.

Conclusion

Here is the paradox of it all: To know real joy in the Christian life, we must feel the pain of death. And, sadly, it is not a onetime experience. How wonderful it would be if we could bury self one time and it would stay dead forever! Instead, we must daily nail self to the cross. And every time we do it, we strengthen our inner self, our spiritual self, which is controlled by the Lord Jesus.

Disciple is certainly an appealing word. But within it there is the discipline of the cross, the denial of self, so that Christ may reign supreme as Savior and Lord.

SUNDAY EVENING, MARCH 29

Title: Hindrances to Spiritual Growth

Text: "Like newborn babies, crave pure spiritual milk, so that by it you may grow up in your salvation" **(1 Peter 2:2 NIV)**.

Scripture Reading: 1 Peter 2:1–3, 11–12

Introduction

A Christian life starts with a spiritual birth experience. You cannot begin a spiritual life merely by making some good resolutions or joining a congregation of believers. Spiritual salvation is much more than developing excellence of character or being a member of a church.

Until you experience a birth from above, you dwell in spiritual death. You do not have the life of God within your innermost being. Until you are born of the Spirit, you are like an unfertilized egg with the potential for spiritual birth. God uses his divine Word to beget you into his family. Some refuse to receive God's Word in faith; consequently, they deprive themselves of this spiritual birth.

Many hindrances and obstacles must be overcome if we are to grow physically from infancy to maturity. The same is true on the spiritual level. We would be wise to recognize some foes that stand across our pathway to spiritual maturity.

I. We have a fallen human nature that makes spiritual growth difficult.

Have you ever known someone who had a congenital defect that prevented him or her from growing to maturity? Most of us have been acquainted with at least one child who had a birth defect that prevented growth to normal maturity. In a very real sense, all of us have a spiritual defect that deters us from being who God wants us to be.

We are all sinners. By using the term *sinners,* we are describing a condition of our being rather than merely describing our conduct. Each of us has within our innermost being a fatal flaw. Because we are sinners, we find it much easier to choose the path that leads downward rather than the path that leads upward. Our natural state encourages us to drift along and to drift downward. Paul described this in Romans 7: "I do not understand what I do. For what I want to do I do not do, but what I hate I do. . . . I know that good itself does not dwell in me, that is, in my sinful nature. For I have the desire to do what is good, but I cannot carry it out" (Rom. 7:15, 18 NIV).

If we fail to recognize the presence of our sinful nature, we may have an overly idealistic concept of self. This oversight can contribute to a negligent, drifting life that does not rise to its spiritual potential.

II. Poor listening habits prevent spiritual growth.

In the parable of the sower (Matt. 13:1–9), Jesus illustrated how the farmer sows his seed on various kinds of soil. The condition of the soil in which the seed is sown largely determines the end product. Jesus closed this parable with the command, "Whoever has ears, let them hear" (NIV).

Jesus later explained this parable as describing how different people hear and respond to the truth of God (Matt. 13:18–23). Only the person who really hears and responds will have an abundant harvest.

    A. *Are you a wayside hearer of God's Word?* Do you refuse to let God's Word penetrate your heart and produce the desired effect?

    B. *Are you a rocky ground hearer?* Do you permit God's Word to enter your heart only in a superficial way?

    C. *Do you let the cares of the world choke out the Word of God?* Does your desire to get ahead in the world cause you to be unfruitful?

    D. *Do you hear and respond to God's Word like good soil being planted with seed?* Do you let his Word germinate and grow and produce a harvest?

How you hear and respond to God's truth will determine the extent of your spiritual growth.

III. The evil world around is a foe to spiritual growth.

John, the beloved apostle, warned his spiritual children about caring too much for the perishables of human existence (1 John 2:15–17). By "the world" he was referring to society as it ignores God and rebels against him. John was pointing out the perishable nature of many material objects that the unbelieving world considers to be of extreme value. He urged believers to think about and to live for things that will abide forever.

In the parable of the sower, Jesus warned about letting the desire for riches and the cares of the world choke out the Word, which brings growth.

IV. The devil is a foe to our spiritual growth (1 Peter 5:8).

Those who ignore or joke about the devil are deceiving themselves and depriving themselves of the resources that God has made available for living a victorious Christian life. Satan would like to see to it that all of us remain in spiritual infancy.

V. Our human tendency to procrastinate hinders growth.

Each believer is responsible for overcoming the obstacles to spiritual growth. We will remain in spiritual infancy if we neglect the means of individual spiritual growth and postpone responding to opportunities for growth provided by the church.

VI. The poor example of others can impede our spiritual growth.

We must be constantly alert so that others' faults and mistakes will not cause us to stumble on our pilgrimage to spiritual maturity. We cannot be held responsible for the actions of others, but we are responsible to God for our own growth.

Conclusion

No one can do your eating for you. No one can do your sleeping for you. No one can do your learning for you. And no one can do your growing for you. Therefore let each of us determine that with the Holy Spirit's help, we will nourish ourselves from God's Word. We will avoid all factors that could prevent us from becoming the competent, mature persons God wants us to be.

APRIL

■ **Sunday Mornings**

Continue the series "The Centrality of the Cross" through Easter Sunday. Then, on the following Sunday, begin a new series titled "The Nature and Mission of the Church," which will run through the first Sunday in May. The New Testament contains many images and figures of speech that describe this divine but human institution for which our Lord died and on which he depends for carrying on his work in the world today.

■ **Sunday Evenings**

"Understanding Christ's Passion" is this month's theme for Sunday evenings. The death of Christ was interpreted only as a great personal tragedy and a political catastrophe by the disciples until the light of God was shed on this event through the doorway of an empty tomb and the presence of a living Lord.

■ **Wednesday Evenings**

Continue the series "Concerning the Gifts of the Holy Spirit."

WEDNESDAY EVENING, APRIL 1

Title: The Gift of Healing

Text: "To another faith by the same Spirit; to another the gifts of healing by the same Spirit" (**1 Cor. 12:9**).

Scripture Reading: James 5:14–16

Introduction

A human being is made up of body, soul, and spirit, or physical, mental/emotional, and spiritual parts. The Lord is interested in all three. To be whole, a person needs health in all three areas. The Bible says, "If we confess our sins, he is faithful and just to forgive us our sins, and to cleanse us from all unrighteousness" (1 John 1:9). This is spiritual healing. But the main point of this message is healing of the mind and body. The gift of healing is the ability to intervene in a supernatural way and cure a person of illness and restore health.

I. First, we need to have a general biblical view of this gift.

A. *Consider some New Testament facts.* The ministry of Christ was one of healing as well as teaching (Mark 1:14–15, 32–34). When Jesus sent out the Twelve and the Seventy, he commissioned them to preach and heal (Luke 9:1–2; 10:9). The book of Acts has numerous accounts of the gift of healing (Acts 3:3; 5:12–16; 8:5–8; 19:11–12), and our text for this message speaks of this ability as a gift of the Spirit.

B. *Consider the nature of healing.* The words in the original text are a double plural—"Gifts of healings"—and obviously refer to many forms of healing, including healings of physical illnesses, spiritual illnesses, and all forms of mental illness as well as such things as nervousness, anxiety, and restlessness.

These gifts of healing are identified with faith. The recipient must have faith—both in God and in human agents. And the healer is to be a person of faith and have the ability to inspire others (Matt. 17:19–21).

C. *Consider the gift and the church.* History reveals that the gifts of healing were practiced in the early days of Christianity. It also reveals that the free exercise of these gifts has gradually waned. Numerous reasons can be given for this decrease, but one is because of lack of faith. History further shows us that some personalities and groups have always held to this gift.

II. A closer study of James 5:14–16 helps us to understand the gift of healing.

A. *The initiative is taken by the sick.* Notice who is called: the spiritual leader of the flock. It is the responsibility of the sick to notify the pastor; this guards against any kind of public display.

B. *The pastor or spiritual leader does two things: prays and anoints the sick person's head with oil.* The application of oil is a symbol of the Holy Spirit, but the pouring of oil can also refer to the use of medication. In modern terms, this would be equivalent to calling the pastor for prayer and the doctor for medical treatment. Oftentimes both are necessary. Prayer seems to be the main thrust of the gift, for it invites God to work on behalf of the ill person.

C. *Spiritual healing takes priority over physical healing.* The spiritual and the physical are often intertwined. Spiritual illness can cause mental and physical illness, and at times, spiritual healing can bring about mental and physical healing. In any case, healing is always for the glory of God.

III. Our attitude toward healing is of vital importance.

A. *Some negatives need to be avoided.* To have a good positive and spiritual attitude about our relation to God, we must realize that not all people are healed. The Bible records instances in which God did not heal even when prayers were spoken. See, for example, 2 Corinthians 12:7–9.

B. *Some positives need to be cultivated.* Christians have been entrusted with a ministry of healing that is in accord with present-day science. One of the greatest needs is for the healing power of God to touch those who are oppressed by the burdens and problems of life. This healing can be effected by prayer, preaching, use of scientific knowledge, and the listening ear.

Conclusion

The gift of healing is invaluable. It may be for one person at one time and for another person at another time. There may be times when a person has this gift and other times when the same person does not. It is the Christian's responsibility to be available for the Holy Spirit's use and bestowal of the gift.

SUNDAY MORNING, APRIL 5

Title: When Death Brings Life

Text: "'I, when I am lifted up from the earth, will draw all men to myself.' He said this to show the kind of death he was going to die" **(John 12:32–33 NIV)**.

Scripture Reading: John 12:20–36

Hymns: "There's a Wideness in God's Mercy," Faber
"Love Lifted Me," Rowe
"O Sacred Head, Now Wounded," Gerhardt

Offertory Prayer: Our Father, we thank you for being our heavenly Father and for showing your love and care for us in so many ways. On this Lord's Day, as we enter the passion week of our Lord's earthly life, we are especially aware of your love in the incomparable gift of your Son. Bless these humble gifts we bring to you as expressions of our love for you, who first loved us. In Jesus' name we pray. Amen.

Introduction

We come today, in our emphasis on the centrality of the cross, to the last week of Jesus' life. It is Monday, the day after he rode triumphantly into Jerusalem on the borrowed donkey. The pilgrims' excitement about Jesus' presence in Jerusalem was running high. They had greeted him on Sunday with palm branches, a practice that had first been used when the Jews celebrated the deliverance of the temple and the city of Jerusalem from the Syrians. Through the years the palm branch had come to be used on coins and in the temple feasts as a reminder of that great victory led by the Maccabeans. So when they waved the palm branches before Jesus, it was a symbolic way of encouraging him to conquer the Romans. They wanted him to be a military savior. They cried, "Hosanna!" which meant "Save us now!"

or "Deliver us now!" But Jesus came riding not on a warrior's stallion, but on a donkey, to symbolize his mission as a man of peace.

I. A strange request.

A. *First, let's consider a strange request coming not from a band of Jesus' own people, but from a company of Greeks.* These were most likely Gentile proselytes who had come as pilgrims to worship in the temple during the Passover. "Now there were some Greeks among those who went up to worship at the festival. They came to Philip, who was from Bethsaida in Galilee, with a request. 'Sir,' they said, 'we would like to see Jesus'" (John 12:20–21 NIV). We are not certain what prompted the Greeks to seek out Jesus, but it is entirely possible that they had been standing in the court of the Gentiles the day before when, with fiery indignation, Jesus had cleared the court of money changers. And even though these Greeks were proselytes and had embraced the Jewish faith, they were not blind to the bigotry and prejudice of the Jews toward the Gentiles. Thus it is possible that they were inwardly amused, as well as outwardly amazed, at what Jesus did!

B. *Whatever the Greeks' immediate reason for seeking out Jesus, something about him created a hunger within their hearts, driving them to find him and talk with him.* They sought out Philip and said, "Sir, we would like to see Jesus." Obviously flustered by the situation, Philip left the Greeks alone until he could confer with someone else. He found Andrew, who suggested that they take the matter to Jesus at once.

II. An amazing revelation.

A. *Not only do we encounter a strange request by the Greeks, but we are faced with an amazing revelation that Jesus gave his disciples.* John wrote, "Jesus replied [to Andrew and Philip], 'The hour has come for the Son of Man to be glorified'" (John 12:23 NIV). Jesus must have been deeply moved by this request from the Greeks. He saw in their coming the beginning of an innumerable host of Gentiles who would believe in him. But before they could believe in Jesus with a true understanding of his ministry, the crucifixion and resurrection had to take place. So Jesus did not receive the company of Greeks at that time. For he was yet a Christ "in the flesh" who had come first to his own people as King of the Jews. In this role, he was not fully ready to be received by the Gentiles, although certain Gentiles, like the Syro-Phoenician woman and the Roman centurion and others, had received him. But before he turned to the Gentiles as a people, the loneliness and rejection of his own people had to occur. He had to be lifted up on the cross and accepted as a sacrifice for sin and not just as "a son of David."

B. *Jesus told Andrew and Philip, "The hour has come."* By this he meant the time was at hand when his mission would be infinitely expanded.

For in just a few days he would die on a cross and be resurrected on the third day, providing once and for all redemption from sin for anyone who believes in him. Jesus continued by illustrating what he meant by his statement "The hour has come for the Son of Man to be glorified." Remember that the Greeks wanted to "see" Jesus. They wanted to be introduced to him, to understand him, to discover his mission. But Jesus implied that they could not "see" him or comprehend his mission—not yet! Why? Jesus knew that at this point these Greeks would see him only as a miracle worker, an appealing teacher, and a potential military leader. They were unable to see him in his role as Savior of the world.

C. *Note the figure of speech Jesus used: "Very truly I tell you, unless a kernel of wheat falls to the ground and dies, it remains only a single seed. But if it dies, it produces many seeds" (John 12:24 NIV).* A kernel of wheat is a small husk covering a small piece of grain. A scientist could tell you everything that is inside that tiny kernel of wheat. But while you look at the grain, you cannot see what is inside! Andrew and Philip could have said, "But Lord, we see you! There you stand among us! We agree with Peter; we believe that you are the Christ, the Son of the living God!" But just as no one can see what is inside a tiny grain of wheat, so they could not see Jesus in the fullest sense of the word. So what do we do with this grain? We put it in the ground, and it dies, disintegrates. But that is not the end of it! Something else happens. We stand aside, and presently a tiny blade appears, then the stalk, the head, and finally the full head of grain.

D. *Jesus' message was that no one could truly see him until he died.* The power and efficacy of his life would not be released until he experienced death. Jesus' life was perfect and sinless, but no one is saved by Jesus' life. He performed many miracles in his daily ministry, but there was no saving power in his ministry. It was simply a demonstration and proof of his deity. It was his *death* that provided salvation. The company of Greeks could not see Jesus yet, but if they waited awhile, they could see him in a way that they could never have seen him before!

III. A positive requirement.

A. *Jesus had said that one cannot find eternal life until first there is a death—his death on the cross.* And following this same theme, he applied the principle to those who would follow him (John 12:25–26). Here is a matter of spiritual priorities. Many Christians are completely earthbound, and their chief concern is with this life, its things, its tangibles.

B. *Then Jesus drove his illustration even closer to home.* He said, "Whoever serves me must follow me" (John 12:26 NIV). Where was Jesus going? He was going to the cross. But where beyond that? He would be resurrected in glory and in triumph! The grain of wheat would fall into the ground and die. And through that death, life would spring forth and a harvest would result.

C. *In summary, what was Jesus saying to us?* First, he was telling us that true life is released only after a death takes place. While the grain of wheat was preserved in safety and security, it was unfruitful. When it was planted in the ground, it bore fruit. It was by the death of martyrs that the church grew in the ancient past. As an old saying puts it, "The blood of the martyrs is the seed of the church." Because they died, the church became the living church. Second, Jesus is saying that only by giving our lives away do we retain life. When Joan of Arc knew that her enemies were strong and that her time was short, she prayed to God, "Lord, I shall only last a year; use me as you can." And finally, Jesus is telling us that only by service comes greatness. At another time, Jesus said, "For it is the one who is least among you all who is the greatest" (Luke 9:48 NIV).

Conclusion

True life is not realized until you identify with God through Jesus Christ. Then you learn that life is found in giving yourself away so that Christ may be top priority. Hear him say to you, "Whoever serves me must follow me; and where I am, my servant also will be. My Father will honor the one who serves me."

SUNDAY EVENING, APRIL 5

Title: Understanding the Cross

Text: "From that time on Jesus began to explain to his disciples that he must go to Jerusalem and suffer many things at the hands of the elders, the chief priests and the teachers of the law, and that he must be killed and on the third day be raised to life" **(Matt. 16:21 NIV).**

Scripture Reading: Matthew 16:13–24

Introduction

Our text reveals that the disciples' recognition of Jesus as the Messiah marked a new departure in Jesus' teaching. After the disciples realized that Jesus was the Messiah, they needed to know what his true mission was. They needed to understand the cross. They had to put away their dreams of a messiah who would come for Israel alone to overthrow its enemies. It was necessary for the disciples to see Jesus as the sin bearer for all humankind and to know that he was the Messiah who would become the Savior of all humankind by way of the cross.

Did his own nation understand the cross? No, they rebelled against the idea of a messiah on a cross. Did his disciples understand the cross? No. Peter's reaction to Jesus' announcement of his coming rejection and death (Matt. 16:22) plainly shows this delusion. Those influenced by Greek philosophers were sure that people belittled God by saying that he could be affected by human actions or pain. Do we understand the cross? No, our understanding falls far short. But we can understand four things.

I. We can understand Jesus' acceptance of the cross.

We cannot pinpoint the time when Jesus first knew that following the Father's will would take him to the cross, but surely he knew at the time of his baptism. Just as baptism pictures a death, burial, and resurrection in our own spiritual experience, so Jesus' baptism prefigured the cardinal events in his own redemptive ministry—his death, burial, and resurrection.

Certainly Jesus knew God's plan for a cross when he fought that great battle with Satan in the wilderness. The devil was willing for him to be a messiah, but not God's Messiah following God's plan. At the time of this titanic struggle, Jesus had already accepted the cross as God's way.

At the beginning of Jesus' ministry, he knew of the cross and had accepted it. Challenged to show a sign when he first cleansed the temple, he replied, "Destroy this temple, and in three days I will raise it up" (John 2:19). John was careful to tell us, "But he spake of the temple of his body" (v. 21).

In Gethsemane when Peter tried to defend his Master with a sword, Jesus asked, "The cup which my Father hath given me, shall I not drink it?" (John 18:11). Here was both the motive and the motto of his entire life. The cross was his choice. "The Son of man must suffer" (Mark 8:31); and the "must" came from God.

II. We can understand history's vindication of the cross.

The cross is not simply an event of two thousand years ago; it is a spiritual fact now. We are involved. Jesus' choice of the cross as God's way to redeem humankind has been vindicated by human experience throughout the centuries. As the mythical mountain of lodestone was supposed to have magnetic properties so powerful that objects that came near were drawn irresistibly to it, so Christ by his cross exerted a magnetic influence on all succeeding generations. He predicted this effect: "And I, if I be lifted up from the earth, will draw all men unto me" (John 12:32). It is impossible to treat Calvary as just another grim episode in history. No other death has so affected us. There was and is a cosmic aspect to Calvary.

A. *The cross reveals our sin.* It reveals the tendencies, the deep-seated conditions within us, that cause spiritual death. It makes the Christian gospel intelligible. A radical rebellion, settled deeply in human nature, called for the most drastic action on God's part to meet and overcome it.

B. *Not only does the cross reveal our sin, but it also reveals God's love.* At the cross, God meets us in love. Jesus had said in words that God is love, but it was on the cross that these words took fire and burned: "God so loved the world, that he gave his only begotten Son" (John 3:16). Every generation finds the cross to be its accuser and its means of salvation.

III. We can understand God's victory through the cross.

In earthly terms, the cross is not a sign of God's majesty and power but an unforgettable reminder of the lengths to which he will go to bring people to him. To God be the glory and victory through the cross.

As great and powerful as symbols can be, the cross was more than a symbol. It was an action. Jesus did something that he alone could do. What did he achieve? He bore the shame of our sin, rebellion, and failure. In the cross, he made available forgiveness, redemption, and release. What he did in that intimate identification with humanity in its sin and sorrow, he still does.

For this reason, we have hope, confidence, and assurance. This divine Christ takes away the sins of the world by his union with every sinner who, by faith, will receive him. Humankind is not deserted. God still ministers to our need. The cross is a victorious, eternal fact.

IV. We can understand our salvation by the cross.

Through the cross, God has given us his earnest concern to save us from sin and death. This is not just one philosophy of life among many others. This is the gospel, the good news.

Although the cross always reminds us of Jesus' death, the philosophy of the cross is a philosophy of life. The cross is life through death. It is finding a new way of life in rejecting the way of self-trust, self-love, and self-assertion. Our salvation, our peace, our fulfillment of God's purpose for us begins with our acceptance of him who died for us. Salvation is of God alone. As Paul put it, "All things are of God, who hath reconciled us to himself by Jesus Christ" (2 Cor. 5:18). Salvation is not anything we can do; it is what God has done for us through the cross. God will give this gift of salvation to anyone who believes, to anyone who puts trust in the crucified Christ.

Conclusion

As we come together tonight, we remember Jesus' cross, but we do more than remember. The cross is the most relevant, most contemporary thing in life. All people must come to terms with that cross that stands to accuse them, to welcome their return to God. Have you come to terms with the cross? Will you do it tonight?

WEDNESDAY EVENING, APRIL 8

Title: The Gift of Helping

Text: "And God has placed in the church first of all apostles, second prophets, third teachers, then miracles, then gifts of healing, of helping, of guidance, and of different kinds of tongues" **(1 Cor. 12:28 NIV)**.

Scripture Reading: Romans 12:1–8

Introduction

Two things should be mentioned about the gift of helping. First, an indefinite number of Christian people may possess this gift. In fact, it appears that all believers may have this one. Second, this particular gift is to be distinguished from others in that it does not have a miraculous character.

I. First, consider some general statements as to what the gift is.

A. *There is no need to elaborate on the meaning.* It simply means to be helpful. The Greek word in 1 Corinthians 12:28 means to take hold of and help. In Romans 12:7 the Greek word takes on the meaning of ministering. It is helpful service.

B. *Think about some areas where such a gift can be used.*
   1. It can be used to serve the troubled, sick, poor, and persecuted. This is where the church can truly represent the Lord. We are to use this gift to minister to these kinds of people in the name of Christ.
   2. It can be used in a special way in the church. Often this gift is used in a quiet, ordinary way. The use goes unnoticed. Examples of this type of worker are secretaries and custodians.
   3. It can be used in building up the church. This is the thought projected in Ephesians 4:12. It is the opposite of tearing down by ridicule, poor cooperation, and inactivity.

II. This gift is identified with the position of a deacon.

A. *The word in Romans 12:7 is the Greek word from which the word* deacon *comes.* The office of a deacon is always that of service, never that of control. Deacons are never a lawmaking body.

B. *The office of a deacon is one of service.* This is a concept that needs to be stressed in contemporary churches. Over the years, the group of "deacons," or corresponding term in churches that do not use that particular term, has evolved into a policy-making body and sometimes even an official board. The gift of helping is one of service. The deacon is a servant.

III. This gift relates to everyone in two basic ways.

A. *Each Christian has a ministry role within the congregation.* For believers to produce as their heavenly Father expects them to, their ministry needs to be well rooted in their faith. Every member of any congregation has something to contribute.

B. *Each Christian is to accept his or her divinely appointed role in the church.* The acceptance of this gift as an endowment from the Holy Spirit will eliminate rivalry and jealousy among church members.

The knowledge of this gift does not have to come by a direct revelation from God in a spontaneous way. It can come through sermons, announcements, appointments, and printed matter.

IV. Consider some general truths concerning this gift.

A. *It is a gift of selflessness.* Although the Holy Spirit gives each believer the attribute of self-esteem, this gift is not for that purpose. This gift is for others, not for the recipient of the gift.

B. *It is a gift of action.* The use of this gift will enable the Christian to act in the right way at the right time.

C. *It is a gift for daily living.* This particular gift is not for the spectacular or for the public eye. It is for day-by-day, week-by-week Christian living.

Conclusion

According to the Bible, every believer has the gift of the Holy Spirit. He dwells in all who trust Christ as Savior. Strong evidence points toward the fact that each Christian has this particular gift of helpfulness. Hopefully all believers will honestly and sincerely use it for the sake of helping humankind and for the glory of God.

SUNDAY MORNING, APRIL 12

Title: The Resurrection of Christ and Our Great Salvation

Text: "Because Jesus lives forever, he has a permanent priesthood. Therefore he is able to save completely those who come to God through him, because he always lives to intercede for them" **(Heb. 7:24–25 NIV)**.

Scripture Reading: 1 Corinthians 15:1–5, 12–20

Hymns: "Christ the Lord Is Risen Today," Wesley
"Low in the Grave He Lay," Lowry
"Jesus Shall Reign Where'er the Sun," Watts

Offertory Prayer: Loving Father, our hearts rejoice today because of the greatness of your love and because of the wonders of your power. We come today eager to respond to your love, wisdom, and power with faith and obedience. We worship you with our hearts and praise you with our lips.

We come bringing tithes and offerings, asking that your blessing be on them to the end that others will come to know Jesus Christ as Lord and Savior. In his name we pray. Amen.

Introduction

If Jesus had not conquered death and the grave, we would not be in this worship service today. Christianity is the faith that claims a living founder. His disciples come together regularly for Bible study, prayer, and worship to experience his living presence in their midst (Matt. 18:20).

Christianity is not just good advice; it is good news from a cemetery. It is good news about God for sinners everywhere. To miss this point is to miss the heart of the gospel. The resurrection of Jesus Christ not only makes possible our great salvation, but it also makes it certain (Heb. 7:25). It is interesting to note how this verse is translated in some modern versions. The *Good News* translation has, "He is able, now and always, to save those who come to God through him, because he lives forever to plead with God for them." J. B. Phillips has this beautiful paraphrase: "This means that he can save fully and completely those who approach God through him, for he is always living to intercede on their behalf."

These inspired words affirm both the ability and the determination of the living Christ to fully save those who come to God by him. This possibility is based solidly on the fact of his conquest of sin, death, and the grave. He will abide forever as our living High Priest in the presence of the Father. Dr. Robert G. Lee, for many years pastor of the Bellevue Baptist Church in Memphis, Tennessee, preached a sermon he called "The World's Blackest Assumption." This black assumption—that Jesus Christ did not rise from the dead—is discussed in Paul's epistle to the believers at Corinth.

1. If Jesus Christ is not risen, the church has no message for a lost world (1 Cor. 15:14).
2. If Jesus Christ is not risen, Christians have nothing to believe (15:14).
3. If Jesus Christ is not risen, the apostles and all subsequent preachers have misrepresented God as having raised Jesus Christ (15:15).
4. If Jesus Christ is not risen, your faith is an empty, worthless shell. (15:17). Did you ever pick up a pecan or hickory nut thinking that it would be filled with a delicious nutmeat only to find that it was an empty shell? That is a picture of your faith if Jesus Christ is not risen.
5. If Jesus Christ is not risen, you are still guilty and under the condemnation that results from sin.
6. If Jesus Christ is not risen, those believers who died with faith in Jesus Christ are perished (15:18). They are gone forever, and we are but whistling in the dark—if Jesus Christ is not risen.
7. If Jesus Christ is not risen, we are very sad creatures because we have built our lives on an illusion.

Thank God that the world's blackest assumption is a falsehood, for in fact Jesus Christ is gloriously risen from the dead.

The empty tomb declared to Jesus' disciples, the Jewish leaders, and the Roman authorities that something had happened to the body that had been buried there. It was the repeated appearances of the risen Christ that completely transformed the hearts and lives of the apostles. They became flaming evangels of the good news that the penalty of sin had been paid, death had been conquered, and Jesus Christ is alive. The risen Christ appeared to his disciples at least ten different times. The thrilling truth of his resurrection gave them a message of hope for a world that was facing despair.

Like the notes of a thousand silver trumpets, the apostles went out to proclaim that Jesus Christ is alive. This was no figment of their imagination. It was no illusion under which they labored. It was no mirage for which they died.

I. The resurrection vindicates Jesus of Nazareth as God's unique Son (Rom. 1:4).

Before his resurrection the apostles believed Jesus to be the Son of God. Following his resurrection and many appearances to them, they knew he was the Son of God to the extent that they put their lives on the line to tell others of his saving grace. Jesus' resurrection proved that his crucifixion was a revelation of divine love for sinners.

When Jesus was crucified, the apostles considered it a personal catastrophe. For their leader it was a public disgrace. For all of them it was a tragic political disappointment.

Only through the doorway of an empty tomb from which Jesus had been raised could God reveal that his Son's death on the cross was a revelation of his great love for sinners.

Christ's crucifixion demonstrated God's boundless love for unworthy sinners. This love is not something we can buy or earn. It is God's free gift. So many people desperately need to be told about the greatness of this love.

Without being aware of it, many people are like Juanito Piring, a former hoodlum who wanted to make up for his sins and had himself nailed to a cross each Good Friday for twelve straight years. Piring, a former gangster and street brawler from the slums of Manila, said he was reenacting the crucifixion for a twelfth year to compensate for the errors of his youth. He said, "I subject myself to this torture to make up for my sins and the sins of others." This sincere but misguided man was seeking to earn something that cannot be earned and to make atonement for sin that has already been atoned for in the death of Jesus Christ on the cross.

II. The resurrection enabled Jesus to intercede for us in God's presence.

The beloved apostle John mentioned this fact when he wrote to encourage his spiritual children to avoid living in sin. "My dear children, I write this to you so that you will not sin. But if anybody does sin, we have an advocate with the Father—Jesus Christ, the Righteous One. He is the atoning sacrifice for our sins, and not only for ours but also for the sins of the whole world" (1 John 2:1–2 NIV). The author of Hebrews wrote of Christ as a mediator who acts on our behalf (9:24). The writer further asserts that Christ has offered himself and continues to offer his sacrificial death as an atonement for the sins of those who accept him as Lord and Savior (10:10–14).

It is by Christ's victorious resurrection from the dead that his ministry of intercession is made possible. He is able to be our Savior from the penalty of sin, from the practice of sin, and eventually from the very presence of sin because he is a living Savior.

III. The resurrection gave believers a living Lord and companion for the road of life.

Jesus Christ is much more than an inspirational memory of one who lived in the past. In the forty days between his resurrection and his ascension, he gave the disciples many indisputable proofs that he had conquered death and the grave (Acts 1:3). He repeatedly encouraged them to wait for a precious gift from the Father God (vv. 4–5).

In the Gospel of the Spirit, as the Gospel of John has been called, Jesus had promised at a time when his disciples could not fully understand his words, "I will not leave you as orphans; I will come to you" (John 14:18 NIV). He was to fulfill this promise on the day of Pentecost when the Holy Spirit would come to reside in the church.

A. *With Peter, we should hear Jesus saying, "Follow me" (John 21:22 NIV).*
B. *With the disciples who were present on the mountaintop, we should hear Jesus giving a divine mandate.* He commanded them to "go and make disciples of all nations, baptizing them in the name of the Father and of the Son and of the Holy Spirit, and teaching them to obey everything I have commanded you" (Matt. 28:19–20 NIV).
C. *We should hear Jesus make a promise to those who give themselves in obedience to his command.* He promised his abiding presence, saying, "Surely I am with you always, to the very end of the age" (Matt. 28:20 NIV).

Conclusion

Yes, Jesus Christ is gloriously alive. He is standing at your heart's door eager to bring God's blessings into your life (Rev. 3:20). Let him come in. Let him go with you along the pathway of your life. Walk with him as he leads you in meaningful living and significant service. Jesus Christ is alive! Hallelujah!

SUNDAY EVENING, APRIL 12

Title: Understanding Our Mission

Text: "As my Father hath sent me, even so send I you" (**John 20:21**).

Scripture Reading: John 20:19–23

Introduction

The greatest act of missions in the history of the universe was God's act of sending his Son into the world to assume our humanity in the incarnation; to live a perfect life as he shared the experience of our race, except for our sins; to win and train those who were to carry on his work; and in the end to die on the cross for our sins, since he had no sins of his own. In that first post-resurrection appearance to his disciples, he conveyed very clearly the mission they were to assume, as he said, "As the Father hath sent me, even so send I you." This is our mission also.

I. How did God intend for this assigned mission to be carried out?

A. *Jesus founded a church.* This fact is recorded in the words he spoke. We also have a record of his work as he "went about doing good" (Acts 10:38). And we have his assurance that "the gates of hell shall not prevail against it" (Matt. 16:18).

B. *This church is described in the New Testament.* The characteristics of the church are fully described. Every church should seek to follow the New Testament pattern. The test in any fellowship of believers is how true its members are to Jesus' teachings, to the examples set forth in the New Testament.

C. *Jesus sent this church, his church, on a mission.* He gave us a task, a commission; the business of a church is to do the work he assigned. What is our mission as his church?

II. Our mission is to share Christ with the world.

In the first verse of his gospel, John wrote, "In the beginning was the Word, and the Word was with God, and the Word was God." John said our mission is to tell the world that all the human mind can know or understand about God is revealed in Jesus Christ. We must learn about God from him.

During World War II, a father and his small son were walking at night through a residential section of their city. The boy noticed in several windows flags with a blue star on a white background, surrounded by a red border. When he asked what this meant, his father replied, "It means that family has a son in the service of his country." When the boy asked about one flag with a gold star, his father explained, "That family had a son who died in the service of his country." After a moment, the boy looked up through a break in the trees and saw a single star framed in a patch of sky. "Look, Daddy," he said, "God had a Son in the service, and his star is a gold star." Deeply moved, the father said, "Yes, Son, God did have a Son in the service, his only Son. And he gave his life too." He did. God's Son died for you and me. Jesus is our message and our only message.

A. *Jesus is our only message because he is our substitute.* He bore the penalty for our sins in our place. As Peter said of him, "Who his own self bare our sins in his own body on the tree" (1 Peter 2:24).

B. *Jesus is our only message because he is our only means of reconciliation.* In his second letter, Paul told the Corinthians, "God was in Christ, reconciling the world unto himself" (5:19). Paul was saying, "Do you see that man writhing in agony on the cross? It is God experiencing that pain, and he is bearing it for you and for me."

C. *Jesus is our only message because he is the only way.* He is the single way of pardon from our sins. The night before he died, Jesus told his disciples, "I am the way, the truth, and the life: no man cometh unto the Father, but by me" (John 14:6).

III. Our mission is to uncover and denounce sin before the world.

We are to pull the mask off sin and show sin before the world for what it is—an ugly, deadly thing. Many false ideas about sin have been introduced in our day. By some it is defined as "maladjustment," an irrelevant mistake made along the way. "Leave it alone," the world says, "and it will be forgotten in time." But as the experience of thousands shows, this is not true. Some say sin is not real at all, but only "the error of the mortal mind." Others preach that we *do* sin but that in the world beyond death we will be given another chance, and in the end none will be lost.

Regardless of what false doctrines may be taught about sin, we have no choice—we must come to terms with it.

A. *Sin is a destroyer.* Sin destroys hearts and homes. Sin ruins friendships, churches, bodies, and minds—even our own immortal souls. Sin shatters relationships, most tragically our relationship to God. Until we repent and seek forgiveness from God, this most vital of relationships cannot be restored; reconciliation cannot occur.

B. *Sin is always worse than we thought it would be as we contemplated it.* When Joseph's brothers stripped him of his coat of many colors and sold him into slavery in Egypt, they got into much more trouble than they had ever imagined. For one, their aged father's grief caused them much worry. They had not realized beforehand how great his anguish would be. The writer of Genesis said, "All his sons and daughters came to comfort him, but he refused to be comforted. 'No,' he said, 'I will continue to mourn until I join my son in the grave'" (37:35 NIV). Joseph's brothers also felt the guilt of their own consciences. As a test to see if his brothers were the same hateful, hardened men, Joseph had Simeon bound before their eyes to be held until they returned with their youngest brother, Benjamin. The brothers said, "We are being punished because of our brother. We saw how distressed he was when he pleaded with us for his life, but we would not listen;

that's why this distress has come on us" (Gen. 42:21 NIV). That was conscience speaking.

Judas's sin was worse than he had thought it would be. The stark horror of what he had done rose up to confront him. He couldn't handle the guilt, so he killed himself. Everyone who rejects Christ will one day realize the seriousness of his or her sin.

C. *Sin cannot be dealt with by human means.* Sin cannot be escaped. Our sin will find us out (Num. 32:23). And sin cannot be hidden. Its consequences will not just go away. "Do not be deceived: God cannot be mocked," Paul told the Galatians. "A man reaps what he sows" (6:7 NIV). Sin, once done, cannot be undone. It can only be confessed and forgiven. We are to explain this fact to the world.

D. *Sin can be overcome, blotted out, its stain removed, only by God's power.* God hates sin. As a great preacher once put it, "God hates sin as we would hate a mad dog on the school ground, as we would hate a rattlesnake in the baby's bed, or as a vulture picking out an infant's eyes." And only God can forgive sin, blot it out, and remove it as far as the east is from the west.

Our mission is to share this knowledge with the world.

IV. Our mission is to define salvation for the world.

We are to preach that Jesus saves. Every Christian should do this by every means available. This is the good news that Jesus "came to seek and to save the lost" (Luke 19:10 NIV).

A. *Salvation is by grace.* "By grace you have been saved" (Eph. 2:8 NIV). This simply means that salvation is God's gift, an unmerited favor. A certain minister once preached a rather lengthy sermon. For twenty minutes he expounded salvation by grace. At the halfway point, he began to expound what sounded like "sinless-perfection doctrine." "Do this, do that and the other," he said, "lest you fall. Don't do this or that or the other lest you lose your salvation." He preached forty minutes: twenty on salvation by grace and twenty on being kept saved by good works. This is a hopeless contradiction. Salvation is by grace—grace alone.

B. *Salvation is through faith (Eph. 2:8).* Salvation is by grace through faith. Faith is the channel through which God's saving grace can operate, the condition that makes his salvation possible. Even the power to exercise faith unto salvation is the gift of God. Paul asked the Corinthians, "What do you have that you did not receive?" (1 Cor. 4:7 NIV).

C. *Salvation is also upon the condition of repentance.* Logically, we can conceive of repentance and faith separately; thus conceived, repentance comes first. But chronologically they occur in a person's life simultaneously. This must be true—else we might have a sinner who has truly repented but who has not exercised faith in Christ or, on the other hand, a believer who has not repented. Neither is possible.

D. *Salvation is manifested in regeneration, or the new birth.* As Jesus said to Nicodemus, "No one can see the kingdom of God unless they are born again" (John 3:3 NIV). "If anyone is in Christ," Paul told the Corinthians, "the new creation has come: The old has gone, the new is here!" (2 Cor. 5:17 NIV).

Conclusion

Some make fun of the doctrine of the new birth as outdated. During a religious gathering in Minneapolis many years ago, a minister who had been pastor of a church in Dallas for fifty years told the group that every year for fifty years he had preached a sermon on the new birth. "Now," he said, "I have put that sermon among my souvenirs and promised God that I will never preach it again. It is outmoded nonsense." The audience applauded. But one member of the audience stood up and said, "I am an ignorant man. I know no Christian doctrine, but I do know that at my home God changed wine into water, whiskey into furniture, hate into love, and a hopeless drunk into a sober man. God changed me."

"Go tell it on the mountain!" This is our mission.

WEDNESDAY EVENING, APRIL 15

Title: The Gift of Administration

Text: "And God has placed in the church first of all apostles, second prophets, third teachers, then miracles, then gifts of healing, of helping, of guidance, and of different kinds of tongues" (**1 Cor. 12:28 NIV**).

Scripture Reading: Romans 12:1–8

Introduction

Leading a group of people is a difficult task, calling for much tact. When a person has the gift of leadership, everything that person does will have visible assurance, natural authority, clear direction, and confirmation by events. A leader will make mistakes, but his or her qualities of leadership are greater than can be expected from natural abilities. This gift of the Spirit is called administration, or leadership.

I. Four New Testament words come under this gift of the Spirit.

A. *Proistamenos (Rom. 12:8).* This is one who takes the lead. It means to stand before or stand over. The person who has this gift is at the head as one who establishes rules and gives directions. A leader is a manager, someone who conducts as an orchestra conductor. Those who have this gift are leaders in all areas of life, especially the church.

B. *Kuberneseis (1 Cor. 12:28).* This is the word for government. It is the same word as "master" found in Acts 27:11 to speak of one who was pilot of a ship. This gift enables one to direct.

C. *Hegoumenos.* This word means to be before, to lead. It is the word for commander or ruler, as is seen in Matthew 2:6. In Hebrews 13:7, 17, and 24, it is used for church leaders. It means the chief person.

D. *Diakonos.* This is the word for "deacon," one who serves. The possessor of this gift is someone who helps others find their proper place in life. A deacon does the right thing without confusion, and a deacon's leadership leads to growth through control.

II. Some qualifications relate to this gift.

A. *First, consider what is not a qualification.* Leading is not being a boss; it is being a servant. Church leaders are never to be power mongers. The gift of administration does not express itself in demagogy, dogmatism, or dictatorship.

B. *Second, consider what are some qualifications.* Paul used the term for pastors and deacons in 1 Timothy 3, where he discussed the qualifications for leadership. He said that a leader must be "above reproach, faithful to his wife, temperate, self-controlled, respectable, hospitable, able to teach, not given to drunkenness, not violent but gentle, not quarrelsome, not a lover of money. He must manage his own family well. . . . He must not be a recent convert. . . . He must also have a good reputation with outsiders" (vv. 2–7 NIV).

Labor or work is another qualification (1 Thess. 5:12–13). The book of Hebrews identifies the gift with service (Heb. 13:7). It is also used of a wealthy person helping the poor (Rom. 12:8).

C. *Third, consider how to arrive at the qualifications that are identified with the gift of administration.* One must possess these qualifications in order to receive the gift. They are evidences of the gift or the use of it.

III. Some responses relate to this gift.

How should Spirit-filled believers respond to spiritual leaders? Three Scripture passages suggest some responses.

A. *First Thessalonians 5:12–13 has two words to describe believers' appropriate response to leaders: "respect" and "highest regard."* This makes for a beautiful relationship and productive work. Regardless of a leader's ability, he or she must have the proper response in order to fulfill the role of administrator.

B. *First Thessalonians 5:17 involves believers praying for their leaders.* Leadership is a lonely role and is difficult at its best. Christians should constantly pray for their leaders.

C. *Hebrews 13 has three words that describe believers' appropriate response to leaders.* Verse 7 says, "Remember." Christians are to care for their leaders. Verse 17 says, "Obey." People obey when they agree to do what is asked of them and when they believe their duties are correct and profitable. To obey is to submit or yield. Verse 24 says, "Salute." This means greet them with dignity, honor, and respect.

Conclusion

The gift of administration benefits all humankind. The more the gift is used and the greater the scriptural response to it, the greater success will be realized. As you reflect on this gift, search your heart and determine your spiritual relation to it.

SUNDAY MORNING, APRIL 19

Title: The Church—The Family of God

Text: "So then, you Gentiles are not foreigners or strangers any longer; you are now fellow citizens together with God's people and members of the family of God" **(Eph. 2:19 GNT)**.

Scripture Reading: Ephesians 2:11–22

Hymns: "A Mighty Fortress," Luther
"Faith of Our Fathers," Faber
"I Love Thy Kingdom, Lord," Dwight

Offertory Prayer: Our heavenly Father, we gather in your house to worship you. We express our gratitude that you are truly our heavenly Father. You gave us life and you sustain us. We are also grateful for the other men and women and children who make up our congregation, our brothers and sisters. In this family of worship, guide us to become the persons you want us to be. We pray in Christ's name. Amen.

Introduction

In this passage, Paul spoke to the church as "the family of God." This analogy has a great deal of meaning and value, and it is supported by a number of other analogies that express the same thing about the nature of the church. In Galatians 6:10 (GNT) Paul referred to the church as "our family in the faith." He admonished Timothy with respect to his pastoral responsibility, "If a man does not know how to manage his own family, how can he take care of the church of God?" (1 Tim. 3:5 GNT). Obviously, the church is a larger family. The church is called the "people" of God (2 Cor. 6:16–18; Heb. 2:14–17; 1 Peter 4:17). The church is also compared to a brotherhood (1 Cor. 6:5; 1 Peter 2:17; 5:9). Also, Jesus referred to the community that followed him in terms of the bride and bridegroom (Matt. 22:1–10; Rev. 19:7).

I. The church is the family—not the building they worship in.

A. *The church is an immediate family.* Most of us were born into a family and grew up with parents and possibly brothers or sisters. We learned the meaning of family in this small, immediate circle. It is the same way with the church. In the New Testament and in our own experience, the church is first of all the small community of believers in a particular place, meeting, worshiping, and serving God.

In the New Testament, of about 114 references to the word *church*, 93 of them refer to these small families of God living in the various communities of the Roman Empire. Our church is the family of God in a particular community.

B. *Growth is part of family life.* There are eight children in my family. We are all grown now and live in various parts of the United States. Most of us have children of our own; some of us have grandchildren. Our mother and father are no longer with us, but our family holds together. We communicate regularly by telephone, and since our oldest sister's home is centrally located, we meet there occasionally.

Although our family is widely scattered in terms of geography, it is still one family. It was that way in the New Testament. At first the people thought primarily of the local congregation. By the time Paul wrote Ephesians and Colossians, however, he realized that all Christians throughout the world were tied together in a family relationship.

C. *The church is a large family with many smaller families.* The church is truly a family. Wherever we may travel and encounter a church, even though they may speak a foreign language, worship in a different way, or have a culture entirely separate from our own, we are at home in that family. The church is the family of God—not a building or organization.

II. The church is God's family.

A. *People are born or adopted into a family.* The New Testament uses both of these terms. John spoke of becoming a Christian as being "born again" (John 3:3). Paul referred to "adoption" (Rom. 8:23; 9:4). Both terms stress our entry into the family of God.

B. *God creates his family.* We don't. Often we think that we build or organize churches. However, new members are born into the church when people hear the gospel under the power of the Holy Spirit. They are convicted of their sins and respond by faith in Jesus Christ. God initiates this even by sending his messenger and his Holy Spirit. We are merely God's servants in bearing that witness.

C. *God also calls the church into being.* Through a mission organization, we may go into a country or city where there are no churches or not enough churches. We may establish a teaching or preaching ministry out of which a church later grows. However, we need to be reminded that the congregation, or church, that emerges does so because God calls it into being. We go on missions only because he sends us. There is response to the Word only as the Holy Spirit works within the hearers. When a church itself is born, no matter how individuals may have been involved, it is God who calls his family into being.

D. *God holds his family together.* In the local church and in the universal church, God the heavenly Father holds his family together. Those of us who are members participate in the family because of our faith in God. Faith in God is the basis for our love for one another. So the church is God's family from beginning to end.

III. The church is truly a family.

A. *A family is a unit composed of various individuals.* Each person has his or her own particular characteristics, and these can often be quite diverse. Members within a family do not always agree, but they are bound together by a bond that is far stronger than human opinion. Though many, we are a family—a unity.

B. *We belong to the family.* Several times in the New Testament the word *belong* is used in connection with our relationship to God and to the church. Human life is made up of "belonging." We do not learn the meaning of human life until we build strong relationships with family members. As we grow older, we desire to be accepted by our peers. Later we enjoy the respect and love of people from many groups and relationships. This means that we derive our meaning in life from belonging to other persons.

We experience this bond of belonging most clearly in the family. Husband and wife belong to each other. Each life would be incomplete unless the other had a claim on that life. Children belong to their parents; parents belong just as much to their children. The bond of belonging does restrict freedom in one sense; yet, in a larger sense, it is the basis of true freedom.

C. *We learn the meaning of love only in belonging.* Again, look at your own family relationships. Look at those who belong to you and to whom you belong. Think of those occasions in which there has been joy in your family. Now think of an occasion full of grief or sorrow. Recall how important it is to intimately belong to another and to have another belong to you.

This is what it means to belong to a church. In the church, we learn to love one another to the extent that we give ourselves to others and accept them into meaningful relationships. Love cannot be known in isolation. It has meaning only in personal relationships. We love God because he first loved us.

D. *In the family, we share.* The human pilgrimage includes both joy and sorrow. A number of years ago, I had the pleasure of serving as interim pastor of a young church in a new area of a large city. The members, who had built or bought homes in the area, came from various church communities. Most of them were relatively young. They cared for one another in times of gladness and grief. I remember one occasion in which a young mother of three was dying of cancer. The other families of the church cared for her and for her three children, helped clean her house, and wept at her funeral as if they had lost a member of their own immediate family. This is the church.

IV. It means much to belong to the family of God.

A. *It means that we acknowledge that we belong to God.* Not only did God create us, but he also redeemed us through Jesus Christ. We are God's creatures. In sin, we believed we could live our lives best without God. This started with Adam and Eve. It led to estrangement and misery. Salvation means that we are restored to God. The relationship of belonging is reestablished.

B. *We cherish belonging to God and to his people.* When we come to know God and the family of God, we have come home. There is no sense of loss in turning our backs on our old kind of life. Rather, there is pure joy because we now realize the relationship with God and others for which we were created. Christians cherish their membership in God's family.

C. *It is God our Father who holds the family together.* When we recognize our heavenly Father, it is easy to recognize that we belong to one another. The differences that could separate us are harmonized if we acknowledge our mutual belonging to God. Because the church is God's family, we belong both to him and to his family.

D. *Only in this family can we grow into the people God wants us to be.* If a child is deprived of a family through the death or separation of his or her parents, some family substitute must be found. A child cannot grow up without a considerable amount of care by someone else. The church is the ideal family in which individual Christians grow up. There we have the right blend of challenge and encouragement. We have approval and correction necessary for healthy growth.

E. *In the family of God, we rejoice at the birth of a new member.* Recently I received a call from a younger member of our family whose first child had just been born. His joy was indescribable. I immediately called other family members to tell them the good news.

Likewise, the church is entrusted with the good news of salvation. We proclaim the gospel of forgiveness throughout the world. In our local community, we rejoice when a person becomes a Christian and is born into the family. This joy is appropriate. Also, when we hear from missionaries in foreign countries that people are becoming Christians, we rejoice from a distance.

Conclusion

Belonging to the family of God is very significant. This family had its origin in the life and teachings and the death and resurrection of our Lord Jesus Christ. We each participate in the family. We make our contribution and pass from the scene, but in a sense, we live on through the family.

Take heart! You are members of God's family. Through your participation, the family lives on.

SUNDAY EVENING, APRIL 19

Title: Recognizing His Identity

Text: "When Jesus entered Jerusalem, the whole city was stirred and asked, 'Who is this?'" **(Matt. 21:10 NIV)**.

Scripture Reading: Matthew 21:1–11

Introduction

On that first Palm Sunday, Jesus, surrounded by a great crowd of followers and others, entered Jerusalem as the King in exact fulfillment of prophecy (Isa. 62:11; Zech. 9:9) to make a final appeal to his own nation. This was his royal entry, and it caused quite a sensation. Matthew said, "The whole city was stirred and asked, 'Who is this?'" (21:10 NIV). For two thousand years, this same Jesus has been invading our complacent little Jerusalems, causing considerable disturbance, and many have been pondering his true identity, asking, "Who is this?"

On the evening of Jesus' resurrection, he appeared to the disciples behind closed doors. He lingered until they recognized him. He came to the Roman Empire and overthrew the Caesars. During the Dark Ages, he came in mystic power to scattered groups. He fortified sorely pressed followers as they proclaimed his truths. He was present during the Protestant Reformation. He came to the eighteenth and nineteenth centuries with stirrings of power and progress. He confronted the twentieth century, and the question was asked, "Who is Jesus?" Now, in the twenty-first century, this amazing man still disturbs us.

Who is this man who examines our policies and motives and dealings with one another? "Who is this?" This question was relevant two thousand years ago, and it is relevant now. There is no easy answer, but we will consider five roles of this mysterious Jesus.

I. Jesus was, and is, a man.

Jesus was born a Jew. His parents were called humble peasants, but they were "of the house and lineage of David" (Luke 2:4). This means that when God became incarnate, he did not assume human flesh in the abstract; he became part of a family. Family membership cuts two ways, so when God came

133

into the world, he entered in such a way as to experience our problem—the family problem. He knew the problem of illustrious relatives, of disgraceful relatives, the problem of "the skeleton in the closet," the problem of mediocrity.

Though born in Bethlehem in fulfillment of prophecy, he grew up in Nazareth in Galilee in a large, devout Jewish family. He had a normal boyhood. He learned his father's trade and was called "the carpenter" (Mark 6:3). He assumed responsibility for the family at his father's death. He learned the lore of his people and the Law and the Prophets as taught by the rabbis. At about thirty years of age, he was baptized (Luke 3:23) and entered into his ministry. Never did a man teach as he taught or live as he lived.

Jesus' body and mind obeyed the laws of normal human development. He met temptations, pondered the cross, slept from weariness, and, exhausted at midday, sat beside a well. Like other men, he had times of great rejoicing, times of hot indignation, and times of deep compassion. At times he was astonished by the people's lack of faith, at other times by their great faith. His soul was nourished by secret prayer, his power was replenished by quiet retreats, and always he lived in humble filial dependence on his Father.

What about Jesus' physical appearance? We have no actual description, but since he worked in a rough occupation, he was probably hard and bronzed.

We see in Jesus the type of manhood we admire: the courage of a valiant soul, the chivalry of a soldier, the genuineness of a true gentleman, and the purity we want to see in our children. Athanasius said, "Christ became human that men might become divine."

II. Jesus is God.

The night before Jesus died, he said, "Anyone who has seen me has seen the Father" (John 14:9 NIV). Jesus is God. A distinguished Jewish rabbi wrote, "For Christians Jesus was born divinely and lived humanly; for Jews he was born humanly and lived divinely." But this is a false distinction, a play on words. Jesus is man. Jesus is God. In the Son, the Father not only acts and speaks, but he is present. Jesus Christ is God himself, uniquely present in human life.

The mysteries surrounding the birth, life, and death of Christ are the mysteries of God. The power of his miracles is God's power. Jesus said, "The works that the Father has given me to finish—the very works that I am doing—testify that the Father has sent me" (John 5:36 NIV). His preaching was the Word of God. His healing hands delivered the infinite mercy and health of God. The forgiveness that Christ imparts is the eternal forgiveness of God. Jesus is God.

III. Jesus is head of the church.

Jesus asked his disciples about the current ideas of his identity. "'But what about you?' he asked. 'Who do you say I am?'" (Matt. 16:15 NIV). Peter's confession was, "You are the Christ, the Son of the living God" (v. 16). Jesus was so pleased with Peter's answer that he said, "Blessed are you, Simon son of Jonah, for this was not revealed to you by man, but by my Father in heaven. And I tell you that you are Peter, and on this rock I will build my church, and the gates of Hades will not overcome it" (vv. 17–18). These are controversial verses about which the Christian world is somewhat divided. But it seems that emphasis has always been placed on the wrong issue. The important thing is that Christ built the church and is therefore its head. Paul told us that Christ loved the church (Eph. 5:25) and purchased it with his own blood (Acts 20:28). In Colossians 1:18 Paul said, "He is the head of the body, the church." In Romans 12 Paul used the physical body to describe the church. He also did so in 1 Corinthians 12, with verse 27 as the key verse: "Now you are the body of Christ, and each one of you is a part of it."

Christ is the head of the church. This means three things.

A. *Christ has absolute primacy in his church.* The members of the body exist to serve the interests of the head.

B. *Christ has supremacy over his church.* Just as the whole government of the body is in the head, so all authority in the church belongs to Christ. He is the supreme ruler of his church on earth. No one else could ever rise to his position.

C. *Christ's church has complete dependence on him.* Just as the human body is lifeless apart from the head, so the church is lifeless apart from Christ.

IV. Jesus is the Savior of the world.

The entire New Testament stems from this fact.

A. *There is no question about Jesus' mission.* Jesus never left the world in doubt about his purpose: "For the Son of Man came to seek and to save the lost" (Luke 19:10 NIV; see also John 10:10; 1 Tim. 1:15).

B. *There is no question about Jesus' motive.* Christ is the sole mediator between God and man (1 Tim. 2:5). John 3:16, the heart verse of the New Testament, expresses his motive clearly: "For God so loved the world. . . ."

C. *There is no question about the early disciples and their faith.* Arrested for preaching Christ after healing a lame man at the temple gate, Peter and John were thrown in jail for the night. The next morning the rulers would have released them in exchange for their promise to keep silent. Instead, Peter preached to the Sanhedrin, charging that they crucified Jesus. Peter affirmed that Jesus was the stone rejected by the builders, which had been made head of the corner. His climax was, "Salvation is found in no one else, for there is no other name under heaven given to mankind by which we must be saved" (Acts 4:12 NIV).

D. *There is no question about Jesus' method, then and now.* "You will receive power when the Holy Spirit comes on you; and you will be my witnesses in Jerusalem, and in all Judea and Samaria, and to the ends of the earth" (Acts 1:8 NIV).

Jesus is the Savior of the world. Today many names are associated with security and salvation. Communism has its plans. Socialism has its doctrines. Democracy has its ideals. Politicians have their promises. The military has its mobile power and its missiles. But humankind can only retrieve; we cannot redeem.

V. Jesus is the constant companion who enables us to serve God and others.

Christ's transforming power has changed lives, and it still changes lives.

A. *Christ helps us understand the Bible.* His Spirit guides us into all truth (John 16:13). He is the key to the Scriptures.

B. *Christ is our model, our example in all things.* Paul told the Corinthians, "Follow my example, as I follow the example of Christ" (1 Cor. 11:1 NIV). Did anyone ever display the qualities or meet the standard set forth in the Sermon on the Mount? Yes, one did—Jesus—and we are to follow his example.

C. *Christ is our constant companion along life's pathway.* He promised his disciples, "I will not leave you as orphans; I will come to you" (John 14:18 NIV). He still does.

D. *Christ's power transforms us into servants of God and others.* To know Christ is to travel a hard road. He does not lead us into a cloister. He will take us by the hand and lead us to Gethsemanes and Calvaries of our own in his service.

Conclusion

To those who obey him, Christ will reveal himself in the conflicts they encounter, and they will learn in their own experiences who he is. Do you know who he is?

WEDNESDAY EVENING, APRIL 22

Title: The Gift of Encouraging

Text: "If it is to encourage, then give encouragement; if it is giving, then give generously; if it is to lead, do it diligently; if it is to show mercy, do it cheerfully" **(Rom. 12:8 NIV)**.

Scripture Reading: 2 Corinthians 1:3–7

Introduction

The word *comfort* is used nine times in our Scripture reading to describe the ministry of encouraging. Encouragement is a gift from God that we are to pass on to others.

I. First, consider the definition of the gift.

A. *The key thought of encouraging is comfort.* The user of this gift excludes all selfish motives and concentrates on helping others. This gift of the Holy Spirit provides believers with the same gift that Jesus and the Holy Spirit possess. In John 14:16 Jesus spoke of himself and the Holy Spirit as being comforters. In our text, Paul spoke of the gift as enabling believers to have that same ability. In 1 John 2:1 Jesus is described as an advocate. In Romans 12:8 believers are described in the same way.

B. *Another concept expressed in encouragement is counseling.* Christians counsel others by urging or warning or reproving. They also counsel by speaking words of encouragement and support. In addition, Christians may counsel by giving an address or recommendation. The idea of counseling is to build up, or edify.

II. Second, consider a New Testament character who illustrates the gift.

The character is Barnabas, known as "the son of consolation."

A. *Barnabas is seen helping Paul in three different ways.*
  1. He endorsed and welcomed an unwelcome convert (Acts 9:23–29). Few things are needed more in this world than to simply know that someone cares. Everyone needs a friend, someone who encourages.
  2. He enlisted Paul as a teacher (Acts 11:22–26). Many people are waiting in the corridors of service to be enlisted. The Holy Spirit endows God's people to find and use these workers.
  3. He developed Paul as a gifted assistant into one who became his superior (Acts 13:50). This is an illustration of someone having this gift to project his feelings away from self to the feelings of others.

B. *Barnabas is seen accepting alien believers who were not welcomed by others (Acts 11:22–26).* When Barnabas saw what the Lord was doing among others, he rejoiced. In this passage, he is referred to as a kind person full of the Spirit and strong in the faith.

C. *Barnabas is seen restoring a youthful dissenter (Acts 15:37).* This action conceivably saved a man in the Lord's work. Through the gift of the Spirit, Barnabas saw the potential in Mark, and through the use of the same gift, he was able to help Mark.

III. Third, observe some general characteristics of the gift.

A. *The gift is one of continuous action.* The use of this gift is a day-by-day, week-by-week activity, not a once-and-for-all action.

B. *The use of the gift has an urgency about it.* Each person with this gift should take it seriously. It is not to be taken lightly. There is too much hurt on the part of people and too much desire to help on God's part to delay using this gift.

Conclusion

People desperately need help, encouragement, and consolation. You, as a Christian, have the gift to provide these things. Use it!

SUNDAY MORNING, APRIL 26

Title: The Church—The Body of Christ

Text: "Just as each of us has one body with many members, and these members do not all have the same function, so in Christ we, though many, form one body, and each member belongs to all the others" **(Rom. 12:4–5 NIV).**

Scripture Reading: 1 Corinthians 12:27; Ephesians 3:6

Hymns: "The Church's One Foundation," Stone
          "Rise Up, O Men of God," Merrill
          "All Hail the Power," Perronet

Offertory Prayer: Our Father, you have given us life, strength, health, and the will and opportunity to work. We now bring to you a portion of our earnings. We pray that you will accept these gifts as expressions of our love for you and commitment to your cause. Use these offerings to carry your good news to others and to bless those for whom you care through Jesus Christ our Lord. Amen.

Introduction

The human body is an amazing creation. Too often we take it for granted and do not express our gratitude to God for his wonderful creation. Gymnasts show an amazing degree of mental focus while their bodies execute difficult and carefully timed feats of coordination. Ice skaters perform with spectacular grace and beauty. Tennis players portray impressive control and concentration. The church, as the body of Christ, needs to operate with the same kind of coordination.

I. The church is like a human body.

   A. *The church is a single functioning organism.* This analogy of the human body correctly introduces us to the church. The church is not an organization made up of many parts assembled together. Rather, it is a living organism that has many parts.
   B. *The church has many diverse members.* In 1 Corinthians 12:12 Paul wrote, "The body, though one, has many parts, but all its many parts form one body" (NIV). Paul went on to illustrate that a foot cannot downplay itself because it is not a hand. An ear cannot say that it doesn't belong to the body just because it is not an eye. Instead, all parts of the body, though diverse, are necessary for the body.

138

In the church, we remain individuals who are quite diverse in nature. It would not be good for us to lose our individuality. In a sense, we have our individual identity only because we are functioning members of the body. Understanding this idea would prevent or solve most problems we encounter in churches today.

C. *The members realize their own importance as it relates to the body.* No organ of the body would have any value or meaning if severed from the body. Paul's argument in 1 Corinthians is precisely this. The hand and the foot have identity simply because of their membership in the body.

In the church, our diversity is a blessing if it is supported by a strong sense of unity. We do not compete with one another; we complement one another. The foot takes the hand where it wants to go. The eyes turn to see what the ears have heard. Not only does meaning depend on the members functioning together; survival depends on it.

II. The body is Christ's body.

We can more easily understand our relationship to the church if we understand the analogy of the body of Christ. The church is Christ's body functioning under his direction; he is the head.

A. *The origin of the church.* The church originated in the life, death, and resurrection of Jesus Christ. There was a people of God in the Old Testament, but the church in the full sense of the word originated in Jesus Christ. Therefore we should not presume to think of ourselves as members of it unless we acknowledge the One who is the head.

B. *How do we become members of the church?* We become members of Christ's church, or body, by being born into his kingdom (John 3:3–7).

C. *An organization is not a church unless it is the body of Christ.* Our land is overcrowded with organizations that call themselves churches. They are tax exempt and have many privileges extended to them by a friendly government. It is not my task or yours to distinguish between churches and the social clubs that call themselves churches. It is, however, our task to make certain we know the difference and that we are related to a body that can rightly be called a church. The church in the broad sense is the body of Christ deriving its origin and its power from him. In a specific instance, a local church is merely an expression of the church in this place and at this time. If it is organized to do our will, we probably should call it our club. If, however, it is the body of Jesus Christ doing his will, we should call it a church.

III. Members of the church are individually important.

A. *Individual members are important to Christ.* Jesus cares for and guides the members of his body. He corrects them when they go astray, and he forgives them when they come back. In him they realize their full meaning.

B. *Members are important to each other.* It is in the church that we find some of the most meaningful relationships in life, some as important as those in our immediate families. Many people would not be able to survive the struggle of day-to-day living without the encouragement and support they receive from other Christians.

C. *Individual members are important to the whole body.* Just as some of the organs of the body are inconspicuous, so are some of the members of the church. Some members stand out as being very prominent in public worship and work. Other members, however, are not visible yet are just as important in the functioning of the body as the prominent members. In some cases they may be more important.

A great lesson is here for those of us who function within the church. We should follow Paul's teaching and utilize the gifts we have for the welfare of the entire body. In so doing, we realize the meaning of our individual lives in terms of the whole body.

IV. The church is dependent on Jesus Christ.

A. *In John 15 Jesus used the figure of the vine and the branches to illustrate his relationship to the church.* He is the vine; we are the branches. No branch can live apart from the vine. In the church, each one of us has a relationship to Christ and to others. Our relationship is that of dependence on him.

B. *Christ is the source of our life and strength.* Just as the vine brings the moisture and nourishment from the earth to the branches, so Christ is the source of our energy and power. Apart from him we would perish.

C. *We depend on Christ for meaning in life.* Next to life itself in importance is meaning. Life must have direction or purpose. Without such meaning we wither away. Jesus Christ is that meaning in our lives.

V. The church is one.

The analogy of the church as the body of Christ stresses the oneness of the church. Certainly it acknowledges the diversity. Moreover, it emphasizes the unity that exists among the diversity. The greatest passage in the New Testament on this theme is Ephesians 4:4–6.

A. *There is one body.* The unity of the church cannot be stated any more clearly than with this statement: "The church is one body."

B. *There is one Spirit.* We often overlook the unifying power of the Holy Spirit because we structure into our church life the cultural and regional prejudices of our own time and place.

C. *There is one hope.* Hope is faith directed into the future. Christians are united in the hope that because Jesus Christ was raised from the dead, we, too, will be raised from the dead and will live with God forever.

D. *There is one Lord.* Jesus Christ is our Lord and Master. We believe in him and obey him. Even when we forget and disobey him, we come back to him in repentance and faith because he is Lord, the head of the body.

E. *There is one faith.* The precious Christian faith is much more than holding an opinion about Christ or believing correct doctrines about Christ and Christianity. It is personal commitment to Jesus Christ on the basis of such doctrines. Within the church there is one faith: commitment to Jesus Christ.

F. *There is one baptism.* Although churches observe baptism in various ways, it is a personal confession of faith in Jesus Christ who died, was buried, and rose from the dead. It is a personal confession that we have died to sin and that we want to walk with Christ. It is a confession that, beyond death, we expect to be raised again.

G. *There is one God.* Jesus Christ is the Son of God. The body of Christ, the church, is held together by God, who is the Father of all humankind.

Conclusion

You and I are members of the body of Christ. We belong to and depend on him. And since we are members of this body, we belong to one another.

SUNDAY EVENING, APRIL 26

Title: Realizing the Resurrection

Text: "As they talked and discussed these things with each other, Jesus himself came up and walked along with them; but they were kept from recognizing him. . . . When he was at the table with them, he took bread, gave thanks, broke it and began to give it to them. Then their eyes were opened and they recognized him" **(Luke 24:15–16, 30–31 NIV)**.

Scripture Reading: Luke 24:13–35

Introduction

Approached from the standpoint of the two disciples who walked with the risen Christ on the road to Emmaus, our Scripture reading is the most beautiful story in the world. Luke told it simply, winsomely, and in great detail because the experience of these two disciples was representative of all of Jesus' followers. This story illustrates that it is possible to see yet not perceive, to behold but not recognize, to have the risen Christ walk beside us without realizing it is truly him.

This story turns on two key verses—Luke 24:16 and 31. There is a dark side to this story: "They were kept from recognizing him" (v. 16 NIV). But there is also a bright side: "Then their eyes were opened and they recognized him" (v. 31 NIV). Heartbreak and sadness gave way to joy and gladness. As clearly as in any record in the New Testament, here are two sides of a coin.

I. The dark side of the coin.

"But they were kept from recognizing him." Imagine it! These disciples were walking beside their risen Lord and did not realize it!

A. *What is the fact here?* Simply that these disciples were in the presence of the greatest reality in history, the reality of the risen Christ, but they did not know it. Can we sit in judgment on them? Is it not pathetic that our own eyes are so often dimmed by unbelief that we fail to realize his presence?

B. *What explains this fact?* The statement "They were kept from recognizing him" does not mean that their physical sight was in any way impaired. Nor does it mean that God had blinded their eyes. Their failure to recognize him was a judgment they had brought on themselves.

1. They were victims of their preoccupation with other thoughts, other things. Obviously they did not expect to see Jesus. They were absorbed in their grief, their frustration, their disappointment.

2. They were victims of their own presuppositions. They said, "We had hoped that he was the one who was going to redeem Israel" (Luke 24:21 NIV). Here they reveal the popular misunderstanding of the role of the Messiah of their hopes. The crucifixion of Jesus was seen as fatal to the hope that he would prove to be the Christ.

3. They were victims of their own unbelief. Their words to Jesus were a confession of obstinate unbelief. They did not expect their Lord to fulfill his own promises, and they refused to believe the word of cheer sent by heavenly messengers.

4. Jesus rebuked them, saying, "How foolish you are, and how slow of heart to believe all that the prophets have spoken! Did not the Messiah have to suffer these things and then enter his glory?" (Luke 24:25–26 NIV). Jesus chided them primarily for not believing the Old Testament. They had failed to believe all that the prophets had spoken, particularly his atoning death and his return to heavenly glory.

C. *What resulted from this fact?* What were the consequences of not recognizing their Lord? How dark is the picture! Because they did not believe the resurrection had truly taken place, they had not experienced its uplifting power.

1. Sadness still ruled their hearts. As the two disciples were talking with each other, Jesus asked, "'What are you discussing together

as you walk along?' They stood still, their faces downcast" (Luke 24:17 NIV).

2. They had abandoned all hope. "We had hoped that he was the one who was going to redeem Israel" (Luke 24:21 NIV). Note the past tense: "We had hoped." Now their hope was gone.

3. The fact that the disciples did not recognize Jesus demonstrates the extreme darkness of unbelief. They continued their speech sadly: "And what is more, it is the third day since all this took place. In addition, some of our women amazed us. They went to the tomb early this morning but didn't find his body. They came and told us that they had seen a vision of angels, who said he was alive. Then some of our companions went to the tomb and found it just as the women had said, but they did not see Jesus" (vv. 21–24 NIV). Note, "It is the third day since all this took place." They did remember Jesus' promise, but they did not recognize him as the risen Christ. To paraphrase their thoughts, "We remember his promise to rise on the third day, but as you can see, he didn't keep his promise." Being disappointed in Jesus is like dwelling in a pit of darkness and doubt.

II. The bright side of the coin.

"Then their eyes were opened and they recognized him" (Luke 24:31 NIV).

A. *What led to their opened eyes, their recognition of Christ?* It happened in a second, but it had its antecedents.

1. First came the revelation of Scripture. Luke reported, "And beginning with Moses and all the Prophets, he explained to them what was said in all the Scriptures concerning himself" (Luke 24:27 NIV). When finally they recognized him, they said, "Were not our hearts burning within us while he talked with us on the road and opened the Scriptures to us?" (Luke 24:32 NIV). Under the magic touch of the Bible's central figure, the Scriptures they had known from childhood were coming alive with light, and they saw the Suffering Servant of the prophet's vision as the very Jesus to whom they had grown close. He who offered himself to God without flaw has a rational claim to be Scripture's best interpreter.

2. First came their burning hearts. How do you define the inspiration of the Scriptures or the quality that makes the Bible different from all other literature? It defies definition, but the witness of God's Spirit in our hearts is the inward glow that confirms the outward revelation. After these two disciples had joined the others in Jerusalem that night, had given their witness, and had heard of the Lord's appearance to Peter (Luke 24:34),

Jesus himself appeared in their midst. Luke wrote, "Then he opened their minds so they could understand the Scriptures" (Luke 24:45 NIV). An open Bible and open minds result in passionate hearts.

3. First came the breaking of bread. The simplicity of Luke's narrative here is instinct with reality and truth: "When he was at the table with them, he took bread, gave thanks, broke it and began to give it to them. Then their eyes were opened and they recognized him, and he disappeared from their sight" (24:30–31 NIV). Was it that familiar, characteristic gesture that gave them their clue, some mannerism reminding them of an unforgotten meal with the Master? A symbol is an interpretation to the heart. Our Lord's symbolic act in that Emmaus cottage was certainly an interpretation to the heart, and two hearts leaped to meet it.

B. *What resulted from their opened eyes, their recognition of Christ?* This was a joyous event. When they did recognize him, when they realized that the resurrection truly had occurred, all of life was changed by the experience. Every shattered hope was reborn. Even uncertainty vanished. The disciples' smoldering hearts burst into flames of joy, and all of life took on a different hue. Note the deep haste that is suggested: "They got up and returned at once to Jerusalem. There they found the Eleven and those with them" (Luke 24:33 NIV).

The disciples were in the grip of the most delightful feeling in the world. Something had happened to them. They had wonderful news to tell, news that would set the hearts of all who heard it on fire with joy; and they couldn't wait to reach Jerusalem so they could share it. In the intense excitement of great joy, they met the Eleven and the others: "Have you heard? Do you know? Isn't it wonderful?" And the disciples replied, "It is true! The Lord has risen and has appeared to Simon" (Luke 24:34 NIV).

Conclusion

Someone has defined the Christian life as a long Emmaus pilgrimage. This is true, for now that he is risen and ascended, geography no longer exists in God's kingdom. A believing heart has everywhere as its Holy Land. Emmaus is anywhere when we meet the risen Lord and welcome him into our hearts.

And when we meet him, we will know him, for we will see him as he is. The resurrection is a historical fact. May God help us realize this fact.

WEDNESDAY EVENING, APRIL 29

Title: The Gift of Giving

Text: "If it is to encourage, then give encouragement; if it is giving, then give generously; if it is to lead, do it diligently; if it is to show mercy, do it cheerfully" **(Rom. 12:8 NIV)**.

Scripture Reading: 2 Corinthians 8:1–15

Introduction

Our consideration of the gift of giving seems to change pace from the study of gifts discussed previously in the series. This type of giving falls into the category of helpfulness rather than being a personal trait. Excitement builds as we continue to study the gifts of the Spirit. We can readily see God's wisdom through his work in the church. By bestowing the gifts of the Spirit, God equips everyone who is needed to do his work in the church.

I. Two words in Romans 12:8 clarify the gift.

A. *The first word is "contributing."* It means to give or share of one's own accord. Giving can apply to all facets of life. Some examples are time, talents, and money. However, it appears that the main use of the gift applies to material things. It is the ability and desire to use the temporal possessions that God has given to us for his glory. The concept of the gift of contributing stresses the ability and desire to give for the good of others and for the glory of God.

B. *The other word is "generously."* The word literally means without fold or crease—that is, wide open. It means to be liberal, not selfish or tightfisted. The gift is to be used sincerely or with delight and without ulterior motives. It is free from inner discord and accompanied by a pure heart.

II. General thoughts that apply to material things add to the understanding of this gift.

A. *The minimal amount for a believer to give is the tithe.* At least two shocking statements relate to tithing. First, it is only a beginning. The Spirit will not limit us to a level of giving below the tithe. Second, the Spirit never contradicts Scripture, which teaches that tithing is the basic proportion for giving.

Also, two motives are seen in the tithing concept. One is the legalistic escape. Some people argue against tithing to cover up covetousness. The other is thinking that tithing is enough. That is not all the Lord requires.

B. *Realizing that the ability to give is from the Spirit establishes the proper attitude toward giving.* Money can be a touchy subject. It has been said that the most sensitive nerve in the human body is the one that goes to the pocketbook. Paul, in 2 Corinthians 8:1–15, gave advice for the use of money. He cited the example of others (vv. 2–8), the example of Jesus (v. 9), the past record (vv. 10–11), the necessity of putting a fine feeling into fine action (vv. 12–13), and the fact that life has a strange way of evening things up (vv. 14–15).

C. *"Where your treasure is, there will your heart be also" (Matt. 6:21).* Christians are indwelt by the Holy Spirit. As they allow the Spirit to control their lives, they demonstrate the gift of giving.

Conclusion

The exercise of the gift of giving exemplifies a real Christian spirit. Let me encourage you right now to give yourself to the Lord Jesus. Make him Lord of your life. Then seek his leadership in the giving of your money.

MAY

■ **Sunday Mornings**

On the first Sunday of the month, complete the series "The Nature and Mission of the Church." On the second Sunday of the month, feature a special Mother's Day message. Finish out the month with three messages with the evangelistic theme "The Good News of God's Glorious Offer." The true shepherd of the flock must not only feed the sheep but must give weekly attention to increasing the flock.

■ **Sunday Evenings**

The theme for Sunday evening messages for May through July is "Jesus Christ as Our High Priest." The book of Hebrews is not the most popular book or the most loved book in the New Testament. In many respects, it is a neglected book. The Jewish, or Old Testament, background that permeates every chapter has probably contributed to its neglect by modern pastors. The book of Hebrews portrays an exalted concept of Jesus Christ. A serious study of this book along with the suggested messages can be most helpful to a congregation.

■ **Wednesday Evenings**

Continue the series "Concerning the Gifts of the Holy Spirit."

SUNDAY MORNING, MAY 3

Title: The Church—The Community of the Holy Spirit

Text: "The Advocate, the Holy Spirit, whom the Father will send in my name, will teach you all things and will remind you of everything I have said to you" **(John 14:26 NIV)**.

Scripture Reading: John 14:15–26

Hymns: "Breathe on Me, Breath of God," Hatch
         "Come, Holy Spirit, Heavenly Dove," Watts
         "Come, Thou Almighty King," Anonymous

Offertory Prayer: Holy Spirit, we need your power within us lest we stumble and fall. Guide us on our way and give us strength as we travel the narrow path of life.

We thank you for providing all our needs and for the ability to give money back into your kingdom. Bless these gifts that they may be used for your work. In Jesus' name we pray. Amen.

Introduction

We often look back to the days of Jesus' life on earth with a bit of regret that we did not get to know him at that time. Sometimes we think our faith would be stronger if we had the opportunity of seeing Jesus. We are probably mistaken. Many of those who saw Jesus did not believe in him.

On the eve of Jesus' crucifixion, he told his disciples, "The Advocate, the Holy Spirit, whom the Father will send in my name, will teach you all things and will remind you of everything I have said to you" (John 14:26 NIV). In other words, Jesus indicated that the Holy Spirit would take his place on earth and would continue all that he had begun.

I. The Holy Spirit is Jesus Christ with us.

    A. *The Spirit of God is the Spirit of Christ.* In the New Testament, we often read the terms *Holy Spirit, Spirit of God, his Spirit,* and *Spirit of Christ.* These terms are synonymous. We will not go astray if we think of the Holy Spirit as Jesus Christ continually living in us in a spiritual way, just as he lived with the first disciples in a natural, physical way.

    B. *The Holy Spirit is present with believers just as Jesus was during his life on earth.* Although the first disciples saw Jesus and walked with him, he was removed from them by his crucifixion. In the Gospel of John, the Holy Spirit is understood as Jesus Christ living with us. The enemies of Christ were able to kill his body, but no one can kill his Holy Spirit. We are assured of his constant presence.

    C. *What is the Holy Spirit like?* The Holy Spirit is God, and God is revealed in Jesus Christ. Therefore the Holy Spirit is like Jesus. If you want to determine whether it is truly the Holy Spirit leading you, ask, "Is this what Jesus would do?" What we know about the Holy Spirit we have learned through the revelation of Jesus Christ.

So we were not left alone when Jesus ascended back to the Father; rather, God is always with us in the presence of the Holy Spirit.

II. The Holy Spirit is our Teacher.

    A. *The early Christians saw Jesus as their Teacher.* He not only taught them the ways of God; he also taught them how Christians should live. His teachings have become the guidelines for the lives of his followers. Jesus' early death did not allow enough time for him to teach them all they needed to know about important subjects. It is remarkable that Jesus, knowing that he would die young, specifically promised that the Holy Spirit would be our Teacher and would continue to teach us after Jesus' departure.

    B. *The Holy Spirit is our Teacher.* We can easily go astray, however, if we think the Holy Spirit teaches us apart from the Bible or the church. The New Testament brings us the teachings of Jesus Christ by inspired writers. The Holy Spirit teaches us partly by helping us to understand the Bible. Sometimes people claim special revelations by the Holy Spirit that are contrary to the teachings of the Bible. If the Bible is faithful to Jesus Christ, then it follows that the Holy Spirit, who continues to teach as Jesus did, will agree with the biblical teachings.

C. *The Holy Spirit is particularly present in the church.* Although our individual Bible study is important and should not be neglected, we often sense the Holy Spirit's presence most keenly in church worship services. He teaches us as we worship and study in the company of others who are also listening.

III. The Holy Spirit leads the church.

A. *The book of Acts gives examples.* Many people think the book of Acts should be named not "The Acts of the Apostles" but "The Acts of the Holy Spirit." If you have read Acts, you know that the Holy Spirit is in charge at every important juncture in the early church. The Holy Spirit led at Pentecost. The Holy Spirit empowered the church as they moved a Jewish foundation to the Gentile world. The Holy Spirit guided and strengthened missionaries in their evangelistic work.

B. *The Holy Spirit leads the church in ministry today.* We often overlook this fact to our own ruin. More important than how much we talk about the Holy Spirit is how much we listen to him as we seek to do his will.

IV. The Holy Spirit is the power within the church.

A. *The Holy Spirit convicts individuals of their sin.* In John 3 we learn that new birth is brought about by the Holy Spirit and the instrumentality of the Word. In other words, when unbelievers hear the gospel being preached, the Holy Spirit drives it into their hearts so they are convicted of their sin and desire to become Christians.

B. *The Holy Spirit empowers Christians to witness.* The only way Christians are able to proclaim the gospel effectively is by the Holy Spirit giving power to their witness.

C. *The New Testament includes many terms describing the Holy Spirit's work.* The Holy Spirit enters us at the time of our conversion. Paul wrote in 1 Corinthians 12:13 that "we were all baptized by one Spirit into one body." The "filling of the Spirit" needs to recur continually throughout our lives. Being "moved by the Spirit" simply means that the Holy Spirit leads or motivates us to do his work.

D. *The Holy Spirit is related to hearing the Word of God.* We learn in Romans 10:17 that faith comes by hearing the Word of God. All missionary and evangelistic work is based on this belief. The Holy Spirit makes this "hearing" possible. Apart from the Holy Spirit, a Scripture passage is merely a lesson in ancient history.

V. The church is a "fellowship of the Holy Spirit."

A. *Worship depends on the Holy Spirit.* We frequently plan our worship services or take part in them unaware that all is in vain unless the Holy Spirit is present. On some occasions we are made aware of the mysterious power of God moving among us and within us. We experience true worship on such occasions. The church is not the church unless the Holy Spirit is moving within it.

B. *The Holy Spirit gives saving power.* He not only convicts sinners of their sin and thereby makes their faith possible; he also gives power to us as we grow in our Christian life.

C. *Without the Holy Spirit, churches become religious clubs.* All too often we think the church belongs to us, and we organize it and do with it as we like. But it is truly the church when the Holy Spirit is moving within the members and its ministry to provide power and direction.

D. *The Holy Spirit makes the church* "the *church*." The entire concept of the church, as it appears in the New Testament as the "family of God" and "the body of Christ," is realized when the Holy Spirit has his way within a congregation. Then the church is known as a fellowship of the Holy Spirit.

Conclusion

If we wish to see the work of Jesus Christ done in our individual lives and in our church, we must be assured of the presence of the Holy Spirit within us—that is, we must be born again—and we must continually seek to be filled with his power.

SUNDAY EVENING, MAY 3

Title: Christ—God's Messenger

Text: "In the past God spoke to our forefathers through the prophets at many times and in various ways, but in these last days he has spoken to us by his Son" **(Heb. 1:1–2 NIV).**

Scripture Reading: Hebrews 1:1–14

Introduction

The letter to the Hebrews was written to prove that the new covenant in Jesus Christ is superior to the old covenant of Mount Sinai. God sent his messenger, Jesus Christ, to establish the new covenant. This introductory chapter to Hebrews overwhelms its recipients with spiritual facts about Christ—God's messenger.

I. Messenger preceded (Heb. 1:1).

God was active in human affairs before he sent his Son. The author of Hebrews gives a summary of divine dealings prior to "these last days" (1:2).

A. *Recipients.* The revelation of God was directed to fathers, the ones who would respond to responsibility by faith, in order for society to have spiritual guidance.
B. *Manner.* The message from God came in a variety of ways. God spoke through a "burning" bush, political decrees, meditations, miracles, natural disasters, and a number of other ways.
C. *Prophets.* The author specifically notes the prophets' role in presenting God's Word to the fathers.

II. Messenger presented (Heb. 1:2–3).

A concise theological treatise concerning Jesus Christ is given in the next two verses of this chapter. He is presented in three realms:

A. *In the cosmic realm.* Christ is revealed to be more than flesh and blood. He is the cosmic Christ, and he has complete rule over the physical universe.
   1. As heir (1:2). Jesus Christ is the heir of all things. This heirship is shared with those who are born again (Rom. 8:17).
   2. As creator (1:2). The role of creator of the universe is attributed to Christ. This is not an uncommon New Testament teaching (John 1:3, 10; Col. 1:16).
   3. As upholder (1:3). God's Son is declared to be the One upholding all things by the power of his Word. There is an obvious force at work in the physical sustaining of the universe that the scientific world has not yet recognized (note Col. 1:17).
B. *In the spiritual realm.* The world of spiritual reality is controlled by Christ. The author of Hebrews gives three major truths regarding the messenger in the spiritual realm.
   1. As glory (1:3). The transfiguration (Matt. 17:1–13) gave us a brief glimpse into the inner glory of our Lord.
   2. As image (1:3). The New Testament speaks of Jesus as being the physical image of the invisible God (John 1:18; Col. 1:15; 2:9). Those who have seen Jesus have seen the Father (John 14:9).
   3. As royalty (1:3). As Christ finished his earthly service, he took a seat "on the right hand of the Majesty on high." This phrase does not imply that there are three Gods on three thrones in heaven. Rather, it simply means that Jesus Christ shares in the royalty of the Trinity.
C. *In the human realm.* Since it is impossible for people to escape sin by their own power, God sent his Son to purge humanity of all iniquity. It seems that the purpose of Jesus' activities in both the cosmic and spiritual realm is fulfilled as he works with people in the human realm. He has once and for all delivered humankind from their enslavement to sin.

151

III. Messenger preferred (Heb. 1:4–13).

The author of Hebrews was aware that his recipients were steeped in Old Testament history and theology. They would be tempted either to reject Jesus as being inferior to the angels of Old Testament fame or to categorize him as being "one among many." The author presented Jesus as God's superior messenger. This highly exalted Person has a superior name (1:4) that should invoke a response of adoration. The author presented Jesus as being superior to God's angels in three ways.

A. *As Son, he is superior to angels.*
   1. Personal declaration (1:5). At no time has God spoken to angels as he did to Jesus when he said, "Thou art my Son."
   2. Social declaration (1:5). God directs a statement to society as a whole as he addresses Jesus in the third person. God wants the world to know that Christ is his Son. "I will be to him a Father." No angel ever received this recognition from heaven.
   3. Theological declaration (1:6–7). The theological word "first-begotten" expresses Christ's supremacy as he relates to all creation. He is superior to angels.
B. *As King, he is superior to angels.*
   1. Eternal rule (1:8). The holy Father declared his Son's rule to be of eternal duration.
   2. Righteous rule (1:8–9). The chief characteristic of his kingdom will be righteousness. Biblical history gives a record of certain angels who have fallen into evil (Isa. 14:12). Not so with Christ.
   3. Glad rule (1:9). Christ imparts gladness to the people he rules.
C. *As God, he is superior to angels.*
   1. Creative activity (1:10). Christ is the agent of creation while angels are results of creation.
   2. Continuing activity (1:11–12). The eternal Christ as compared to the temporal universe points out his superiority to creation (including angels).
   3. Courtly activity (1:13). A capstone in the comparison of Christ to angels is found in the verse regarding his position in "court." The enemies of righteousness will serve as his footstool. No angel can ever attain this position of glory.

Conclusion

Though angels are inferior to Jesus, that certainly does not mean they are without purpose. God planned for angels to be ministering servants to those who become heirs of salvation. God has a plan for every member of his creation. Though we might think of ourselves more highly than we ought, we find peace when we adapt our wills to that of Christ.

WEDNESDAY EVENING, MAY 6

Title: The Gift of Mercy

Text: "If it is to encourage, then give encouragement; if it is giving, then give generously; if it is to lead, do it diligently; if it is to show mercy, do it cheerfully" **(Rom. 12:8 NIV)**.

Scripture Reading: Matthew 5:1–7

Introduction

The use of this gift is one of the most beautiful services a Christian can perform. It can be used to give hope, encouragement, and determination. Jesus is our best example of One who practices mercy.

I. First, consider some general characteristics of mercy.

A. *It is a quality attributed to God.* "Rend your heart and not your garments. Return to the LORD your God, for he is gracious and compassionate, slow to anger and abounding in love, and he relents from sending calamity" (Joel 2:13 NIV). Micah also emphasized God's mercy: "Who is a God like you, who pardons sin and forgives the transgression of the remnant of his inheritance? You do not stay angry forever but delight to show mercy" (7:18 NIV). The trait of God pointed out in these two passages is his benevolent feeling toward humankind. Notice the phrases "slow to anger," "pardons sin," and "forgives the transgression."

B. *It is a quality believers are commanded to have.* "He has showed you, O mortal, what is good. And what does the LORD require of you? To act justly and to love mercy and to walk humbly with your God" (Mic. 6:8 NIV). Luke 6:36 says, "Be merciful, just as your Father is merciful" (NIV). As Christians, we each possess the gift of mercy. We simply need to cultivate our skill of using it.

C. *It is a gift of the Holy Spirit (Rom. 12:8).* At this point, we should remind ourselves of the true purposes of all gifts of the Spirit. They are used to honor Jesus, build up the church, complement and supplement one another, and accomplish God's will in the lives of his children. They are to be used in accordance with Scripture.

II. Second, consider what the gift of mercy includes.

A. *It is the ability to be compassionate.* Mercy is cheerful love toward suffering members of the body of Christ. It means to bear one another's burdens and alleviate one another's distress. Mercy is not allowing others to get what they deserve.

B. *These are some characteristics of mercy:*

1. Pity or sympathy. Pity is more than just feeling sorry for someone. It is a deep-down, sustained compassion. It is kindness but more. Pity is showing love under the Holy Spirit's guidance. It is acting in Christ's name with the motive of glorifying God.
2. Action. Jesus was moved with compassion. He healed the blind, the crippled, and the diseased. He was not just stirred emotionally by their needs. Mercy is demonstrated when a person sees a need and acts to meet that need. It is considerably more than words.
3. Cheerfulness. Mercy radiates sunshine. It is the opposite of doing a service grudgingly.
4. Strengthening. Christians, in using this gift, are always giving strength to others and imparting hope. The use of this gift never damages or destroys.
5. Hope. Hope is an important ingredient of life. Without it there is little, if anything, left in life. As Christians show mercy, they put a spark in those who are downcast.

III. The use of this gift applies to all areas of life.

 A. *It applies to the physical.* Institutions such as hospitals and orphanages are ministries of mercy, and Christians who meet the physical needs of others demonstrate the gift of mercy.

 B. *It applies to the social.* A basic human need is to know someone who cares. Using the gift of mercy means showing love to others. Loneliness is a terrible ailment, but mercy can help heal those who have emotional scars.

 C. *It applies to the spiritual.* Soul-winning and evangelism use the gift of mercy. Church enlargement and outreach are other ways of using the gift of mercy.

Conclusion

 People throughout the world are hurting. Their hearts ache and their bodies are diseased. Their stomachs are empty and their souls are thirsty. Those of you who believe in Jesus Christ have the gift of mercy. Use it!

SUNDAY MORNING, MAY 10

Title: Mary: A Model for Modern Mothers

Text: "Greetings, you who are highly favored! The Lord is with you" (**Luke 1:28 NIV**).

Scripture Reading: Luke 1:26–35, 46–56

Hymns: "Faith of Our Mothers," Patten
    "He Leadeth Me," Gilmore
    "O Love That Wilt Not Let Me Go," Matheson

Offertory Prayer: Holy and loving Father, we thank you for the beauty of this spring Lord's Day morning. Gracious is your love and generous is your kindness. We rejoice today in all that you mean to us and all that you have done for us. We come today in worship, bringing not only our prayers, but also our tithes and offerings, asking that you receive these gifts and bless them to the advancement of your kingdom. Grant us this day a reverent, worshipful spirit with ears that truly hear and hearts that responds positively to your will. In Jesus' name. Amen.

Introduction

We should look for models to imitate in the Scriptures. Today, on Mother's Day, let us look at Mary, the mother of our Lord, as a great model of motherhood. Let us discover something about her faith and faithfulness. Let us consider the fruit of her motherhood so that we may identify some factors that contributed to her success as a mother.

I. Mary was chosen for a mission (Luke 1:28).

Mary became the mother of Jesus by way of a miraculous conception. Jesus was born of a virgin. He had an earthly mother without an earthly father.

Because of his love for us, God chose to become flesh and blood, and to do so, he came as a baby, born by a miraculous virgin conception. But it was not Mary's virginity alone that qualified her uniquely for becoming Jesus' mother.

    A. *Mary was a devout worshiper of the true God.*
    B. *Mary was pure in mind and heart and body.*
    C. *Mary was humble, realizing her dependence on God.*
    D. *Mary was obedient to God's will.*
    E. *Mary was willing to do what God had planned for her.*
    F. *Mary had an attitude of gratitude.* She was thankful that God used her to further his work.
    G. *Mary was consistent and self-controlled.* These are qualities needed by modern mothers as well as by the mother of Jesus.

II. Mary was chosen to be a model.

Mary was not just chosen for a mission; she was also chosen to be an example for other mothers.

    A. *Mary responded positively to God's plan for her life.* Once she knew God's will, she desired to participate as God had planned.
    B. *Mary magnified the Lord in song for his goodness and mercy.* God puts a song in the hearts of those who trust him.
    C. *Mary worshiped the mighty God of Israel (Luke 1:49).* Mary's God was no weakling. He was the great God, the creator of the universe. He was God on the throne, and she responded to his authority.

D. *Mary worshiped the merciful God (Luke 1:50).* Humanity needs mercy more than justice. God is eager to forgive and to help the undeserving.

E. *Mary worshiped the helping God (Luke 1:54).* God's love expresses itself in a persistent attitude of goodwill and helpfulness to his people. The psalmist described the God of Israel as "a very present help in trouble" (Ps. 46:1). Mary felt this assistance from God, and she became a helper to him in his work of helping others.

III. Mary suffered the pains of motherhood.

Much pain is associated with the birth experience. Even greater pains lie along the pathway of life for some mothers, and Mary endured these pains.

A. *When Jesus was twelve years old, Mary found it difficult to understand him (Luke 2:49–50).* Mary could sympathize with modern mothers of teenagers.

B. *Later Mary's other children were indifferent to Jesus' true identity.* They did not accept him to be who and what he really is until after his resurrection.

C. *Mary no doubt felt much pain when Jesus was rejected by the people of his hometown, Nazareth (Luke 4:28–29).*

D. *Mary suffered the horrible shame of seeing her Son arrested, falsely accused, convicted, condemned, and crucified.* "There stood by the cross of Jesus his mother" (John 19:25).

In no way can we fully comprehend the agony in Mary's heart during these terrible hours of Jesus' suffering.

IV. Mary worshiped a risen and ruling Savior.

After Jesus' resurrection from the dead, Mary was present with those who had rejoiced in his victory over death. She was with them as they prayed in anticipation of the Holy Spirit's coming (Acts 1:14).

Conclusion

Mary is an excellent model for contemporary mothers.

Hers was a life of great faith, made evident by her song called the Magnificat, which was recorded by Luke (1:46–55).

Mary's heart was in tune with God as she was constantly open to his will. Her prayer was dialogue rather than monologue.

Mary believed that God's will was good, and that it was something to desire instead of something merely to undergo.

Mary, as a good role model for mothers everywhere, encourages us to purity, prayer, and participation in God's will.

SUNDAY EVENING, MAY 10

Title: Christ—The Humiliated One

Text: "We do see Jesus, who was made a little lower than the angels for a little while, now crowned with glory and honor because he suffered death, so that by the grace of God he might taste death for everyone" **(Heb. 2:9 NIV)**.

Scripture Reading: Hebrews 2:1–18

Introduction

The new covenant could be established only by the death of the Testator (Heb. 9:16). God is the one establishing the new covenant. The God of heaven cannot die. For the covenant to become effective, God left the safety of heaven in the person of Jesus Christ and took on himself the form of man. God as true man could die. This is what happened to Jesus at Calvary.

The taking on of human form was a humiliating experience for Jesus Christ. Yet he did it so that we might have eternal life. In this particular chapter of Hebrews, the humiliation of Jesus Christ is vividly brought home to the reader.

I. By the passiveness of humankind (Heb. 2:1–4).

God's position is that of glory and honor. Everyone should respond to him in reverence and worship. When Jesus appeared in human form, this perplexed the minds of his day. Jews were tempted either to neglect or to reject this historical Jesus as the true God. Shame was inflicted on Jesus as the Jews failed to accept him as God's Son. The writer of Hebrews dealt with the problem of apathy toward Jesus Christ.

A. *Neglect of the message (2:1).* Christians are challenged to give special attention to the message of God. To ignore the message is, in essence, to declare it of no importance to the soul.

B. *Validity of the message (2:2).* In building his case against those who neglect Jesus, the author maintained that the law of judgment and wrath had been properly applied by God in the past. God's message is valid.

C. *Warning of the message (2:3).* People may humiliate the person of Jesus Christ by ignoring the entire fact of his death, burial, and resurrection. Yet God is not the one who suffers; it is people who suffer. This message has been confirmed by the testimony of first-century believers and should not be rejected by present readers.

D. *Proof of the message (2:4).* Along with the introduction of Jesus Christ and the new covenant, God gave additional signs and wonders to prove that the message was from him.

II. By the position of angels (Heb. 2:5–9).

The author went to special lengths in chapter 1 to reveal Jesus' superiority to the angelic world. In this chapter on the humiliation of Christ, the author mentioned that Jesus was made "a little lower than the angels" (2:9).

  A. *The original relationship (2:5)*. In preparing readers for the position of humiliation that our Lord assumed ("lower than the angels"), the author emphasized that the future was placed in the hands of Jesus and not the angels. This humiliation was temporary.
  B. *Taking a place of humility (2:9)*. The process of humiliation was accomplished by the voluntary will of Jesus Christ. He endured this shame by the grace of God.
  C. *Purpose of humiliation (2:9)*. Jesus' crucifixion was recognized by a crown of glory and honor. Jesus tasted death on behalf of all humankind so that those who believe in him do not have to face eternal death.

III. By the participation of Christ (Heb. 2:10–17).

Jesus willingly participated in the humiliation process that caused him to become flesh and blood and to die a vicarious death. Several matters are detailed in this passage that reveal his desire to secure salvation for humankind, even through humiliation.

  A. *Captain of salvation (2:10)*. Jesus desired to lead many people to the way of salvation. He had to become the captain of their salvation. To carry out this role, he had to suffer.
  B. *Identity with humankind (2:11–13)*. The author of Hebrews drew an affinity between the Sanctifier and the ones sanctified. Jesus is pictured as being in total identification with people, as "he is not ashamed to call them brethren."
  C. *Submission to death (2:14–15)*. The ultimate in Jesus' humiliation came when he submitted himself to death. He had to enter the realm of death, or kingdom of darkness, to destroy it from within.
  D. *Voluntary activity (2:16)*. This verse literally means that Jesus took on himself the care and concern of "the seed of Abraham." He could have been indifferent, but his very nature compelled him to take action.
  E. *Priest of reconciliation (2:17)*. It was necessary for Jesus "to be made like unto his brethren" so that he could be our faithful and merciful High Priest. This was the only way he could secure reconciliation for humankind.

Conclusion

The humiliation process gave Jesus the opportunity to experience the same temptation that people face (Heb. 2:18). Consequently, he is able to come to people's aid, not on a theoretical basis, but on an experiential basis. He encourages his followers to a life of victory because he won total victory for them as he experienced life and death in the flesh.

WEDNESDAY EVENING, MAY 13

Title: The Gift of Evangelism

Text: "So Christ himself gave the apostles, the prophets, the evangelists, the pastors and teachers" **(Eph. 4:11 NIV)**.

Scripture Reading: Acts 21:1–8

Introduction

The gift of evangelism is a gift that each Christian should cherish and use enthusiastically. The world waits for people of God to share the good news of Jesus Christ.

I. First, consider the meaning of evangelism.

A. *Three New Testament words are closely related.*
1. *Evangel* means good news. This is the message to be declared, the gospel of salvation.
2. *Evangelical* indicates the spirit of the message. Its spirit calls attention to the message itself.
3. *Evangelist* refers to the bearer of the message, the one who has the gift to proclaim the good news.

B. *In this message* evangelist *and* evangelism *will be used interchangeably because both the message and the messenger are gifts of the Spirit.*

C. *The concept expounded is that of proclaiming good news.* Believers who use this gift of the Spirit proclaim in an effective way. The message of Christ will be shared in such a way that people will respond to the Holy Spirit's call, commit their lives to Christ, and become disciples. The fruit of an evangelist is a determining factor as to whether the gift is in operation or the person is operating on his or her own.

II. Consider some basic qualifications for evangelism.

A. *Evangelists must meet several spiritual requirements.* First, they must be born again. Jesus must be real in their lives, and they must have faith, clean character, reverent enthusiasm, and humble dedication.

B. *Evangelists must meet certain physical requirements.* They must communicate a message that appeals to both the intellect and emotions and that embodies doctrinal content.

C. *Evangelists must meet some fruit-bearing requirements.* Fruit bearing may be different from what some evangelists desire or expect. It is their responsibility, under the Holy Spirit's guidance, to proclaim Jesus as Savior and Lord. But it is the One who gives the gift who also gives the fruit—that is, convicts people of their sin and draws them to Christ.

III. Consider those who possess this gift.

    A. *Evangelists may be placed in three categories.* These are professional evangelists, those who make their living by full-time evangelistic efforts; evangelistic pastors—all pastors should fall into this category, but some seem to be more gifted in this area than others; and laypersons who engage in outreach.

    B. *The Bible teaches that all believers have this gift.* The Lord equips all his children to tell others of his redemptive love. It is a natural thing for people who have been born again to bear testimony to their experience.

Conclusion

Considering the millions of lost people in the world today, it is urgent that those who have the gift of evangelism exercise it. Hopefully thousands of people who love the Lord and want to see his kingdom grow will consecrate themselves to the use of this gift.

SUNDAY MORNING, MAY 17

Title: What Is a Born-Again Christian?

Text: "Jesus answered him, 'Truly, truly, I say to you, unless one is born anew, he cannot see the kingdom of God'" (**John 3:3 RSV**).

Scripture Reading: John 3:1–15

Hymns: "Love Divine, All Loves Excelling," Wesley
            "Let Jesus Come into Your Heart," Morris
            "I Hear Thy Welcome Voice," Hartsough

Offertory Prayer: Holy Father, we are not worthy to come into your presence, and yet we rejoice that through Jesus Christ you have given us access to the very throne room of your grace and power. We thank you that we can participate in extending your work beyond our immediate sphere of influence. Bless these gifts to the end that others will come to know Jesus Christ as Savior and Lord. In his name we pray. Amen.

Introduction

The term "born-again Christian" has had national and even international attention since former US president Jimmy Carter acknowledged publicly that he is a born-again Christian. Since that time there have been many commentaries on what it means to be a born-again Christian. One curious writer addressed a letter to Ann Landers with an inquiry, "In plain barroom language, explain what it means to be a 'born-again Christian.'" Ann Landers, who was Jewish, replied as if she were an evangelical Christian with the answer, "It means that you have let Jesus Christ come into your heart."

Not all people who think they are born-again Christians are born-again Christians.

1. To merely believe in God does not mean that you are a Christian.
2. To live a morally upright life and be a decent neighbor does not mean that you are a born-again Christian.
3. To be reared in a godly Christian home does not mean that you are a born-again Christian, for physical birth and a good environment do not bring us into God's family.
4. To be baptized does not mean that you're a born-again Christian.
5. To be a church member, even a very good one, does not guarantee that you are a born-again Christian.

I. What is the birth from above?

A. *The new birth is a divine change wrought in the heart of a believer by the Holy Spirit of God.*
B. *The new birth is a complete change wrought in the innermost being of a believer by the Holy Spirit.* This change is not a partial or installment event.
C. *The new birth is a permanent change wrought in the heart of a believer upon entering into a new relationship with God.*

II. Why does everyone need the new birth?

A. *Jesus said that it was absolutely essential if one would see and enter into the kingdom of God.* He spoke these words to Nicodemus in John 3.
B. *Our present spiritual condition requires that we experience this birth from above.* Until this birth is experienced, one is spiritually dead, being devoid of the spiritual life of God.
C. *God's holy nature requires that we experience this birth from above so that we might have fellowship with him.* It is in the new birth that we become partakers of the divine nature. Apart from this new birth, we do not have a nature that would enable us to love God and enjoy his fellowship.

III. What does the new birth do for or to a person?

Most definitely the new birth does not make one perfect or infallible.

A. *The new birth introduces one into the family of God (John 1:12; Gal. 4:6; 1 John 3:1–2).* We become part of a human family by physical birth, and we become part of God's family by spiritual birth.
B. *The new birth brings eternal life as a present possession to the believer (John 3:36; 5:24).* Eternal life is not a reward that is bestowed on us at the end of the way as a result of great faithfulness and sacrifice. Eternal life is the gift of God through faith in Jesus Christ, and it comes to us in the moment of our faith response to Christ (Rom. 6:23).
C. *The new birth brings the Holy Spirit of God into the heart of the believer (1 Cor. 3:16; 6:19; 1 John 4:13).* The Holy Spirit takes up residency within the

heart of a believer at the moment of new birth so that he might direct the believer in God's great redemptive work and reproduce within that believer the character of Jesus Christ.

D. *The new birth makes spiritual growth possible (1 Peter 2:1–2).* Until the new birth has been experienced, it is impossible to grow spiritually.

E. *The Holy Spirit brings us under the correction and chastisement of our Father God (Heb. 12:4–10).*

After we become the children of God, God deals with our sins as a father would deal with the sins and mistakes of his child. Because he loves us, he chastises us to bring us into conformity with the image of his Son, Jesus Christ.

IV. How can we be sure that we are born again?

A. *Are you trusting Jesus Christ as Savior?* Have you put your trust in him and in him alone for your salvation? Or are you trusting yourself to get the job done? You can only be sure of a born-again experience if you are trusting Jesus Christ.

B. *There are some distinctive marks of the twice-born.* Do you have these characteristic features?

1. Do you have an appetite for the things of the spiritual life? Do you hunger for the Word of God? Do you hunger for fellowship with the people of God? An absence of these would indicate either spiritual illness or the absence of life.

2. Do you love God and God's people (1 John 3:14; 4:19)? If you do not love God and his people, you should be disturbed about your spiritual condition.

3. Do you have an aversion for sin? Do you want to avoid sin and eliminate it from your life (1 John 2:1; 3:9)? If you find deep within your heart a sincere aversion for doing that which is wrong, this is one of the evidences that you have been born of the Spirit and that God's nature dwells in you.

4. Do you have an ambition to please God in all of your life? If you can honestly answer in the affirmative, these are evidences that indeed you have experienced the new birth.

V. How can one experience the new birth?

A. *You must come to Jesus Christ in faith that trusts him.* Accept him to be what he claims to be. Decide that you will depend on him to do what he offers to do and what he has promised to do.

B. *To come to Christ means that you turn from a life of selfishness, sin, and self-destructiveness and that you make the decision to let Jesus Christ become Lord of your life.* Turn from self-righteousness and from the wickedness that will destroy you, and commit your life to Jesus Christ. Claim him as your very own. Confess him before others and identify yourself with him.

Conclusion

Nicodemus, a very good man, needed the new birth. The Samaritan woman, described in John 4, a very fallen woman, also needed the new life that the new birth brings. All of us are somewhere between these two extremes. And between these two extremes, all of us can come to Christ and experience the new birth.

SUNDAY EVENING, MAY 17

Title: Christ—The Apostle and High Priest

Text: "Christ is faithful as a son over God's house. And we are his house, if indeed we hold firmly to our confidence and the hope in which we glory" **(Heb. 3:6 NIV).**

Scripture Reading: Hebrews 3:1–19

Introduction

The focal point of Christianity is Jesus Christ. The author of Hebrews encourages the recipients to give consideration to this Jesus. He identifies him as both the Apostle and High Priest of our profession. Much of the letter emphasizes Jesus as our High Priest. Chapter 3 stresses the apostleship of our Lord.

The word for "apostle" means "one sent forth with orders." Jesus Christ was sent from the Father with orders to secure salvation for lost humankind. This chapter depicts Jesus as that great Apostle who is eventually rejected in unbelief (3:12). Take note of this Apostle.

I. Characteristics of the Apostle (Heb. 3:2–6).

Four characteristics are given in this chapter regarding the Apostle of God that set him apart from all other apostles.

A. *Faithful to the Father (3:2).* Jesus Christ was faithful to the Father, who had designated him as the Apostle. Even though the Son is a member of the Godhead, his ministry is still under the direction of the Father. He had a responsibility to follow divine orders. This he did, even as Moses did.

B. *More worthy than Moses (3:3).* The author of Hebrews is aware of the great loyalty the readers had to Moses. He maintains that the subject of the new covenant, Jesus Christ, is worthy of more honor than Moses. He implies that Christ, not Moses, is the builder of the house.

C. *Creator of all (3:4).* The writer expands the building concept as applied to the Apostle to include "all things." An outstanding biblical fact about Jesus Christ is his creative activity as declared in John 1:3 and Colossians 1:16.

D. *Over his own house (3:5–6)*. In a discussion about the assembly of God's people (his "house"), Moses was said to be faithful "in" his house, while Christ was faithful "over" his house. The simple prepositions indicate the responsible positions held respectively by Moses and our Lord.

II. Challenges of the Apostle (Heb. 3:7–14).

As the great Apostle of our profession, Jesus places several specific challenges before those who choose to follow him. These challenges summarize his basic appeal to the church.

A. *Challenge to obedience (3:7–11)*. The example of the wilderness disobedience was never far from the minds of those who knew of God's dealings with Israel. Repeatedly the appeal is made to avoid another "day of temptation in the wilderness." The readers are again reminded of God's anger as he dealt with the Israelites and his consequential judgment when he said, "So I sware in my wrath, They shall not enter into my rest." One of the Apostle's specific challenges is to obey God.

B. *Challenge to belief (3:12)*. An attempt is made to remove all unbelief from the minds of God's people. This unbelief causes one to depart from the living God. The implied teaching is that belief attracts one to the living God.

C. *Challenge to exhortation (3:13)*. The Apostle's message emphasizes the value of Christian fellowship. The body of Christ should encourage individual members to grow spiritually. This support must be maintained daily—it will help members to resist becoming involved in sin.

D. *Challenge to steadfastness (3:14)*. Christ is the picture of steadfastness, the symbol of security. As we live our lives in confidence and consistency, we actually emanate a major facet of Christ's character.

III. Condemnation of the Apostle (Heb. 3:15–18).

The One sent to "speak for God" is portrayed as likening the present generation to the wayward children of Israel.

A. *Hardness of heart (3:15)*. God warns people of the danger of hardening their hearts to his ways.

B. *Provocation of heart (3:15–16)*. When people harden their hearts against God, they provoke God, causing him to become angry with them.

C. *Grief of heart (3:17)*. God's anger always causes him to be grieved with his creation. He is hurt when people disobey his commands. After all, God always desires the very best for his creatures.

D. *Condemnation of heart (3:18)*. Those who harden their hearts and reject God's way are condemned by their own actions. God is grieved at their unbelief and declares that they shall not enter into his rest.

Conclusion (Heb. 3:19)

That unbelievers are not able to enter God's rest is not God's fault. The weight of the whole matter is not on the loving, uncompromising ministry of the Apostle, but on the unbelief of sinners.

WEDNESDAY EVENING, MAY 20

Title: The Gift of Preaching

Text: "So Christ himself gave the apostles, the prophets, the evangelists, the pastors and teachers" **(Eph. 4:11 NIV).**

Scripture Reading: 1 Timothy 3:1–7

Introduction

Someone has written the following description, titled "The Pastor's Easy Job."

> His job is something like a football in a big game; he is knocked on one side and then on the other.
>
> If he writes a postcard, it is too short; if he writes a letter, it is too long; if he has his messages printed, he is a spendthrift.
>
> If he attempts to safeguard the interests of the church, he is trying to run things; if he does not, he is allowing things to go to the dogs.
>
> If he attends extra meetings of the church, he is an intruder; if he does not, he is a shirker.
>
> If the attendance is slim, nobody likes him anyway; if he tries to help, he is a pest.
>
> If he calls for the offering, all he thinks about is money; if the offering is not good, he is to blame.
>
> If he is in a smiling mood, he is frivolous; if he is serious, he is a sorehead.
>
> If he seeks advice, he is incompetent; if he does not, he is bullheaded.
>
> If he mixes with the members, he is too familiar; if he does not, he is too ritzy.
>
> So, ashes to ashes, dust to dust; if others won't do it, the pastor must. (Author unknown)

The pastor, in the final analysis, is accountable to God. His or her successes or failures are not to be determined by a person, committee, or congregation, but by how faithful he or she is to God.

I. Three words in the New Testament describe the office of a pastor.

A. *The first word is* overseer. This word comes from the Greek word *episcopos*. It is translated "bishop" and is used to describe the *work* of a pastor.

B. *The second word is* elder. This word comes from the Greek word *presbuteros* and is translated "elder." It is used to describe the *dignity* and *rank* of the office.

C. *The third word is* pastor. This word comes from the Greek word *poimen* and means "shepherd." It refers to the *relation* of the pastor to his or her flock.

II. No Scripture indicates that a pastor is to be perfect.

No pastor can be perfect.

A. *The book of Jeremiah speaks of a pastor's imperfections.* Jeremiah 2:8 tells of a pastor's transgressions, and 10:21 tells of a pastor's rashness and failure to seek the Lord.

B. *First Timothy also speaks of these imperfections.* In this passage the descriptions of a pastor's work are stated in a positive way. However, the implication of the negative is also present.

III. The pastor has specific duties.

A. *The pastor's ministry includes three spheres.*
   1. The pastor is to work in the sphere of the church. The church is a pastor's main habitat of service, in which he or she presides as an administrator and teacher. The pastor is officially set aside by the church to perform these duties.
   2. The pastor is to maintain a godly home life (1 Tim. 3:5). If a pastor is not successful in the home, he or she will not be successful in the church. Pastors are to provide a Christian environment for their families.
   3. The pastor is to function in the real world (1 Tim. 3:7) and to be respected by others in ordinary day-to-day tasks.

B. *The pastor's ministry involves three objectives.*
   1. The pastor is to guide God's people. One of the chief duties of a leader is to guide, instruct, and counsel. This is done by public speaking, personal interviews, and in group settings.
   2. The pastor is to feed God's people. The principal responsibility of the user of this gift is preaching. By preaching God's Word, a pastor feeds his or her flock. The pastor also nourishes them in other ways as occasions arise.
   3. The pastor is to guard or protect God's people. False doctrines are being preached everywhere. A pastor's congregation inevitably sees these false ideas on television, the internet, and in books and magazines. A pastor is to protect God's people from being misled.

C. *The pastor acquires many traits as a result of this gift.* Notice in 1 Timothy 3:1–7 such qualities as being above reproach, able to teach, good at managing, prudent, respectable, and temperate.

IV. The congregation must relate to the pastor's use of this gift.

A. *Hebrews 13:17 gives two admonitions.* One is to obey or to agree with what one is told to do. The other is to submit or comply even when things are contrary to one's opinion.

B. *Hebrews 13:18 gives an admonition to pray.* For the Lord to use a pastor effectively, his or her congregation must pray for their spiritual leader.

C. *First Timothy 5:17 gives an admonition to honor.* This can apply to monetary support, but it also encompasses words of commendation and encouragement.

Conclusion

Few positions in all the world are more significant than a pastor's. God gives this gift to some by the Holy Spirit. May those who have the gift use it with dignity and honor.

SUNDAY MORNING, MAY 24

Title: The Great Salvation That Creates Fellowship

Text: "His disciples followed him. And on the sabbath he began to teach in the synagogue; and many who heard him were astonished, saying, 'Where did this man get all this? What is the wisdom given to him? What mighty works are wrought by his hands!' . . . And they took offense at him" **(Mark 6:1–3 RSV)**.

Scripture Reading: Luke 4:16–30

Hymns: "Rejoice—The Lord Is King," Wesley
"What a Friend We Have in Jesus," Scriven
"Lord, Speak to Me, That I May Speak," Havergal

Offertory Prayer: Holy Father, You are the giver of every good and perfect gift. Today we accept life itself as a gift from your loving hand. We thank you for the gift of eternal life and for the abiding presence of your Holy Spirit, who would teach us what our Lord taught and enable us to implement those teachings. Help us this day to follow the counsel of our Lord and live our lives as a service to you and others. In Jesus' name. Amen.

Introduction

Our great salvation includes more than the salvation of our souls, which is the free gift of God when we put faith and trust in Jesus Christ as Lord and Savior. It includes more than new bodies and a heavenly home, which our Lord is preparing for those who love him. Our salvation involves living the heavenly way of life here and now in the power of the risen and living Lord.

It is by Jesus' substitutionary death and his victorious resurrection that he saves us from the penalty of sin. It is by the Holy Spirit's authoritative teaching as heaven's infallible and inerrant Teacher and by his work within our hearts that we experience spiritual transformation. Paul declared concerning those who have experienced the new birth that God has "predetermined that they shall be conformed to the image of his son" (cf. Rom. 8:28–30). While this purpose will not be completely accomplished in this life, God is at work to bring about this spiritual transformation here and now.

The great salvation that our Lord came to make possible is a salvation from fear and hate and prejudice. This salvation creates a brotherhood and a fellowship among people of diverse backgrounds, cultures, and colors. Jesus came that the human family might truly become the family of God, but people have not always welcomed this thought in actual practice.

How do you respond to the implication that God is the Father of all people who come to him through faith in Jesus Christ? Can you accept them as brothers and sisters? Do you respond to them with the kind of love that the Master Teacher requires?

I. Jesus was and is the Master Teacher who came from God to give wisdom to believers.

Jesus is the way to the highest possible human happiness. His great teachings contain the truth of God concerning all the issues of life that challenge us. He came that we might have life in abundance in the here and now as well as eternal life beyond (John 10:10). Heaven is not merely a residence; it is primarily a relationship between the believer and God. Heaven should be a way of life for those who recognize Jesus Christ as more than just a soul Savior who permits us to have a ticket to heaven. He wants the heavenly way of life to become real to us today.

II. Jesus, the Master Teacher, spoke with authority (Matt. 7:28–29).

   A. *Jesus spoke with the authority of his own unique person.*
   B. *Jesus spoke with the authority of one filled with and under the control of the Holy Spirit.*
   C. *Jesus taught with the authority of one who came with the absolute truth from God.*
   D. *Jesus spoke with the authority of one captivated by pure love.*

By his teachings, our Lord comes to correct us, inform us, and change our lives. He wants to instruct our minds, stir our emotions, and affect our will as we make the decisions that will be pleasing to him. To be a true follower of Jesus Christ, we must let his teachings determine our attitudes, actions, and ambitions.

III. Our Savior would save us from ugly and cruel prejudices toward others.

Most of us are unwilling to admit that we have ugly prejudice in our minds and in our lives. Around the world between every class and color and condition, prejudice, hate, and fear hinder the coming of God's kingdom in the hearts and lives of people. Jesus, heaven's Master Teacher, has a word for us at this point.

A. *In his treatment of the Samaritan woman at the well, Jesus crossed racial, gender, religious, and cultural barriers (John 4).* He did this to minister to one who was considered by many as a worthless, immoral derelict. In Jesus' kindness to her, he not only ministered to her but also taught his disciples that God loves Samaritans.

B. *In the experience with the ten lepers who were cleansed, Jesus revealed that praise and worship of those from this hated race was pleasing to him (Luke 17:11–19).* We should extend acceptance to all who are acceptable to our Father God. As we do so, we will experience not only the fellowship of God but the fellowship of his family as well.

C. *In the parable of the good Samaritan, our Lord revealed that the service of this hated foreigner was to be commended and was also to be imitated (Luke 10:29–37).*

D. *The conversion of the Roman soldier Cornelius is perhaps the most dramatic demonstration in all of the New Testament that reveals how God would have us relate to people of other colors, cultures, and conditions (Acts 10–11).* As a result of this experience, Peter gave voice to a pronouncement that has revolutionary significance. "Truly I perceive that God shows no partiality, but in every nation anyone who fears him and does what is right is acceptable to him" (Acts 10:34–35 RSV). Two entire chapters of the New Testament are given over to the conversion of Cornelius and his family. This is not accidental or incidental. The living Lord through the ministry of the Holy Spirit was trying to teach his church some of the things that he had wanted to teach them during his earthly ministry.

Conclusion

The words of our text declare, "His disciples followed him" (Mark 6:1 RSV). Are you willing to let Jesus, heaven's Master Teacher, deliver you from ugly prejudice, destructive fear, and hate? Only as we do so can he bring about the great salvation that can be ours right now.

Following Jesus begins with belief in him and continues with listening to him and obeying him as heaven's Master Teacher day by day.

SUNDAY EVENING, MAY 24

Title: Christ—The Believer's Rest

Text: "Let us then approach God's throne of grace with confidence, so that we may receive mercy and find grace to help us in our time of need" (**Heb. 4:16 NIV**).

Scripture Reading: Hebrews 4:1–16

Introduction

The author of Hebrews considered a major problem confronting New Testament Christians as he studied the Ten Commandments. Moses wrote that those who fear God are to "remember the sabbath day, to keep it holy" (Ex. 20:8). New Testament Christians emphasize keeping Sunday ("the first day," 1 Cor. 16:2) as a day of worship, not Saturday (the seventh day). This chapter discusses the basic meaning behind keeping the "seventh day." The key to this whole concept is the word "rest." God rested on the seventh day (Heb. 4:4). The writer of Hebrews interprets the idea of "rest" for believers as being found within the person of Jesus Christ (4:9–11, 16). Consequently, this chapter presents the teaching that if a person is involved in God's "rest," it will be within a relationship with Jesus Christ.

I. The reality of God's rest (Heb. 4:1–10).

In chapter 3, the author warned that anyone who rejects God's ways will not be allowed to enter into his rest. The author revealed the reality of God's rest to the readers.

A. *Fact of concern (4:1–2).* The writer was concerned that certain recipients of this letter might not be involved in God's true rest.

B. *Identity of God's rest (4:3–9).* The foundational idea of God's "rest" lies within God's creation activities (4:3). After six days of work, God finished creation. He then rested on the seventh day (4:4). God desires his creation to share in his rest (4:5–6). The way to enter this rest is through belief, or faith, in God (4:6). Joshua's followers did not find the desired rest. God had had a future revelation that would meet the inner needs of humankind (Matt. 11:28–29; Heb. 4:9, 15–16). The nature of this promised rest is found in Jesus Christ.

C. *Availability of rest (4:10).* God's rest is available to everyone. To enter into this rest, however, people must not try to achieve it by their own good works. No one can earn it by performing righteous deeds (Titus 3:5–7). Only by faith can anyone share in God's rest (Eph. 2:8–9).

II. The need for God's rest (Heb. 4:11–13).

A. *Hunger created (4:11).* The author seems to have contradicted himself in verses 10 and 11. But there is no contradiction. The impossibility of attaining God's rest is asserted in verse 10. In verse 11, though, he encouraged his readers to hunger for this rest. Their hunger should not involve an attempt to win God's rest, but a sincere seeking of God's way.

B. *Word revealed (4:12).* It seems appropriate that a statement regarding the dynamic power of God's Word is inserted in the context at this point. What humans cannot accomplish through their personal efforts, God accomplishes through his Word.

    C. *God observed (4:13)*. Again, an astounding revelation is given. God's very character calls for him to examine people's hearts. God perceives their inner faith and responds with the gift of rest.

III. The way of God's rest (Heb. 4:14–16).

The recipients of the letter were not left to search out the intricacies of God's rest. Rather, the writer presented the way through which this rest is made available to humankind.

    A. *Heavenly source (4:14)*. People's needs are met by a heavenly High Priest. He supersedes our highest expectations. It is his responsibility to extend to us God's rest.

    B. *Compassionate source (4:15)*. People's hungers are satisfied by a loving High Priest. His desire for us is far superior to our desires for ourselves. It is his duty to provide us with God's rest.

    C. *Approachable source (4:16)*. People's ineptness tends to make them shy away from approaching God. Yet God longs for us to draw near to him.

Conclusion

When individuals submit to God's will, they find help in time of need. This is the essence of God's "rest." People are no longer dependent on themselves. They no longer experience their own failures. They rely on God and enjoy his strength. This is God's rest for us.

WEDNESDAY EVENING, MAY 27

Title: The Gift of Wisdom

Text: "To one is given by the Spirit the word of wisdom; to another the word of knowledge by the same Spirit" (**1 Cor. 12:8**).

Scripture Reading: Proverbs 4:1–7

Introduction

Why is it that someone who is obviously much less intelligent is able to do more than someone who is more intelligent? The subject of this message—the gift of wisdom—is the answer. This wisdom comes from the Holy Spirit.

I. Consider the meaning of wisdom.

    A. *It is to be understood in relation to knowledge.* Knowledge is information, and wisdom is the right use of that information. Knowledge has no use unless it is applied. Wisdom is the application of knowledge.

    B. *It is to be understood in relation to some basic concepts.*

1. Wisdom never creates confusion, envy, or strife but always creates harmony and peace. Wisdom, as a gift of the Spirit, is to create unity in the church.
2. Wisdom is always used in a cheerful way. Paul said in Galatians 5:22 that joy is a fruit of the Spirit. A gloomy attitude is not in keeping with the gift of wisdom.
3. Wisdom denotes quality and not activity. Anyone can be active, whether he or she is indwelt by the Holy Spirit or not. Only a gift of the Spirit is a source of wisdom that results in quality.
4. Wisdom shapes character. It epitomizes a pious manner and finds expression in the knowledge of the Word.
5. Wisdom consists of the thoughts of God embodied in Christ. These characteristics are for the enlightenment of the soul. This is the business of believers who have the gift of wisdom.

C. *Wisdom as a gift of the Spirit is different from that of the flesh.* Humans possess a wisdom apart from the gift of the Spirit. But true spiritual wisdom is from God. Several passages of Scripture confirm this fact (1 Cor. 1:20; 2:5–6; 3:19; 2 Cor. 1:12; James 3:15).

II. Consider how this gift relates to life (Acts 6:10).

A. *Wisdom is given to believers for defense.* Those who follow Jesus are subject to hostility (Matt. 10:17–20; Acts 4:1–22; 6:8–15). When they are so confronted, they need help making a defense. This is the use of the gift of wisdom.

B. *Wisdom is given to believers for answers to unbelievers (1 Peter 3:15).* One of the greatest challenges Christians face is witnessing to unbelievers. It is impossible to do this in many situations without the gift of the Holy Spirit.

C. *Wisdom is given to believers for problem situations (James 1:5).* The use of this gift dissolves tension in groups. It clarifies objectives and shortens processes.

D. *Wisdom is given to believers for practical conduct.* Ephesians is an excellent Scripture reference for this fact. The first three chapters are dedicated to doctrine and the last three to the application of it.

Conclusion

The wisdom discussed in this message is always mediated through the Holy Spirit. He not only enables one to stand for oneself, but also to convey understanding to others as it relates to salvation. The Holy Spirit gives believers the ability to effectively apply this wisdom to their own lives and to others (Rom. 16:19; 1 Cor. 3:18; Eph. 5:15–17; James 3:13).

SUNDAY MORNING, MAY 31

Title: Guess Who's Coming to Dinner

Text: "Behold, I stand at the door and knock; if any one hears my voice and opens the door, I will come in to him and eat with him, and he with me" **(Rev. 3:20 RSV)**.

Scripture Reading: Luke 14:15–24

Hymns: "God, Our Father, We Adore Thee," Frazer
            "The Light of the World Is Jesus," Bliss
            "Blessed Redeemer," Christiansen

Offertory Prayer: Holy Father, you have been so gracious and generous to us. Today we thank you for the glad consciousness of forgiven sin. We thank you for the joy of being members in your family. Serving you and helping others know the great salvation that is offered through Jesus Christ is a privilege. As we worship with our tithes and offerings, we pray that you will add your blessings to them so that your kingdom might come in the hearts and lives of men and women, boys and girls, to the ends of the earth. For we pray in Jesus' name. Amen.

Introduction

A 1967 Academy Award–winning movie was titled *Guess Who's Coming to Dinner.* The film portrays the story of a girl from a wealthy white family who becomes engaged to a black man. The parents consider themselves to be very liberal-minded but at times appear otherwise, making for both some painful and some comical aspects.

How would you respond if someone invited you to a dinner where the special guest was Jesus Christ, the Son of God? How would you react to the possibility of inviting him into your home for a meal? How would you react if you received an invitation to attend a banquet at which Jesus Christ was serving as the host?

It is interesting to note in the words of our text that Jesus Christ invites himself to come into our lives. He offers to sit as a guest at the table that we would place before him. In turn he would serve as the host for a banquet that he would provide for us.

It is significant that our Lord would describe conversion and the Christian life in terms of a banquet experience in which both he and the guests would enjoy feasting and fellowship together. How tragic it is that many look upon the Christian life as a famine instead of a feast.

I. There is a stranger at the door.

The door is pictured as the entrance into one's heart and life. Each of us as individuals have control over that door. We can open the door, or we can keep it closed. To each of us is given the privilege and the responsibility of choice.

A. *We need this Stranger in the house of our life as much as we need health, and even more.*

B. *We need this Stranger in the house of our life as much as we need wealth, and even more.*

C. *We need this Stranger in the house of our life more than we need friends, as important as they are.*

D. *We need this Stranger in the house of our life as the dominant member of our family.* He can greatly enrich our family life if we will let him in.

II. Who is this Stranger who wants to come to dinner?

He who stands at the door of our heart repeatedly and patiently is no figment of human imagination. He is no fictitious character from some religious novel. The Stranger at the door is the man of Nazareth whose claims, character, and conquest of death and the grave prove that he is the Son of God. He came in human flesh to reveal God's grace, love, and power.

This Stranger at the door is the creative Lord who comes for his own place in the center of the heart of his creatures. He comes not as an intruder, but as the One who has the privilege of ownership by right of creation and preservation. He wants to claim his own by virtue of his redemptive love.

III. What does this Stranger at the door want to do?

A. *This divine Stranger wants to come into your life.* He wants to come in through the door. He is not satisfied merely to look in.

B. *This divine Stranger wants to be your Savior and Lord.* He wants to bring you the gift of forgiveness and bestow on you the gift of eternal life. He wants to bring into your innermost being his precious Holy Spirit to be your Teacher, Guide, and Helper.

C. *This divine Stranger wants to become your friend.* Christ takes the initiative in coming to us in order that he might get acquainted with us, but even more so in order that we might become acquainted with his transforming and enriching presence.

D. *This divine Stranger wants to make our life complete.* From the days of Adam, people have been but a fraction of what the Creator God meant for us to be. The living Christ came to heal the wound inflicted by sin. He came so that by his death and resurrection he might return us to our Creator. Life without him is incomplete, unhappy, unfruitful, and unsatisfying.

This wonderful Stranger wants to reclaim you for God's glory and to recreate within you the nature of God. He wants to rescue you from the sin that is so destructive to you and to restore to you the joy and happiness that God meant for you to have.

IV. What must you do regarding this Stranger?

You may decide simply to ignore him and to have nothing to do with him.

You may decide to neglect or postpone making any decision concerning this divine Guest who wants to come into your life.

You may deliberately decide to reject him and have nothing to do with him. Most likely this would be your reaction if you consider him to be some kind of thief who wants to rob you and take something from you. You will probably reject him if you consider him to be some kind of bully who wants to mistreat you and subordinate you to his selfish will.

The way of wisdom is to recognize this Guest at the door as the divine Son of God who comes with the gifts of heaven for you.

Conclusion

With an ear attentive to his knocking at the door, respond with the faith that is willing to accept him and with the joy that is willing to welcome him into your life. This divine Stranger alone can bring to you the gift of forgiveness that is full and free and forever. He alone can bring you the gift of eternal life and make you a member of God's family. And he alone can teach you the truth of God that will help you to live an abundant life in the here and now. Treat him not as an enemy who wants to invade your life with destructive purposes. Instead, welcome him as the Friend who loves you so much that he was willing to die for you. Accept him as being so divine that he conquered death and the grave and lives forever to be the loving Lord of your life.

SUNDAY EVENING, MAY 31

Title: Spiritual Discernment Offered

Text: "Son though he was, he learned obedience from what he suffered and, once made perfect, he became the source of eternal salvation for all who obey him" **(Heb. 5:8–9 NIV).**

Scripture Reading: Hebrews 5:1–14

Introduction

The main point of this Scripture passage is found in verse 11. The writer is saddened by the lack of spiritual discernment among the people. A keen spiritual sensitivity is essential in believers' lives. The goal of this passage is to encourage the readers "who by reason of use have their senses exercised to discern both good and evil" (Heb. 5:14).

I. Aid to spiritual discernment (Heb. 5:1–4).

Scripture spoke historically to its immediate situation, and it speaks prophetically to all future circumstances. God used an earthly high priest as an example to teach the recipients of the Hebrews letter. This man, as God's minister, aided believers in their development of spiritual discernment.

A. *Ordained by men (5:1).* A high priest was set apart by men to minister to them. A high priest experienced the same basic needs as those to whom he ministered.

B. *Man of infirmity (5:2).* A high priest also had the same weaknesses as those to whom he ministered. He took part in the same ignorance, the same iniquity, and the same obstinacy.

C. *Man of sacrifice (5:3).* A high priest was not above personal sin. He was aware of his spiritual needs. Consequently, the sacrifices he offered to God were for his own sake as well as that of others. His spiritual discernment involved inward as well as outward wrongs.

D. *Called by God (5:4).* An outstanding characteristic of a high priest is that although he was ordained by men, he was called by God. The position of high priest was not something a man took on himself. He was appointed by God to aid others in spiritual discernment.

II. Source of spiritual discernment (Heb. 5:5–10).

As an earthly high priest was an aid to spiritual discernment, the heavenly High Priest, Jesus Christ, is the source of spiritual discernment. Awareness of God and his activities is found in a personal relationship with Jesus Christ.

A. *Begotten of God (5:5).* Christ did not seek glory for himself. Rather, God appointed him to the divine task of serving as our supreme High Priest. As the Father is the paternal source of the Son, so Christ is the source of our faith.

B. *After Melchizedek (5:6, 10).* The high priesthood of Christ was as unique as that of the Old Testament priest Melchizedek. Christ, like Melchizedek, was distinct in origin, order, and function. He was not of the order of the Aaronic priesthood.

C. *Obedient through suffering (5:8).* Trials and tribulations develop a sensitive spirit. Though Christ was by nature in total obedience to his Father, he was made even more aware of the Father's will through hardships and suffering. As the Son of God developed, so the sons and daughters of God must develop in spiritual discernment. We develop as we obey God.

D. *Secured salvation (5:9).* No moral imperfections existed within Jesus, yet his life was one of continually growing awareness. When he reached full spiritual discernment (perfection), "he became the author of eternal salvation." This happened as Jesus died on the cross as the ultimate sacrifice. The resulting salvation is limited only to those who obey him.

III. Exhortation to spiritual discernment (Heb. 5:11–14).

A. *Need revealed (5:11).* The author was intensely aware that his readers were "dull of hearing." They were in dire need of the spiritual discernment available through Christ.

B. *Cause of need (5:12–13).* The Christian community had failed to make spiritual progress. Instead of advancing into a new spiritual dimension, they kept reverting to a review of the fundamentals of the New Testament faith.

C. *Key to growth (5:14).* An advantage to mature Christian living is the ability to enjoy the "strong meat" of God. The key to attaining spiritual growth is simple: we must exercise the spiritual insights we already possess. When we respond to the light God has allotted us, we then receive additional light.

Conclusion

The author gave the formula for developing spiritual discernment in verse 14. We need to be like "those who by reason of use have their senses exercised to discern both good and evil."

JUNE

- ## Sunday Mornings

  The theme for Sunday mornings this month is "The Church and the Modern Family." On the Sunday preceding Independence Day, incorporate a message on liberty.

- ## Sunday Evenings

  Continue the series "Jesus Christ as Our High Priest."

- ## Wednesday Evenings

  Complete the series "Concerning the Gifts of the Holy Spirit."

WEDNESDAY EVENING, JUNE 3

Title: The Gift of Knowledge

Text: "To one is given by the Spirit the word of wisdom; to another the word of knowledge by the same Spirit" **(1 Cor. 12:8)**.

Scripture Reading: 1 Corinthians 12:1–8

Introduction

The gift of knowledge, which we will consider in this message, is needed by everyone. Each Christian has the gift to some degree.

I. Just what is the gift of knowledge?

A. *It is the ability to assimilate facts.* A person's whole self is involved, not just his or her mind. Knowledge is one experience or a series of experiences. It may include emotions like grief and sadness, or joy and happiness.

B. *It is the ability to differentiate facts.* People who have the gift can take one fact or statement and distinguish it from others. This is especially true in the area of doctrine. Spiritual knowledge is needed to distinguish doctrines such as sovereignty and mercy.

C. *It is the ability to disseminate facts.* Here the gift is closely related to the gift of wisdom. Those who have the gift of knowledge know how to spread the good news of Jesus.

II. The gift of knowledge is in reference to believers' relation to God.

A. *The Holy Spirit dwells only in believers; therefore, only Christians have this gift.* People other than Christians have knowledge, but they cannot have spiritual knowledge apart from the Holy Spirit giving it to them.

B. *The Holy Spirit gives the gift through human communication.* This is the ability to appraise and judge things as they are. People who have the gift are able to distinguish between imagination, emotional disturbance, or subjective feelings. They are able to clarify a passage of Scripture as it relates to Bible truths. Knowledge differentiates the spiritual and legalistic.

C. *The Holy Spirit gives the gift to distinguish between true and false.* Christians who have the gift are able to know the difference between genuine and false piety and between godliness and self-righteousness. The gift has a special application in the areas of Christian maturity and evangelism.

III. Some dangers arise when using the word *gift* as it relates to the gift of knowledge.

A. *Some think that because this gift is a gift, it is instantaneous.* The gift of knowledge is more the ability to get knowledge than the instantaneous possession of it.

B. *Believers get knowledge by the gift of the Spirit in various ways.*
1. Knowledge is attained by listening. The psalmist said, "Be still, and know that I am God" (Ps. 46:10). God has a lot to say to those who will listen.
2. Knowledge is attained by studying. Paul said, "Study to shew thyself approved unto God" (2 Tim. 2:15).
3. Knowledge is attained by applying. Peter said, "Giving all diligence, add to your . . . knowledge" (2 Peter 1:5).

Conclusion

We are cautioned against assuming that we know. We should make sure we are the right kind of students under the right kind of teacher. The Holy Spirit gives the gift of knowledge.

SUNDAY MORNING, JUNE 7

Title: Let Us Encourage One Another

Text: "Let us consider how we may spur one another on toward love and good deeds" **(Heb. 10:24 NIV)**.

Scripture Reading: Hebrews 10:19–25; 12:1–2

Hymns: "Praise Him! Praise Him!" Crosby
"Fairest Lord Jesus," Willis
"Make Me a Channel of Blessing," Smyth

Offertory Prayer: Holy and loving Father, we approach your throne, reminded that you are the giver of every good and perfect gift. We thank you for life. We thank you for the work that we have the privilege of doing and for the witness that we have the privilege of giving. We thank you for the gift of time. We are humbled as we think of your many blessings to us. Today we give ourselves as an offering to you to express our gratitude and love. Help us to live each day for the purpose of serving and helping. Accept our tithes and offerings for the advancement of your kingdom's work. We pray in Jesus' name. Amen.

Introduction

In a sermon titled "The Need for Encouragement," Dr. W. Truett declared that no one is exempt from the need to be encouraged by others. This is particularly true in family circles. Husbands need encouragement from their wives and vice versa. Mothers need encouragement from their children. Children need constant encouragement from both parents.

It is interesting to note how our text is translated by various versions. The King James Version puts it, "Let us consider one another to provoke unto love and to good works" (Heb. 10:24). *Provoke* means "to arouse to action, to excite, to stir up the feelings." The word is often used with reference to arousing one to anger, but in our text it is a strong word used to encourage love and good works.

The Revised Standard Version translates the verse, "Let us consider how to stir up one another to love and good works." "Stir up" means "to move, to excite, to agitate."

The *Good News* translation translates our text, "Let us be concerned for one another, to help one another to show love and to do good." To be concerned is to show interest or care. To help is to provide assistance.

The New International Version puts it, "Let us consider how we may spur one another on toward love and good deeds." To spur is to prompt or motivate.

Whatever the version used, the verse urges us to help one another practice self-giving love and perform good works for God and others.

I. Let us encourage one another.

    A. *This imperative is all inclusive in its necessity.* Every one of us will need encouragement during the coming week as we attempt to achieve various goals. Achievement is always the result of overcoming obstacles.

    B. *This imperative is all inclusive in its application.* God's will is for each of us to be a cheerleader for others.

        1. Husbands and wives should encourage each other as they work toward a happy and successful marriage.

        2. Parents should encourage their children, especially through words of appreciation. Too often parents are overly generous with criticism and stingy with encouragement.

        3. Children can greatly encourage their parents by their choices and their conduct.

4. Teachers have a marvelous opportunity to encourage students to achieve excellence, and students also can be a great encouragement to their teachers.
5. In employer-employee relationships, there is much room for improvement in encouraging each other.
6. Good coaches are those who can encourage their team as a whole to strive for excellence.
7. All Christians should consider themselves part of God's cheering squad to encourage other Christians.

II. Why is continuous encouragement needed?

An illness that often goes undetected afflicts many of us. It is called depression. People have a tendency to become discouraged even while doing helpful and significant work. Why is this so?

A. *Some reasons within ourselves make living by the principle of love and helpfulness difficult.* By nature we are immature and self-centered. We find it easier to hate than to love. We find it easier to quit than to continue. We must overcome these inward inclinations. The right kind of encouragement can help us.
B. *Some reasons outside ourselves make living by the principle of love and helpfulness difficult.* We live in a self-centered world that measures success largely in terms of having and acquiring and accomplishing. There is not much encouragement for people to be anything other than self-centered.
C. *Some reasons even within the Lord's work make it difficult for us to devote ourselves to a life of loving helpfulness to others.* The sinful world in which we live provides no encouragement. The devil will do everything he can to create discouragement, despair, and defeat. Spiritual progress is always an uphill experience. The prevailing spirit of the world urges us to float downstream, and it is always hard to swim upstream.

The author of Hebrews marshals the spiritual leaders of the past in chapter 11, which has been called faith's Hall of Fame, so that they may cheer us on as we run the race that has been set before us (Heb. 12:1–2).

Conclusion

Let us encourage one another to have greater faith in God. Let us share with others our relationship with Jesus Christ so that we might impart to them the benefits of our faith.

Let us encourage one another to make a sacrifice for God and for others. The measure of our sacrifice is the measure of our love and our faith. Until we are willing to sacrifice for our God and for others, our faith will not have much opportunity to develop.

Let us encourage one another to dedicate ourselves to spiritual values. We live in a world that emphasizes materialistic values. The greatest values, however, are in the heavenly realm. It has been said that one's interest will always follow one's dollars. If this is true, we can be sure that our heart remains in God's work by investing in his church with our tithes and offerings. Let us encourage one another to live with eternity in mind rather than living with no thought for tomorrow.

Let us encourage one another to be concerned for others' souls. We can witness to those who come into the circle of our personal influence. We can contribute to missions and other organizations that take part in bringing men, women, and children to a personal relationship with Jesus Christ.

Let us encourage one another to involve ourselves in loving service so that we will truly be worth something to God and to others.

May the Lord enable us to cheer one another onward as he seeks to encourage us. And may he always put his Spirit within us and on us.

SUNDAY EVENING, JUNE 7

Title: Christ's Challenge—Perfection

Text: "Therefore let us move beyond the elementary teachings about Christ and be taken forward to maturity, not laying again the foundation of repentance from acts that lead to death, and of faith in God, instruction about cleansing rites, the laying on of hands, the resurrection of the dead, and eternal judgment. And God permitting, we will do so" **(Heb. 6:1–3 NIV)**.

Scripture Reading: Hebrews 6:1–20

Introduction

By nature we are sinful creatures (Rom. 5:12), so we can never be perfect through our own efforts. Yet through the power of God we are always to move in that direction. The author's purpose in this chapter was to challenge believers to aim for perfection. To achieve this end, he presented the goal, gave reason for the struggle, and then revealed three instruments available to Christians in this adventure.

I. The goal is given (Heb. 6:1–8).

Great explorers, whether in the fields of mathematics, science, or travel, have all shared a common element. They have been driven to explore the unknown by some underlying goal in their lives. Jesus appeals to this segment of nature as he guides the writer of Hebrews to define a goal for believers.

A. *The ultimate (6:1).* God's ultimate intent is for Christians to "be taken forward to maturity" (NIV). He wants us to experience his complete character of holiness.

B. *The immediate (6:1–3).* For Christians to reach the ultimate, they must start where they are. One common fault of new Christians is that they remain in immature faith. We are tempted to keep working on our spiritual foundation instead of building on the foundation that God has already given us. Time and energy are wasted when we neglect to construct the actual building because we are busy remodeling the foundation. The author said to start building on the foundation immediately rather than constantly going back to "nurse" it.

C. *The impossible (6:4–8).* The writer gave an aside on a prevalent apostasy being witnessed in that day. He warned of a group who had experienced certain phases of the pre-salvation ministry of God with people. Yet they had not responded in faith to the salvation offered. Note the change of persons in the pronouns used here. They are in the third person plural in the King James Version ("those," "they," "them," "themselves"). But when the writer spoke of the Christian, he used the first personal pronoun. This change in language clearly indicates that those involved in the apostasy were never members of the true Christian community. The word "impossible" in verse 4 cannot mean anything else.

II. The encouragement is given (Heb. 6:9–12).

Christians are encouraged to follow Christ even against the discouraging backdrop of apostasy.

A. *The potential present (6:9).* Believers are able to accomplish great things for God. The main reason for this potential is that those who are saved can be victorious.

B. *The reward offered (6:10).* The greatest of all incentives is to receive God's recognition. He does not let our efforts go unnoticed.

C. *The diligence encouraged (6:11–12).* Christians have a witness to their immediate environment. They should always be regarded as persons of diligence, pursuing worthwhile goals in life.

III. The instruments are given (Heb. 6:13–20).

The Bible should be regarded as an instruction manual from God to humans. If God wants us to accomplish something, not only will he reveal the goal to us, but he will also give us the means to attain his desired objective. Three instruments are provided in this chapter to aid believers in reaching perfection.

A. *God's promises (6:13–16).* God's promises are awesome. As they were available to Abraham, so they are present for our benefit. His promises guide us through the darkest of circumstances.

B. *God's counsel (6:17).* God counsels believers daily through the ministry of his Holy Spirit.

C. *God's hope (6:18–19).* A formidable instrument given to believers is hope, which keeps us anchored to the solid Rock, Jesus Christ.

Conclusion

The life of perfection must be the life "within the veil." Our forerunner guiding us to that righteous life is none other than Jesus Christ.

WEDNESDAY EVENING, JUNE 10

Title: The Gift of Faith

Text: "To another faith by the same Spirit; to another the gifts of healing by the same Spirit" **(1 Cor. 12:9).**

Scripture Reading: Hebrews 11:1–6

Introduction

To be saved we must have saving faith. After we are saved, we need faith to do God's work. Most Christians do not have the faith they need or want to carry on their Lord's work. We need to develop the art of completely letting God control everything. This is the gift of the Holy Spirit.

I. Three kinds of faith are used in the Bible.

    A. *The first is natural faith.* This is mental recognition and assent, the inborn element of belief. It is the kind of faith mentioned in James 2:19, which notes that even demons believe.

    B. *The second is saving faith.* This is committal of the soul to Christ for salvation, faith that unites a person to God. It is saying yes to God's Word as it relates to the soul's salvation.

    C. *The third is faith that lays hold of God's promises.* This is the gift of the Spirit. This does not mean that the Spirit does not give saving faith also; rather, it means that to lay hold and act on God's promises is a special gift. All believers have this gift to some degree, but some use it more than others.

II. Consider what it means to lay hold of God's promises.

    A. *Two biblical illustrations help to explain the concept.*

        1. 1 Kings 18:36–39. "Answer me, LORD . . . so these people will know" (v. 37 NIV). The strange and daring was done. As Elijah laid hold of God's promises in faith, a miracle happened. Many people became believers in Jehovah God as a result.

        2. John 11:41–46. "Father, I thank you that you have heard me . . . that they may believe" (vv. 41–42 NIV). Jesus is the example of faith here. As a result, one of the most amazing miracles of all time occurred.

    B. *Another illustration also helps to elaborate the idea.*

A classic example of the gift of faith refers to the life and ministry of George Mueller, who by faith operated an orphanage in Bristol, England. He cared for ten thousand orphans over sixty years, receiving $5 million in the process. He began his work with only two shillings in his pocket. Without once making known any need, he received enough to build five large homes, able to house two thousand orphans, and to feed the children day by day, all by faith and prayer. Never did they go without a meal. Often the pantry was bare when the children sat down to eat, but help always arrived in the nick of time. (Leslie B. Flynn, *19 Gifts of the Spirit* [Wheaton, IL: Victor, 1974], 141.)

C. *Laying hold of God's promises is applicable to all areas of life.* God's promises can be claimed by an individual or a collective group such as the church. The concept relates to the granting of peace of mind, the performance of a spiritual duty, the provision of economic necessities, and the restoration of physical health.

III. Two specific ideas apply to the use of this gift.

A. *The gift enables believers to better achieve what they could do to a degree without it.* For example, a church can launch a mission project on sheer facts. People need Christ, people are available to start a church, and it is the right thing to do. But faith is exercised in claiming God's promise to supply every need. Then bold action can and will be taken that is not possible without the gift.

B. *The gift enables believers to do things they are unable to do without it.* The use of this gift makes the impossible possible. The Bible says, "With God all things are possible" (Matt. 19:26). Here the human desire must correspond with God's desire.

The use of this gift gives hope to a hopeless situation. Hopelessness is closely associated with helplessness. God helps the helpless. The use of the gift of faith makes an unendurable situation endurable. Some situations are beyond the human ability to bear. With this gift, these problem situations can be dealt with successfully.

Conclusion

The gift of faith is coupled with prayer. Even though it is God's prerogative to give the gift, when believers desire more faith, ask for it, cultivate their use of it, and use it for God's glory, they experience a greater outpouring of it.

SUNDAY MORNING, JUNE 14

Title: The Church in Your House

Text: "Paul, a prisoner of Christ Jesus, and Timothy our brother, To Philemon our dear friend and fellow worker—also to Apphia our sister, to Archippus our fellow soldier—and to the church that meets in your home: Grace to you and peace from God our Father and the Lord Jesus Christ" **(Philem. 1–3 NIV)**.

Scripture Reading: Romans 16:1–5

Hymns: "To God Be the Glory," Crosby
        "Christ Receiveth Sinful Men," Neumeister
        "Once for All!" Bliss

Offertory Prayer: Holy Father, we thank you for your beautiful love and your gracious purpose for us. We rejoice in this good day you have made. We will be glad in it and serve you with enthusiasm. We come to worship you by offering the adoration of our hearts and the praise of our lips. We come bringing our energy and our efforts in the form of these tithes and offerings for use in furthering your kingdom's work. Bless these gifts that we place on the altar for you today as expressions of our desire to be completely at your disposal. In Jesus' name. Amen.

Introduction

Is there a church in your house? Has the church ever met at your home? Would the church be welcome in your house?

Various statements in the New Testament indicate that house churches were numerous in the early days of Christianity. We find Aquila and Priscilla and the church that met at their house sending greetings along with Paul to the church in Corinth. When Paul sent his letter to the church in Rome, he sent special greetings to the church that met in Aquila and Priscilla's home.

The Greek word *ekklesia* has at least three meanings in the New Testament. It is used to refer to all Christians in a house (Rom. 16:5), all Christians in a city (1 Cor. 1:2), and all Christians in the world (Col. 1:24). It is used mostly to refer to a local congregation of baptized believers.

The New Testament records five different instances in which a whole household experienced conversion and baptism.

1. The household of Cornelius (Acts 10:44–48).
2. The household of Lydia (Acts 16:15).
3. The household of the Philippian jailer (Acts 16:30–34).
4. The household of Crispus (Acts 18:8).
5. The household of Stephanas (1 Cor. 1:16).

In our day we have emphasized the personal responsibility of each individual to put faith in God. Perhaps we have neglected to appeal to a whole family about accepting Jesus Christ in order for them to become Christians as a unit.

Where is the church? In answering that question, do you automatically think of a street address or a place where a building has been constructed for purposes of worship and Bible study? The New Testament never focuses on a place, but rather on people. Have we secularized our homes and isolated them from the living and powerful presence of Jesus Christ so that we never visualize the church as being in our house?

Some people see their homes as nothing more than service stations where they drive in, fill up their tanks, and leave. Some treat their homes like they are restaurants or bars. They are places to eat and drink and renew the physical energy necessary to carry on daily activities. Some picture their houses as nothing more than motels where they sleep. Some think of their houses as hospitals where those who are ill or hurting receive care. Some manage their homes as if they are recreation centers. They are places to have a good time. Others use their homes as if they are offices or factories. They see them as places where they work and do what they must to earn a living.

Have you ever stopped to think about your house as being a place where the church meets to carry on God's work and to experience his blessings?

The church is not simply a structure, a street address, a place.

I. The church is where God's people are.

Missionary Bruce Conrad tells about driving up to the home of some Native Americans in one of the western states. A little boy recognized him, rushed to the door of his house, and shouted to his mother, "Here comes the church." The little boy did not know the missionary's name, but he did know the nature of his business. The church is wherever God's people are. If you recognize and respond to the implications of being the people of God, your home will become a dwelling place of the church.

II. The church is where biblical teaching is conducted.

In New Testament days the church was not a building where people went to hear a sermon. The church was the church when people met together to study the teachings of Jesus Christ and the instructions of his apostles. Believers were following the great tradition of their spiritual forefathers. Moses had said to the Israelites, "These commandments that I give you today are to be upon your hearts. Impress them on your children. Talk about them when you sit at home and when you walk along the road, when you lie down and when you get up" (Deut. 6:6–7 NIV).

Every believer needs to see his or her home as a place where biblical truths should be taught and studied and implemented. In that sense your house can become as sacred and as important for spiritual education as a building dedicated specifically to that purpose.

III. The church is where Christian fellowship is enjoyed (Acts 2:42).

In the early church, food was shared between the early disciples as they visited the temple. They broke bread from house to house, eating and sharing together (Acts 2:42, 46). These early disciples shared not only their food, but also their experiences and insights into the purposes of God. They shared a common faith in Jesus Christ and a common experience of being indwelt by the Holy Spirit. They shared the momentous task of telling others about God's wonderful work in their hearts and lives.

IV. The church is where prayers are offered (Acts 2:42; 12:5, 12).

Jesus had quoted the Old Testament, declaring that God's house was to be a house of prayer. Do you pray to the heavenly Father and listen as he speaks to your heart? Do you invite friends into your home for prayer, that you might join together in intercessory prayer for others?

V. The church is where praise is given to God (Acts 2:47).

Parents should consistently praise God for his many blessings while their children are present. Likewise, Christians should not hesitate to tell visitors in their home how much they appreciate God's goodness. How long has it been since you offered praises to God in the presence of your visitors?

VI. The church is where conversions take place (Acts 2:47).

Has anyone been saved in your home besides one of your children? Have you ever used your home as a place to share with someone what Jesus Christ means to you?

A conversion can take place in your home just as it can take place in someone else's home or in the church if the good news of God's love is presented to those who need it.

Conclusion

What about the church in your house? Will you let your home become a place where the church meets and functions? Will you make it a place where the people of God are welcome?

SUNDAY EVENING, JUNE 14

Title: Christ—The Superior High Priest

Text: "Because Jesus lives forever, he has a permanent priesthood. Therefore he is able to save completely those who come to God through him, because he always lives to intercede for them" (**Heb. 7:24–25 NIV**).

Scripture Reading: Hebrews 7:1–28

Introduction

The readers of the letter to the Hebrews were aware of the Jews' high priesthood system. They also knew of a special historical priest named Melchizedek. Now they were learning about the high priesthood of Christ. This chapter compares the three separate high priesthood systems to prove that Christ is the superior High Priest. We need none other than Jesus Christ.

I. The priesthood of Melchizedek (Heb. 7:1–7).

A. *Priest of God.* Melchizedek's outstanding designation was "priest of the most high God" (7:1). It is significant to the Levitical system that this man was recognized by Abraham, the father of Israel.

B. *King of righteousness (7:2).* This mysterious Melchizedek was also the king of Salem (ancient city of Jerusalem). His reign was one of righteousness. The people he ruled could trust his judgment.

C. *King of peace (7:2).* The result of Melchizedek's reign was peace. The people of his kingdom profited under his great rule.

D. *Unlimiting facts (7:3).* Some interesting statements have been made regarding Melchizedek. The most feasible way to interpret this verse about his being "without father, without mother" is to understand that all other priests were required to have a genealogical record proving their heritage. This was not so with Melchizedek. No records gave details about his origin, family, life, or death.

E. *Superior to Abraham (7:4–7).* Abraham paid tithes to Melchizedek. The priest blessed Abraham in return for the tithes. The author concluded that the greater always blesses the lesser; therefore Melchizedek was greater than Abraham.

II. The priesthood of Levi (Heb. 7:8–12).

The author was establishing the idea that Jesus is superior to Melchizedek. In the process, he also pointed out that the priesthood of Melchizedek was superior to that of Levi.

A. *In obeisance to Melchizedek (7:8–10).* The author reasoned that when Abraham gave tithes to Melchizedek, all future generations of Abraham (including the yet unborn Levi) also shared in this experience through him. This would mean that Levi gave tithes to Melchizedek through his grandfather Abraham.

B. *Less than perfect (7:11).* The way the author posed the question clearly indicates that the priesthood of Levi was not perfect.

C. *To be replaced (7:11–12).* Though it may be a note of dismay to the Levitical priesthood, the author wrote, "If perfection could have been attained through the Levitical priesthood—and indeed the law given to the people established that priesthood—why was there still need for another priest to come, one in the order of Melchizedek, not in the order of Aaron?" (v. 11 NIV).

III. The priesthood of Christ (Heb. 7:13–27).

The heart of the whole matter is the high priesthood of Christ.

A. *Of the tribe of Judah (7:13–14)*. The superior High Priest came from the tribe of Judah, not the tribe of Levi. Moses had not indicated that this would happen.

B. *Like Melchizedek (7:15–17)*. The special emphasis of this characteristic is that Christ's authority is based on "an endless life," not a carnal law.

C. *Strength replaces weakness (7:18–19)*. The superior High Priest was destined to replace the weaknesses of the old system with strength that would result in perfection.

D. *Priest by an oath (7:20–21)*. Christ was made High Priest through an oath by the Most High God. This was not so with the Levitical system.

E. *Eternal priesthood (7:22–24)*. The Levitical priests faced an inevitable death. Christ did not. He has an unchangeable priesthood that continues forever.

F. *Offered himself (7:25–27)*. The Levitical system required animal sacrifices. Christ offered himself as the Lamb of God, the only sacrifice needed to bring salvation to everyone. Sacrifice and High Priest are welded together in the person of Jesus Christ.

Conclusion

The Son was set apart as High Priest by the oath of God himself (7:28). This is an eternal act. Because of this High Priest who intercedes on our behalf, we can have eternal security.

WEDNESDAY EVENING, JUNE 17

Title: The Gift of Tongues

Text: "To another the working of miracles; to another prophecy; to another discerning of spirits; to another divers kinds of tongues; to another the interpretation of tongues" **(1 Cor. 12:10)**.

Scripture Reading: 1 Corinthians 14:1–28

Introduction

Few issues have ever risen in a local church that are more divisive than speaking in tongues. Because of the gravity of the subject, I will discuss it in two messages rather than one.

I. Speaking in tongues is a gift of the Holy Spirit (I Cor. 12:10).

A. Glossolalia *is the technical term for this gift*. It is a compound of two Greek words, *glossa*, which means tongue, and *lalia*, which means speech or speaking.

B. *General references to the term are ecstatic utterances and strange tongues.* The common reference in contemporary usage is charismatic. The definition of this term varies with the insights, schools of thought, and historical setting of the person making the explanation.

II. Speaking in tongues has several New Testament references.

A. *The Pentecostal experience (Acts 2:1–13).* The word "other" is found in verse 4. The words, "speak in his own language," are in verse 6, "own tongue" in verse 8, and "our tongues" in verse 11.

    Some exegesis will help here. In verse 4 the word is simply "other." In verse 8 it is "tongue," or dialect, and in verse 11, it is the plural "our tongues." We may conclude that this biblical reference is to the language of the people who heard the disciples.

B. *The Caesarean experience (Acts 10:44–48).* The word in verse 46 refers to inanimate things. It means to give sounds. Applying to a person, it simply means to speak, or the ability to express oneself. The word "tongues" is plural for "tongue." The conclusion is that these were ecstatic utterances intended for the Gentile world.

C. *The Ephesian experience (Acts 19:1–6).* In verse 6 the word "spoke" (NIV) is what is known in the Greek as both a first person singular and third person plural imperfect active. The word for "tongues" in verse 6 is the same word in Acts 10:46 and is simply the plural for "tongue." Here more than one person is speaking.

III. Some conclusions may be drawn from these studies.

A. *The Greek words throughout refer to languages and dialects.* Where the plural is found, it is in the multiple—that is, multiple number of languages and dialects.

B. *Historically, the use of multiple languages and dialects that were originally the language of people developed into ecstatic utterances.* This is sometimes the situation among charismatics today.

Conclusion

    Spirit-controlled believers will be careful about their attitude toward others in regard to their philosophy in the use of this gift. If certain people believe in speaking in tongues, they should be tactful toward those who do not. Likewise, if certain people do not believe in speaking in tongues, they should be tactful toward those who do. All Christians must keep in mind that the purpose of the gifts is for edification of the church, and proper use of the gifts will build up the church.

SUNDAY MORNING, JUNE 21

Title: The Forgotten Father

Text: "Then Joseph being raised from sleep did as the angel of the Lord had bidden him" **(Matt. 1:24)**.

Scripture Reading: Matthew 1:19–25

Hymns: "God, Our Father, We Adore Thee," Frazer
"Faith of Our Fathers," Faber
"All the Way My Savior Leads Me," Crosby

Offertory Prayer: Our Father in heaven, we thank you that we may be called your children—heirs of God and joint heirs of Jesus Christ. We thank you for our fathers who have given good gifts to us. Even more we are thankful that you are our heavenly Father who gives the Holy Spirit to his children. Accept these tithes and offerings as tokens of our love for you. And grant, Father, that your Spirit may fully bless and guide our lives. In Jesus' name we pray. Amen.

Introduction

When Christmas rolls around, the spotlight settles on baby Jesus; his mother, Mary; the shepherds; the angels; and the Magi. Have you ever heard a sermon about Joseph, Mary's husband, who functioned as Jesus' human father? In my entire library, I have only one printed sermon on him.

The Roman Catholic Church has canonized Joseph, calling him St. Joseph. But Protestantism has virtually ignored him. He deserves better. He must have been a remarkable man of God to be chosen from all men on earth to serve as Jesus' earthly father. Let us use the occasion of Father's Day to give him honor.

Matthew recorded the most information about Joseph. He was a descendant of David, so royal blood coursed through his veins. He maintained a dignity and kindness that reflected his family heritage. He witnessed Jesus' birth, saw the shepherds' adoration, and led Mary and the baby to Egypt to escape Herod's slaughter of infants. Joseph took Jesus to the temple at least twice—once in his infancy and again when he was twelve years old. Jesus called Joseph "father" and was subject to his authority. Joseph feared God and worked hard to support his family in a rustic town disdained for its obscurity and provincialism.

Joseph disappeared from the historical accounts of the Gospels. It is likely that he died when Jesus was a young man; and Jesus, as the oldest son, assumed the responsibility of Joseph's carpenter shop and the support of his family. He did not stop working as village carpenter until his younger brothers were old enough to take over. Then he entered his public ministry.

Although little is written about Joseph, we find plenty of facts to know that he was a great man.

I. Joseph was a just man.

"Then Joseph her husband, being a just man . . ." (Matt. 1:19). The Bible tells us with frankness and tact of Jesus' conception by the Holy Spirit.

A. *Joseph was sensitive to society's moral standards.* He could not ignore what people would think and say. All his life he had been abiding by this high standard. Apparently Joseph had no dynamic, overwhelming personality. He was a good man with ordinary abilities, but he put those abilities in God's hands, and God used him. God wants to use you in the same way.

B. *Joseph was sensitive to his own reputation.* When people say, "I don't care what people think as long as I think I'm right," they are only trying to fool themselves. Being right is most important, but what others think of you is also important. You truly may be right, but if people think you are wrong, you may have lost your opportunity to help them. A godly person's reputation is very important.

C. *Joseph was sensitive to Mary's plight.* "While he thought on these things . . ." (Matt. 1:20). He delayed any rash judgments and did not want to believe the worst. He kindly considered Mary's dilemma and was willing "to put her away privily" (Matt. 1:19) if that would protect her from the cruel gaze of hostile neighbors. His emotional balance in this crisis is amazing.

II. Joseph was sensitive to a heavenly vision.

Like Paul, Joseph was not disobedient to his vision from heaven. A supernatural birth required supernatural proof. After his dream, he had no further doubts and unreservedly accepted Mary as his wife. They had perfect faith in each other.

III. Joseph was a faithful father.

He provided Jesus with a human example for his sublime teachings about God as our heavenly Father. John Stuart Mill could not pray the Lord's Prayer because he had experienced brutal, unreasonable discipline by his callous father. To think of God as a Father like his father was uncomplimentary to God.

Jesus seemed to warmly remember Joseph's generosity to his children: "If you, then, though you are evil, know how to give good gifts to your children, how much more will your Father in heaven give good gifts to those who ask him!" (Matt. 7:11 NIV).

Conclusion

Jesus' parable of the prodigal son (Luke 15:11–32) is perhaps most revealing. This moving story could also be called "the parable of the loving father." The best part of the story is the boy's return from a far country. We know that the father never ceased to watch for him, for "when he was yet a great way off, his father saw him" (v. 20). The father "ran," denoting his own eagerness for reconciliation. He joyfully welcomed his son back home with a robe, ring, shoes, and a joyous feast. The father said to his other son, "Thy brother . . . was lost, and is found" (v. 32).

Jesus said that God is like that. Though you may have wandered away from him, he is a loving Father who longs for your return. He will forgive you and restore your place as his son or daughter if you will turn from your old life and look to him.

SUNDAY EVENING, JUNE 21

Title: Christ—Mediator of a Better Covenant

Text: "We do have such a high priest, who sat down at the right hand of the throne of the Majesty in heaven, and who serves in the sanctuary, the true tabernacle set up by the Lord, not by a mere human being" (**Heb. 8:1–2 NIV**).

Scripture Reading: Hebrews 8:1–13

Introduction

A covenant is an agreement between two or more parties. The Bible is built on two major covenants between God and humankind, the old and the new. Hebrews 8 compares the covenants. Both were acceptable to God when he so designated them to be applicable to humankind. The prominent difference is that the old covenant was simply a shadow of the new covenant. The mediator of the covenant of realism is Jesus Christ.

I. Position of the Mediator (Heb. 8:1–2).

A mediator is one who tries to bring two separate parties to harmony on the same subject. A priest also acts as a bridge between two points. Therefore the concepts of mediator and priest carry the same basic idea of intercession. Jesus Christ held a unique position that allowed him to become the mediator of a better covenant.

    A. *Heavenly High Priest (8:1).* Jesus occupies a heavenly seat. His intimacy with the Father qualifies him for the task of mediation.

    B. *Minister of the sanctuary (8:2).* As mediator Jesus serves at the heavenly sanctuary. He has total access to the Father's throne.

    C. *Architect of realism (8:2).* Jesus ministers in the true tabernacle. His actions are not based on a type system. He not only founded the "real" tabernacle (John 1:3) but continues its worship as well. He is qualified to present a new and better covenant to humankind.

II. Performance of the Mediator (Heb. 8:3–6).

The author of Hebrews mentions the weaknesses of the old system. He then gives a very concise statement regarding Christ's performance as mediator.

    A. *Weakness of the earthly (8:3–5).*
1. Needed gifts (8:3). The Levitical priesthood had to secure gifts for the sacrifice. They were not sufficient within themselves to sacrifice to God.
2. According to law (8:4). The Levitical priesthood was restricted by law in their system of sacrifices. Jesus superseded the law.
3. Servants of shadows (8:5). Even with their best intentions, the Levitical priests served only a "shadow of heavenly things."

    B. *Minister of realism (8:6).* Quite a contrast lies between the two areas of service. The Levitical priesthood served in the shadows, while Christ had "a more excellent ministry." He served in total realism. There were no shadows in his place of ministry.

III. Promise of the Mediator (Heb. 8:6–9).

A promise is only as true as the person making it. When God promises something, it is as realistic as a historical incident. The mediator's ministry is built on promises from God.

    A. *The better covenant (8:6–7).* The new covenant that is mediated by Christ is superior to the old covenant. It is established on "better promises" (promises involving more divine revelation of Christ).

    B. *The inadequate old covenant (8:8).* The very reason for the introduction of the new covenant is that the old covenant had faults. Only an inspired writer could reveal this, for anyone else would have been accused of blasphemy.

    C. *The basis of the new covenant (8:9).* The people under the old covenant had broken their agreements with God, so God felt it necessary to bring a new covenant to his people.

IV. Productions of the Mediator (Heb. 8:10–12).

This particular passage notes three things the mediator accomplished through the new covenant.

    A. *Spiritual covenant (8:10).* The mediator places God's laws in the hearts and minds of the people, not on tablets of stone. It is a spiritual experience.

    B. *Universal knowledge (8:11).* Any person has the privilege of knowing God if the conditions of salvation are met.

    C. *Overwhelming love (8:12).* The mediator is also capable of showing love and forgiveness. It is valuable to know that an all-knowing God is able to forget our sins.

Conclusion

The new covenant superseded the old covenant through Jesus Christ. The old covenant was "ready to vanish away" (8:13). We are under the law of grace and love, not the legalism of Sinai.

WEDNESDAY EVENING, JUNE 24

Title: The Gift of Tongues (continued)

Text: "To another the working of miracles; to another prophecy; to another discerning of spirits; to another divers kinds of tongues; to another the interpretation of tongues" (**1 Cor. 12:10**).

Scripture Reading: 1 Corinthians 14:1–28

Introduction

Studying the gift of tongues is both fascinating and challenging. The conclusions to which one comes are exciting yet soul searching. Believers must consider the subject humbly and with a receptive heart and mind.

I. Paul gives specific instructions for the use of tongues (I Cor. 14).

A. *When considered a mark of divine approval, speaking in tongues may arouse jealousy among church members.* Some who have this gift may be tempted to develop a pious attitude and consider those who do not exercise the gift as less spiritual, resulting in confusion and disorder in the church.

B. *When considered a mark of divine approval, speaking in tongues may result in self-display rather than edification of the church.* Communication is essential in worship services. If we are to build others up, they must be able to understand what we are saying. As Paul explained, "Anyone who speaks in a tongue does not speak to people but to God. Indeed, no one understands them; they utter mysteries by the Spirit. . . . Anyone who speaks in a tongue edifies themselves, but the one who prophesies edifies the church. I would like every one of you to speak in tongues, but I would rather have you prophesy. The one who prophesies is greater than the one who speaks in tongues, unless someone interprets, so that the church may be edified" (1 Cor. 14:2, 4–5 NIV). For believers to be edified, there is little place for self-importance.

C. *When considered a mark of divine approved, speaking in tongues may have an adverse effect on the outside community.* Non-Christians should benefit from worship. "Tongues, then, are a sign, not for believers but for unbelievers; prophecy, however, is not for unbelievers but for believers. If the whole church comes together and everyone speaks in tongues, and inquirers or unbelievers come in, will they not say that

196

you are out of your mind? But if an unbeliever or an inquirer comes in while everyone is prophesying, they are convicted of sin and are brought under judgment by all, as the secrets of their hearts are laid bare" (1 Cor. 14:22–25 NIV).

D. *When considered a mark of divine approved, speaking in tongues carries some limitations.* No more than two or three people should speak in tongues at the same time. No one should speak aloud unless an interpreter is available.

II. History records some interesting observations of the gift.

A. *Speaking in tongues is a valid experience in the lives of some.* Others should be careful to avoid negative remarks in regard to such experiences. Speaking in tongues is valid emotionally and psychologically, and this is beneficial. Different people have different experiences, but no one is ever to disrupt the unity of the church.

B. *Subjective experience alone is not adequate concerning the gift.* Obviously a feeling of well-being alone is not sufficient to declare any event as valid. Feelings are fickle. Experiences must be objective as well as subjective.

C. *Negative and positive results have been observed in the use of the gift.* Dependency on a charismatic leader rather than on Jesus Christ is dangerous. God does not give direction in a magical way, but in a rational way. Often the usage of the gift alienates rather than unites.

Conclusion

The criterion that determines the validity of speaking in tongues is whether it is building up the church. Another way to evaluate the use of tongues is to discover what the fruits of such experiences are (Gal. 5:22–23). In conclusion, Dr. John P. Kildahl said:

> My glossolalia research has convinced me that it is a learned behavior which can bring a sense of power and well-being. It may also lead to excesses resulting in community disruption. It is the use of glossolalia which determines whether or not it is constructive.
>
> Micah said that true religion was to do justice, love kindness, and to walk humbly with God. If the practice of glossolalia produces these fruits, then it appears to me to be a responsible use of the experience. (Quoted in Michael P. Hamilton, ed., *The Charismatic Movement* [Grand Rapids: Eerdmans, 1975], 142.)

SUNDAY MORNING, JUNE 28

Title: Forms of Freedom

Text: "Stand fast . . . in the liberty wherewith Christ hath made us free, and be not entangled again with the yoke of bondage . . . ye have been called unto liberty; only use not liberty for an occasion to the flesh, but by love serve one another" **(Gal. 5:1, 13).**

Scripture Reading: Galatians 5:1–3, 13–16

Hymns: "A Mighty Fortress Is Our God," Luther
"America the Beautiful," Bates
"Mine Eyes Have Seen the Glory," Howe

Offertory Prayer: Our Father, we thank you for the freedom for which others sacrificially gave themselves, which demands our constant vigilance and consistent practice, which all people aspire to enjoy, and which is fully found only in and through your Son, Jesus Christ, in whose name we pray. Amen.

Introduction

Nearly two and a half centuries ago, a few men assembled in Philadelphia endorsed the words of Thomas Jefferson that prefaced one of the major political revolutions in human history, words that stir the feelings of people who seek and value freedom: "We hold these truths to be self-evident, that all men are created equal, that they are endowed by their Creator with certain unalienable Rights, that among these are Life, Liberty, and the pursuit of Happiness."

Freedom is the ideal in every age. Where do we seek it? How do we exercise it? Let's consider some forms that peoples' quests for liberty take.

I. Some seek freedom by force.

A. *People who want freedom for themselves seek it through force.* What they want, they take. They respect neither the person nor the property of others. Their sole intent is to satisfy their own lusts, whatever their nature.

B. *The philosophy of this quest is that "might makes right."* It is the philosophy of the bully who demands that others give in to his wishes. He uses verbal force or threats when possible, physical force or violence when necessary.

Force cannot bring freedom. When people get on top by force, they become the victims of two forces against which they have no protection—a lust for more power and a fear of those below them who aspire for freedom through the overthrow of those in power. Lust and paranoia hold the bullies captive. The bullies gain deliverance from lust and paranoia only as they succumb to another bully. As Jesus said: "All they that take [or live by] the sword shall perish with the sword" (Matt. 26:52). The "fastest gun in the West" was a wanted man—wanted by every gunman who wanted the reputation of being the fastest. Likewise, the team that brags about being number one is the one other teams want to beat.

C. *The exercise of raw force inspires in its victims a yearning for real freedom.* When English officials used imprisonment in 1667 in an effort to force William Penn to give up Quaker views, he said, "The jail will be my grave before I'll change one jot. . . . The Tower was the worst argument to use against me; for whoever may be right or wrong, those who use force can never be right."

II. Most seek freedom through law.

A. *Civilized society cannot exist where each does what is right in his or her own eyes (Judg. 21:25), where personal whim and force are the only guides to social conduct.* One theme of human history is the futility of force, the law of the jungle. Another is the quest for rules or laws for ordering society.

B. *The Declaration of Independence is history's best-known statement of this quest; the US Constitution and its Bill of Rights are the most celebrated expressions of its achievement.* One states, the other assumes, that "the Laws of Nature and of Nature's God entitle" people to the equality to which all people are created; that government's purpose is to secure human rights; that government derives its just or lawful powers "from the consent of the governed"; that public officialdom, which is insensitive to human rights and humane laws—in 1776, a king—is a threat to freedom, as a train of twenty-seven abuses and usurpations proves; and that lovers of freedom through law look "to the Supreme Judge of the world for the rectitude of . . . intentions," rely "on the protection of divine Providence," and "pledge to each other . . . Lives . . . Fortune and . . . sacred Honor." The Constitution rests on the premise that government's powers are dangerous when concentrated, so it distributes them: the legislature has the power to make laws; the executive, to administer them; and the judiciary, to interpret them. The Bill of Rights rests on the premise that some rights are beyond the reach of government's power.

C. *The philosophy of freedom through law is, as President Gerald R. Ford phrased it in his inaugural address, that "right makes might"—that is, right laws are a beneficent force, essential to civil tranquility, domestic peace, and social harmony.*

D. *Law provides limited freedom at best.* It marks the boundaries within which one can operate freely but beyond which one cannot go. Often it appears in the negative: "Thou shalt not. . . ." For law to work, all must be equally subject to it; also, officials must administer it even-handedly. We are not free to obey the laws we like and transgress those we dislike. Whoever seeks freedom under law—whether it be the Jewish law, which Paul, in Galatians, contrasted with the gospel and viewed as a tutor preparing for the gospel, or some other law— "He is a debtor to do the whole law" (Gal. 5:3). Sometimes we yearn for more freedom than law can provide, and we feel like applying to law what the song applies to other things—"Don't Fence Me In."

E. *Anyone acquainted with the changing concept and practice of law in the last two and a half centuries cannot avoid the conclusion that law is capable of abuse and that it can be a force that tyrannizes peoples' persons and spirits.* Law is no better than those who make, execute, and interpret it, supported by people who have confidence both in the laws and in public officials. The US system rests on the view that God implanted a law in nature and that government's laws are to be consistent with it. In the mid-1800s, the "historical school" viewed law as the expression of folk custom, a view that served nationalism—one law for the English, another law for Germans, another law for the French, another law for Americans, and so on. Later the "analytical school" viewed law as something consciously created by lawyers, the state as the entity with sole power to create law, individual "rights" as nothing more than concessions granted by the state, and compulsion, not justice, as the criterion of law. Still later, the "pure theory" school emphasized the procedure by which the state enacts law, not the substance of law, as the clue to law; if lawmakers employ the "pure" procedure or form, law is valid, whatever its nature. Such a view of law provided the basis for several twentieth-century dictatorships, one of them being Adolf Hitler's Third Reich, which acted according to positive or government-made law in all matters but violated elemental laws of nature.

F. *However essential good laws, applied equally to all and administered even-handedly, are to ordered society, law cannot give people the full freedom for which they yearn.* So one prays as Katharine Lee Bates prayed for America: "God mend thine every flaw, confirm thy soul in self-control, thy liberty in law."

III. Anyone can find freedom in grace, available through faith and expressing itself in love.

a) *Freedom is available to anyone who believes in the gospel of Jesus Christ.* This is the theme of Galatians, a letter written in the heat of controversy between those who tried to make Gentile Christians observe Jewish Levitical and ceremonial laws (Judaizers) and those who insisted that God's grace, which leads one to believe in Jesus Christ, frees one from law's tyranny and liberates the spirit so that he or she can voluntarily accomplish only what law cannot achieve because of compulsion (Paul's party).

b) *Spiritual freedom can exist even when human law constricts.* When Paul wrote in prison, "I have learned, in whatsoever state I am [abasement or abundance], therewith to be content" (Phil. 4:11), he was a freer man than Emperor Nero, who was torn between his own ego drives and his fear of enemies. Madame Guyon, imprisoned by Louis XIV for ten years (1695–1705), said it well:

> My cage confines me round;
> Abroad I cannot fly;
> But though my wing is closely bound,
> My heart's at liberty.
> My prison walls cannot control the flight,
> The freedom of the soul.
> Stone walls do not a prison make,
> Nor iron bars a cage;
> Minds innocent and quiet take
> These for a hermitage;
> When I am free within my heart
> And in my soul am free,
> Angels alone that soar above
> Enjoy such liberty.

c) *Love is the companion of faith.* "There is no fear in love; but perfect love casteth out fear" (1 John 4:18). Where there is no fear, there is freedom.

d) *Love fulfills what law at its best can only aim at.* Law and officials are a terror to evil works, not to good works (Rom. 13:3). The ideal which the best of laws seeks to attain by observing negative prohibitions ("Thou shalt not . . .") is attained only by observing the positive demands of love: "Thou shalt love thy neighbor as thyself" (Gal. 5:14; Rom. 13:9).

e) *If the Son of God makes us free, we are free indeed (John 8:36)!* And from that time on, we are never the same. For, like our Master, we then minister as servants to others (Matt. 20:28).

Conclusion

If you want freedom, seek it where it can be found—not in force, however strong; not in law, however good; but in faith, which expresses itself in love.

SUNDAY EVENING, JUNE 28

Title: Christ—The Testator

Text: "How much more, then, will the blood of Christ, who through the eternal Spirit offered himself unblemished to God, cleanse our consciences from acts that lead to death, so that we may serve the living God!" **(Heb. 9:14 NIV)**.

Scripture Reading: Hebrews 9:1–28

Introduction

Technical aspects of instituting a new covenant are considered in this chapter. The author said, "Where a testament is, there must also of necessity be the death of the testator" (9:16). The testator is one who effects a covenant (testament). Each covenant has its own conditions for agreement, and these must be met for the covenant to be valid. Death on the testator's part is declared to be the condition of the covenant. Jesus Christ gave validity to the new covenant by his death.

To fully appreciate the Testator's ministry, one must have knowledge of the old covenant. The end result of the Testator's new covenant is the promise of an even greater relationship between God and humankind (9:28).

I. The old covenant (Heb. 9:1–10).

A wise minister always starts with a congregation where they are and brings them to the place where they ought to be. This is the approach of the author of the letter to the Hebrews. He begins with "the first covenant" and its "ordinances of divine service, and a worldly sanctuary" (9:1).

A. *Setting (9:2–5).* The writer to the Hebrews gives the physical setting of the tabernacle. The structure, its arrangement, and its furnishings are described in simple form.

B. *Procedure (9:6–7).* The writer also presents a brief description of the procedure used by the priests to administer the things of God. Emphasis is placed on the fact that the priest had to offer a sacrifice for himself as well as for the people.

C. *Meaning (9:8–10).* The first tabernacle was only a figure of the heavenly tabernacle. The entire system of Levitical sacrifice pointed to the need for a new covenant, since the way into the heavenly Holy of Holies was not yet made manifest. Another agreement between God and humankind was thus expected.

II. The new covenant (Heb. 9:11–28).

The new covenant was brought into being out of necessity. God's old covenant did not fail, but the people failed in their response to it.

A. *Founded on realism (9:11).* Christ came to establish the new covenant on "a greater and more perfect tabernacle." His ministry was not to be built on shadows, but on the realistic certainty of God.

B. *Founded on his blood (9:12–28).* The heart of the whole matter was the Testator's action. How was he to accomplish his mission? It had to be done through the shedding of his blood.

   1. Entered the Holy Place (9:12–13). Christ entered the Holy Place of God through his own blood and obtained our eternal redemption. He was the ultimate sacrifice.

   2. Purges the conscience (9:14). The Testator offered himself

flawless as a sacrifice for our sins. Because of this, we are able to have our consciences purged from dead works and inspired to serve the living God.

3. Seals the testament (9:15–23). Christ's sacrificial action on the cross met all demands for the new covenant. The tenet is given that "almost all things are by the law purged with blood; and without shedding of blood is no remission" (9:22). Jesus Christ shed his blood. As Testator he met the requirements of the new covenant, and he did so out of love for lost humanity.

4. Appears before God (9:24). The Testator did not minister before a man-made structure. But upon his death, he went "to appear in the presence of God for us."

5. One time sufficient (9:25–28). In contrast to the priests of the old covenant, the Testator of the new covenant needed to suffer only one time. "So Christ was once offered to bear the sins of many" (9:28).

III. The future relationship (Heb. 9:28).

The relationship of the future cannot be called a covenant because the Testator will not die again. Yet there is a glorious future for those who believe in Christ.

A. *Promise to the expectant.* A promise is given to those who expect future happiness through Christ.

B. *Present covenant involves sin.* The new covenant required Christ's death to deliver humankind from sin.

C. *Future relationship without sin.* The future relationship will not involve sin. Jesus will not come to minister to a sinful world. Rather, he will return to rescue his redeemed for eternity.

Conclusion

The horror of Jesus' death as Testator emphasizes his love and our shame. The hope of his second coming emphasizes his love and our honor.

JULY

■ **Sunday Mornings**

"Lessons from the Upper Room" is the theme for the Sunday morning messages this month.

■ **Sunday Evenings**

From the days when Adam and Eve were driven from the garden, people have been in need of a mediator who could bring them back to God. Jesus Christ is the one mediator between God and man. Complete the series of messages from the book of Hebrews titled "Jesus Christ as Our High Priest."

■ **Wednesday Evenings**

One of the great tragedies of life is the inability or the neglect of a father to pass on to his children the benefits of his experience. Fathers must instruct, warn, and encourage their children. Wednesday evening messages from John's first epistle are titled "The Counsel of a Spiritual Father to His Children." This series will continue through September 23.

WEDNESDAY EVENING, JULY 1

Title: The Christ We Preach

Text: "We proclaim to you what we have seen and heard, so that you also may have fellowship with us. And our fellowship is with the Father and with his Son, Jesus Christ" **(1 John 1:3 NIV)**.

Scripture Reading: 1 John 1:1–4

Introduction

First John is the most intimate letter in the New Testament. Although John touched on many fundamental doctrines and truths within the Christian faith, it was not his purpose to write a treatise, as was most often true with the apostle Paul. First John deals with family matters. We might compare it to a letter from a father to his small children who need to be encouraged, perhaps reprimanded, and mostly to be reminded that God is love and that they are to manifest God's love constantly through their lives.

Yet there was an immediate reason why John wrote this letter when he did. A group of so-called Christians known as Gnostics were perpetrating a heresy within the church. They were teaching that all matter is inherently evil, and God, being good, could have nothing to do with evil matter. Therefore they taught that God could not have been incarnate in the body of Jesus. They said that Jesus only appeared to have lived in the flesh, that he was nothing more than a phantom. To John this false teaching was taking the heart out of the Christian faith. So his letter is a manifesto—that is, it proclaims what was shown and proved in the life of Jesus Christ.

In the prologue to John's letter (1:1–4), he told us three things about Jesus, and then he developed these truths in the remainder of the letter.

I. John said that Jesus is the source of our life (1 John 1:1–2).

A. *John plunged into a series of proofs attesting to Jesus' humanity.* First, he said that he and his fellow disciples *heard* Jesus speak. The verb *heard* is in the perfect tense, which means they had heard Jesus not just one time, but repeatedly, and his words had been etched in their hearts.

B. *Next John declared that he had seen Jesus.* The word John used for "seen" means more than having received a visual image on the retina of the eye. It means that he had understood, perceived, discerned. Then John said, "which we have looked upon." Here he used another word that means to gaze at with wonder, awe, or reverence.

C. *Finally, John said that he had "handled" Jesus with his hands.* This is the word Jesus used after his resurrection to prove to his disciples that he was not a spirit but that he had a body (Luke 24:39). First John 1:2 is an expansion of what John said in verse 1. Jesus, the source of our life, has been manifested, and there is no way that his existence, death, or resurrection can be denied!

II. John said that Jesus is the subject of our preaching (1 John 1:3).

A. *In verse 1 John spoke of the "Word of life."* These words were the dawn that broke through the darkness of sin. But now the dawn became noonday splendor as John identified the Word of life as Jesus Christ, God's Son. And this Christ is the One whom we have seen with the eyes of our souls and heard through the living words of Scripture.

B. *John said something that shocked every God-fearing Jew who would not so much as pronounce the name of God.* He said, "Our fellowship is with the Father." How dare a sinful creature presume that he can fellowship with the almighty God of creation!

C. *The secret lay in the blessed intercessor, Jesus Christ.* He introduced people to God as "the Father." Our fellowship with God as heavenly Father comes through our relationship with his Son, Jesus Christ. Therefore Jesus, and Jesus alone, is the subject of our preaching.

III. John wrote about sharing our faith (1 John 1:4).

A. *Note the order here: Real joy comes after fellowship with God, his Son, and his children has been established.* This unique relationship enables us to experience true joy.

B. *Jesus desired that his followers have joyful hearts.* Never in the Bible are Christians instructed to be depressed or pessimistic. One of the goals Jesus had in mind as he taught his disciples was for them to experience joy (John 15:11).

C. *What was the joy that filled Jesus' soul?* It was the completion of our salvation (Heb. 12:2). Likewise, our joy is based on the finished work of Jesus on the cross. Salvation and joy are inseparable. This contagious joy adds an effective note to the sharing of our faith.

Conclusion

This is the Christ whom we preach. He is the source of our life, the subject of our preaching. Because of who he is, we share our faith so that others may know this joy unspeakable!

SUNDAY MORNING, JULY 5

Title: Upper Room Lessons on Love

Text: "A new command I give you: Love one another. As I have loved you, so you must love one another. By this everyone will know that you are my disciples, if you love one another" **(John 13:34–35 NIV)**.

Scripture Reading: John 13:31–38

Hymns: "Love Divine," Wesley
           "O God, Our Help in Ages Past," Watts
           "My Jesus, I Love Thee," Featherstone

Offertory Prayer: Our Father, we thank you for the gift of life. We realize that every breath we breathe is by your grace. We acknowledge our stewardship of the things you have placed in our care. The gifts we give today are simply a loving expression of our stewardship. We pray that the church will be wise in distributing these gifts for the maximum advancement of your kingdom. In Jesus' name. Amen.

Introduction

Today we enter into the sacred place of the upper room where Jesus instituted the Lord's Supper. Here Jesus taught his disciples just before his crucifixion (John 13–17), here the devil won a victory over Judas, here Jesus met with his disciples after the resurrection, and here the disciples prayed and the Holy Spirit set the fires of Pentecost. Our message will be confined to John 14–17, the account of Jesus' last evening with the Twelve.

We see in our reading that Jesus was facing the agony of the cross, and it is evident that the disciples were not ready for the work he was committing to them. They were dense, weak, jealous of one another, and hungry for power. Judas was struggling with Satan. The disciples still didn't understand about the Messiah or their mission (cf. Matt. 16). They had to learn quickly and adequately. The first lesson they needed to learn was the meaning of love (John 3:1–31)—Jesus' love and their love.

I. Jesus explained the relationship between love and service (John 13:1–5).

In the upper room during the passion meal, Jesus demonstrated his love. John 13:1 in the New International Version says, "Having loved his own who were in the world, he loved them to the end." His hour had come. Here was Jesus, "the Lamb slain before the foundation of the world," ready to die a redemptive death. He would soon no longer be with his disciples physically. He needed to show them that "He loved them [and continuously loves them with His perfect love] to the end (eternally)" (John 13:1 AMP). Compare Romans 5:6–8 and Ephesians 3:14–19. So Jesus did the work of a servant as he washed their feet. John 13:6–11 gives Peter's reaction, as he misunderstood the Master's actions.

Jesus then interpreted the meaning of his actions (13:13–17). A servant must not expect better treatment than his Lord. There is only one kind of greatness, the greatness of service—true humility. Our love is shown by our willingness to do whatever is necessary to advance Christ's kingdom—even if it involves humiliating service.

II. Jesus appealed to Judas with longsuffering love (John 13:18–30).

Judas must have been the perfect actor and the perfect hypocrite—he deceived everyone but Jesus. After revealing that a disciple would betray him, Jesus gave a morsel to Judas. To give a morsel at a meal was a mark of goodwill. Judas must have been on Jesus' left, the place of highest honor kept for the most intimate friend. Again and again Jesus must have quietly appealed to Judas, but Judas remained unmoved, impervious to this appeal of love. This scene beautifully displays the attitude Jesus expects us to have. Real Christlike love always seeks the best for everyone.

III. Jesus taught them that love meant going to the cross, which would be followed by great glory (John 13:31–33).

The disciples had to learn that the Christian way is not the easy way. To bring redemption to the world and glory to God, Jesus had to bear a cross. Soon the disciples would see Jesus dying on the cross, for he was now seen as a God who was not only concerned about people but was actually involved with people. God *would* glorify Jesus through the resurrection and his return to glory. And the disciples would often face a cross as they carried on Christ's work—and Jesus would glorify them.

IV. Jesus gave his disciples a command to love one another (John 13:34–35).

This was Jesus' farewell command. We are to keep on following his examples of love (agape).

Jesus loved his disciples selflessly and sacrificially. Sometimes we think love is meant to give us happiness. In the long run, it does, but it may bring pain or demand a cross. Jesus also loved his disciples understandingly. He knew them and he still loved them. Jesus loved his disciples forgivingly even when Peter later denied him and the others forsook him in his time of need. They were blind and insensitive, slow to learn, and lacking in understanding, but there was no failure in them that Jesus could not forgive. As he loved, so are we to love.

Conclusion

Jesus knew the future of the kingdom depended not on the brilliance and greatness of his followers, but on their loving one another as he loved them. So it is today. The first lesson in the upper room is love.

SUNDAY EVENING, JULY 5

Title: Christ—The Living God

Text: "Let us draw near to God with a sincere heart and with the full assurance that faith brings, having our hearts sprinkled to cleanse us from a guilty conscience and having our bodies washed with pure water" **(Heb. 10:22 NIV)**.

Scripture Reading: Hebrews 10:1–39

Introduction

People with spiritual perception are aware of two major activities of God: he expresses his love in many ways, yet he also expresses his displeasure and wrath to those who reject him. The author of Hebrews was aware of God's wrathful activity. He wrote, "It is a fearful thing to fall into the hands of the living God" (Heb. 10:31).

The Scripture passage under consideration reveals several things that the living God does for and to humankind.

I. Cancels out the old (Heb. 10:1–8).

As noted in earlier passages of Hebrews, Christ canceled out the old covenant and ushered in the new covenant.

A. *A shadow only (10:1).* The old covenant was only a shadow of the good things yet to come. A type may represent but never replace the real thing.

B. *Needed repeating (10:2–3).* The sacrificial system under the old covenant did not satisfy once and for all. Sacrifices had to be offered repeatedly.

C. *Faulty offering (10:4–6).* The very fact that people had to offer sacrifices for sin hurt God. He first desires obedience from people, not sacrifice.

D. *Built on law (10:7–8).* The old covenant was built on the foundation of law. God established the new covenant on the law of grace and love.

Jesus canceled out the old covenant by fulfilling it in the establishment of the new covenant.

II. Conquers by the new (Heb. 10:9–17).

The way Christ conquered the old covenant was to bring in the new covenant.

A. *Doer of God's will (10:9).* Jesus sought to follow God's will his entire life. This involved making a new covenant.

B. *God's will sanctifies (10:10).* The major objective of God's will was to provide salvation for everyone who would accept it. We are set apart for God as a result of Jesus' ultimate sacrifice.

C. *One sacrifice satisfies (10:11–12).* The fact that the single sacrifice of Christ was sufficient is so important that it is repeated over and over.

D. *Enemies conquered (10:13).* Though a minister of concern and love, Jesus' actions brought his enemies into subjection.

E. *Sins banished (10:14–17).* When Christ establishes the new covenant within believers' hearts, he no longer remembers their sin.

III. Charges up the believers (Heb. 10:18–25).

Any courage not received from God is a faulty courage. The living God encourages Christians in their daily walk.

A. *Boldness to enter (10:18–21).* When sin is conquered, all guilt and shame are stripped from the soul. In its place comes a boldness to enter the intimate presence of God.

B. *Draw near in assurance (10:22).* Godly courage instills assurance in his children's hearts.

C. *Hold fast in profession (10:23).* Steadfastness is developed in believers' lives. Through faith they remain true to God's calling.

D. *Exhorting one another (10:24–25).* When people set things right between themselves and God, they are then more able and willing to share with others.

IV. Challenges the sinners (Heb. 10:26–31).

Sinners will never be able to elude God's condemnation and wrath. They will be "dressed down" by the almighty God.

A. *Deliberate sin (10:26).* Sinning on purpose will draw God's anger.

B. *No more sacrifice (10:26).* If someone rejects the sacrifice of Christ, God has no other system of sacrifice to offer for that person's sins.

C. *God's alternative (10:27–30).* God warns rebellious people about his jealous anger. His divine vengeance threatens those who desecrate "the blood of the covenant."

D. *Message of sobriety (10:31).* The living God is to be feared by unbelievers.

V. Compliments the attainers (Heb. 10:32–37).

Jesus does not forget his beloved followers. He comforts those who obey him in faith.

A. *Past illumination (10:32).* Listen to the master artisan as he tenderly points out deeds of the past apprentice.
B. *Past endurance (10:32–33).* He is gracious to remind those under trial of their former glories and victories.
C. *Past compassion (10:34).* The living God made note of the compassion his followers had previously shown to others.
D. *Present needs (10:35–36).* God's will involves immediate solutions to present needs.
E. *Future expectations (10:37).* God's greatest act will be seen in Christ's physical return to redeem his people.

Conclusion (Heb. 10:38–39)

The challenge for Martin Luther was "the just shall live by faith." This spiritual formula is still reaching people for Jesus Christ.

WEDNESDAY EVENING, JULY 8

Title: The Center of the Circle

Text: "If we walk in the light, as he is in the light, we have fellowship one with another, and the blood of Jesus Christ his Son cleanseth us from all sin" (**1 John 1:7**).

Scripture Reading: 1 John 1:5–10

Introduction

"Light" is a favorite word of John's—used not only in his letters, but also in his gospel. He saw God and light as inseparable. He literally illuminated his letters and gospel with light as again and again he used that symbolism for God and truth.

As we consider 1 John 1:5–10, we find that John, in effect, drew a circle with God at the center. He is the source of the light that fills the circle; darkness, with its evil, is beyond the circumference of the circle. Then, with the compassion typical of his great heart, John invited sinful humanity, by nature prisoners of darkness, to enter the circle of light and approach God at its center.

I. Let's examine the light and its source (1 John 1:5).

A. *Where do we find the first manifestation of God as "light"?* We must flip back to Genesis 1:3: "God said, Let there be light: and there was light." What preceded that light? The emptiest, most hopeless scene the human mind could ever conjure. The author of Genesis wrote,

"The earth was without form, and void; and darkness was upon the face of the deep" (1:2). Then what happened? God's very presence, which is light, enveloped that murky chaos and creation began.

B. *Listen to John's words in the prologue of his gospel.* "In him was life; and the life was the light of men. And the light shineth in darkness; and the darkness comprehended it not" (John 1:4–5). The Old Testament revelations of God as light were but fingers pointing to the perfect revelation of God in his Son, Jesus Christ.

C. *What did people see when Jesus came to earth?* As their eyes were opened to the truth, they saw his glory. And what was that glory? The glory of the Father in heaven, and that glory was overflowing with grace and truth. That "light," which is synonymous with Jesus, pierced the darkness, and evil forces of darkness tried in every way to put out his light. But they could not! Even when Jesus was dying on the cross and they thought his light would fade away, it shone all the brighter, for it lightened the dark chasm that had separated people from God. So the Bible's victory shout is, "God is light, and in him is no darkness at all"!

II. Let's discover the darkness and its expression (I John 1:6, 8, 10).

A. *Whenever Scripture says that people walk in "darkness," it refers to sin—that which separates people from God.* In verse 6 John declares that if anyone claims to have fellowship with God while simultaneously living in habitual sin, he is a liar in both word and deed. The tense of the verb "walk" speaks of habitual action, something done repeatedly as a lifestyle. Christians may temporarily step into darkness, but because of their new nature, they are miserable until they return to the light.

B. *John teaches an elementary lesson in verse 8.* The very first step to God that a sinner must take, which is the hardest step of all, is to say, "I am a sinner." Such an admission goes against the grain of human nature. Yet anyone who refuses to admit that he or she walks in darkness is without hope in this world and in the world to come. Note also that the word is "sin," and not "sins." God is not so much interested in an unbeliever's specific acts of sin as he is in the sinful human nature that separates the unbeliever from God.

C. *Verse 10 contains John's most serious statement regarding sin and its expression in human nature.* A person who says that he or she does not sin is calling God a liar, for as Paul said, "All have sinned, and come short of the glory of God" (Rom. 3:23). Such a deceived person does not comprehend God's truth at all.

III. Let's hear the invitation and its results (I John 1:7, 9).

A. *The word "walk" expresses habitual action.* Someone who has formed the habit of daily walking "in the light" as Jesus is in the light gives evidence of a radical change in lifestyle. No longer is there a compatibility with darkness in daily conduct. In verse 7 John teaches an amazing reciprocity: Not only can we have fellowship with God, but he can have fellowship with us!

B. *In verse 9 John tells Christians what to do about sin in their lives.* They are not to despair nor to believe that they will be lost again because they have sinned. Rather, they are to confess their sins. Unbelievers are instructed to "believe" (John 3:16), but Christians have already believed. When they sin, they are to "confess"—agree with God about their sins. As a result, God will "forgive us our sins, and . . . cleanse us from all unrighteousness." John was talking about receiving forgiveness after committing a specific sin. After Christians confess, fellowship is restored and God cleanses them from all defilement accompanying the sin.

Conclusion

A circle of fellowship is illumined by God's pure light. In the circle's center is Jesus Christ. When we repent of our sin and believe that Jesus died for our sin and rose from the dead, we are admitted to that circle. We do not become perfect. Sometimes we wander to the circumference and temporarily step into darkness. But all is not lost! There is a way back to the center of the circle.

SUNDAY MORNING, JULY 12

Title: Upper Room Lessons on Heaven

Text: "Do not let your hearts be troubled. You believe in God; believe also in me. My Father's house has many rooms; if that were not so, would I have told you that I am going to prepare a place for you? And if I go and prepare a place for you, I will come back and take you to be with me that you also may be where I am. You know the way to the place where I am going" **(John 14:1–4 NIV).**

Scripture Reading: John 14:1–15

Hymns: "Guide Me, O Thou Great Jehovah," Williams
"The Wayfaring Stranger," Old Southern Melody
"Face to Face," Breck

Offertory Prayer: Our Father, we are humbled before you as we think of the provisions you have made for us. We acknowledge your wondrous love that prompted you to send your only Son to procure eternal life for us. We do not give today to earn salvation, but we give out of gratitude for our salvation and so that Christ may be shared with others. In Jesus' name. Amen.

Introduction

We often face the age-old question of life after death. Deep down in every heart this question must be answered in order for one to prepare to live.

Historian and essayist Ernest Renan said, "The day in which the belief in the afterlife shall vanish from the earth will witness a terrific moral and spiritual decadence. There is no lever capable of raising an entire people if once they have lost faith in the immortality of the soul."

The story is told that when the gospel was first carried into Britain by the messengers of the cross, a striking incident took place at the court of Edwin, the king of Northumbria. The great hall was lighted with torches and a crowd had gathered to hear what the teachers of this new religion had to say. A grim earl asked, "Can the new religion tell us what lies beyond death? Man comes out of the mystery of eternity, passes through the light of this world, and disappears into the mystery of eternity beyond. Does this new religion tell us what lies beyond death?" Job asked this same question. And in the New Testament, Paul gave the answer: "Christ Jesus . . . has destroyed death and has brought life and immortality to light through the gospel" (2 Tim. 1:10 NIV).

Jesus' disciples were also troubled about what happened after death, for Jesus had been telling them that he was going to die on a cross and that the Father would glorify him. In the Gospel of John, Jesus said, "My children, I will be with you only a little longer. You will look for me, and just as I told the Jews, so I tell you now: Where I am going, you cannot come" (13:33 NIV).

In John 13:36 Peter asked Jesus, "Where are you going?" John 14 is Jesus' answer. He sought to comfort his disciples about what was soon to take place. He wanted to strengthen them for the difficult times in their future. He promised them a home with him forever.

Now let's note five simple facts.

I. Jesus called for his disciples' trust.

Jesus never promised his disciples an easy way of life. In fact, he told them that following him would bring many difficulties.

> "I am sending you out like sheep among wolves. Therefore be as shrewd as snakes and as innocent as doves. Be on your guard; you will be handed over to the local councils and be flogged in the synagogues. On my account you will be brought before governors and kings as witnesses to them and to the Gentiles. But when they arrest you, do not worry about what to say or how to say it. At that time you will be given what to say, for it will not be you speaking, but the Spirit of your Father speaking through you.
>
> "Brother will betray brother to death, and a father his child; children will rebel against their parents and have them put to death. You will be hated by everyone because of me, but the one who stands firm to the end will be saved." (Matt. 10:16–22 NIV)

Jesus also said, "Whoever wants to be my disciple must deny themselves and take up their cross and follow me" (Matt. 16:24 NIV).

But at the same time, Jesus informed his disciples that their trials would be worth it all. And as we go through hardships in this life, we must keep our eyes on Jesus and completely trust him.

II. Jesus pointed out his function.

"I am going there to prepare a place for you." Jesus was blazing the way for the disciples. He cleared the way so they could follow in his steps. The author of Hebrews spoke of Jesus as "our forerunner" (6:20), a word translated from the Greek *prodromes*. In the Roman army, the *prodromoi* were the reconnaissance troops. They went ahead of the main body to blaze the trail and make it safe for others to follow. Jesus explained to his disciples that he was blazing the way to heaven so his disciples could follow in his steps. And his resurrection and ascension prove his point.

III. Jesus encouraged his disciples by telling of his ultimate triumph.

"I will come back. . . ." History will have a consummation—that being Jesus' final victory.

Listen to Revelation 1:4–8:

> John,
> To the seven churches in the province of Asia:
> Grace and peace to you from him who is, and who was, and who is to come, and from the seven spirits before his throne, and from Jesus Christ, who is the faithful witness, the firstborn from the dead, and the ruler of the kings of the earth.
>
> To him who loves us and has freed us from our sins by his blood, and has made us to be a kingdom and priests to serve his God and Father—to him be glory and power for ever and ever! Amen.
>
> "Look, he is coming with the clouds,"
>   and "every eye will see him,
> even those who pierced him";
>   and all peoples on earth "will mourn because of him."
>   So shall it be! Amen.
>
> "I am the Alpha and the Omega," says the Lord God, "who is, and who was, and who is to come, the Almighty." (NIV)

IV. Jesus promised his disciples that they will be with him forever.

In Revelation 21:1–4 (NIV) John said:

> Then I saw "a new heaven and a new earth," for the first heaven and the first earth had passed away, and there was no longer any sea. I saw the Holy City, the new Jerusalem, coming down out of heaven from God, prepared as a bride beautifully dressed for her husband. And I heard a loud voice from the throne saying, "Look! God's dwelling place is now among the people, and he will dwell with

214

them. They will be his people, and God himself will be with them and be their God. He will wipe every tear from their eyes. There will be no more death or mourning or crying or pain, for the old order of things has passed away."

V. Jesus told his disciples that he is the way to heaven (John 14:4–6).

Jesus is the way—the only way. Jesus is the truth—the only truth. Jesus is the life—the only life. Jesus alone is the way to the Father. He alone can lead us into God's presence without shame or fear.

Conclusion

Jesus' promise to prepare a place for us is made certain by his resurrection. In a way, Jesus' resurrection is the pledge of our own resurrection. We are linked to him forever.

Long ago I read these memorable lines:

> When I am to die,
> "Receive me," I'll cry,
> For Jesus has loved me,
> I cannot tell why;
> But this I do find,
> We two are so joined,
> He can't be in heaven,
> And me left behind.

One day Jesus will fulfill the promise of the Scriptures. "You will fill me with joy in your presence, with eternal pleasures at your right hand" (Ps. 16:11 NIV). He has gone to prepare a place for us, and he is preparing us for the place.

SUNDAY EVENING, JULY 12

Title: Faith—Way of a Good Report

Text: "These were all commended for their faith, yet none of them received what had been promised. God had planned something better for us so that only together with us would they be made perfect" **(Heb. 11:39–40 NIV).**

Scripture Reading: Hebrews 11:1–40

Introduction

Every believer wants to have a good report before the Lord. The author of Hebrews declares that through faith believers are given a good standing before God. What is faith? It may be defined as the foundation of hope. It is the evidence of those many features of life (trust, love, fidelity, and so on) that go unseen by the physical eye (11:1).

This chapter is a compilation of teachings on faith. Faith helps believers obtain good reports in several matters (11:2).

I. In matters pleasing to God (Heb. 11:3–6).

Faith is necessary for God to be pleased. This is true as we try to comprehend life.

A. *An acceptable creation (11:3).* The Bible says that God created the world (Gen. 1:1; John 1:3). Through faith we accept this fact. The author presents a fascinating detail that "things which are seen were not made of things which do appear." God created something out of nothing. Only God could do that.

B. *An acceptable sacrifice (11:4).* The story of Cain and Abel is repeated to teach what kind of sacrifice is acceptable to God.

C. *An acceptable life (11:5).* The mystery surrounding Enoch's departure is used to illustrate the part faith plays in a life acceptable to God.

D. *Summary statements (11:6).* This is one of the most powerful verses in Scripture. It speaks of the absolute, essential nature of faith. Faith is necessary even for a simple belief in God.

II. In matters prepared by God (Heb. 11:7–16).

God uses circumstances to test believers' faith. It is not uncommon for believers to experience difficulty. In each of the following instances God prepared a test for his followers.

A. *A universal flood (11:7).* God allowed a flood to test a whole generation. Noah responded in faith and survived.

B. *A strange land (11:8–10).* Abraham was called by God to leave the security of home and travel to a strange land. By faith he was given a new land.

C. *A closed womb (11:11–12).* God had promised Abraham that he would become a great nation, yet Sarah, Abraham's wife, was not able to bear a child. Through faith this difficulty was overcome.

D. *Summary statements (11:13–16).* Strangers and pilgrims survived the earthly trek because, by faith, they desired a better country where God would be called their God.

III. In matters preserved in God (Heb. 11:17–22).

God places a protective arm about certain aspects of the Christian's experience. He does not depend on humans for certain matters.

A. *A hope in resurrection (11:17–19).* The hope of resurrection is always instigated by God. Abraham had faith that God would raise his son Isaac from the dead if the sacrifice of the child was necessary.

B. *A hope in blessing (11:20).* People may help us in times of need, but real spiritual blessings come from God as we put our faith in him.

C. *A hope in worship (11:21).* No worship is valid unless the person involved is exercising faith in the one true God.

D. *A hope in death (11:22).* Human strength ends at death. Faith in God and in Jesus Christ provides hope for eternal life after death.

IV. In matters proposed by God (Heb. 11:23–38).

When God promises victory, he makes a way for it to be attained. We gain the good report of victory only through faith.

A. *A conquering of fear (11:23–28).* God desired for Moses to conquer his fears and live a triumphant life. Through faith Moses was enabled to defeat fear and uncertainty.

B. *A conquering of adversaries (11:29–30).* Many things blocked Israel's progress from Egypt to the promised land. These obstacles were overcome by faith.

C. *A conquering of circumstances (11:31).* Rahab had a sinful occupation. But through faith in God she was given a very responsible position in biblical history.

D. *Summary statements (11:32–38).* An overwhelming list of saints is presented, bearing testimony that the way of a good report is by faith.

Conclusion

Although each of these recorded saints had received a good report by faith, the new covenant in Jesus Christ promised even more (Heb. 11:39–40).

WEDNESDAY EVENING, JULY 15

Title: Establishing the Fellowship

Text: "My little children, these things write I unto you, that ye sin not. And if any man sin, we have an advocate with the Father, Jesus Christ the righteous" (**1 John 2:1**).

Scripture Reading: 1 John 2:1–2

Introduction

Paul said in his letter to the Ephesians, "For it is by grace you have been saved, through faith—and this not from yourselves, it is the gift of God—not by works, so that no one can boast" (Eph. 2:8–9 NIV). This is perhaps the simplest yet most profound statement in the Bible in regard to the new birth. However, Satan, in his sinister determination to distort every truth in God's Word, has caused many to think that God's grace is cheap permission for a Christian to sin.

In other words, Satan tries to tell people, "You could never meet God's standards. Why even try?" Or else he says, "God is a loving heavenly Father, and he understands your human weakness. Don't take sinning so seriously. God will always forgive." Either of these attitudes toward sin in a Christian's life will produce a devastating effect. It will destroy fellowship with God and will prevent a Christian from growing and maturing in the faith. Inevitably these attitudes will cause a Christian to doubt his or her salvation and relationship with Christ.

Therefore, in the first two verses of chapter 2, John talked about "establishing the fellowship" that should exist between God and his people.

I. John declared that the privilege is shared by all believers.

A. *"My little children . . ." (2:1).* Note the sudden change in John's manner. Up to this point in his letter, he had maintained a certain formality. He used the form "we" instead of the personal "I." He laid down some very positive guidelines regarding darkness and light—sin and righteousness. He plainly said that Christians must confess their sins—there is no "blanket forgiveness" provided for Christians even though they are children of God. Their sins must be dealt with individually and specifically.

B. *John called his readers "little children" six times throughout his letter.* Jesus also used this phrase when he was talking to his disciples. Children are usually teachable, and little children are even more in need of careful guidance. So, in essence, John told the recipients of his letter, "Little children, as God has spoken to me, let me lead you step-by-step through this business of dealing with sin in your lives and establishing and maintaining fellowship with your heavenly Father."

II. John introduced the prohibition in this personal relationship.

A. *"These things write I unto you, that ye sin not" (2:1).* The verb tense that John used concerning sin has much significance. The verb tense in "If any man sin," suggests committing a certain sin at a certain time. John was not talking about habitual sinning. In other words, John considered sin in a Christian's life not as recurrent but as unusual and definitely infrequent.

B. *So John basically said, "Don't fall into sin.* Avoid it like the plague. But *if you do* become trapped by Satan in a weak moment, don't give up! Don't think that all is lost!" Satan has deluded many Christians into believing that they cannot live victoriously because they seem to succumb so easily to certain temptations. Sometimes they give in and resign themselves to lives of spiritual defeat. This is just as Satan would have it. Many Christians sit on the sidelines because they have convinced themselves that they cannot live a meaningful Christian life.

III. John revealed the provision God has made for his children.

A. *"We have an advocate with the Father, Jesus Christ the righteous" (2:1).* This is one of the most comforting statements in the entire letter. The word "advocate," in this context, means "one called to your side." It was used to indicate a legal counsel, one who undertakes the cause of another. Yet there was a far deeper meaning when the word was applied to Jesus, seated in heaven at the right hand of the Father. In his relationship to us, he is not just a legal counsel, for we are his! He died on a cross for us; he redeemed us with his blood.

B. *John said that we have an advocate "with the Father."* The word "with" literally means "facing." Our advocate is facing the Father in heaven when he pleads our cause. This means that he is always in fellowship with the Father to plead the cause of Christians who have sinned.

C. *In verse 2 John reminded us of a basic truth: that Jesus "is the propitiation for our sins."* The word "propitiation" has a simple meaning. The guilt of sin separated people from God. On the cross, Jesus assumed that guilt and paid the penalty with his own blood. He removed the cause of alienation between God and humankind. Jesus satisfied the demands of God's broken law. "Propitiation," then, simply means "satisfaction."

Conclusion

In essence, John was warning Christians against sin. Satan is ever waiting for opportunities to tempt and seduce God's people. Sometimes we fall victim to his wiles. When we do, a loving and understanding God has made provision. Jesus is our advocate; he will, upon our repentance, plead our cause before the Father and restore broken fellowship.

SUNDAY MORNING, JULY 19

Title: Upper Room Lessons on Jesus' Promises

Text: "Don't you believe that I am in the Father, and that the Father is in me? The words I say to you I do not speak on my own authority. Rather, it is the Father, living in me, who is doing his work" **(John 14:10 NIV).**

Scripture Reading: John 14:7–31

Hymns: "Holy, Holy, Holy," Heber
"Standing on the Promises," Carter
"'Tis So Sweet to Trust in Jesus," Stead

Offertory Prayer: Dear Lord, we thank you for fulfilling the promise that we would have the living presence of Jesus in our daily walk in life. As we give our tithes and offerings today, we pray for those who serve on the mission fields of the world. Help us to be faithful in our living, in our giving, and in our witnessing. In Jesus' name. Amen.

Introduction

Jesus had been preparing the disciples for his imminent departure, and he told them why he was going—to prepare a place for them (John 14:2). His assurance of coming back for them calmed their hearts, but at the same time they wondered how they would cope during his absence. Every day Jesus had been with them answering their questions, directing their thoughts, settling their arguments, and strengthening them by his presence. Now he would be leaving them. They would be like helpless orphans. As a partial explanation, Jesus told his disciples, "You know the way to the place where I am going" (14:4 NIV). But Thomas asked, "Lord, we don't know where you are going, so how can we know the way?" (14:5 NIV).

Jesus gave a more complete answer, which contains many promises.

I. The promise of knowing the Father through Jesus (John 4:5–11).

If you know Jesus, you know God. The knowledge of Jesus that stops with the man and the martyr, the teacher and the brother, is only a partial knowledge of him. In Jesus we see the Father.

You probably have seen a little boy who looked, talked, and walked like his father. What do you say about the boy? You likely remark, "He is the spitting image of his daddy." To see Jesus is to see the Father.

If you want to know how God feels about fallen humanity, see Jesus as he talked with the woman at the well. If you want to know how God feels about those who are sick and suffering, see Jesus healing the blind, the crippled, and the leper. If you want to know how God feels about grief, see Jesus at the tomb of Lazarus. If you want to know how God feels about children, listen to Jesus say, "Let the little children come to me" (Luke 18:16 NIV). If you want to know how God feels about sinners, see Jesus dealing with Zacchaeus in Luke 19:1–10.

II. The promise of greater works (John 14:12–14).

The disciples had seen Jesus do many miraculous works, but he encouraged them by saying that they would do even greater works. Did they? Yes, look at what happened on the day of Pentecost. Jesus wanted them to know that his power would reside in them.

III. The promise of a helper, the Holy Spirit (John 14:15–24).

Jesus promised not to leave the disciples as helpless orphans. He promised that through the Spirit he would come to them. He promised them an abiding presence that would bring love and obedience (14:21–24; cf. Acts 1–3; 1 Cor. 3:16–17).

IV. The promise of blessings through the Holy Spirit (John 14:25–26).

Jesus promised the Holy Spirit as the Advocate (v. 26). An advocate is one who is summoned to assist someone in a court of justice. The Advocate was to be Christ's representative—in his place. He would guide the disciples into truth and help them recall everything Jesus had told them (v. 26). During the events that unfolded in the lives of the apostles, they did remember the words that Jesus had spoken to them before his crucifixion—and they understood them in a new light.

V. The promise of peace (John 14:27–31).

Jesus did not promise his disciples that their lives would be easy. The peace Jesus promised was a triumphant overcoming of difficulties and problems. The world thinks of peace as being where there is no pain or sorrow—a peace of escape. The peace Jesus gives is *shalom*, which means everything that makes for our highest good. It is a peace that is independent of our outward circumstances.

Archibald Rutledge visited an old man living alone in an isolated area. He said to the man, "You must mind being all alone like this." The old man looked up and answered, "Mr. Rutledge, I'm not exactly alone. I miss all who are gone, but I'm not alone."

Rutledge replied, "Someone else has been here to see you then—I'm mighty glad to hear it."

"Captain," said the old man, "you know who I mean. He was my first Friend in life and he will be my last—same as he is to you. Jesus doesn't come to see me; he stays with me all the time. I'm not lonely."

The abiding presence of Jesus in your life brings peace.

Conclusion

Today by faith you can appropriate the promises Jesus made to the disciples in the upper room.

SUNDAY EVENING, JULY 19

Title: An Exhortation to Remember

Text: "Therefore, since we are surrounded by such a great cloud of witnesses, let us throw off everything that hinders and the sin that so easily entangles, and let us run with perseverance the race marked out for us" **(Heb. 12:1 NIV)**.

Scripture Reading: Hebrews 12:1–29

Introduction

In the letter to the Hebrews, the new covenant through the person of Jesus Christ has been introduced. The last two chapters of Hebrews are messages of exhortation. Four special exhortations are found in chapter 12: readers are encouraged to heed a race to be run, a chastisement to be endured, a challenge to be accepted, and a city to be experienced.

I. A race to be run (Heb. 12:1–4).

The Christian life may be compared to an athletic contest that takes place in a major arena. The Christian is the athlete, and the Christian life is the contest.

A. *The witnesses (12:1).* The race is to be run in an arena before many spectators who share an unusual feature. Just as the race is a test of faith, so all who witness it are people of victorious faith. The great "cloud of witnesses" refers to the people of faith who are noted in chapter 11.

B. *The race (12:1).* Preparations must be made for the race. Just before the starting gun is sounded, the runner must remove the training weights. In the case of this race, these are the sins that "so easily beset us." The runner's conduct during the race must be that of patient endurance. The course is planned by someone else, and the runner is faulted if he or she moves out of the designated field.

C. *The example (12:2–3).* Young athletes study the forms and mannerisms of those who have succeeded in their field. So we study the life of Jesus Christ. He is the pinnacle of spiritual success. He both authored and finished our faith. If we are to live by faith, we must study him with the desire to be like him.

D. *The goal (12:4).* The goal of all Christians is to so resist sin and temptation that they will shed blood if necessary to be successful.

II. A chastisement to be endured (Heb. 12:5–11).

Discipline plays an essential role in rearing a child. It is also necessary in a Christian's spiritual development. Believers are challenged to endure chastisement from the Lord.

A. *The fact (12:5).* The Lord disciplines his own. Chastisement is part of the parent-child relationship.

B. *The reason (12:6–8).* God chastens his children because he loves them. Parents must share their experiences with their children. Discipline is a system that encourages children to respond to their parents. This applies to our relationship with the heavenly Father.

C. *The result (12:9–11).* God disciplines us so that we may profit from his experiences. He wants us to partake of his holiness.

III. A challenge to be accepted (Heb. 12:12–21).

The heart of exhortation is the challenge to be victorious in daily living. The readers are encouraged to have the proper walk, attitude, and guide.

A. *Proper walk (12:12–13).* Circumstances tend to push believers toward defeat, but they are exhorted to strengthen their feeble hands and knees. The readers are encouraged to help other believers who have faltered so that the fallen may be healed.

B. *Proper attitude (12:14–15).* Three relationships are given in this passage. Individuals must seek to maintain peace with others. They must always be aware of God's grace. And they must protect themselves against bitterness.

C. *Proper guide (12:16–21).* Some allow fleshly impulses to guide their steps, as did Esau; others choose to follow the way of God, as did Moses.

IV. A city to be experienced (Heb. 12:22–27).

In this passage believers are given a glimpse of their glorious future.

A. *Heavenly scene (12:22–24).* The heavenly scene is depicted as Mount Zion. There is the city of the living God, the heavenly Jerusalem, and a vast company of angels. Praise his name!

B. *Earthly acceptance (12:25).* The readers are exhorted to accept this heavenly scene as a future reality. The materialism of this world often obscures future hopes unless faith in Jesus Christ intervenes.

C. *Godly judgment (12:25–27).* The author warned of God's judgment to seal the great truths of Christianity in the readers' minds.

Conclusion

Verses 28 and 29 challenge believers to serve God acceptably with godly fear and reverence. This exhortation is emphasized by yet another reminder of God's awesomeness.

WEDNESDAY EVENING, JULY 22

Title: The Tests of Fellowship

Text: "We know that we have come to know him if we obey his commands. . . . Anyone who claims to be in the light but hates his brother or sister is still in the darkness" **(1 John 2:3, 9 NIV)**.

Scripture Reading: 1 John 2:3–14

Introduction

As a preface to his instructions concerning irrefutable proof of one's abiding fellowship with God in Christ, John exhorted believers to avoid sin and be conscious of Satan's ever-present efforts to tempt and seduce children of God. But realizing that the sinful nature is still present with us even though our souls are redeemed, John reminded his readers that all is not lost when we sin. God has made provision, through the advocacy of Jesus, our great High Priest, who is seated at God's right hand in heaven. With that incomparable truth established, John proceeded to set forth two tests that will prove that a person has fellowship with God.

I. The first test is that of obeying God's commands (1 John 2:3).

A. *"Know" is a very special word.* It is more than just being acquainted with someone. It describes a continuing relationship that has deepened and become more intimate because of experiences shared. We might illustrate this way: Here is an individual whom you and I met at the same time on the same day. We made his acquaintance, learned his name, and perhaps discovered something about him. A relationship was established. But then I went away and never saw that person again. On the other hand, you cultivated the relationship. You saw this individual almost every day. You became fast friends and shared many experiences together. Both of us know this person, but my knowledge of him is only as a passing acquaintance. You really know him because you have experienced life situations together. This is the knowledge of God to which John referred.

B. *How can we be sure that we know Christ?* By a natural desire to keep his commands. John was not indicating a dutiful act of obedience, as a slave obeys his master, with no feeling. Rather, he was advocating obedience based on who Jesus is and who he has become to us. John was talking about constantly keeping or guarding God's Word. This requires daily meditation on Scripture.

C. *In verse 5 John said that whenever someone takes God's message to heart, the love of God has reached its full stature in that person.* Jesus said, "If ye love me, keep my commandments" (John 14:15). Love, in its very essence, is a reciprocal experience. The perfect ideal of love involves two parties. We must express love to another, and that person in turn must respond with love. This is what John meant when he said that when we obey God's Word, we are responding to the love that has caused God to reach out to us in the first place.

II. The second test is that of loving one another (1 John 2:9).

A. *We must clearly understand the kind of love to which John referred.* He was not talking about the affection we have for those whom we like and with whom we have things in common. Loving those who are lovable requires no effort. John was talking about the kind of love expressed by the word *agape*, self-sacrificing love that does not first consider whether that love will be returned. Its interest is entirely for the well-being of the person to whom the love is expressed.

B. *How do we love others who are not lovable or those who are hostile or insulting or offensive?* It happens naturally, spontaneously, because it comes out of the overflow of love produced in our hearts because of our obedience to God's Word. If we obey God's Word, he will fill us to overflowing with his love—and it is with *that* love that we will automatically love others.

C. *John added, almost as an afterthought, that when a Christian loves others, he has no "occasion of stumbling in him" (2:10).* In other words, when we show love to others, no stumbling blocks are in our way to keep us from growing in grace, from advancing from glory to glory in our Christian lives.

Conclusion

Two things, inseparably related, assure us of continued fellowship with God: first, a habitual obedience to God through the keeping of his commands; and second, a habitual loving of others, which becomes the natural outflow of our obedience to God.

SUNDAY MORNING, JULY 26

Title: Upper Room Lessons on Relationships

Text: "I am the vine; you are the branches. If you remain in me and I in you, you will bear much fruit; apart from me you can do nothing" **(John 15:5 NIV)**.

Scripture Reading: John 15:1–27

Hymns: "Come, Thou Fount," Robinson
"More Love to Thee," Prentiss
"I Surrender All," Van de Venter

Offertory Prayer: Loving Father, you loved us even before we were born. We thank you for loving us through our earthly family and through your church. We thank you for sending your Son to show your love by dying on a cross for us. We thank you for your Holy Spirit who draws us ever closer to you. We thank you for bringing us to this house of worship today that we might adore you and receive the blessings you have for us. We come now bringing our tithes and offerings as tokens of our love and expressions of our desire to share with you in your work of blessing people everywhere. Through Jesus Christ our Lord we pray. Amen.

Introduction

Slip into the upper room where Jesus and his disciples are spending their last moments before Jesus' arrest and crucifixion. First, put yourself in Jesus' place. Suppose you are about to leave your disciples and you must give them last-minute instructions on how to carry on your work—and they are slow learners. What would you say to them? Or suppose that you are one of those disciples and you are heartbroken at the thought of your Lord going away. You are confused, frustrated, and overwhelmed by all that is happening.

In the upper room, Jesus tells his disciples that they must not only understand the meaning of love, but they must love one another as he has loved them. He promises them a home forever with him. In the meantime, he will be with them every step of the journey. In their future hours of discouragement, they will remember his gracious promises. He wants them to comprehend the blessings, privileges, and responsibilities resulting from their personal relationship with him.

I. The disciples' relationship with Christ (John 15:1–11).

A. *Jesus used many metaphors to illustrate himself, his work, and relationships.* For example: light, John 8:12; door, John 10:7; shepherd, John 10:11; vine, John 15:1.

B. *Jesus said, "I am the vine; you are the branches."* He wanted his disciples to understand that no external qualifications can set a person right with God—only a personal relationship with Jesus Christ can do that. Grape vines are common in Israel. Each year the vines are cut back to conserve the plant's life and energy. Branches not bearing fruit are cut off. The main point Jesus wanted to get across was that his disciples had to draw strength from him and him alone. He said, "Apart from me you can do nothing" (15:5 NIV). In verse 7 he indicated that those who abide in Christ and have Christ's words abiding in them may ask what they want and it will be done, simply because they will ask nothing out of accord with the mind of Christ. Jesus then called them to remain in his love and keep his commands.

C. *What are some results of this vine-branch relationship?*
1. Bear much fruit (vv. 4–5).
2. Receive prayer power (v. 7).
3. Glorify the Father (v. 8).
4. Obey his commands (cf. Ex. 20; Matt. 5–7).
5. Become full of joy (v. 11; cf. John 1:1–4; 2:1–6).

Our happiness can reach no higher than when we share the joy that Christ felt because of being loved by his Father and doing his will. For Christians, all of life's relationships must grow out of our personal relationship with Jesus.

II. The disciples' relationship with one another in Christ (John 15:12–17).

These disciples had a common tie—Jesus.

A. *They were chosen by Christ (v. 16).* We are God's people. Later the apostle Peter, who was in the upper room that night, wrote to discouraged Christians, "You are a chosen people, a royal priesthood, a holy nation, God's special possession, that you may declare the praises of him who called you out of darkness into his wonderful light" (1 Peter 2:9 NIV).

B. *Their relationship was characterized by genuine love (vv. 12–13, 17).* In the New Testament, individual Christians could not describe their lives without the term "one another." They were to bear "one another's" burdens (Gal. 6:2); admonish "one another" with psalms, hymns, and spiritual songs (Col. 3:16); comfort "one another" (1 Thess. 4:18); exhort "one another" (Heb. 3:13); pray "one for another" (James 5:16); and love "one another" (1 Peter 1:22). For enrichment and stability, you must experience the fellowship of your local body of Christ—your church.

C. *Their relationship was characterized by obedience to Christ (v. 14).*
D. *They were friends, partners with Christ (v. 15).*
E. *They were continuous fruit bearers (v. 16).*

III. The disciples' relationship with the world (John 15:18–27).

Jesus knows what lies ahead for his disciples, and he warns them. Jesus tells his people what they can expect. The Gospel of Mark records just a sample:

"You must be on your guard. You will be handed over to the local councils and flogged in the synagogues. On account of me you will stand before governors and kings as witnesses to them. And the gospel must first be preached to all nations. Whenever you are arrested and brought to trial, do not worry beforehand about what to say. Just say whatever is given you at the time, for it is not you speaking, but the Holy Spirit.

"Brother will betray brother to death, and a father his child. Children will rebel against their parents and have them put to death. Everyone will hate you because of me, but he who stands firm to the end will be saved." (13:9–13 NIV)

Jesus told his disciples that the world hated him first (John 15:18, 22–25). He explained that the world's hatred of them was proof that they were not of the world (v. 19). He further conveyed that they were sharing their Master's lot. Later Peter wrote, "Dear friends, do not be surprised at the fiery ordeal that has come on you to test you, as though something strange were happening to you. But rejoice inasmuch as you participate in the sufferings of Christ, so that you may be overjoyed when his glory is revealed" (1 Peter 4:12–13 NIV).

Then Jesus told his disciples that their suffering would bear good witness to Christ (John 15:27). The time would come when Christians would be called to burn a pinch of incense and say, "Caesar is Lord." But they would refuse to do this. Instead, they would testify, "Jesus is Lord." And persecution would follow because Christians put Christ first.

Jesus knew that if people were permanently bonded together by him, he could trust them with his work until he came again.

Conclusion

Go to your spiritual upper room and learn the lessons Christ Jesus has for you to learn!

SUNDAY EVENING, JULY 26

Title: The Word of Exhortation

Text: "May the God of peace, who through the blood of the eternal covenant brought back from the dead our Lord Jesus, that great Shepherd of the sheep, equip you with everything good for doing his will, and may he work in us what is pleasing to him, through Jesus Christ, to whom be glory for ever and ever. Amen" **(Heb. 13:20–21 NIV).**

Scripture Reading: Hebrews 13:1–25

Introduction

The letter to the Hebrews closes with a personal exhortation to its recipients. You may feel the very heartbeat of applied Christianity as you read these twenty-five verses. The closing remarks encourage believers to accept certain factors of the Christian experience, each of which is aimed at developing spiritual maturity within the Christian community.

I. Acceptance of person (Heb. 13:1–6).

The heart of Christian worship is the personal experience someone has with God. Yet the outward manifestation of this worship causes an individual to be properly related to others. Consequently, a high priority on God's list is to encourage individuals to accept others with concern and respect.

A. *Brothers and sisters (13:1).* If Christians cannot love one another, who can they love? This is a legitimate question that must be asked in every local church. The readers are exhorted to "let brotherly love continue."

B. *Strangers (13:2).* The Christian community must never become self-centered. God frequently sends strangers into our midst. These strangers may be God's blessings in disguise.

C. *Prisoners (13:3).* When someone has been found guilty and punished for some crime, he or she must not be forsaken by the local church. Also, many Christians are being punished by oppressive governments for their spiritual stand. We must share in their suffering.

D. *Mates (13:4).* The author was direct in speaking of the sanctity of sex within marriage. Husbands and wives must continually show their love for each other.

E. *Self (13:5–6).* As Christians, we have a valuable ministry to ourselves. First, we must learn to be content. Second, we must learn to overcome fear by trusting in God. This care for self should never be neglected.

228

II. Acceptance of authority (Heb. 13:7, 17, 24).

The early Christian community had a profound respect for their clerical leadership. The letter to the Hebrews spells out three responsibilities the laity has in relationship to the clergy.

    A. *Remember leaders (13:7).* Church leaders need the prayers of the people they serve. As you follow their leadership, consider also the end result of their witness.

    B. *Obey leaders (13:17).* God has made ecclesiastical leaders responsible for guiding churches in the faith. Consequently, the laity should honor this God-given responsibility with obedience.

    C. *Greet leaders (13:24).* Leaders find themselves in lonely places. Church members should not hesitate to greet them warmly or express heartfelt appreciation.

III. Acceptance of doctrines (Heb. 13:8–16).

It does matter what you believe! The author encouraged the Christian community to accept basic Bible doctrines.

    A. *Centrality of Jesus (13:8).* The doctrine of Jesus Christ is central to the Christian faith.

    B. *Centrality of grace (13:9).* A believer's heart is secured by God's grace. Without grace, no one could experience a personal relationship with God.

    C. *Centrality of the blood (13:10–16).* The author of Hebrews could not overemphasize the necessity of Christ's sacrificial blood on Calvary's cross.

IV. Acceptance of blessings (Heb. 13:18–23).

God offers many blessings to his followers. Certain conditions accompany these blessings, and believers must respond to God in order to receive them.

    A. *In prayer (13:18–19).* When you intercede for others in prayer, their happiness becomes yours.

    B. *In doxology (13:20–21).* The closing words of the letter are a prayer of blessing for its recipients.

    C. *In fellowship (13:22–23).* Fellowship in the name of Christ causes those involved to receive blessings.

Conclusion

The letter to the Hebrews concludes with a universal desire of concerned hearts: "Grace be with you all" (13:25). May this verse motivate each of us to spread this marvelous grace to the world.

WEDNESDAY EVENING, JULY 29

Title: Counterfeit Christianity: What Is It?

Text: "All that is in the world, the lust of the flesh, and the lust of the eyes, and the pride of life, is not of the Father, but is of the world" **(1 John 2:16)**.

Scripture Reading: 1 John 2:15–17

Introduction

One of the most distasteful and unpleasant words in the human vocabulary must be the word *counterfeit*. We usually think of that which is counterfeit as being something purposely designed to deceive. Even more devious than those who ply their counterfeiting trades in the marketplaces of the world are those guilty of counterfeiting in the spiritual realm. The tragedy connected with this kind of counterfeiting is that many times those involved are victims rather than agents! For Satan is the master counterfeiter of all time. He seizes vulnerable people, deceives them by his devilish wiles, and victimizes them in this business of counterfeiting spiritual realities.

In today's Scripture reading, John exposed the essence of counterfeit Christianity.

I. John introduced a strange kind of love.

A. *What "world" was John talking about?* It was not the world of nature, the beauty of which often defies the descriptive powers of the most gifted poet. Rather, John was speaking of the "world system," the total of human life that exists apart from God, alienated from or hostile toward God. The forces of evil in this world system seduce men and women away from God and righteousness. The system is ordered, not haphazard. Much of it is cultured, intellectual, even religious.

B. *John was aware of the evil power of the world system.* Throughout his gospel and letters, John repeatedly dealt with this subject. In his gospel, he said that the world is in the dark. He quoted Jesus' words "I am the light of the world: he that followeth me shall not walk in darkness, but shall have the light of life" (John 8:12). The world is in the dark because it does not know *God* (John 17:25); it does not know *Christ* (John 1:10); it does not know the *Spirit* (John 14:17); and it does not know or understand *Christians* (1 John 3:1).

C. *What "love" for the world was John talking about?* Surprisingly, it was agape love—a self-sacrificing kind of love. This is an example of how Satan can counterfeit that which is spiritual. Just as Christians who are filled with agape love offer themselves to God's perfect will, so those who are victimized by Satan offer themselves to the false brilliance of the world. A sad example of this kind of love is seen in the

230

case of Demas, one of Paul's coworkers (see 2 Tim. 4:10). Paul used the word *agape* to describe Demas's love for the world.

II. John talked about a strange manifestation of this love.

A. *Verse 16 briefly defines the world system, the* kosmos. First is the desire to have things—"The lust of the flesh." "Flesh" refers here to the depraved human nature that governs a person's will, reason, and emotions. As desperately as unbelievers may try to please God, they cannot. Paul said, "The mind governed by the flesh is hostile to God; it does not submit to God's law, nor can it do so. Those who are in the realm of the flesh cannot please God" (Rom. 8:7–8 NIV).

B. *Second is the desire to have whatever attracts the eye.* John called this "the lust of the eyes." It may express itself in an inordinate desire for fine clothes, a new car, a larger home, or power to control all that one sees. Slaves to this sin worship at the altar of mammon!

C. *Third is the desire to be—"The pride of life."* The word translated "pride" is the same word used in James 4:16 and translated "boastings." It amounts to the arrogant, proud dependence on one's own achievements, intelligence, resources, or wealth. These sins are always surrounding us. James said, "Each person is tempted when they are dragged away by their own evil desire and enticed. Then, after desire has conceived, it gives birth to sin; and sin, when it is full-grown, gives birth to death" (James 1:14–15 NIV).

Conclusion

John summarized, "The world and its desires pass away, but the man who does the will of God lives forever" (1 John 2:17 NIV). John meant that the world would pass in a futile show. In spite of its glitter and appeal, it will not last; it is headed for destruction. But those who continue to do God's will because it has become their lifestyle will abide forever!

AUGUST

■ **Sunday Mornings**

The Old Testament prophets were not so much spokesmen for the future as they were for their generation. They were also the proclaimers of timeless truths about God, humankind, and the critical issues of life. "The Modern Message of the Minor Prophets" is the theme for the Sunday morning messages from August through October. Continue the series of messages based on the books of the Old Testament known as the Minor Prophets. The theme is "The Modern Message of the Minor Prophets."

■ **Sunday Evenings**

"Standing Firm under Stress" is the suggested theme for messages based on texts from Peter's first epistle. Peter knew what it meant to be under pressure, and he wrote to people who were under the pressure of persecution. His book speaks to the personal needs of God's people today. This series will run through September.

■ **Wednesday Evenings**

Continue the series of messages from 1 John using the theme "The Counsel of a Spiritual Father to His Children."

SUNDAY MORNING, AUGUST 2

Title: Prophets—Yesterday and Today

Text: "Surely the Sovereign LORD does nothing without revealing his plan to his servants the prophets. The lion has roared—who will not fear? The Sovereign LORD has spoken—who can but prophesy?" **(Amos 3:7–8 NIV).**

Scripture Reading: Amos 3:3–8

Hymns: "I Love to Tell the Story," Hankey
"Bring Them In," Thomas
"Make Me a Channel of Blessing," Smyth

Offertory Prayer: Our Father, you have provided the night for rest, and you have created the day for work. You have given us the privilege of giving. Keep us ever mindful that part of Christian growth is investing ourselves, through our money, in sharing the gospel here at home and around the world. Draw our hearts to you so that we may love your kingdom and recognize our place as citizens in it. Use the money that we bring for spreading the gospel message. Bless those who will be enabled to work for you because we bring our gifts this morning. We pray in Jesus' name. Amen.

Introduction

The roll call of Israel's prophets includes its most illustrious heroes, from Abraham to Jesus. In one sense, all of God's leaders are prophets, since the Hebrew word *nabi*, which is translated "prophet," comes from a Hebrew root meaning "to speak." In a large context, then, anyone who speaks for God is a prophet. Therefore Abraham (Gen. 20:7) and Moses (Deut. 34:10) are prophets; and prophetesses such as Miriam (Ex. 15:20) and Deborah (Judg. 4:4) are also in the noble succession.

Included in Israel's history is another group whom Bible scholars call "false prophets." Jesus used the term in his Sermon on the Mount (Matt. 7:15). These false prophets were intensely nationalistic and were optimistic concerning the nation's destiny whether or not its people obeyed the Lord's commands.

A true prophet was distinguished by saying "thus saith the Lord," which was his authority for preaching. On the other hand, each prophet had his own individuality and was related in a definite way to the time in which he lived. He saw the future and interpreted it in the light of God's will. Yet he also saw the present and declared God's purpose for his own generation. We should never debate whether the prophets were "foretellers" or "forthtellers," for in fact they were both—uniquely equipped by God and infallibly guided by him.

I. The prophet as a person.

A. *God did more than send messages to Israel.* He sent people. The sermon one delivers is never any stronger than the life one leads. An older preacher told a younger preacher that he would take him on a preaching expedition. They walked through the town for several hours. When they finished, the young man said, "When are we going to start preaching?" The older man replied, "We have been preaching. Everywhere we have walked, people have seen us and have reflected on the kind of life we live. Remember, young man, that the greatest sermon you'll ever preach is in the life you live." This follows very closely some words I remember from our college president to the ministerial society when I was a student. He said, "The greatest sermon you'll ever preach will be some day when you walk down the streets of the city or town where you are a pastor. You won't hear it, but someone will remark to a friend, 'There goes our pastor. He is a man who lives what he preaches.'"

B. *God's prophets were people of unquestionable integrity.* There was absolutely no question about their moral standards. For one of God's prophets to be dishonest was completely out of the question. An old cliché, often attributed to Ralph Waldo Emerson, says, "Your actions speak so loudly I can't hear a word you say."

II. The prophet as a called person.

A. *Old Testament prophets shared one thing in common.* Each was called of God. These calls did not all come in the same way. Isaiah's call came within the dignity and refinement of the temple ritual. Amos was called in the bleak desert as he pondered the injustice that prevailed in the land. Hosea's call came as the aftermath of a broken heart and broken home when his wife had been unfaithful. Jeremiah was called when he was a young lad, hardly able to cope with the situation. Habakkuk's call came as he pondered God's seeming indifference to the prosperity of the wicked and the suffering of the righteous.

B. *Each of these calls has one unifying fact.* The prophet was not to speak in his own name nor in his own strength. God vaccinated Isaiah against being overly optimistic when he volunteered for service. On the other hand, he immunized Jeremiah against discouragement when the reluctant young man hesitated to take on such a difficult assignment.

In our day, it is no different. John Henry Jowett, in *The Preacher: His Life and Work*, said about the call to be a prophet, "The call of the Eternal must ring through the rooms of his soul as clearly as the sound of the morning bell rings through the valleys of Switzerland calling the peasants to early prayer and praise." When the divine calling rests on a young prophet, he has no alternative. But unless a man is called to be a prophet, he should remain a Christian layman and not attempt that to which God has not called him. When George Truett was in his prime, a man said to him, "I don't understand how a man can devote his full time to being a preacher." Dr. Truett replied, "I agree with you, sir. You do not understand." But God's prophets understand. They have been called. They have no alternative. They must be prophets.

III. The prophet's message.

If one wished to summarize the prophetic message in one phrase, one might say that the Old Testament prophet's task was to keep before the people the character and nature of God. In doing this, he included every aspect of the truth revealed to him in order that he might fully present it to the people. Three things were always present in the prophet's message.

A. *God is holy.* Any definition of deity must begin with this indisputable truth. The word *holy* means "other than," but it also means more. The moral nature of God is included in his holiness. A people will become like the god they worship. This is why the Canaanites were an extremely immoral people. Their god was a sex symbol, and their worship was tied up with physical immorality, even the rituals of the service itself being nothing more than a sexual orgy. But Israel's God never had a character flaw. Whatever else the prophet said, his message was never inconsistent with this basic truth about his God.

B. *God is active in history.* He punishes the wicked and vindicates his righteous. To a prophet, the greatest heresy imaginable would have been to presume that God was absent from his world and incapable of intervening at a given moment. God established law for running his world, but he was never subject to those laws. God stood in the shadows, always keeping watch over his own people and always present to punish evil.

C. *God is merciful and redemptive.* Both Old Testament prophets and modern-day preachers are responsible for condemning sin, but they must also communicate God's love and mercy for repentant sinners. A vital part of every Old Testament prophet's message was God's redemptive work. God had chosen the Jewish nation as an instrument to bring the Redeemer into the world. To the Jews, he was the promised Messiah. Each prophet made his own distinct contribution concerning the Messiah, and the messages of all the prophets were linked by a unity of theme. God would intervene in history and bring deliverance to sinful people.

Conclusion

The prophets of Israel were probably the nation's greatest contribution to the world besides Jesus Christ himself. No other group of people or organization can compare with them. We cannot draw an exact line of comparison between Israel's prophets and today's preachers, but many similarities are present. True prophetic preaching is more than merely predicting events in great detail. Those who strongly support God's will are prophetic men and women. They speak forth God's Word for the day in which they live. Firmly yet lovingly they warn a sinful world that sin will bring destruction and that forgiveness is available to those who turn to Jesus Christ.

SUNDAY EVENING, AUGUST 2

Title: Introduction to the First Epistle of Peter

Text: "Grace and peace be yours in abundance" **(1 Peter 1:2 NIV)**.

Scripture Reading: 1 Peter 1:1–2; 5:12–14

Introduction

For nine successive Sunday evenings you are invited to enjoy the blessings that come from a study of 1 Peter. Tonight we begin with an introduction.

I. Who wrote the letter?

"Peter, an apostle of Jesus Christ" (1 Peter 1:1). The internal evidence confirms that Peter is the writer, and his authorship makes this letter the universal testimony of primitive Christianity. Peter was brought to Jesus by his brother, Andrew (see John 1:29–42). Jesus predicted that he would become like a rock in character. Along with Andrew and James and John, Peter was called from the fishing business to full-time ministry (see Matt. 4:18–22; Mark 1:16–20; Luke 5:1–11). He was one of the Twelve whom Jesus chose from his disciples and named as apostles (see Luke 6:12–16).

Peter called himself "a fellow elder and a witness of Christ's sufferings who also will share in the glory to be revealed" (1 Peter 5:1 NIV). In 2 Peter 1:1 he called himself "a servant and an apostle of Jesus Christ."

II. Through whom was the letter written?

"With the help of Silas, whom I regard as a faithful brother, I have written to you briefly" (1 Peter 5:12 NIV). Silas was Paul's traveling companion and amanuensis. Some of Silas's style can be detected in the letter.

III. To whom was the letter written?

A. *"To God's elect, exiles scattered throughout the provinces of Pontus, Galatia, Cappadocia, Asia and Bithynia" (1:1 NIV).* The letter was directed to those who had journeyed from their homeland because of conquest, trade, or some other reason (cf. Acts 2:5–11).

B. *Peter addressed himself to "God's elect."* He referred to the saved people dispersed in the Roman provinces of Asia Minor, an area that is now Turkey.

C. *Note the Trinity in their salvation (1:2).*
1. The foreknowledge of God the Father.
2. The sanctification of the Spirit.
3. The sprinkling of the blood of Jesus Christ.

Compare Exodus 12:12–14; Psalm 51:7; and Matthew 26:28. Are not these all symbols of what God does to cover our sins?

IV. Where was the letter written?

Peter wrote the letter in Babylon. "She who is in Babylon, chosen together with you, sends you her greetings, and so does my son Mark" (5:13 NIV). Peter considered Mark as his son in the ministry. The Gospel of Mark was written through the eyes of Peter. Is Babylon a mystical substitute for Rome? Later in the book of Revelation it is so used. Why not the literal Babylon? There is no reason why Peter should not have journeyed as far to the east as Paul did to the west.

V. When was the letter written?

The date of writing is not entirely clear. A good guess would be AD 64 or 65. The Roman emperor Nero died on June 9, AD 68. The letter reflects the persecution that had begun in Nero's reign in AD 64 and spread to the provinces. Peter seemed to be familiar with the earlier letters of Paul but not with the Pastoral Epistles.

VI. Why was the letter written?

"I have written to you briefly, encouraging you and testifying that this is the true grace of God. Stand fast in it" (5:12 NIV). Although Peter's theme was "the true grace of God," his purpose seems more practical than doctrinal. He was exhorting and witnessing. His purpose was to cheer and strengthen scattered Christians who were enduring fiery trials (see 1 Peter 1:6–7; 2:12; 4:12–13; 5:10 for evidences of persecution).

Conclusion

The salutation of the letter illustrates how the gospel unites both Jew and Gentile into "one new humanity out of the two, thus making peace" (Eph. 2:15 NIV). "Grace" was the usual salutation in letters among the Gentiles. "Peace" was the salutation in letters among the Jews. Christianity filled both with content before unknown. Grace, which had meant greeting, became the unmerited love and mercy of God. Peace became the peace that passes human understanding—peace between God and humans through Jesus Christ and, as a result, between humans.

WEDNESDAY EVENING, AUGUST 5

Title: Counterfeit Christianity: Its Results

Text: "They went out from us, but they did not really belong to us. For if they had belonged to us, they would have remained with us; but their going showed that none of them belonged to us" **(1 John 2:19 NIV)**.

Scripture Reading: 1 John 2:18–23

Introduction

Today's advertisers use newspapers, magazines, billboards, radio, television, and the internet to increase their share of the market by showing the superiority of their products over those of their competitors. In a sense, that is what John did in the latter part of 1 John 2. As we discovered in our last study, starting at verse 15, John referred to false religions, or "counterfeit Christianity." He had already identified the parts of a false religion, showing how the very love of God is counterfeited. Now, beginning at verse 18, John was holding up "Brand X" and exposing its inferiority to real Christianity. He also described those who promote such sinister deception.

I. The enemy is plainly revealed before the church (1 John 2:18–19).

A. *Paul warned in 2 Thessalonians that the "man of sin" (the Antichrist of whom John spoke) will be revealed in the last days (2:3–12).* Probably this is what John was referring to in verse 18. But lest the readers think there will be no satanic opposition until that time, John said, "Even now many antichrists have come. This is how we know it is the last hour"

(v. 18 NIV). In other words, John meant that those with the spirit of the Antichrist were already at work in the world.

B. *In verse 19 John was painfully explicit in regard to these pretenders.* He revealed that they hold membership in the church. They go through the motions of worship and participate in church events, but theirs is the spirit of Judas Iscariot, who was so deceptive in his role as a disciple that none of the other eleven disciples suspected that he was an enemy of Christ until the night before the crucifixion. The time had come for these impostors to separate themselves physically from the church because they were never part of the body spiritually. At some point they had given intellectual assent to the lordship of Christ, but their hearts had never confirmed their profession.

C. *These people were "apostates."* They were unbelievers who had mentally adopted the doctrines of the Christian faith but had never been united to the church by a personal relationship with Jesus Christ. John said, "They were not of us" (v. 19). Their source was not in the body of Christ, which is composed of true believers only.

II. Disciples are reminded of who they are and what they possess (I John 2:20–21).

A. *John reminded believers, "You have an anointing from the Holy One, and all of you know the truth" (v. 20 NIV).* He was elaborating on a certain ministry of the Holy Spirit—that of enlightening believers concerning the meaning of God's Word. John was basically saying, "As for *you* (as opposed to antichrists), you are anointed by the Holy Spirit, and you know the truth."

B. *In verse 21 John merely expanded on what he had just said.* This was his purpose in writing—not to instruct the ignorant but to remind believers of what they already knew.

III. The traitor is identified clearly and unmistakably (I John 2:22–23).

A. *The Bible teaches that Satan is the father of lies (John 8:44).* His approach is always based on what is false and misleading. The greatest lie Satan has ever perpetrated is that Jesus is not the Christ. He tries to spread this lie in many ways. In our day, he takes the intellectual, rational approach by denying the virgin birth of Christ.

B. *But what about these blessed names,* Jesus *and* Christ? The name *Jesus* comes from a Hebrew word, *Yeshua,* which means "Jehovah saves" and proclaims the deity, humanity, and vicarious atonement of our Savior. *Christ* means "the anointed one" and is a translation of the Hebrew word from which we get *Messiah.* Jesus was anointed by the Father and designated as Savior; he was the acceptable sacrifice for the sins of the world.

Conclusion

What are the results of "counterfeit Christianity"? The denial that Jesus is the God-man, born of a virgin, who was crucified for our sins and rose the third day to overcome death. Those who deny these basic cardinal truths about Jesus Christ have a counterfeit religion.

SUNDAY MORNING, AUGUST 9

Title: Privilege Means Responsibility

Text: "You only have I chosen of all the families of the earth; therefore I will punish you for all your sins" **(Amos 3:2 NIV)**.

Scripture Reading: Amos 3:1–8

Hymns: "Give of Your Best to the Master," Grose
"Our Best," Kirk
"To the Work!" Crosby

Offertory Prayer: O God, you are both mighty and merciful. We are grateful that you want only sins to cease and not sinners. We are grateful that you have provided redemption through your Son and that you are willing to pour your mercy on us if we will but receive it in repentance and faith. We worship you now with our gifts. May we be generous, even as you have been. Forgive us when we are self-centered and fail to realize that a Christian's distinguishing mark is love for others. Give us grace to take courage for the future and to dedicate not only our money but ourselves to your service. We pray in Jesus' name. Amen.

Introduction

Amos was from the southern kingdom, but his ministry was to the northern kingdom. He came from the desolate country south of Bethlehem. His hometown, Tekoa, was located on a hill about 2,700 feet high. The east side sloped down to the wilderness of Judah. To the southeast a deep valley ran to the Dead Sea. Amos had two occupations—both humble ones. He "followed the flock" (Amos 7:15), which indicates he was not a wealthy sheep owner, although he may have been prosperous enough to hire an assistant when he went to Bethel. He was also "a gatherer of sycamore fruit" (v. 14).

Amos, growing up under the discipline of the desert, developed stern convictions. He did not always have a sweet spirit but preached caustically against sin. He pointed to the certainty of judgment.

I. Israel was a privileged nation.

No nation had ever been blessed more abundantly than the people to whom Amos spoke. From their beginning they had been the object of God's revelation and love. God had disciplined his people through natural disasters

239

and had led them to repentance. God had revealed his righteousness to them by allowing them to conquer the land inhabited by the Canaanite tribes. God's love was reflected in the prophets who had warned them of imminent danger.

God chose Israel, not Assyria with its military might, nor Egypt with its civilization and culture. His purpose in choosing Israel was to make them a kingdom of priests and a holy nation. His ultimate purpose, moreover, was to bring, through the people, redemption to the world by Jesus Christ. Israel's position as a highly favored nation was attained solely by God's grace. Israel did not deserve either this position or God's unique favor. But God chose this nation, and to be chosen was a great privilege.

II. Some people are chosen today.

Throughout the centuries God has, in his wisdom and sovereignty, given special gifts to certain people. An Arab Christian guide in Israel asked me one day, "Why did God choose Isaac instead of Ishmael?" He continued, "Ishmael was, as far as the Bible indicates, a much more desirable person as human attainments go. Yet God chose Isaac."

I replied, "Why did God choose Jacob instead of Esau? Esau was probably the more likable of the two boys. Why did God choose Judah instead of Joseph?" I then said, "Why did God choose me, sinner that I am and unworthy as I am?" The answer to these questions rests in the wisdom, sovereignty, and grace of God.

Yes, God chooses to bless some people with unique abilities and opportunities. Of course, all people have talents, but we must face realistically the fact that some people seem to have more than their share of natural gifts.

Those who live in the world today have privileges and opportunities unheard of a century ago. The average American has a much higher standard of living than a wealthy person who lived half a century ago. Modern conveniences make life easy, comfortable. All of us, even those who live modestly, are highly privileged, but some are especially favored.

III. God expects much from the favored.

The statement Amos made concerning privilege and responsibility followed a sermon he delivered as recorded in the first two chapters of his book. He had listed six of Israel's neighbors: Damascus, Gaza, Tyre, Edom, Ammon, and Moab. He outlined the characteristic sin of each and then warned of divine judgment. He next turned to Judah with a similar message. Just as Israel was basking in the sunlight of their superiority, Amos warned Judah of the coming judgment (see Amos 2:4–5). He then pointed out that the northern kingdom, though more prosperous, was no better than Judah or the surrounding countries. Judgment was certain because she had abused her privileges.

Whether Amos began a new sermon with the third chapter or completed the same one, we have no way of knowing, nor is it important. We can be sure, however, that what he said about the peril and price of privilege (3:2) applies to both Israel and Judah. God had redeemed all twelve tribes from bondage. The entire country, though now a divided kingdom, had received blessings from generation to generation. Therefore God must deal with the two kingdoms based on how they used the good things that had been given to them.

Children who are reared in homes of unusual opportunity have a higher responsibility. Those who have been saved from deep sin have a great obligation. Those who have good jobs and a comfortable living standard must recognize God's hand on them. Shallow and superficial people abuse privileges. Mature people recognize the importance of staying humble and grateful to God.

IV. Where are you?

Everyone listening to this message can honestly say, "God has been good to me." Now the penetrating question is, "How far along the line of maturity have you come? Are habits that hurt and even destroy still a part of your lifestyle? Do you cling to things, or do you let things cling to you that keep you from being your best and attaining all that God wants you to have?"

Most people, somewhere in their life cycle, wake up to life's meaning. The tragedy is that so many wait until the opportunity for a full life has slipped away. When we do this, we have limited time in which to realize our full potential. Marie Antoinette, wife of Louis XVI, remained a silly, privileged girl for too long. When the French Revolution broke and her world collapsed, she faced calamity and death. At that time, she matured quickly and turned into a brave, strong woman. The tragedy is that, as one of her biographers said, "She played with life and never wrestled with it." Another writer said, "One wonders what would have happened in history if Marie Antoinette had faced her troubles sooner and become a woman before it was too late." Often, when we waste a year in our youth, it takes three to five years to gain it back.

Where are you? When a farmer fails to go out in March and April with his plow and break the ground, sow the seeds, and cultivate the plants, he will starve before winter is gone. The Bible speaks of a pool being stirred by an angel and the need for a person to step into the pool at that time in order to be cured (John 5:4). With some opportunities, it is now or never. When we abuse our privilege or fail to use it, tragedy results.

Conclusion

Of course, the greatest tragedy is that of failing to receive the Savior when we have the privilege of hearing the gospel. Years ago an advocate of foreign missions said that no person has the right to hear the gospel twice until everyone has heard it once. Unfortunately, some hear it several times but fail to respond. We who live where the good news is preached often should beware lest we become hardened and take it for granted. John Greenleaf Whittier wisely asked,

Forever around the Mercy Seat
The guiding lights of love shall burn;
But what if, habit-bound thy feet
Shall lack the will to turn?

What if thine eyes refuse to see,
Thine ear of Heaven's free welcome fail,
And thou a willing captive be,
Thyself thy own dark jail?

—*"The Answer"*

Privilege means responsibility. Wise people take advantage of the opportunities of their lifetime during the lifetime of their opportunities.

SUNDAY EVENING, AUGUST 9

Title: God's People Have a Living Hope

Text: "Praise be to the God and Father of our Lord Jesus Christ! In his great mercy he has given us new birth into a living hope through the resurrection of Jesus Christ from the dead" **(1 Peter 1:3 NIV).**

Scripture Reading: 1 Peter 1:3; 3:15; 5:10

Introduction

Hope, along with faith and love, is one of the three permanent graces of a Christian (see 1 Cor. 13:13). Peter had experienced the death of hope when Jesus was crucified and the renewal of hope when Jesus was resurrected. Peter praised God that he has "begotten us again unto a lively hope by the resurrection of Jesus Christ from the dead" (1 Peter 1:3). Note especially the word "again." Hope had died and was revived by Jesus' resurrection.

I. The death of hope.

A. *Hope died for Peter when Jesus died.* Peter had affirmed Jesus as the Messiah, the Son of God (see Matt. 16:16). He misunderstood the nature of the Messiah (see Matt. 16:21–23), but he was loyal to Jesus (see John 6:66–69; 13:37). During Jesus' trial and crucifixion, "Peter followed afar off" (Luke 22:54), but he did follow. Although the look on Jesus' face after Peter denied him (see Luke 22:61) broke Peter's heart, he still believed and had hope. Concerning Jesus' crucifixion, Mark 15:31–32 says, "The chief priests and the teachers of the law mocked him among themselves. 'He saved others,' they said, 'but he can't save himself! Let this Messiah, this king of Israel, come down now from the cross, that we may see and believe'" (NIV). Peter probably expected Jesus to do just that. But when Jesus died, hope died. It was night. Perhaps none of the disciples expected Christ to rise again, even though he repeatedly had told them that he would.

B. *Hope died for the other disciples when Jesus died.* Note some illustrations from Scripture:

    1. "Mary Magdalene, Mary the mother of James, and Salome bought spices so that they might go to anoint Jesus' body. . . . They were on their way to the tomb and they asked each other, 'Who will roll the stone away from the entrance of the tomb?'" (Mark 16:1–3 NIV). When the angels at the empty tomb reminded them of Jesus' promise to rise on the third day, "they remembered his words" (Luke 24:8).

    2. The disciples refused to believe the women's report about the empty tomb and the angels "because their words seemed to them like nonsense" (Luke 24:11 NIV). However, Peter and John did run to the tomb to find out about the grave robbery. Peter saw "the cloth that had been around Jesus' head. The cloth was still lying in its place, separate from the linen. Finally the other disciple . . . also went inside. He saw and believed" (John 20:7–8 NIV). This is evidence that John had not believed before this experience.

    3. Cleopas and his unnamed companion had no hope. Referring to Jesus who had been crucified, they said, "We had hoped that he was the one who was going to redeem Israel. And what is more, it is the third day since all this took place" (Luke 24:21 NIV).

II. The revival of hope by Jesus' resurrection.

A. *Jesus' appearances:*

    To the women (Luke 24:1–8)

    To Mary Magdalene (John 20:1–18)

    To Cleopas and another (Luke 24:13–32)

    To Simon Peter (Luke 24:33–35; 1 Cor. 15:5)

    To all the disciples except Thomas (Luke 24:36–43; John 20:19–25)

    To all the disciples the next Sunday night (John 20:26–31)

    To seven disciples by the Sea of Galilee. Jesus repeated the miraculous draw of fish, as at Peter's call to the ministry, and reaffirmed Peter's apostleship (John 21).

    To about five hundred, at once, perhaps at a mountain in Galilee as Jesus had appointed before his death (Matt. 28:16–20; 1 Cor. 15:6)

    To James, the half brother of Jesus (1 Cor. 15:7)

    To the disciples at Jerusalem, then at the Mount of Olives and the ascension (Luke 24:44–53; Acts 1:3–12)

B. *Peter and the other disciples now knew that Christ lived.* They witnessed to this truth even to the point of exile and martyrdom.

C. *Their Scriptures had been reinterpreted by Jesus.* He opened their minds so they could understand the Scriptures. He showed them in the Old Testament, "This is what is written: The Messiah will suffer and rise from the dead on the third day, and repentance for the forgiveness of sins will be preached in his name to all nations, beginning at Jerusalem" (Luke 24:46–47 NIV).

D. *Jesus commissioned them to preach the gospel to all nations.* They were to start in Jerusalem, then go to Judea and Samaria, and then to the whole world. They were to wait in Jerusalem for the Holy Spirit to inaugurate the gospel age. They obeyed, and at Pentecost the Holy Spirit came as promised (see Matt. 28:18–20; Luke 24:48–49; John 20:21; Acts 1–2).

Conclusion

Christian hope is reasonable. Every reason for believing in God the Father and God the Son is a reason for hope. Every experience of God the Holy Spirit is a reason for hope, including one's salvation and the witness of the Holy Spirit. And the witness of Peter and others whose hope was revived by Jesus' resurrection is a reason for hope.

WEDNESDAY EVENING, AUGUST 12

Title: Counterfeit Christianity: Its Antidote

Text: "See that what you have heard from the beginning remains in you. If it does, you also will remain in the Son and in the Father" **(1 John 2:24 NIV)**.

Scripture Reading: 1 John 2:24–29

Introduction

The temptation to be faithless is the number one problem among Christians—and it always has been. This is the sinister counterfeit Satan has so successfully perpetrated in a variety of ways among believers. He often uses other people in his determination to weaken a Christian's faith. One person he uses is the cynic, who raises doubts in the Christian's mind. This person has the syrupy "Did God really say . . . ?" (Gen. 3:1 NIV) approach of the Tempter. Then there is the hypocrite who looks like a Christian and talks like a Christian but whose conduct is inconsistent. Satan also uses popular views to distort the truth. For example, "One religion is just as good as another as long as you are sincere." Or, "You have to be realistic. The Bible doesn't always mean what it says." Or, "You don't need to go to church to be a Christian." John gave an antidote for the problem of faithlessness.

I. The first antidote John gave is the abiding of the Word (1 John 2:24–26).

A. *How does Jesus become real to a new believer?* Through Scripture! What are some of the first, basic truths we learn? That Jesus is God's Son,

244

that he died on a cross for our sins and rose the third day, and that he promised to return to receive us unto himself. Along with these great truths is the amazing realization that God knows us by name and is always available to hear our prayers and answer them according to his will. But it doesn't take long for Satan to start whispering doubts to a young Christian.

B. *What is the antidote for these attacks from Satan?* John simply said to hold fast to that which we learned at the beginning of our pilgrimage with God. Stay in the Word! John used the word "abide," which means to remain in the sense that one is at home, comfortable, and conversant with Bible truths. We are not merely to "taste" the Word; we are to ingest it, depending on the Holy Spirit to help us digest it so that it can be absorbed into our lives.

II. The second antidote John gave is the anointing of the Spirit (1 John 2:27).

A. *John referred to "anointing" as the coming of the Holy Spirit at salvation to abide in us.* This anointing, or initiation, is never repeated. Yet we may grieve the Holy Spirit by disobedience and sin, thus allowing self to usurp the Spirit's leadership.

B. *Because of the anointing of the Holy Spirit we receive at salvation, John said, "You do not need anyone to teach you" (v. 27 NIV).* He meant that we do not constantly need to be taught the elementary truths of the gospel, for that is one of the Holy Spirit's vital ministries. Also, the Holy Spirit provides a glorious "check and balance" within us. He is always present to verify the teachings we do receive from others.

III. The third antidote John gave is the coming of Jesus (1 John 2:28–29).

A. *John reminded his readers that the next great event on eternity's calendar is the second coming of Jesus.* He did not set any date; rather, he was saying, "Whenever he comes—and it could be at any moment—be found living in such a way that you will not be ashamed to stand before him!"

B. *Actually, Christians should live before God as Enoch did.* The Bible says that Enoch walked with God, and he was not found, for God took him (Gen. 5:24). Enoch lived in such close and constant communion with God that his transition from earthly existence to heavenly existence was a very simple thing. This is how we should live.

Conclusion

What part does God's Word play in your life? Does it "abide" within you? And what about the Holy Spirit? Does he have complete control in your life? Do you anticipate Jesus' coming with joy? Are you living so close to him, consistently walking by his side, that his coming will be a welcome transition?

SUNDAY MORNING, AUGUST 16

Title: Grace That Is Greater Than Our Sin

Text: "I will heal their waywardness and love them freely, for my anger has turned away from them" **(Hos. 14:4 NIV)**.

Scripture Reading: Hosea 3:1–5

Hymns: "There's a Wideness in God's Mercy," Faber
"Amazing Grace," Newton
"Grace Greater Than Our Sin," Johnston

Offertory Prayer: Our Father, we are grateful that your works are great and your ways are true and just. Most of all, we are grateful that you are merciful. We thank you this morning for all your blessings on our work. We express our gratitude both for your temporal blessings that are reflected in our material possessions and for the eternal riches of your grace that make salvation possible. We bring our money not only to symbolize our devotion but to tangibly express our desire to help advance your kingdom. We pray in Jesus' name. Amen.

Introduction

One outstanding Old Testament scholar said, "Hosea picked up where Amos left off." By this he meant that Amos was a stern preacher of righteousness, but Hosea saw beyond God's stern demands to his mercy and grace.

Several years ago a minister preached on God's demand for holiness in life. As he held the standards high, a broken, sinful woman seated in the second row spoke up spontaneously, "But what if we can't do these things? What if we're weak? Is there any hope?"

The book of Hosea says there is hope. Even if we have stooped as low as Gomer, Hosea's wife, who was immoral and unfaithful, God's grace is sufficient to take away our guilt. Just as God told the prophet of Israel to go and buy his erring wife from slavery, so God believed in his nation Israel and so he believes in us today. In fact, he cared so much for us that he sent his Son to die on a cross that a lost world might be saved.

I. God has all kinds of preachers.

Even as no snowflake is exactly like another when observed under a microscope, no two personalities are quite alike. God uses each of us as we are and gives us strength to conquer personal weakness. Amos and Hosea are two cases in point; they illustrate the fact that God delights in diversity and never tries to fit one person into another one's mold.

    A. *Amos.* He was rustic, often caustic, reflecting the type of background from which he came. Hosea, on the other hand, was either from the city or from a high-class rural community. Where Amos condemned sin fiercely, Hosea stressed forgiveness. Amos saw sin as a transgression of God's law, but Hosea saw sin as a breach of relationships and a failure to love properly. Never has the fact that the heart makes the preacher been more clearly portrayed than in the lives of Amos and Hosea. It would not be fair to say that Amos was hard and unforgiving, but we can safely say that he placed more emphasis on conforming to a standard than on repenting and receiving God's love. Even when he invited the people of Israel to repent, his words consisted of "prepare to meet thy God" (Amos 4:12).

B. *Hosea.* He was more than a preacher who cried for justice. He presented mercy. He found God's unending love through his own domestic tragedy. As he was led to forgive his sinful wife, a revelation burst in his mind, opening his lips and making him a gentler prophet. God gave him a broken heart so he could understand God's broken heart. Hosea learned that the fundamental difference between God and humanity is not God's power versus our lack of it, his greatness that dwarfs our smallness, nor his omniscience that exposes our ignorance. Rather, God's greatest attribute is his unconditional love that shames our own conditional love.

On the other hand, Hosea was not an emotionalist with no iron in his blood nor rigor in his gospel. To think of Hosea as mild or weak would be a terrible mistake. He had a passion for righteousness that was just as vehement as that of Amos. He diagnosed the moral and social diseases of Israel and did not hesitate to announce that remedies were desperately needed. But his last word was forgiveness, not judgment. He knew that God smites to save and cuts to heal.

II. Tears can become telescopes.

During prosperous times in our lives, we seldom learn many lessons. When sorrow comes, however, we understand things that God wants us to know. Hosea's life, as much as any other in the Bible, illustrates this truth. As a young man, he married Gomer, and they had children. At some stage, Gomer became unfaithful. Some scholars suggest that Gomer's third child, and maybe even her second, were products of her infidelity. Whether or not this is true, we do know that Gomer, after bearing three children, left Hosea for a life of immorality. The matter broke Hosea's heart. As a result, he wrote a beautiful poem, found in chapter 2 of his book, with this incident as its background.

Sometime later, perhaps after many years had passed, God commanded Hosea to go find his wife. He did as God commanded and bought Gomer back from the slave market. Hosea took her home and restored her to the former position she had held in the house. However, he first made her endure a probation period in which she proved herself a faithful wife.

Hosea learned many lessons from this experience.

A. *The nature of sin.* Hosea discovered that sin is not against arbitrary decrees but against the love relationship. He applied this to his nation's spiritual condition. The people of Israel were guilty of more than breaking the Ten Commandments. They were guilty of breaking God's heart.

B. *The essence of religion.* During Gomer's absence, Hosea learned another truth. He came to understand the essence of religion. What does God want from his creation? Well, what does a husband want in his wife? Not merely someone to wash the dishes, vacuum the floor, and do the laundry. He could hire a maid to do these chores. A man wants companionship with his wife. Likewise, God does not want from his creation merely perfunctory obedience to the external requirements of religion. Instead, he wants a person's devotion, which establishes fellowship between the two. Hosea then understood that God desired Israel to return to him so that a loving fellowship might exist between the two.

C. *The heart of God.* A third lesson Hosea learned was the greatest! He discovered something about God's heart. The chief characteristic of our Creator is that he is also our Redeemer. God chose Abraham to make a great nation from him. God had one specific goal in mind: to bless all nations through Abraham's seed. The ultimate seed, through whom the world would be blessed, is Jesus Christ. In him we learn the fullness of a truth that is brought to us in part throughout the Old Testament. God is merciful, and he delights in forgiving people when their repentance is genuine and their faith is sincere.

III. Why and how does God do it?

A. *Why?* The answer is found in Hosea 11. In this beautiful poem on God as a loving Father, Hosea traces the anguish of a father whose son has rebelled against him. God, as the Father, said that he will not cast off his people (11:8–9). The latter part of verse 9 explains why God will not make judgment his last word. Hosea, speaking for God, said, "I am God, and not man."

B. *How?* How does God forgive? Although he is God and not man, in Jesus Christ, he is both God and man. Hosea, more than any other Old Testament prophet, anticipates the gospel of God's grace through his Son. In Jesus Christ we see Hosea going to the marketplace and buying back his erring loved one. The chapter expresses that even though we have gone astray, God is always ready to forgive.

Conclusion

Only one thing is greater than our sins—God's grace. More than love, grace is undeserved love. We love those who are lovely, but God loves even those who are unlovely. Paul said, "Very rarely will anyone die for a righteous man, though for a good person someone might possibly dare to die. But God demonstrates his own love for us in this: While we were still sinners, Christ died for us" (Rom. 5:7–8 NIV). The most cherished hymns of the Christian faith have always been those that tell of God's forgiving love. We who are saved never tire of hearing the gospel story. We are warmed every time we hear of how someone like Hosea would forgive his wife after she had disgraced him. The greatest story of all, however, and the one to which Hosea points, is that of our Savior, who knew no sin, becoming sin so that we might be the righteousness of God in him!

SUNDAY EVENING, AUGUST 16

Title: Kept by the Power of God

Text: "To an inheritance incorruptible, and undefiled, and that fadeth not away, reserved in heaven for you, Who are kept by the power of God through faith unto salvation ready to be revealed in the last time" (**1 Peter 1:4–5**).

Scripture Reading: 1 Peter 1:3–5

Introduction

As a lake reflects an image, Peter's writings reflect his experience. Peter had lost face but not faith with his denials of his Lord. Jesus, true to his promise, had kept Peter from Satan. Peter is now busy strengthening the brethren (see Luke 22:31–32).

I. Who are the kept?

    A. *Not:*
1. Those on whom worldly fortune has smiled.
2. Those who are politically powerful.
3. Those exempt from earthly ills and misfortune.

    B. *But:*
1. Scattered, persecuted Christians in the provinces of Asia Minor (1 Peter 1:1–2, 6–8).
2. The elect. This is a term for saved persons. God, to be God, must be sovereign. Humans, to be humans, must be free. God has provided a way of salvation by which a person is free to accept or reject his grace. God does not elect that some will be saved and some lost; but he "gave his only begotten Son, that whosoever believeth in him should not perish, but have everlasting life" (John 3:16).

You can "make your calling and election sure" (2 Peter 1:10). Follow the instructions in 2 Peter 1:1–10. "Hereby we do know that we know him, if we keep his commandments" (1 John 2:3). One simple explanation of election is: "God votes for you. The devil votes against you. You cast the deciding vote."

II. Who keeps them?

God, by his power. God pledges his power, as manifested in raising Jesus from the dead, to keep the elect (1 Peter 1:5). Peter had learned to trust God. So had Paul (2 Tim. 1:12) and Jude (Jude 24–25) and Jesus (John 10:27–30).

III. From what are they kept?

A. *From spiritual defeat.* For example:
   1. Peter (Luke 22:31–32; Acts 4:3; 5:17–42).
   2. Stephen (Acts 7:54–60).
   3. Paul (2 Cor. 12:7–10).

B. *From the devil's power.* Satan has no power except by God's permission (Job 1:6–12; 2:1–6; Luke 22:31–32). God can bring good out of what seems to be evil (Rom. 8:28–39).

IV. How are the elect kept?

"Through faith" (1 Peter 1:5). Faith is a necessary condition rather than an arbitrary one. Faith is willingness to put one's life in God's hands. "Without faith it is impossible to please him [God]" (Heb. 11:6). Faith is willingness to be kept. The bank cannot keep one's money unless one deposits it in the bank. God cannot keep a person unless the person is willing to be kept.

V. Kept for what? What is the end of our keeping?

A. *"Unto salvation" (1 Peter 1:5).*
   1. Salvation as a past experience (John 3:16; Rom. 8:1; Eph. 2:8–10).
   2. Salvation as a present experience (Rom. 13:11; Phil. 2:12–13).
   3. Salvation as future consummation "at the appearing of Jesus Christ" (Matt. 25:31–46; 1 Peter 1:7; 1 John 3:1–3).

B. *"An inheritance" (1 Peter 1:4).*
   1. Incorruptible. Not subject to decay, as are all things on this earth (Matt. 6:19–21).
   2. Undefiled. The first paradise was defiled by sin. Sin will not enter the heavenly paradise.
   3. Heavenly treasure that cannot fade away (1 Peter 1:4).
      a. Hear Jesus (John 14:1–3).
      b. Hear Paul (1 Cor. 2:9; Phil. 3:20–21; 2 Tim. 4:6–8).
      c. Hear John in Revelation.
         (1) A holy place (Rev. 21:1–3; 22:1–5).
         (2) Exempt from weariness (Rev. 7:16).
         (3) Exempt from pain (Rev. 7:17; 21:4).
         (4) A place of service (Rev. 7:15).

Conclusion

God keeps the heavenly home for those who are kept for it.

When I was a boy, I went with my father to see his boyhood home on the farm, which he had not visited for many years. I had heard him describe it as a place of pure delight, so our visit was very disappointing. The house was dilapidated. My father said, "We can at least get a drink from the spring." But we found the spring choked by debris. You see, the house was vacant. No one kept it. But we have a heavenly home reserved for us. The Lord has prepared it and keeps it for us "who are kept by the power of God through faith unto salvation ready to be revealed in the last time" (1 Peter 1:5).

WEDNESDAY EVENING, AUGUST 19

Title: Bearing Family Traits

Text: "Dear friends, now we are children of God, and what we will be has not yet been made known. But we know that when he appears, we shall be like him, for we shall see him as he is" **(1 John 3:2 NIV).**

Scripture Reading: 1 John 3:1–10

Introduction

In our text, John was talking about spiritual family traits. When we are born again, we receive new life—not biological life, but spiritual life. And just as our biological life is "programmed" into our genes, so our spiritual life is predetermined by God to produce certain characteristics. For example, Paul said in Romans 8:29, "For those God foreknew he also predestined to be conformed to the image of his Son" (NIV).

However, just as in the physical growth process certain things such as illness or injury can change one's hereditary development, so in the spiritual realm disobedience and sin can cause us to slow down or even abort the spiritual growth that God desires us to experience. Throughout the New Testament, we find many passages that remind us of the spiritual family traits we should develop in our lives. John revealed four things about these spiritual family traits that God programmed into us when we were born again.

I. First, John told us what we are (1 John 3:1).

A. *John was amazed by what God has done for sinful humanity.* "What great love the Father has lavished on us" (NIV). In other words, John was saying that nothing else in human life even faintly resembles the love that God has shown to humankind.

B. *What is it about this love that so astounded John?* "That we should be called children of God! And that is what we are!" (NIV). The word "called" here literally means "styled." When we are born again because of God's great love, the Holy Spirit begins to style us so that day by day we come to resemble children of God and cease to look like children of the world.

II. Next, John told us what we will become (1 John 3:2–3).

A. *John used a hint of caution in these verses.* It is almost as if John were saying, "Now Christians, a wonderful thing has happened as a result of God's amazing love. But we have not arrived yet! Many rough places need to be smoothed out, many attitudes and ideas need to be altered."

B. *A Christian's spiritual mirror is God's Word.* We are never flattered when we see ourselves in relationship to God's Word. But the positive note in this experience is that we are becoming more like our Lord every day. We have no idea what the finished product is going to be, but we do know that we will be like Jesus!

C. *John said that we are continually cleansed when we have this hope.* As the hope within us purifies our hearts, we are brought closer and closer to that state of purity required to stand in God's presence.

III. Then John told us what we should avoid (1 John 3:4–9).

A. *John outlined four things about sin in these verses.* He explained what sin is, what sin does, why sin is, and where sin originates. Unless we properly understand what John was saying about sin, this can be the most frightening passage in the Bible. We must remember that the difference between a believer who sins and an unbeliever who sins is that the unbeliever can sin without remorse. Unbelievers continue to sin because that is their unredeemed nature. Christians, however, cannot sin without feeling convicted by the Holy Spirit.

B. *John broke through the dark cloud with a word of triumph.* "The reason the Son of God appeared was to destroy the devil's work" (v. 8 NIV). We are not strong enough to fight against sin by ourselves, but in Christ "we are more than conquerors" (Rom. 8:37).

IV. Last, John told us what we must reflect (1 John 3:10).

A. *How do we truly reflect our kinship to God?* First, we do what is right. We reflect a joyful, spontaneous relationship with Christ demonstrated by the "good works" we perform in Christ's name.

B. *Second, we reflect our kinship to God by loving one another.* This is not just affection for others; it is loving them in spite of who they are or what they have done. This kind of love has a redeeming quality; it seeks to lift others up and heal their heartache and pain.

Conclusion

Are the marks of Jesus Christ and the family of God on you? Are you daily reflecting Jesus by your good works and by your love for others?

SUNDAY MORNING, AUGUST 23

Title: What Is True Religion?

Text: "He has shown you, O mortal, what is good. And what does the LORD require of you? To act justly and to love mercy and to walk humbly with your God" **(Mic. 6:8 NIV)**.

Scripture Reading: Micah 6:6–15

Hymns: "God of Grace and God of Glory," Fosdick
"In Christ There Is No East or West," Oxenham
"Let Others See Jesus in You," McKinney

Offertory Prayer: Our Father, even as you have conquered death by the resurrection of your Son, so you have enabled us to conquer death by our relationship with you through Jesus. Every Lord's Day is a reaffirmation of our resurrection faith. And every gift we bring is a reaffirmation of our dedication to your purposes. Bless those who give and the causes that are supported by our gifts. Give us greater faith to trust you to provide for our needs. Make us willing to give you the tithe that you have said is holy unto you. We pray this in our Savior's name. Amen.

Introduction

The minor prophet Micah preached during the same general period as the major prophet Isaiah. But Micah began his ministry about ten years after the great son of Amoz heard God's call in the temple after the death of King Uzziah. Micah labored in the small town of Moresheth about twenty-five miles southwest of Jerusalem, while Isaiah spent his time mostly in the capital city of Jerusalem. Although these men were contemporaneous and not far apart geographically, like Amos and Hosea, they present a contrast of personalities. Isaiah was an aristocrat, and royal blood likely flowed through his veins. Micah, with no such heritage, was a man of lowly origin, a son of the soil. Isaiah was the friend and confidant of royalty, while Micah associated with the poor and never lost the common touch. Isaiah saw God's purposes as aligned inseparably with Jerusalem, but Micah had about the same regard for the city as a southern plantation owner has for New York City. Isaiah was concerned with national and international politics, while Micah was burdened with moral and ethical righteousness. God had a place for both men.

Micah's book has three main divisions. In chapters 1–3, he traced the root and results of sin, concluding with the clear statement that the city of Jerusalem would "be plowed as a field, and . . . become heaps" (3:12). In chapters 4 and 5, however, he spoke of God's goal in history. In chapter 5, he painted a beautiful picture of the coming Messiah, even naming the city in which he would be born (5:2). The last two chapters of the book gather the threads and weave them together into a comprehensive summary.

Many scholars believe that the greatest single statement of the Old Testament is found in Micah 6:8: "What does the LORD require of you? To act justly and to love mercy and to walk humbly with your God" (NIV).

I. Act justly.

One main emphasis of the Old Testament prophets was on proper treatment of others. God's ideal for his country was a society in which every citizen had a good standard of living but no one exploited a neighbor to increase his or her own wealth. The laws that Moses established were designed to protect the rights of the underprivileged. Though slavery was permitted, the Hebrew laws concerning slavery were far more protective of the oppressed than the laws of any of Israel's neighbors, including the great Hammurabi Code.

The last resort of oppressed people has always been the court of law. When people feel that their rights are being violated, they may appeal to a court of equity and have an unbiased judge rule regarding their condition. The situation in Israel, however, had become tragic. Judges were bribed by the rich to render a decision for them against the poor. The main theme of Amos's preaching had been the need for justice. Perhaps the key verse of his entire prophecy was "Let judgment run down as waters, and righteousness as a mighty stream" (Amos 5:24).

Micah picked up on Amos's theme and made it a major part of his message. When he spoke of Jerusalem's coming destruction, he gave as one of the principal reasons, "Her leaders judge for a bribe, her priests teach for a price, and her prophets tell fortunes for money. Yet they look for the LORD's support and say, 'Is not the LORD among us? No disaster will come upon us'" (Mic. 3:11 NIV). Any nation is about to crumble when its courts become corrupt. When justice is perverted other iniquities follow quickly. The core of Jesus' ministry was his love for the common people, who heard him gladly, and he desired that they be treated properly by those who had authority over them. To act justly is to treat others with honor and integrity. This is a basic aspect of living for the Lord.

II. Love mercy.

Although justice is important, something is needed to temper its severity. Mercy has been called the benevolence that disposes a person to overlook personal injury or to treat an offender better than he or she deserves. Here, however, the word has a much wider range of meaning. The Hebrew word for "mercy" was a favorite word in Hosea's vocabulary. Often the word is translated "lovingkindness." We should never regard justice and mercy as opposite. Rather, one involves the other. Justice is the foundation of God's throne, but mercy is an inseparable part of his character. In many ways the term is parallel to the Christian word for "love."

One thing should be stressed about mercy: we must love it. Only then can it become a pervading principle of our lives. When we love mercy, we stay busy helping those who are burdened. Mercy supplies our motivation for living. Mercy is never strained. Instead, it drops as the gentle rains of heaven. We do not say, "I will be merciful." Mercy becomes part of our character like the dew spreads over the grass.

III. Walk humbly with your God.

Where Amos considered religion as ethical, bringing forth justice, and Hosea considered it as emotional, bringing forth love, Micah saw one other characteristic. A truly religious person is deeply spiritual, walking in fellowship with his or her Creator. This concept was emphasized in Isaiah's messages to Israel. He saw God highly exalted, and to him a person's greatest sin was to walk in the pride of his or her own countenance rather than in humble submission to God.

To become rightly related to God involves repenting of our sins after we sense that all is not well with us. To feel comfortably complacent and satisfied that we are all right with God is like dry rot at the root of our lives. The only attitude a sinful person can express in the presence of the Almighty is humility. When someone comes before God with this attitude, he or she will find forgiveness in Jesus Christ. We have said too little about repentance; therefore we are short on humility. This means we are also short on true fellowship with God. Micah considered humility a fundamental part of God's command to humankind.

Conclusion

What is your answer to God's appeal? Surely as we discover these commands, we must humbly confess that we are sinners. The purpose of a statement such as Micah 6:8 is not to urge us to strive after good works, but rather to help us see our sinful condition so we can turn to the Savior. Following the new-birth experience, these goals—to act justly, love mercy, and walk humbly with God—must not be ignored. God expects the very best from us. Someone remarked concerning a Christian many years ago, "To look into his face was a benediction, because one saw there manifested the glow of a real holiness." Some of his last words were, "I have always tried to help you live more Christlike lives."

SUNDAY EVENING, AUGUST 23

Title: The Problem of Undeserved Suffering

Text: "In all this you greatly rejoice, though now for a little while you may have had to suffer grief in all kinds of trials. These have come so that the proven genuineness of your faith—of greater worth than gold, which perishes even though refined by fire—may result in praise, glory and honor when Jesus Christ is revealed" **(1 Peter 1:6–7 NIV)**.

Scripture Reading: 1 Peter 1:6–7; 2:19–25; 3:8–18; 4:12–19

Introduction

The age-old problem we are going to look at this evening is undeserved human suffering. Suffering for one's own sins seems just, but how can God be good and still allow suffering or death by disease, earthquakes, famine, flooding, and other natural causes? A good Christian contracts cancer; a baby is born blind. Why? Why?

This is perhaps the most difficult question about God. In fact, we cannot answer it. But our faith should be encouraged by the mere fact that this is a problem to us. We intuitively believe that God should be good, holy, and powerful. Jesus, the supreme example of an innocent person suffering, revealed God as good. The noblest Christians of all time (many who came to faith through suffering) affirm with Paul, "We know that in all things God works for the good of those who love him, who have been called according to his purpose" (Rom. 8:28 NIV).

I. Some attempted solutions.

A. *Some escape the problem through atheism or some form of materialism.* Unbelief has its problems too. The design and order of the universe and human intelligence argue for the intelligence of a creator. If God is not good, then the goodness in his universe is a puzzle. How can we account for happy homes, healthy children, a loving Savior, and the spiritual intuition that God is good?

B. *Some deny that sorrow, sin, and death exist.* "These are errors of a mortal mind," they say. Pain seems real, as anyone knows who has been to the cemetery. As one said, "If he did not die, why did they bury him?"

C. *Some lay all pain and suffering on the devil.* A fine Christian couple whose baby fell from a window to his death said, "The devil did it." The Bible teaches that Satan can act only with God's permission. God is far stronger than the devil. This approach solves nothing.

II. Some reasons to trust in God's goodness.

A. *God knows all.* We have only partial knowledge. We see the dark cloud from beneath. God sees the sun shining on it from above. Job and his friends wrestled with the problem of suffering, and Job concluded that God is so great and wonderful, as evidenced by his creation, that we can trust him in all circumstances (see Job 38–40; 42:1–6).

Such trust can be seen in the illustration of a father and his little boy walking deep into the woods. The father asked, "Son, do you know the way home?" The boy replied, "No, Father, but you do."

B. *Suffering may be used for growth in faith and character.*

1. As a hot fire is necessary to separate dross from pure gold, the fire of suffering is used to purify faith (1 Peter 1:6–7).

      2. Satan was allowed to sift Peter as wheat is threshed to separate grain from chaff. The process was not pleasant, but it did not hurt the wheat (Luke 22:31–32).

            Paul prayed earnestly for the removal of a thorn in his flesh (possibly eye disease) that he thought was hurting his ministry. God did not take away the thorn, but he did give grace to bear it. Paul lived to see that his suffering of the thorn made him a better minister (2 Cor. 12:7–10).

  C. *Suffering may be used to reclaim a backslider or convict the unsaved (Heb. 12:5–11).*

          A young mother died unexpectedly a few days after giving birth to a child. It seemed like an absolute tragedy. However, her death caused her father to be convicted of his sin and he became a Christian. Because her death was necessary to convict his hard heart, it was good.

  D. *Suffering may be used to make individuals more sympathetic.* If this world had no pain or suffering, there would be no concern or sympathy. How callous we all would be!

  E. *Suffering helps Christians to understand Jesus' suffering (1 Peter 2:19–25).* He is the supreme example of the innocent suffering for the guilty. Jesus thanked God for the privilege of being the Savior (Matt. 26:26–28). He believed that God would bring good out of evil, and so he did. Jesus endured the cross and discovered joy (Heb. 12:2). He fulfilled God's promise spoken through Isaiah about the Messiah, "After he has suffered, he will see the light of life and be satisfied" (Isa. 53:11 NIV).

  F. *Suffering for Jesus' sake causes those who suffer to be truly blessed.* They know that God knows all about it and that he stands on the side of those who have been loyal to him at any cost (Matt. 5:10–12; 1 Peter 3:8–18; 4:12–19).

Conclusion

Have faith in God. Believe in Jesus. Jesus was sure about God. How could anyone be as good as Jesus if God were not good?

"All kinds of trials" last only "a little while." But "praise, glory and honor" will last forever (1 Peter 1:6–7 NIV). Jesus said to Peter, "You do not realize now what I am doing, but later you will understand" (John 13:7 NIV).

Many believers who have the strongest faith in God are those who have suffered most. This should encourage us to trust God and never be afraid.

Wednesday Evening, August 26

Title: The Proof of Kinship

Text: "The one who keeps God's commands lives in him, and he in them. And this is how we know that he lives in us: We know it by the Spirit he gave us" (**1 John 3:24 NIV**).

Scripture Reading: 1 John 3:11–24

Introduction

John spoke of one's love for another as "a new command" (1 John 2:8 NIV). How can a command be both old and new? It is old in fact but new in freshness; it is old in principle but new in practice. As Christians grow in grace and in the knowledge of Jesus Christ, each new day brings the light of greater knowledge—and at the same time, a new unfolding of the unfathomable depths of his love! In other words, the command to "love one another" (1 John 3:11) comes from one of the oldest known laws of God to humankind (Lev. 19:18), but it becomes a refreshingly new command as it is restated and demonstrated in Jesus Christ. Therefore the ultimate test of one's Christianity is whether he or she loves others. If we study our Scripture reading, we find that John described this love in four ways.

I. First, we find that it is a spontaneous love (1 John 3:14).

A. *A Christian's love for others should be an involuntary, spontaneous act of the heart.* One should not have to say, "I will make myself love my fellow Christians. They have ignored me, insulted me, and wronged me, but I will love them if it kills me!" If that is the way we love others, we are not showing a spontaneous love. Instead, we are trying to make ourselves love others merely by human effort. This is an impossible feat.

B. *In verse 14 John said that this spontaneous love proves that we have been born again as God's children.* "We know that we have passed from death to life, because we love each other. Anyone who does not love remains in death" (NIV). Spontaneous love means that we are spiritually alive, born into God's family with other Christian brothers and sisters. So when we see our brothers and sisters in Christ, we reflexively reach out to them in love!

II. Second, we find that it is a sacrificial love (1 John 3:16).

A. *To "perceive" means "to know by experience."* We do not know about the love of God simply because we have read what the Bible has to say about it. Rather, as believers in Jesus Christ, we have experienced the love of God.

B. *The identifying quality of God's love, which every believer has experienced, is that Jesus "laid down his life for us."* This was, on Jesus' part, an act of the will. Jesus' life was not wrested away from him by evil men who pursued him as a hunter stalks an animal. Jesus said, "I lay down my life—only to take it up again. No one takes it from me" (John 10:17–18 NIV). Then John said, "We ought to lay down our lives for the brethren." By so doing we imitate the love of Christ in our lives. We literally allow Christ to love through us, even if it means giving our lives for him!

III. Third, we find that it is a sharing love (1 John 3:17–18).

A. *Here John became very practical about Christian love.* He had been talking about such high and lofty acts as giving one's life for another for Jesus' sake. Now he introduced the fact that we can show a sharing love to others in many different ways. These are not necessarily heroic acts; nonetheless, they demonstrate the love of Christ. John also spoke of those who have "material possessions" (v. 17 NIV), or material blessings from God, that we tend to take for granted. If we are so blessed, then see others in need and neglect to help them, "how can the love of God be in [us]?" (v. 17 NIV).

B. *John's summary of practical Christian love in verse 18 is classic.* He is not saying that we should not use kind, warm words of encouragement to express our love to a needy brother or sister. He is simply saying that those words must be accompanied by warm deeds! Every pious, religious word in the world cannot take the place of one genuine act of Christian love.

IV. Fourth, we find that it is a satisfying love (1 John 3:22–24).

A. *The Bible is filled with precious promises God has given to us, particularly promises regarding prayer.* But often these promises are accompanied by certain conditions. In verse 22 the promise is, "[We] receive from him anything we ask" (NIV). How wonderful! But what is the condition? "We keep his commands and do what pleases him" (NIV).

B. *John was not talking about sinless perfection.* He was describing the state of Christians who, as far as they know, have no unconfessed sin in their lives. They are under the control of the Holy Spirit. When this happens, John said that Christians will have "confidence before God" (v. 21 NIV). They will have courage, freedom in speaking, and boldness to stand before God in prayer. The love of God in them is a satisfying love.

Conclusion

A chorus we often sing states the truth of tonight's message simply yet profoundly: "They will know we are Christians by our love." The world will recognize the sincerity of our faith not by our churchmanship or outward piety, but by the expression of love we exhibit toward one another.

SUNDAY MORNING, AUGUST 30

Title: Neutrality Is Nauseating

Text: "On the day you stood aloof while strangers carried off his wealth and foreigners entered his gates and cast lots for Jerusalem, you were like one of them" (**Obad. 11 NIV**).

Scripture Reading: Obadiah 1–16

Hymns: "Who Is on the Lord's Side?" Havergal
"Am I a Soldier of the Cross?" Watts
"Onward, Christian Soldiers," Baring-Gould

Offertory Prayer: Our Father, we are grateful that you always hear our cry when we are troubled. You never turn your back on us however deep our need. You renew our strength as we depend on you. Because of our resources in Christ, we can meet any situation victoriously. As we bring our gifts this morning, may we remember afresh all that you have done for us in Jesus Christ. You have given us a new song. May we sing it well, and may we give our gifts now to share with others the beautiful melody that comes from a transformed life. We pray in Jesus' name. Amen.

Introduction

Scholars have tossed the book of Obadiah back and forth, sometimes not knowing what to do with it. Some consider it an indignant oration. This, however, is not a fair appraisal. Obadiah was filled with righteous indignation. The Edomites had failed to help the Israelites when the city of Jerusalem was assailed by a foreign power. More than that, Edom probably gloated, since the prophet said, "You should not gloat over your brother in the day of his misfortune" (Obad. 12 NIV).

Bad blood had existed between Edom (the descendants of Esau) and Israel (the descendants of Jacob) for many centuries. Several times their armies had marched from one country to another. This time, however, the Edomites merely looked on as some other enemy assaulted the Israelites.

I. Righteous indignation.

Of course, it is wrong to hate! Never is there justification for showing any spirit toward someone except that of love. Yet we are justified in properly evaluating people's attitude toward God's moral law and making some value judgments. Obadiah was God's prophet. He saw the proud Edomites, who were safely nestled in the mountains where no enemy could reach them, make no attempt to help when the Israelites were attacked. Perhaps they rationalized by saying, "We haven't hurt anyone. We simply didn't want to get involved."

Obadiah felt strongly about their neutrality. He would have agreed with poet Marguerite Wilkinson, who said:

> I never cut my neighbor's throat;
> My neighbor's gold I never stole.
> I never spoiled his house or land,
> But God have mercy on my soul!
>
> For I am haunted night and day
> By all the deeds I have not done.
> Oh unattempted loveliness!
> Oh costly value never won!

II. Evil will be punished.

The Edomites were a race of bandits who lived among the rocky crags and natural fortresses near the Dead Sea. They would swoop down on a trading caravan, plunder it, and retreat to the security provided by their strategic geographic location. They were constantly waiting for anyone to pass by, even straggling Israelites, and striking like an eagle strikes its prey, would dash swiftly upon them in murderous hate.

Who are the Edomites of our day? Are they not the ones settled in secure positions who privately engage in crooked politics, gambling rings, illegal drugs, human trafficking, and other crimes that destroy society? How arrogant they are! They firmly hold the destiny of many people and grip a city, county, or even larger area tightly in their clutches. The forces of decency seem powerless before them.

God, however, has a word for people like this, spoken through Obadiah: "'Though you soar like the eagle and make your nest among the stars, from there I will bring you down,' declares the LORD" (Obad. 4 NIV).

III. The source is pride.

Edom's dwelling seemed impregnable. This fostered pride and arrogant self-confidence. Those who think they cannot be touched by the limitations of humanity often do terrible things. Proud people are presumptuous. They say, "Who shall bring me down to the ground?" (Obad. 3), but God said that he will "destroy the wise men out of Edom" (Obad. 8). No one can shake a fist in God's face and ignore the basic laws of humanity. God is present in human affairs. Everyone is answerable to his law. He sees every violation of both law and duty. Some may think they can actively pursue wickedness or look on indifferently when others' rights are violated, but God, in his time, will rectify matters. Obadiah said, "The day of the LORD is near for all nations. As you have done, it will be done to you; your deeds will return upon your own head" (Obad. 15 NIV).

IV. The kingdom is coming.

Although sometimes God seems to delay his work, in his good time he will make his people victorious. The enemy may actively oppose God's people or harm them simply by failing to come when they need help. Either position is despicable in God's sight, and both will be punished. Actually, the neutral person is never completely neutral. A close study of verses 10 through 14 shows that the Edomites were more than neutral. They antagonized, irritated, and even worked against Israel. It is that way every time!

But God always has the last word. The prophet said, "But on Mount Zion will be deliverance" (Obad. 17 NIV). Of course, the greatest fulfillment of that verse is the deliverance from sin that was made possible by Jesus' death on the cross. God's people always win the victory! We should trust him and remain faithful.

Conclusion

Does anyone mistreat you? Are you suffering because of your loyalty to God? If so, wait and you will see God's deliverance. When you become depressed, read his Word often. Underline passages that emphasize the truth of God's faithfulness to his people. Never despair! Those who actively oppose you or stay neutral when they could help you will not win the victory. God will win it, and you will also if you are on his side and seeking to do his will.

SUNDAY EVENING, AUGUST 30

Title: The Salvation of Souls

Text: "Receiving the end of your faith, even the salvation of your souls" **(1 Peter 1:9)**.

Scripture Reading: 1 Peter 1:9–12

Introduction

Salvation is the most important consideration for every person. The very thought that our faith will "result in praise, glory and honor when Jesus Christ is revealed" fills us "with an inexpressible and glorious joy" (1 Peter 1:7, 8 NIV). The goal of our faith, its wonderful consummation, will be the ultimate salvation of our souls (v. 9).

Salvation is also important to God. The salvation of souls was planned in God's heart before the foundation of the world. He determined that humans would be created in his spiritual image, eternal souls who would have freedom of choice. He elected to provide a Savior, Jesus Christ, who would live, die, and rise again. Jesus is an adequate Savior (1:18–25). God also elected that everyone who trusts in Jesus as the Son of God will be sanctified by his Holy Spirit, redeemed by the blood of Christ (v. 2), and "kept by the power of God through faith unto salvation ready to be revealed in the last time" (v. 5).

I. The salvation of souls was the subject of Old Testament searching and revelation (1 Peter 1:10–12).

The Old Testament prophets prophesied under the influence of the Holy Spirit.

    A. *Content of the revelation.*
        1. What did they reveal?
           a. That the Christ would suffer.
           b. That the Christ would be glorified.
           c. That the Gentiles would be saved.
        2. Where did Peter get his sermon? He was present in the upper room when Jesus, just risen from the dead, preached it to the disciples (see Luke 24:44–48).

3. What are certain passages Jesus must have used?
   a. That the Christ would suffer (Ps. 22; Isa. 52:13–53:12).
   b. That the Christ would be glorified (Ps. 110; Isa. 9:6–7).
   c. That the Gentiles would be saved (Gen. 12:1–3; Pss. 47, 67).
B. *Nature of the revelation.*
   1. The prophets searched diligently (1 Peter1:10).
   2. They were aware that while speaking to their own generation, they were also speaking for later generations, and that while speaking to their own people, they were also speaking to the Gentiles (v. 12).
   3. The details as to the times and the exact condition of the times were not revealed to them (v. 11). The Old Testament prophets did not seem to distinguish between the first and second advents of the Messiah with a gospel age between.
   4. They must have had in mind a near fulfillment, which in many instances is now not clear to us. God had in mind a larger meaning. For example, Isaiah's prophecy in Isaiah 7:14–17 must have had an immediate reference to Ahaz. God had in mind a fulfillment with reference to Jesus that was not in Isaiah's mind. As Matthew explained, "All this took place to fulfill what the Lord had said through the prophet: 'The virgin will be with child and will give birth to a son, and they will call him Immanuel' (which means, 'God with us')" (Matt. 1:22–23 NIV). The point is not that events fulfilled what the prophet said, but that they fulfilled what God had said through the prophet.

II. The salvation of souls is the subject of New Testament preaching (I Peter 1:12).

A. *God uses certain people to preach the gospel just as in times past he used certain people to prophesy.*
B. *The Holy Spirit assists preachers as they proclaim the message just as he assisted the prophets.*
C. *The message of the prophets and the message of preachers is the same—the suffering and glory of Christ.*
D. *The purpose of both prophecies and preaching is the salvation of souls.*

III. The salvation of souls is the subject of angelic inquiry (I Peter 1:12).

According to Peter, angels are interested in God's plan. Note Paul's affirmation of angelic interest: "We have been made a spectacle to the whole universe, to angels as well as to human beings" (1 Cor. 4:9 NIV). "God was manifest in the flesh, justified in the Spirit, seen of angels" (1 Tim. 3:16). And Jesus declared, "I tell you, there is rejoicing in the presence of the angels of God over one sinner who repents" (Luke 15:10 NIV).

Conclusion

The salvation of souls is the most important thing in the world. It is the object of God's revelation, of the Holy Spirit's work, and of the Lord's coming. It is the only reason for our pilgrimage here on earth, to save our souls and to help save the souls of others. "How shall we escape, if we neglect so great salvation?"

SEPTEMBER

- **Sunday Mornings**

    Continue the series "The Modern Message of the Minor Prophets."

- **Sunday Evenings**

    Complete the series "Standing Firm under Stress" from First Peter.

- **Wednesday Evenings**

    Continue the series "The Counsel of a Spiritual Father to His Children" from 1 John. On the last Wednesday evening of the month, begin a series of expository messages based on the book of Exodus that reveals God's concern for his people. "The God Who Reveals Himself in Times of Need" is the suggested theme for this series. This series will run through the end of the year.

WEDNESDAY EVENING, SEPTEMBER 2

Title: Identifying the Impostors

Text: "Dear friends, do not believe every spirit, but test the spirits to see whether they are from God, because many false prophets have gone out into the world" (**1 John 4:1 NIV**).

Scripture Reading: 1 John 4:1–10

Introduction

Nothing is simple about Satan. This archenemy of God and humankind likes nothing better than to be portrayed as a red-skinned simpleton with horns and a pitchfork to be laughed at and joked about. He feels quite comfortable when he is linked to the Halloween setting, complete with witches and goblins and ghosts. He is equally at home with cultured intellectuals, who smile condescendingly at the "myth" of Satan, regarding him merely as a superstitious carryover from primitive religion. But the truth of the matter is that "Satan is alive and well." In every generation he updates his wiles and methods of attack.

Nevertheless, Christians have every reason to rejoice in the fact that Satan is marked for defeat. Just as a wounded animal in the forest is more dangerous and ferocious than at any other time in its life, so it is with Satan, who has been mortally wounded by Jesus Christ. The death-dealing blow was inflicted when Jesus cried from the cross, "It is finished" (John 19:30). Satan is marshaling every evil supernatural power at his disposal to keep unbelievers blinded from the truth.

In our passage for tonight's study, John outlined four ways in which we can identify the impostors, the instruments of Satan.

I. First, John said that we must recognize our enemy (1 John 4:1, 3).

A. *Note that John said we are not to "believe every spirit," but we are to "test the spirits" (NIV).* We may infer that many false spirits exist in the world, and we need to be aware of them. One is the "human spirit," which is subject to satanic influence until it comes under the control of Jesus Christ. Another spirit is "the spirit of the world" (1 Cor. 2:12), or the "world system," which is dominated by Satan, or "the god of this world" (2 Cor. 4:4). Also active in the world are "evil spirits," or demon powers, who are emissaries of Satan.

B. *What should we do about these spirits?* John said that *we* are to "try the spirits." That phrase literally means "to put to the test." Verse 3 constitutes the test: "What do you think about the Messiah?" (Matt. 22:42 NIV). Anyone who does not believe that Jesus Christ is God in the flesh is anti-God.

II. Next, we must realize our identity (1 John 4:2, 4).

A. *Here is the positive side of the test we have just discussed.* When we confess our sin and place ourselves at the mercy of God, the Holy Spirit regenerates us, giving us new life. This, in turn, makes it possible for us to believe and confess that Jesus is the Christ.

B. *Verse 4 is a beautiful reiteration of verse 2.* John said that the Holy Spirit's presence in a believer's life is superior to and more powerful than any other spirit in the universe. Each of us can say with Paul: "I can do [everything] through him who gives me strength" (Phil. 4:13 NIV).

III. Then John said that we must emphasize the truth (1 John 4:5–6).

A. *John presented a stark contrast in these verses.* On one side are those of the world system, whose thoughts and actions are dominated by Satan. On the other side are those of us who belong to God and who are indwelt by his Spirit. God gives us spiritual understanding so we can "recognize the Spirit of truth and the spirit of falsehood" (v. 6 NIV).

B. *Two classes of listeners hear the truth and accept it.*
   1. Unbelievers who yield to the conviction of the Holy Spirit and receive the Word in all its life-changing power.
   2. Believers who are already indwelt by the Holy Spirit. One of the Spirit's ministries is to enlighten believers of God's truth.

IV. Finally, we are to publicize the gospel.

A. *This is our message!* Christianity is a way of life based on the fact that even though we did not love God, he loved us and sent his Son to be the payment for our sins.

B. *This is a kind of love that we cannot understand.* It is to be experienced, and when we experience a life filled with this love, we experience God, who covers our sinful past and seals our future forever.

Conclusion

In summary, John has told us that Satan is real; he is committed to keeping unbelievers lost and to harassing Christians. We must realize who we are, for he who is in us is greater than any force of evil in the world (1 John 4:4). We must emphasize the truth of God, because that is the truth that sets us free (John 8:32). Finally, we must share the good news that "God was reconciling the world to himself in Christ" (2 Cor. 5:19 NIV).

SUNDAY MORNING, SEPTEMBER 6

Title: God Will Wait—but Not Forever

Text: "The Lord is slow to anger, and great in power, and will not at all acquit the wicked" **(Nah. 1:3)**.

Scripture Reading: Nahum 1:1–8

Hymns: "There's a Wideness in God's Mercy," Faber
"Grace Greater Than Our Sin," Johnston
"Though Your Sins Be as Scarlet," Crosby

Offertory Prayer: Our Father, we pray that the many wonderful teachings of your Word will never be wasted on us. We humbly acknowledge that we are sinners. We have fallen short of your perfect will for our lives, and we have rebelled against things that you have provided for our good. Because we are redeemed, we know the joy of forgiveness. We bring our tithes and offerings that the gospel may be preached everywhere. Bless the work in our community and bless the causes that we support through our gifts. We pray in Jesus' name. Amen.

Introduction

The repentance of Nineveh under Jonah's preaching was short-lived. Within little more than a century, Assyria had once again turned to sin, reveling in crime and debauchery. God sent a second Hebrew prophet to them, but by this time they had sunk so deep into sin that Nahum considered their destruction imminent.

Nineveh had to be destroyed. God's holiness and power were at stake. The arrogant capital of Assyria had to be judged because the One who controls the forces of nature must not and certainly cannot allow the guilty to remain unpunished.

When did Nahum preach? He foretold Nineveh's destruction, which occurred in 612 BC. He reminded the people that they were no better than the people of Thebes (3:8 NIV), who were carried away into captivity in 663 BC. Therefore Nahum must have preached between these two dates.

Like Obadiah, Nahum saw utter destruction for one of Israel's arch-enemies. Those who attack Nahum's book as unworthy of a place in the prophetic canon are grossly unfair. They base their conclusions on invalid presuppositions. Individuals are not self-righteous because they condemn sin, nor are they blind bigots because they are loyal to their nation and the revelation they possess of God. One is justified in crying out when justice is perverted or morality scorned. God's prophets must declare God's judgment, not because they delight in condemning but because they must uphold God's holiness and sovereignty. They also must encourage their fellow worshipers who are seeking to live in accordance with God's commands. Nahum was a great man who has an important place in both history and prophecy.

I. God is real.

Although each prophet was uniquely conscious of Jehovah's presence in the world, Nahum in a very special way saw his work and spoke graphically of it. Nahum's God was no absentee deity. Jehovah was neither aloof nor apathetic, as one dwelling far off in a distant heaven. The most deadly danger that any nation can face is the moral skepticism that belittles the significance of God's personal presence in the world.

II. God is a stronghold.

Life has more than summer days of ease and prosperity. Winter comes, and when it does, we need a strong defense to weather the storms of life without disaster or disgrace. In our days of weakness, as well as in our days of sorrow and sin, God provides his infinite care. When we are oppressed by a sense of inadequacy, we find our sufficiency in God. If he does not remove that which disturbs us, he gives us grace to bear it. We need to learn this truth and remind ourselves of it often. Many years ago, Dr. Len G. Broughton, while riding on a train with a Supreme Court judge, said, "Judge, you are a man of wide reading and broad sympathy. You possess an abundant amount of knowledge. Can you tell me in a single sentence why we are having so much crime in this country?" The judge replied, "Yes, I can. I think I can do it in a single sentence. Men have lost the consciousness of God." If losing the consciousness of God's holiness causes crime, losing the consciousness of his love can cause great depression. God is a stronghold for us in our time of need.

> Above us are the eyes that never slumber,
> That work against whatever hurts or harms;
> Around us are His mercies without number,
> And underneath the everlasting arms.
>
> Above us are the hands that once were riven,
> That broke the spell of Satan's coming charm;

268

A round us are the pledges He has given,
And underneath the everlasting arms.

Above us are the wings of His protection,
The blessed hope that stills our dread alarms;
Around us are the fruits of His affection,
And underneath the everlasting arms.

—*W. M. Czamanske*

III. God is patient.

Even when God sees entrenched evil and knows it must be punished, he does not rush in arbitrarily and with intense wrath destroy the sinner immediately. He warns! He never smites without first threatening. He is even slow to threaten. After warning, he is slow to sentence the criminal. Once he has given the sentence, he is slow to carry it out. Why? Because God is both great and good. He is both holy and merciful. Paul asked, "Do you show contempt for the riches of his kindness, forbearance and patience, not realizing that God's kindness is intended to lead you to repentance?" (Rom. 2:4 NIV). If God were less than the God of mercy he is, he would have sent terrible judgment on all the world long ago. Instead, he waits and gives sinners every possible chance to realize the folly of their ways and repent.

IV. God will not wait forever.

God had showed mercy to Nineveh. The Assyrian Empire was one of the bloodiest that has ever existed in the world. The cruel acts of its people were unbelievable and even unspeakable. God sent one prophet, Jonah, and the nation repented. How long that repentance lasted we do not know, but probably a very short time. It seems that only one brief period in Assyrian history leaves room for this repentance. Nineveh had turned back to sin, yet God continued to wait, hoping the people would return to him. Perhaps other prophets were sent of whom we have no record. Surely the people of Nineveh were not without a message from God during the many corrupt years after their apostasy, which followed their repentance under Jonah's preaching. But now, in Nahum's day, God's patience became fully exhausted. Nahum had declared that doom was imminent. The people of Nineveh could expect to reap what they had sown. The three chapters of Nahum represent three separate words from God. In chapter 1, we see the destruction of Nineveh *decreed*. In chapter 2, we see the destruction of Nineveh *described*. In chapter 3, we see the destruction of Nineveh *defended*.

Let sinners who continue to reject Christ take warning. We never know when it will be too late for repentance. An ancient rabbi said to his people, "Repent the day before you die." They replied, "But we do not know the day of our death." The rabbi answered, "Then repent today!"

Conclusion

Has God been unusually good to you in spite of the fact that you have ignored him and failed to commit your life to Christ as your Savior? If so, maybe this message today is a special word from God to you. God loves everyone, but this does not mean that everyone will be saved. True, the Bible says that God is not willing that anyone should perish but that all should come to repentance. But elsewhere in his Word, he spoke clearly concerning the necessity of repentance and faith in order to secure salvation. Do you realize that you are lost, yet you still hesitate to make a decision for Christ? Do not misinterpret God's goodness nor his patience with you. He withholds punishment as long as possible because he wants you to know that he loves you. But do not misunderstand his kindness! He desires that you repent. Perhaps Satan's greatest appeal is to tell sinners that they have plenty of time. Maybe they do, but maybe not! One thing is certain. The sooner you become a Christian, the sooner you enjoy an abundant life. The only safe thing to do, considering life's uncertainty, is to be saved now. God waits in mercy, but he will not wait forever for your decision!

SUNDAY EVENING, SEPTEMBER 6

Title: Exhortation to Consecration

Text: "Therefore, with minds that are alert and fully sober, set your hope on the grace to be brought to you when Jesus Christ is revealed at his coming" **(1 Peter 1:13 NIV)**.

Scripture Reading: 1 Peter 1:13–2:8

Introduction

A little boy was very excited as he viewed a circus for the first time. He reported to his grandmother, "If you ever went to just one circus, you would never go to a prayer meeting again." But that was a child's appraisal, because Grandmother had a great joy that he could not yet understand.

Why be a Christian? Why be holy? Why be persecuted for Jesus' sake? How do you answer people who say, "It is futile to serve God. What did we gain by carrying out his requirements and going about like mourners before the Lord Almighty?" (Mal. 3:14 NIV).

What did Peter say? His reply is in God's grace providing an eternal plan of salvation, past, present, and future, as outlined in 1 Peter 1:1–12. The word "Therefore" (NIV) in our text points back to God's gracious plan as the ground of Peter's call to holiness.

I. As children of God the Father, be obedient (I Peter 1:13–25).

A. *What are we as Christians exhorted to do?*
   1. Have "minds that are alert" (v. 13 NIV). Be ready to accomplish God's will.

270

    2. Be "fully sober" (v. 13 NIV). Live moderately.

    3. "Set your hope on the grace to be brought to you when Jesus Christ is revealed at his coming" (v. 13 NIV).

    4. "Do not conform to the evil desires you had when you lived in ignorance" (v. 14, see 1 Peter 2:1).

    5. "Be holy, because [God is] holy" (vv. 15–16).

    6. "Live . . . in reverent fear" (v. 17). God is worthy of reverence.

    7. Be obedient to God the Holy Spirit, especially as he leads you to love others unconditionally.

  B. *Why are Christians exhorted to consecration?*

    1. Jesus is coming (v. 13). He will return to end the gospel age. He also comes to believers at death.

    2. We are children of the heavenly Father. God is holy, so we need to act in such a way that we are recognized as his children (vv. 14–17; see Matt. 5:9).

    3. The price paid for redemption (vv. 18–23; cf. 2 Cor. 5:14; 1 John 4:19).

    4. God can be trusted. His word is sure (vv. 24–25; see Isa. 40:8).

II. As babies in Christ, grow (1 Peter 2:1–3).

No one is born fully developed, either physically or spiritually. Babies are not expected to walk and talk at birth. They are expected to take nourishment and grow. God has provided "pure spiritual milk," his Word, so that by it we may grow up in our salvation now that we have tasted that the Lord is good (v. 2 NIV). When one is born again, that person comes into the kingdom of God as a spiritual baby. He or she needs to take nourishment and grow (see Pss. 34:8; 119; Matt. 4:4; 1 Cor. 3:1–3; 2 Tim. 2:15; Heb. 6:5).

III. As living stones, be the living temple of God (1 Peter 2:4–8).

In this bold passage, the believers are conceived as living stones built on Jesus Christ, the foundation stone, to form a living temple in which God dwells.

In the light of Peter's experience at Caesarea Philippi (see Matt. 16:13–23), it is interesting that he did not consider himself to be the foundation of the church, but rather he understood Christ to be. Isaiah 28:16 and Psalm 118:22 are the Old Testament Scriptures quoted, but Peter was preaching what he learned from Jesus as recorded in Matthew 21:42–44.

The religious leaders who were supposed to be experts rejected Jesus as a stone set aside. God made him the head of the corner (vv. 6–7; cf. Acts 2:36). Peter had preached this sermon before (see Acts 4:8–12). Paul had essentially the same idea in Ephesians 2:19–22. Jesus is the head of the corner for believers, but he is a stone of stumbling to the disobedient.

Conclusion

This message does not conclude. It continues next week with further illustrations of the nature of the Christian life and additional reasons why Christians should be consecrated.

WEDNESDAY EVENING, SEPTEMBER 9

Title: Love versus Fear

Text: "There is no fear in love; but perfect love casteth out fear: because fear hath torment. He that feareth is not made perfect in love" **(1 John 4:18)**.

Scripture Reading: 1 John 4:11–21

Introduction

Through Jesus Christ, God revealed himself to humans. Through the Holy Spirit, God indwells humans. In tonight's study, we shall see three grand and glorious things about this unique relationship between God and his people. First, we shall see the *gift*; then we shall discover the *gain* (what we have "gained" in receiving this gift); and finally, the *glory*, the inexpressible result of our continuing relationship with God through the Holy Spirit's presence within us.

I. Let's examine this incomparable gift of God to the believer (1 John 4:12–13).

A. *The first part of the gift is expressed outwardly.* "If we love one another, God dwelleth in us." We prove our faith to the world by loving one another—or, more specifically, by letting God love others *through* us. I may "like" you or "dislike" you; that is beside the point. You may "detest" some of my ways; that, too, is beside the point. The simple, earthshaking truth John has given us is that God dwells in us *only* if we love one another in spite of who or what we are!

B. *The second part of the gift is expressed inwardly.* It concerns the assurance we need constantly that we are the children of God. How do we know that we are his? Because he has given us his Holy Spirit. Upon our repentance, God "baptized," submerged, us into his family. Furthermore, the verb phrase, "He has given" (NIV), is a perfect tense, indicating that the gift was a permanent one, given to us at a point in the past to be forever ours.

II. But then, there is the gain (1 John 4:17).

A. *What do we "gain" in this relationship with God that transforms us and makes us his children?* The word is *boldness*, and it is one of the most important words in the New Testament. Luke said in the book of Acts that the religious authorities were amazed at the "boldness" of Peter and John (4:13). The disciples "spake the word of God with boldness" (Acts 4:31). We are invited, as God's children, to "come boldly unto the throne of grace" (Heb. 4:16). And this "boldness" is neither a brashness nor a reckless presumption, but a "freedom of speech" God has given believers through the presence of his Spirit indwelling them.

B. *Another dimension of this boldness is revealed in verse 17.* Christians will have boldness "in the day of judgment." Because of their relationship with God through Christ, they will have no reason to fear at the judgment. Paul said plainly in 2 Corinthians 5:10 that "we must all appear before the judgment seat of Christ; that every one may receive the things done in his body, according to that he hath done, whether it be good or bad."

III. Finally, let us see the glory of it all (I John 4:18–21).

A. *What kind of "fear" was John talking about in verse 18?* It is possible that he was talking about fear at the thought of judgment. But where there is "perfect love" (and it is perfect because it is God's love in us and not our own), there is trust, confidence, and assurance. Just as darkness cannot exist in the presence of light, so fear cannot reign where there is love.

B. *There is no torment like that produced in a person who lives in fear.* There is a fear of tomorrow, a fear of death, a fear of judgment. And because sin alienates people from God, it is the fear of unbelievers toward a God whom they do not know and whom they cannot call "Father."

C. *The glorious promise is that "perfect love casteth out fear."* When we surrender to God and are able to allow God to love *through* us, there can be no fear. The love of God within us destroys and dissipates fear.

Conclusion

If you are a Christian, you have already received the greatest gift of all—salvation by grace through faith. But have you received the gift John talks about, which ought to be operative in the life of every Christian? Are you letting Christ love others through you, and are you receiving constantly the assurance that you belong to God because of his Spirit within you? Have you gained a "holy boldness," a freedom to share your faith with others? Are you free from fear because God has shed abroad his love in your heart?

SUNDAY MORNING, SEPTEMBER 13

Title: God Deals with Sin

Text: "The great day of the LORD is near . . . a day of wrath" (**Zeph. 1:14–15**).

Scripture Reading: Zephaniah 1:2–18

Hymns: "Depth of Mercy! Can There Be," Wesley
"Pass Me Not, O Gentle Savior," Crosby
"Though Your Sins Be as Scarlet," Crosby

Offertory Prayer: Our Father, we are grateful that you have given us victory over sin. We rejoice that you have sent Jesus Christ to remove the dread of death. We bring our tithes and offerings to you this morning and pray that they will be used to take the message that in Jesus Christ is both life and power. Let this message bring assurance to the doubting and comfort to the weak. We thank you that enduring faith may replace doubt in the lives of those who are able to hear the gospel because of our gifts. In Jesus' name we pray. Amen.

Introduction

The name *Zephaniah* means "Jehovah hides." Some scholars believe his parents gave him this name because he was born during Manasseh's reign in Judah, a time of immorality and sin. Persecution against God's people was so great that perhaps children of righteous parents actually had to be hidden to prevent them from being killed.

Two significant things are noted about Zephaniah. First, his family tree is traced back four generations to Hezekiah, probably the great king of Judah. Second, he prophesied during the reign of Josiah, a good king (639–608 BC) who discovered an ancient law book in the temple in the eighteenth year of his reign (621 BC) and immediately started a program of moral and spiritual reform. Since Zephaniah condemned the sinful practices that were abolished by Josiah's order, it is generally agreed that he preached prior to 621 BC. This would make him an early contemporary of Jeremiah, who preached in the thirteenth year of Josiah's reign (626 BC).

I. God's presence cannot tolerate sin.

Although we find a few hopeful passages in Zephaniah's book, its main theme is God's judgment of sin. Zephaniah "hit the ground running" as he began his preaching. In Zephaniah 1:2 he declared, "I will utterly consume all things from off the land, saith the LORD." He then started to list the various groups that must face judgment.

A. *Humans, animals, birds, and fish will be cut off.* Those engaged in idolatrous worship, those who had backslid, and those who had never sought the Lord in the first place—all must give an account to the God of holiness.

B. *Another group was singled out for condemnation.* These were complacent people who did not really believe that God would do anything. Zephaniah characterized them as people who thought, "The LORD will not do good, neither will he do evil" (1:12).

C. *Zephaniah teaches us one great lesson.* All people, no matter who they are, who are rebelling against God's will must suffer the consequences of

274

their sin. God has ordained a moral law that says sinners will suffer. This law will never be repealed, because it is part of God's holy character. The wages of sin are death and always will be!

II. God urges people to repent.

A. *Zephaniah realized and told the people that God is always available.* Though we may be alienated from God and distant from one another, we can be brought close by true repentance. Certainly repentance, either on a national level or an individual one, is the only safeguard against destruction.

B. *Repentance requires self-examination.* We must know ourselves thoroughly. We must be honest with ourselves as we determine where we stand in God's sight. Everything worthless in both our hearts and conduct must be destroyed. If we do not judge ourselves by repenting, we will be judged by God. Any earnest search of our lives will reveal sin. We must be willing to forsake that sin and follow the Lord. The phrase "gather together" (2:1) indicates a religious assembly and therefore implies that confession of sin should be public. This is in harmony with New Testament teaching, for Jesus said we should confess him publicly.

III. Why seek the Lord?

Four purposes for seeking the Lord were relevant in Zephaniah's day and are equally important for us.

A. *We seek God to know him.* Jesus said, "This is eternal life: that they know you, the only true God, and Jesus Christ, whom you have sent" (John 17:3 NIV). Throughout the Old and New Testaments, emphasis is placed on having a heart that knows God.

B. *We seek God to enjoy him.* First, of course, we must be reconciled. We cannot rejoice in the Lord until we have accepted Christ's atonement for our sins. Only then can we draw near to God, finding great joy, and our souls be satisfied by his blessings. Living in his favor, his lovingkindness is meaningful for us.

C. *We seek God to serve him.* Our constant prayer should be the words that Paul spoke on the Damascus Road, "Lord, what wilt thou have me to do?" (Acts 9:6). We do not have to wait until we get to heaven to receive our reward for service. Keeping God's commandments and giving ourselves in devotion to him brings us joy.

D. *We seek God to be more like him.* An old truism says, "We become like that which we constantly admire." As we love God and worship him faithfully, we will find ourselves becoming more like him. We cannot reproduce in our lives some of God's attributes, such as omniscience, omnipresence, and omnipotence, but we can progressively come to resemble his moral attributes. As we grow in the Christian life, we can become renewed after the image of him who creates us in righteousness and true holiness. To seek the Lord means to become more like him.

IV. Purity follows repentance.

A. *Zephaniah closed his recorded preaching with a word of hope.* He saw the people returning to the Lord. Judgment had scattered the nation, but he saw Israel restored. He also looked beyond and saw the Gentiles being converted. God would gather for himself a people of "pure language" (3:9) so that they might call on the name of the Lord and serve him wholeheartedly.

B. *Purity means a refined character and conversation.* Pure language implies a pure life, for the mouth speaks from the abundance of the heart. At the Tower of Babel the people's tongues were confused because of pride. At Pentecost, however, the people were united as they spoke in "other tongues." The only hope for a fragmented world to be unified is through a genuine turning to God.

Conclusion

God's day will be a time when he has the final word. To sinners it will be a day of reckoning. No escape is possible from the penalty that accompanies sin. The day of the Lord will bring the inexorable certainty of the moral law that "a man reaps what he sows" (Gal. 6:7 NIV).

On the other hand, for those who turn in repentance, the horrible threat of punishment becomes lost in the wonderful message of God's love. God will break the power of sin. The darkness of the day of the Lord, a day of judgment and terror, will give way to the radiant life of his grace. As Zephaniah anticipated God's great forgiveness, he shouted, "Sing, O daughter of Zion; shout, O Israel; be glad and rejoice with all the heart" (3:14).

SUNDAY EVENING, SEPTEMBER 13

Title: God's Chosen People

Text: "You are a chosen people, a royal priesthood, a holy nation, God's special possession, that you may declare the praises of him who called you out of darkness into his wonderful light. Once you were not a people, but now you are the people of God; once you had not received mercy, but now you have received mercy" **(1 Peter 2:9–10 NIV)**.

Scripture Reading: Exodus 19:3–6; Titus 2:11–14; 1 Peter 2:9–10

Introduction

Peter had exhorted the scattered Christians in the Roman provinces to consecrate themselves to Christ on the basis that they were:

1. Children of God the Father (1 Peter 1:13–25).
2. Believers in Christ who ought to grow (1 Peter 2:1–3).
3. Living stones in the living temple (1 Peter 2:4–8).

He now called for consecration on the basis that they are God's chosen people. This relationship may be plotted as a dot within a circle. The circle completely owns the dot. God completely owns his people.

I. God's chosen people.

The text designating Christians as God's chosen people is almost identical with the words of God spoken through Moses at the foot of Mount Sinai designating Israel as God's chosen people (Ex. 19:3–6). The people of Israel misunderstood the nature of their covenant relationship. They thought that they were better than the Gentiles. They generally thought that they had been elected to salvation rather than to service. In the main, they persecuted and killed God's representatives, culminating in the crucifixion of Jesus.

In the parable of the wicked husbandmen (Matt. 21:33–46), Jesus epitomized their sad history of poor stewardship. He indicated the end of Israel's special relationship in the words, "Therefore say I unto you, The kingdom of God shall be taken from you, and given to a nation bringing forth the fruits thereof" (Matt. 21:43). Our text informs us that the nation, or people, who now have a similar relationship to God as the chosen people are the Christians.

II. The nature of God's chosen people.

  A. *God had called his people out of darkness into his wonderful light.* They had come from heathenism to Christianity (cf. Rom. 9:24–26; Eph. 5:8; Col. 1:12–13). Was Peter familiar with these writings of Paul, or did these writers independently develop the same ideas?
  B. *They were:*
    1. "A chosen people" (1 Peter 2:9 NIV), an elect race corresponding to spiritual Israel, Abraham's children by faith (see Gal. 3:22–29).
    2. "A royal priesthood" (1 Peter 2:9 NIV). Every Christian is a priest. He or she needs no one to go to God on his or her behalf. We say that officers in Christ's church are bishops, presbyters, deacons, and so on, but not priests.
    3. "A holy nation." Holy means set apart, dedicated to God.
    4. "God's special possession" (1 Peter 2:9 NIV). In Titus 2:14 Paul wrote, "[Christ] gave himself for us to redeem us from all wickedness and to purify for himself a people that are his very own, eager to do what is good" (NIV).

III. The purpose of God's election (1 Peter 2:9).

The purpose is "that you may declare the praises of him who called you out of darkness into his wonderful light" (1 Peter 2:9 NIV). When God first chose Israel at Sinai, the reason was not that God loved Israel more than the Gentiles. "For all the earth is mine" (Ex. 19:5) is one of the reasons God gave for calling Israel as a special people. God's election of Israel was a method for reaching all nations. God's election of Christians is a method for reaching the heathen with the gospel.

Conclusion

The purpose of one's life is to glorify God. Election is not to salvation but to service. The Christian is to bear fruit. God desires his chosen people to be missionaries to all people. If God's people become rebellious and sinful, he may raise up another people who will accomplish his purpose.

WEDNESDAY EVENING, SEPTEMBER 16

Title: That Which Overcomes

Text: "Whatsoever is born of God overcometh the world: and this is the victory that overcometh the world, even our faith" **(1 John 5:4)**.

Scripture Reading: 1 John 5:1–12

Introduction

In the section of John's epistle that we will be studying tonight, John had some probing things to say about faith in the life of a believer. He gave us the *preamble* of faith—the foundation, the basic premise, the "launching pad" of a faith that identifies one unmistakably as a member of the family of God. Then, increasing the pressure of his spiritual scalpel, John talked about the *practice* of faith—that which, without words, speaks eloquently of one's relationship with God. Finally, he gave the *principle* of faith, driving down some pilings on which to build the superstructure of one's faith.

I. First, let's examine John's preamble of faith (1 John 5:1).

A. *John stated a basic truth: "Whosoever believeth that Jesus is the Christ is born of God."* In other words, he was saying that those who have truly experienced the new birth are those who not only have given intellectual assent to the incarnation, but who also have received in their hearts this truth. They know, with experiential knowledge, that Jesus came in the flesh and lived a sinlessly perfect life on earth.

B. *In the last phrase of this verse, John's underlying theme emerges.* The NIV translates it, "Everyone who loves the father loves his child as well." Here is the greatest equation in the Bible. *Loving God equals loving his children!* John was talking about spiritual family love—not love for the lost person, which is a redemptive, compassionate love. Rather, John was presenting a complete cycle: When I love God, I love his children.

278

II. In verses 2–5, John became very practical and talked about faith.

A. *Here is a second equation: Loving God equals keeping his commandments.* What had John done? He had taken the first equation—"Loving God equals loving his children"—and changed it from an attitude into an action. In other words, I can *say* to you that I love God and consequently his children, and I can fool you, but I cannot fool God. But if I "keep his commandments" and do those things he has told me to do in his Word, you can *see* that and know that I am sincere. That is faith in practice and not just in word.

B. *Now let us reiterate what we have learned previously regarding this love of God in us that flows out to our brothers and sisters.* It is *spontaneous*; that is, it is explosive, filled with joy and overflowing. Love is not done out of duty but flows naturally from the constrainment of joy.

C. *Then John said that keeping God's commandments is not a "grievous" experience.* God's commands are not burdensome. For most people, rules and regulations are unpleasant. We chafe under them; we resent them. But John said there is a difference with the commandments of Jesus. Because his commandments are given in love, they are a delight and not a burden!

III. In verses 6–12 John set forth the principle of faith.

A. *The principle of faith in God is based on two facts about Jesus that John referred to by the use of the words "water" and "blood."* "Water" refers to Christ's baptism by John at the beginning of his public ministry. By this act, it was declared to the world that Jesus was the Messiah. From that moment, the steps of Jesus were ever and always toward the cross. So then, if the "water" represents the commencement of Jesus' earthly journey, the "blood" stands for the culmination of it all on the cross. Thus the principle of Christian faith has been dependent from the beginning on the saviorhood of Jesus and on his atonement for sin through his blood shed on the cross.

B. *The victory shout comes in verse 12: "He that hath the Son hath life; and he that hath not the Son of God hath not life."* When we start to exercise and practice the faith God gave us when we were born again, we begin to feel a power and a peace that provides spiritual buoyancy. We can say, "This is the life!" Why? Because we have the Son, the Lord Jesus Christ, living within, on the throne of our heart!

Conclusion

Many Christians do not "practice" their faith. It lies dormant within them. As a result, they have no joy. They cannot say, "This is the life!" in regard to their Christianity. They have no spontaneity in their love for their fellow Christians. Often they become miserable and defensive in their Christian lives—sometimes even afflicted with self-pity. The practice of one's faith is the overcoming power in life.

SUNDAY MORNING, SEPTEMBER 20

Title: God's Grace Is Marvelous and Mysterious

Text: "I will restore to you the years that the locust hath eaten" **(Joel 2:25)**.

Scripture Reading: Joel 1:2–14; 2:21–27

Hymns: "Lead, Kindly Light," Newman
"Have Faith in God," McKinney
"Great Is Thy Faithfulness," Chisholm

Offertory Prayer: Our Father, we know that you love the world you have made, and you love every person who lives in it. As we worship the beauty of your holiness this morning, we realize that many do not know Jesus Christ as Savior. We pray that our gifts may be used to share the gospel with those who are lost. We thank you that we know the gift of salvation through your Son. Inspire us to so live and give that through us many who are enslaved by chains of sin may be set free, and many who are living in darkness may come to know him who is the Light of the World. We pray this in Jesus' name. Amen.

Introduction

Everyone knows which prophet is connected with a "great fish." Jonah! But do you know who is connected with a plague of locusts? Joel! When did he preach? Most conservative scholars believe he was one of the earliest prophets to Israel, preaching sometime between Jonah and Amos or perhaps even before Jonah.

Joel preached during a time when the land was strongly influenced by priests. He often referred to religious rituals and matters associated with formal worship. His book begins with a description of various calamities that had come on the land. He then issued a solemn call to repentance. Most scholars agree that the material in the book after 2:17 represents the time following the people's repentance. The Lord becomes compassionate and promises restoration and blessing.

One should read the whole book at one time, for it is very possible that its three chapters represent one great sermon. The most notable thing about the book is the picture it draws of God's grace and his willingness to pour out his Spirit on the people when they turn in earnest repentance to him.

I. Desperation.

Joel opened his message with an alarming cry. The land was completely devastated and the situation was desperate. No one could remember anything like it. The great-grandchildren of those living would hear about the terrible plague of locusts that stripped the land of its vegetation and left it scorched.

To Joel these events represented God's chastening hand on the nation.

280

Rather than mentioning specific sins, he proclaimed that God's moral law had been violated. He left it to God's Spirit to impress on the people the individual sins they had committed.

Sin always brings punishment! The moral law of sin and judgment affects unregenerate people. God's chastening hand comes to his own children. The situation in Israel is existentially symbolic of the life of every person who lives in rebellion to God. Sin brings crisis!

II. Invitation.

a) *No prophet of God properly condemns sin or threatens judgment unless he also gives an invitation to repent and experience God's forgiveness.* The Hebrew prophets never hesitated to cry out against evil, both national and personal. On the other hand, they were just as eager to proclaim their God as "gracious and merciful, slow to anger, and of great kindness" (2:13). Although several isolated verses in the first section urge the people to cry to God, the actual call to repentance is found in the middle of the second chapter.

b) *Deliverance from the penalty and power of sin is based on one's willingness to sincerely repent.* In order to repent, one must realize that sin is more than a series of acts; it is a broken relationship with God. Robert G. Lee made a significant distinction between sin and sins. He said, "Sins are the visible results which come from sin. Sin is a state and refers to the depraved nature . . . sins are acts, the result of, a fruit of, the sinful nature." Dr. Lee emphasized the point further with prolific parallelism:

> Sin is character, but sins are in conduct. Sin is the center, but sins are the circumference. Sin is the root, but sins are the fruit. Sin is the fountain, but sins are its flow. Sin is the tree, sins are fruit of the evil tree. Sin is the unstrung root, sins are the jangling inharmonies produced therefrom. Sin is the evil lungs, sins are the polluted and poisonous breathings that come from every gasp of the lungs. Sin is the contaminated reservoir, sins are the streams that flow therefrom carrying pollution and disease as they go. Sin is source, sins are secretions. Sin is the old nature, sins are the manifestation of the old nature. Sin is what we are, sins are what we've done. Sin is the fact, sins are the act.

> In other words, sin is an affair of the heart, and the need is not for ritual reformation nor a change in worship methods, but heartfelt sorrow for sin, genuine repentance, and full surrender to God's purpose. When people come to understand the spiritual nature of forgiveness, they will rend their hearts and not their garments (2:12–13).

III. Restoration

    A. *God never refuses one whose heart is truly repentant.*

        1. From a national standpoint, God loved Israel and was "jealous for his land" (2:18). Starting with 2:18, Joel spoke in a comforting way. The locusts, which were seen as punishment from God because of sin, would be driven away. The land would be glad and rejoice. A great future was in store for Israel.

        2. The message is also for individuals. In fact, every message from God is ultimately for individuals. Sins would be forgiven and fellowship with God would be restored. The people would know that God was in their midst and that he was their God. They would never be disappointed in him. One statement by Joel regarding the restoration is strange but very important. He said, "I will restore to you the years that the locust hath eaten" (2:25). This statement is more than just a promise of fertility to the land—it is a great promise for each individual. God's grace is an unusual thing. One prophet told the returning exiles that they had received from the Lord's hand double for all their sins (Isa. 40:2). Moses reminded the people of his day that with God's help one could chase a thousand, but two could chase ten thousand (Deut. 32:30). Gideon's three hundred put to flight the entire army of the Midianites.

           The sweetness and inward joy that forgiveness brings is marvelous! Those who taste such joy know God's love in a unique way. Such forgiveness makes people remarkably sensitive to the spiritual weaknesses of others. Those who have been forgiven much can love much and give themselves in service in an exceptional way, compensating for years wasted in sin.

    B. *We must be careful, however.* It is always better not to have sinned so deeply. The scars remain although the sins are forgiven. We may tend to express an overbearing zeal that could be emotionally unhealthy. Extremism will defeat or seriously damage our well-meaning witness. On the other hand, we are thrilled at the prospect of God restoring the years that the locusts have eaten. We should never limit the matchless power of God's grace. With him all things are possible.

Conclusion

God is always present in the life of a nation. He uses a collective group of people as long as they can be used, and he earnestly desires to see nations continue forever in his will. Israel was used by God in a unique way to bring Jesus into the world. He lovingly watched over the nation because he had chosen it as his instrument.

The greatest lesson in Joel's prophecy should be the message directed to individuals. Sin brings judgment, but God's grace brings forgiveness, resulting in joy, peace, and the outpouring of God's Spirit. We must remember that although God loves those who are undeserving, they must repent of sin to receive salvation.

SUNDAY EVENING, SEPTEMBER 20

Title: The Christian Pilgrim

Text: "Dearly beloved, I beseech you as strangers and pilgrims, abstain from fleshly lusts, which war against the soul; having your conversation honest among the Gentiles: that, whereas they speak against you as evildoers, they may by your good works, which they shall behold, glorify God in the day of visitation" **(1 Peter 2:11–12)**.

Scripture Reading: 1 Peter 2:11–3:12

Introduction

Christians are to be in the world but not of it. Jesus refused to pray that his disciples should be removed from the world. "My prayer is not that you take them out of the world but that you protect them from the evil one" (John 17:15 NIV). The world needs Christians (cf. Matt. 5:13–16), and the Christian probably needs the world.

Peter addressed his Christian readers as "strangers and pilgrims."

I. The nature of the pilgrimage.

A. *Pilgrims are citizens of heaven.* "We, however, are citizens of heaven, and we eagerly wait for our Savior, the Lord Jesus Christ, to come from heaven" (Phil. 3:20 GNT). As citizens of the kingdom of heaven, the pilgrims are subject to the King. They are exhorted to live in this temporary abode in accord with the will of the Lord of their eternal home (cf. Heb. 11:8–10, 13–16). For this cause they will "abstain from fleshly lusts, which war against the soul" (1 Peter 2:11).

B. *Pilgrims are witnesses.* They seek to get others to join them in the Christian journey. Peter exhorted believers, "Your conduct among the heathen should be so good that when they accuse you of being evildoers, they will have to recognize your good deeds and so praise God on the Day of his coming" (1 Peter 2:12 GNT).

II. Some areas of the pilgrim's responsibility.

A. *Civic responsibilities (1 Peter 2:13–17).*

1. It is in accord with God's will that civil governments exist. The purpose of government is "for the punishment of evildoers, and for the praise of them that do well" (v. 14).

2. Christians are not anarchists. They are to submit to the civil authorities as part of their duty to God. "Submit" is a military

283

metaphor that pictures an army arranging itself in proper order for battle. All of the soldiers cannot be generals if the army is to accomplish its purpose.

3. Peter's general admonition, "Submit yourselves to every ordinance of man for the Lord's sake," must be tempered by what Peter did. When the authorities overstepped the bounds of God's will for civil government and charged Peter and John not to speak at all or teach in the name of Jesus, they answered, "Whether it be right in the sight of God to hearken unto you more than unto God, judge ye. For we cannot but speak the things which we have seen and heard" (Acts 4:19–20). Jesus' great affirmation, "Render therefore unto Caesar the things which are Caesar's; and unto God the things which are God's" (Matt. 22:21), indicates that duties to God and duties to government ought not to conflict with each other. When government oversteps its bounds, then Christians must obey God.

B. *Master and slave relationships (1 Peter 2:18–25).* Peter did not seem to question the institution of human slavery, nor did other Christians for many centuries. Today in our country and in countries around the world, Christians are on the front lines in the fight against sex slavery and human trafficking, the modern-day forms of slavery. Commanding a slave to suffer a bad master is quite different from suffering for Jesus' sake or for righteousness' sake as commanded in Matthew 5:10–12.

C. *Home relationships (1 Peter 3:1–7).* In the Hebrew world, the patriarchal family was not questioned. Peter did not question it. Within the system he suggests:

1. Wives can win their husbands to Christ by a good example (v. 1).
2. Beauty of character is more important than outward beauty. "Let it be the hidden man of the heart" (v. 4).
3. Husbands have a Christian obligation to be kind to their wives. "Giving honour unto the wife" (v. 7).
4. Peter acknowledged that both the husband and the wife are equal spiritually in God's sight as "heirs together of the grace of life" (v. 7). The teaching of Jesus in Matthew 19:4–6, quoting with approval Genesis 2:24, and his advocacy of the single standard in John 8:1–11, leads us to believe that his will is that both men and women be considered as equals and full partners in the home.

Conclusion

Our pilgrimage is important. In it we prepare for heaven. In it we influence others. The example and teaching of Christ are our guide, and his will is love (see Matt. 22:35–40).

WEDNESDAY EVENING, SEPTEMBER 23

Title: That You May Know

Text: "These things have I written unto you that believe on the name of the Son of God; that ye may know that ye have eternal life, and that ye may believe on the name of the Son of God" (**1 John 5:13**).

Scripture Reading: 1 John 5:13–21

Introduction

The spiritual leaders who, through the generations, have consistently pointed people to God have been those who possessed an unshakable faith in God, in his Word, and in his promises. They *knew* the God whom they served; they *believed* in him; and when they spoke they communicated that confidence and assurance to others. Genuine Christianity is based on a know-so relationship with God through Jesus Christ. (From John's repeated use of "we know" comes the term "know-so." We *know* certain things about Jesus, *so*, or therefore, certain things are true.)

In the closing verses of John's epistle, he revealed *four things* we can know for certain. As he wrote, there is no hint of hesitation; here was a man who knew and knew that he knew.

I. First, John spoke about our eternal safekeeping (1 John 5:13).

A. *John declared his purpose in writing his gospel in John 20:31.* He showed how one can *receive* eternal life by believing that Jesus is the Christ. His purpose in writing 1 John was that we may *know* that we have it.

B. *To the people whom John originally wrote his letters, these words were shining beacons in a world of pagan darkness.* The believers were surrounded by people whose lives were saturated with mythology and superstition, and who believed in many gods, most of whom were characterized as jealous, angry, and immoral. These Christians were under constant attack; they were opposed, criticized, ridiculed, and persecuted. Obviously, there were some who had come to doubt their salvation.

C. *Therefore, against these continual onslaughts of doubt with which Satan has attacked every generation, John lifts his voice with ringing assurance.* "You can *know* that you have eternal life!" How? "By *these things* which I have written unto you" (5:13). What are "these things"? He has spoken of the settled-sin question (1 John 1:9), of our keeping his commandments (2:3), of the love shed abroad in our hearts (3:11), and of the witness of the Holy Spirit (4:2, 13).

II. Then John gave a second thing of which we can be certain: answered prayer (1 John 5:14–15).

A. *This is one of the Bible's most important statements on prayer.* Of the three vital things John taught about prayer, the first is that there must be

285

a *conviction* about prayer. "This is the confidence that we have in him." We are not to believe that prayer is just a probability. It is not an exercise to be engaged in as a last resort. We are to believe in the efficacy of a genuine prayer life.

B. *Second, there is a condition that accompanies prayer.* "If we ask any thing according to his will, he heareth us." He will not answer just because we ask. There is a certain way in which we are to ask—and that is "according to his will." Our asking will be according to his will when it is according to his Word.

C. *Third, this kind of praying brings a conclusion.* "And if we know that he hear us, whatsoever we ask, we know that we have the petitions desired of him." Prayer, offered according to God's conditions, brings us what we ask for. As a matter of faith, we have what we ask for the moment we ask. But as a matter of fact, the answer may be long in coming.

III. John included here another dimension of faith, another privilege that is ours: intercessory concern (1 John 5:16–17).

A. *These are awesome and chilling words.* In keeping with the context in which John had been writing, we can assume that the "sin unto death" is that sin committed by the unbelievers who were saying that Jesus was not God come in the flesh. They were denying the incarnation. They had intellectually received the Word, and like those described in Hebrews 6, they had "tasted" of heavenly things. But they had not become "new creations," whereby they were able to say with conviction that Jesus is the Son of God, the Christ.

B. *Engaging in intercessory prayer is a privilege and a solemn duty for Christians.* We can intercede in prayer on behalf of not only our brothers and sisters in Christ, but also on behalf of unbelievers who may be tottering on the rim of eternal destruction.

IV. Finally, John closed this thrilling epistle on a note of triumph.

He said that Christians can know ultimate victory in spite of the power and harassment of Satan (5:18–21).

A. *John was describing believers, and the phrase "sinneth not" is in the present tense.* It refers not to the committing of an *act* of sin, but to a continuous lifestyle of sin. Believers will err along the way but will not pursue the habit of sinning. Rather, they will generally strive toward godliness. Why? Because they watch over, or guard, their spiritual lives. They are alert to temptation.

B. *In verse 19 John said that Christians have a special identity.* "And we know that we are of God." Christians belong to a new generation of people, to a new order of life. Often they are in the minority, but the hope of the world lies in the declaration of Christ through this minority, which Jesus called "the salt of the earth" and "the light of the world."

Conclusion

John concluded his letter in a rather unusual way: "Little children, keep yourselves from idols." An "idol" is anything that comes between God and me, any substitute for God. It may be a desire, an ambition, a pleasure, even a friend. As long as anything in my life is causing an "eclipse" of my Lord, I am powerless as a Christian. I am vulnerable to Satan's attacks. But once the channel is cleared and there is "nothing between my soul and the Savior," all is well! Then *I can know* whose I am because of the unhindered witness of God's indwelling Spirit.

SUNDAY MORNING, SEPTEMBER 27

Title: Take Your Doubts to the Lord

Text: "How long, LORD, must I call for help, but you do not listen? . . . I will look to see what he will say to me" **(Hab. 1:2; 2:1 NIV)**.

Scripture Reading: Habakkuk 1:1–2:3

Hymns: "Have Faith in God," McKinney
        "O God, Our Help in Ages Past," Watts
        "Faith Is the Victory," Yates

Offertory Prayer: Our Father, give us wisdom to distinguish between your way and the world's way. May we never cling to false or foolish hopes, but always open our hearts to receive the abundant joy that is found only in Jesus. May we remember the richness of your ways when we are tempted to put self above service to others. Keep us from being so foolish as to trust our own resources. Help us realize that true security is found in you alone. We pray in Jesus' name. Amen.

Introduction

Most of the Old Testament prophets said "thus saith the LORD" with certainty. However, Habakkuk, like Jeremiah, dared to ask "Why?" in regard to some phases of the Lord's work. Habakkuk preached shortly before Nebuchadnezzar first invaded Judah in 605 BC. His name means "embracer," which scholars suggest spoke symbolically of his "wrestling with God" or "embracing the philosophical problems of the nation." He had a deep understanding of his fellow citizens' increasing sinfulness. Also, he had a high concept of the ideal life, including work, enjoyment of fellowship with the Lord, and industry based on equity and justice. One scholar said, "Habakkuk had a keen insight into the wickedness of his people and a thorough conviction of the only possible cure: faith in the promised Redeemer." The book of

Habakkuk falls into three natural divisions. Chapter 1 presents Habakkuk's problem. Chapter 2 gives God's answer. Chapter 3 expresses the prophet's praise; it is one of the most superb poems in its concept of God and beauty of language to be found in the Old Testament.

I. The prophet's problem (Hab. 1).

The first chapter is dialogue between Habakkuk and the Lord. The prophet raised a timely problem.

A. *Had God forgotten the righteous people and ceased to care?* Habakkuk lived during a time when vanity, lies, and injustice prevailed. For a long time he had cried out to the Lord concerning the inequity of the land, but he had received no explanation. In chapter 1, he complained, "How long, LORD, must I call for help, but you do not listen? Or cry out to you, 'Violence!' but you do not save?" (v. 2 NIV). He continued by pointing out to the Lord that "the law is paralyzed, and justice never prevails. The wicked hem in the righteous, so that justice is perverted" (v. 4 NIV).

B. *The age-old problem of why the righteous suffer and the wicked prosper is still with us today.* In every generation, we see this problem reenacted. God, however, had an answer for Habakkuk. He is neither indifferent nor inadequate; rather, he is on the field just when he seems most invisible. Even as he listened to Habakkuk's complaint, the Lord was raising up a nation to be the rod of his chastening hand. Judah had had a brief respite while the balance of power had been changing hands in international politics.

But the days of Assyria were numbered, and Babylon would soon be knocking on Judah's door with one purpose in mind—conquest. Habakkuk's description of the Chaldean army on the march is quite graphic. A bitter and hasty nation with no regard for human life or social values, the Babylonians arrogantly glorified their own strength and performed acts of unspeakable cruelty to accomplish their ungodly aims.

C. *The Lord's answer, rather than helping Habakkuk, intensified his problem.* How could a God of holiness permit his people, even though they were disobedient, to be annihilated by a brutal and godless executioner? Judah was sinful, but for God to use the monstrous Babylonians as his agent of punishment seemed inconsistent with his holiness. This second problem, like the first, is relevant to our day. Of course, atheists have no such problem. Only those who believe in God are confronted with the paradox of prosperous evildoers and suffering saints. Is there an answer?

II. The prophet's perception (Hab. 2).

A. *In verse 1 Habakkuk determined to wait for an answer.* He intended to stand at his watch and see what the Lord would say. He was not disappointed. The Lord told Habakkuk to write down the vision that would come to him so the people could read it, reminding him that its fulfillment would come in God's good time.

B. *Verses 4 through 19 depict Babylon's destruction.* God had not abdicated his moral character to pagan people. Not only would sin be punished, but also sin would punish itself. God has established a world so morally constituted that history repeatedly testifies to the self-destructiveness of sin. We are not just punished *for* our sins. Quite often we are punished *by* our sins. God would use Babylon as an instrument to chasten his people, but the pagan king would think that his victory was due to his own ability. After God used him, God would discipline him and finally destroy him.

C. *Verses 6 through 19 announce a series of "woes."* These were "taunt songs" to the ones who glorified themselves in pride and ignored the basic laws of morality. The last verse of chapter 2 is a word from God to Habakkuk. The prophet needed to realize that God was in his holy temple working his sovereign will, and the earth needed to trust God and keep silent.

III. The prophet's prayer (Hab. 3).

A. *Habakkuk was satisfied once he understood God's long-range plan.* He may have felt like the poet Ella Wheeler Wilcox who wrote:

> I know there are no errors
> In the great Eternal plan;
> And all things work together
> For the final good of man.

And as she wrote in another poem:

> The world will never adjust itself
> To suit your whims to the letter;
> Some things will go wrong, your whole life long,
> And the sooner you know it the better.

> It's folly to fight with the Infinite
> And go down at last in the wrestle;
> The wiser man shapes into God's plan
> Like water shapes into a vessel.

B. *Habakkuk was now ready to sing praises to his great God.* The last chapter of his book contains this majestic hymn.

According to Habakkuk, God is alive and active even though external events seem to indicate the opposite. Ultimately decency wins. In due time, right always prevails. Habakkuk's brief prophecy closes with a lyrical outburst. His poem begins with vivid imagery, describing the Lord's wondrous works in the world. It concludes with a portrayal of the security and soaring power of those who live in intimate fellowship with God. Of course, Habakkuk had to wait for full vindication, but he would do so quietly, confident in the integrity of God's government. Even though disaster and destruction awaited him, Habakkuk came to realize that he could trust implicitly in his Lord.

Conclusion

What is Habakkuk's message for us? We should believe our beliefs and doubt our doubts, never making a skeptic's mistake of believing our doubts but doubting our beliefs. Habakkuk's faith was fortified and his insight was purified when he was willing to wait for God's answer to him. God honors and rewards anyone who sincerely seeks the truth. He will not leave such a person hopeless and with unanswered questions. Individuals who have access to true spiritual power are not those who have never had a doubt. Rather, they are those who have examined their hearts honestly and faced their doubts candidly, emerging victorious with a tender spirit and complete confidence.

Habakkuk's experience tells us that we should not deny or hide our doubts. Far less should we be ashamed of them. We will need all of eternity to understand infinity, but we can use our doubts and rise on them to higher concepts of God than we ever believed were possible.

SUNDAY EVENING, SEPTEMBER 27

Title: A Call to Christian Living

Text: "Forasmuch then as Christ hath suffered for us in the flesh, arm yourselves likewise with the same mind" **(1 Peter 4:1)**.

Scripture Reading: 1 Peter 4:1–11; 5:1–14

Introduction

A call to Christian living is always in order. The ground of the appeal is the example of Christ. "Forasmuch then as Christ hath suffered for us in the flesh. . . ." The "then" is like an arrow pointing back to 1 Peter 3:18–22, where Peter presented the truth that "Christ also hath once suffered for sins, the just for the unjust, that he might bring us to God" (1 Peter 3:18). The appeal is, "Arm yourselves likewise with the same mind." Compare Paul's appeals in Romans 12:1–2 and Philippians 2:5–11.

The difficult passage in 1 Peter 4:1, "For he that hath suffered in the flesh hath ceased from sin," when taken with verse 2 seems to mean that one who has armed himself with the mind of Christ, so that he is willing to suffer persecution for his faith, has rest from sin as his goal in life. He no longer spends his life in the sinful pursuits of the lust of the flesh but now makes the aim of his life the doing of God's will.

I. The heathen do not understand the call (I Peter 4:3–4).

A. *It is natural for the unsaved person to pursue sinful lusts.* The varieties of sins from which Christians had repented are listed as follows:
1. "Lasciviousness" or "licentiousness" (RSV) means without morals. It describes such acts as filthy words, indecent bodily movements, lewd sex acts, and so on.
2. "Lusts" or "passions" (RSV). In themselves "lusts" may be good or bad. Desire for the will of God is good, but the desires here condemned are "human lusts," of which Peter had written in 2:11: "Abstain from fleshly lusts, which war against the soul."
3. "Excess of wine" or "drunkenness" (RSV).
4. "Revellings" refers to drinking parties.
5. "Banquetings" or "carousing" (RSV) is another word Peter used for wild drinking parties.
6. "Abominable idolatries" or "lawless idolatry" (RSV). All idolatry is abominable, but especially that which promotes drinking and lust in the name of religion.

B. *A Christian's abstinence from sin is a silent rebuke to those who sin.* The heathen speak evil of the Christian because of this (1 Peter 4:4).

II. Every person will give account of himself to God (I Peter 4:5–6).

The import of this passage seems to be that all without exception are to be judged by God. Those now dead had the gospel preached to them while they were alive, so they (as well as those now living) will be judged according to the lives they lived in the flesh. Those who, while yet in the flesh, truly trusted Christ will share the eternal life of God in the Spirit.

III. Christian living demands faithfulness (I Peter 4:7–11).

A. *The imminence of Christ's return encourages faithfulness.* "But the end of all things is at hand" (v. 7). How near Peter did not say. He urged readiness, as did Jesus (Matt. 24:42) and Paul (1 Thess. 5:6). It may be drawing near as God counts time. In that case, as Peter explained, "One day is with the Lord as a thousand years, and a thousand years as one day" (2 Peter 3:8).

Not only is it true that one should be ready to meet the Lord when he comes at the end of the age; but since death may come at any time, one should be ready to meet the Lord at death.

B. *More important than the time when one meets the Lord is the certainty that one will.* So we are to be ready by:
1. Being sober (v. 7), that is, keeping a sound mind, and "watch [ing] unto prayer."
2. "Above all things have fervent charity [unfailing love] among yourselves; for charity [love] shall cover the multitude of sins" (v. 8). "Above all" means above all other duties to one's fellow

291

humans. It does not take precedence over the first commandment to love God. Proverbs 10:12 was probably in Peter's mind: "Hatred stirs up conflict, but love covers over all wrongs" (NIV). Love seeks to extinguish strife as water puts out a flame. Love judges others most charitably.

3. "Practice hospitality ungrudgingly to one another" (v. 9 RSV).
4. "Good stewards of the manifold grace of God" (v. 10). God has given many gifts, talents, and abilities to believers for ministering. God is still the owner, and believers are but trustees of God's unmerited gifts, which are to be used for the good of others in his name.

Illustrations in verse 11 are, first: If one's gift is speaking, let him or her use it, not for self or for novelty, but in conformity to the Word of God. The "oracles of God" are used in Acts 7:38 to refer to the Mosaic law, in Romans 3:2 to refer to the Old Testament, and in Hebrews 5:12 to refer to Christ's teaching. Second, if one's gift is serving, let him or her do it not for pride or self-glory, but with the humble acknowledgment that one's ability to help is a trust from God.

Conclusion

The purpose of Christian service is "that God in all things may be glorified through Jesus Christ, to whom be praise and dominion for ever and ever. Amen" (1 Peter 4:11). See also the doxologies in 1 Peter 5:10–11 and 2 Peter 3:18.

WEDNESDAY EVENING, SEPTEMBER 30

Title: God Will Take Care of You

Text: "During that long period, the king of Egypt died. The Israelites groaned in their slavery and cried out, and their cry for help because of their slavery went up to God. God heard their groaning and he remembered his covenant with Abraham, with Isaac and with Jacob. So God looked on the Israelites and was concerned about them" **(Ex. 2:23–25 NIV).**

Scripture Reading: Exodus 1:1–2:25

Introduction

The experiences of God's people in Egypt teach many truths about God. One of the most delightful traits of God is his providence. God took care of Israel from their first moment in Egypt until their movement out of Egypt.

Jacob's family came to Egypt to escape a famine in the land of Canaan. There they were reunited with Joseph, the son of Jacob, who had been sold by his brothers. Joseph had attained a high political standing in Egypt. Pharaoh gave Joseph's family the land of Goshen as a place of permanent residence. For several years the Israelites prospered and multiplied. After Joseph's death, another pharaoh, who did not know Joseph, came to power. This pharaoh was threatened by the Israelites, so he forced them into hard labor. The good life of Israel turned to disappointment.

God had displayed his providence in past years. The Israelites had experienced the marvelous care of God. Now, during the atrocious experience of an arrogant pharaoh, God displayed himself as the God who would ultimately take care of his people.

The providence of God prevails over those who trust him. Let us notice some insights about the providence of God.

I. God's providence endures time (Ex. 1:1–7).

Often, as time passes, it seems that God has forgotten his people. Time lapsed, and God's people grew weary with a day-by-day existence of bondage.

A. *The apparent silence of God.* The care of God seemed evident to Jacob and his sons when they were reunited with Joseph. The family of Jacob could easily detect the care of God over Joseph. They could see God's care over them as he led them to Egypt for food and for a family reunion.

The family of Jacob died. "Then Joseph died, and all his brothers, and all that generation" (Ex. 1:6 RSV). Jacob's offspring belonged to the family of God. They inevitably wondered if God cared for them. They heard about God's great care and concern over their family. Now they wondered if God had forgotten them. God was apparently silent over their Egyptian bondage.

During critical times in the lives of God's people, we often feel that God is silent. This is especially true during times of injustices from others when we wish that God would act immediately.

B. *The inevitable working of God.* The story of Israel's bondage in Egypt demonstrates that God works in his time. In the providence of God, he did not deliver them with the first cry of bondage. God moves and works in his way. Israel wanted immediate action, but God worked on his own time schedule. For hundreds of years he allowed the people to multiply. Then he selected and prepared a leader.

Time does not erase God's providence. God may appear silent at times, but he is always working. God will inevitably work for his people.

II. God's providence withstands assaults (Ex. 1:8–22).

During times of assault, the enemy seems stronger than God. To the Israelites, Pharaoh's strength seemed stronger than Jehovah's might. Further investigation into God's providence demonstrates that God is stronger than any enemy.

A. *The assault of the enemy.* God permitted Pharaoh's assault on Israel. During the time of Pharaoh's persecution, the people groaned and questioned the strength of the Lord. Pharaoh used three methods to destroy Israel. First, he sought to break their spirit by making the Hebrews a servant people (Ex. 1:8–14). Second, he sought to persuade Hebrew midwives to betray their own blood (Ex. 1:15–21). Third, he attempted to destroy all the male children born to a Hebrew family (Ex. 1:22). Without a doubt, Pharaoh's power seemed preeminent.

B. *The power of God.* God is stronger than any foe. The entire exodus story demonstrates the superiority of God over any power. Two Hebrew midwives, Shiphrah and Puah, expressed their faith in God's supremacy by refusing to obey Pharaoh's order to kill Hebrew babies at birth. These women saw a King greater than Pharaoh.

The poet James Russell Lowell expressed faith in God's power.

Truth forever on the scaffold
Wrong forever on the throne.
Yet, that scaffold sways the future
And, behind the dim unknown
Standeth God within the shadow,
Keeping watch above His own.

III. God's providence defied explanation (Ex. 2:1–25).

Reading the birth account of Moses causes one to realize the unseen forces of God at work. There can be no logical human explanation for the events surrounding Moses' birth and life. God's providence defies explanation.

A. *God's intervention.* Since the call of Abram out of Ur of the Chaldees, God had a special purpose for Israel. During the years of the patriarchs, he worked out his plan. God's plan of deliverance seemed to be reduced to a slender thread—just a tiny baby set adrift on a river in a fragile basket. But God was going to execute his intention through the means of unlikely prospects.

B. *God's miraculous works.* The events surrounding the birth of Moses are filled with the strange working of God. God preserved a baby from Pharaoh's murderous plot and even saw that Moses was discovered by Pharaoh's daughter. Furthermore, he provided Jochebed, Moses' mother (Ex. 6:20), to rear him in the ways of Jehovah. One cannot look at the events in Exodus 2 without acknowledging God's marvelous providence. It defies explanation.

Conclusion

You need not be dismayed in troublesome times. God will take care of you. He will provide his strength; and you will experience his unseen power at work in your life.

OCTOBER

- **Sunday Mornings**

  Continue the series "The Modern Message of the Minor Prophets."

- **Sunday Evenings**

  The suggested theme for Sunday evening sermons this month is "Some Personal Portraits of Peter." Many people greatly value a family picture album, and the study of a spiritual biography can be compared to looking through a photo album. This series of messages, biographical in nature, contains lessons that can help each of us day by day.

- **Wednesday Evenings**

  Continue the series "The God Who Reveals Himself in Times of Need."

SUNDAY MORNING, OCTOBER 4

Title: God's Work Must Go On

Text: "Is it a time for you yourselves to be living in your paneled houses, while this house remains a ruin?" **(Hag. 1:4 NIV)**.

Scripture Reading: Haggai 1:2–8

Hymns: "To the Work!" Crosby
         "We'll Work Till Jesus Comes," Mills
         "I Know That My Redeemer Liveth," Pounds

Offertory Prayer: Our Father, help us to accept all things that we have as a sacred trust. Give us the grace to stop any attempt to serve both God and mammon. May we center our lives in Christ and place our full trust in him. May we strive to make his perfect will our goal. Make us truly aware of your presence as we give, and may our tithes and offerings promote peace and goodwill as Christ is received as Lord in the lives of those who hear the gospel because of our gifts. We pray in Jesus' name. Amen.

Introduction

The temple in Jerusalem was burned in 586 BC. Those who remained from the previous deportations (605 and 596 BC), with a few exceptions, were carried captive to Babylon. For more than half a century, the Jews remained in this foreign country. Though separated from their native soil, they managed to survive. Babylon gave them a limited amount of freedom, allowing them to build their houses, cultivate their gardens, and work at jobs according to their wishes.

In 539 BC, Cyrus the Great conquered Babylon. One of his first official acts was to issue a decree permitting the Jews to return to their homeland. They began the trip with great anticipation but became disappointed when they saw Jerusalem. Nothing was left of its former glory, which they had rejoiced about in their songs during the exile. The walls were heaps of refuse. The temple was a pile of charred stones. The streets were overgrown with weeds.

After their initial reaction of discouragement, the Jews went to work setting the altar on its old site and offering sacrifices as in earlier days. Then they began to rebuild the temple. However, enemies caused the work to cease by order of the Persians, who had granted the Jews permission in the first place. For approximately fifteen years nothing was done. The people worshiped amid the debris of an unfinished building. Yet they did build houses for themselves and provide for their own comfort. Then the prophet Haggai appeared on the scene.

I. God's house is as important as our houses.

    A. *Throughout history the issue of "institutionalism" has arisen.* Since God is spirit, it is more important to have our hearts in tune with him than to have fancy places of worship. But another fact is equally true. God's people need a house of worship. Billy Sunday used to say, "You may tell me that you can worship God as well on a fishing bank on Sunday morning out among nature as you can in a plush place of worship. I tell you that perhaps you can, but you won't!" Another person has said that a man can probably have high and noble concepts of God coming out of a sand trap on the thirteenth hole of a golf course at 11:00 on Sunday morning, but chances that he will are not very great. God's people need to worship, and they need a house in which to worship.

    B. *The way people treat God's house often indicates their love for him.* It may be true that sometimes religious people "overinstitutionalize" and must be called back to simple faith, as Jeremiah called his people in the temple sermon (chaps. 7, 26).

    C. *A greater danger is that people may fail to provide an attractive and functional place of worship.* When Haggai came on the scene, the Jews had started to rebuild the temple but quit. Is anything more distressing than to see a house of God half finished? The prophet looked at the people's homes. He saw that they had taken care of their personal needs regardless of the economic adversity that had come their way. Why should they dwell in comfortable homes and let God's house lie in waste? It is not right to serve God with the leftovers in any area of our lives. He deserves the firstfruits of our time, talents, money, and enthusiasm. God's work must go on. We cannot wait until we have everything in our own lives satisfactorily arranged before taking care of the spiritual needs in our community.

II. God's money is not our money.

A. *The people of Israel had done a very wrong thing!* Times had become tough, and they had siphoned the part of their money that should have been dedicated to God into satisfying their own desires. Haggai said, "Now this is what the LORD Almighty says: 'Give careful thought to your ways. You have planted much, but have harvested little. You eat, but never have enough. You drink, but never have your fill. You put on clothes, but are not warm. You earn wages, only to put them in a purse with holes in it'" (1:5–6 NIV).

The prophet's words were important. A spiritual law is present in the world that applies to all people but particularly to God's redeemed family. When we spend God's money on ourselves, the result is tragic. People used to say, "God has a way of collecting his tithe." They were right!

B. *Those who dedicate God's money to God usually spend their own money wisely also.* Those who are so disorganized that they fail to give God the firstfruits of their income are confused about their priorities. God's money is his, and we can never be happy until we realize this fact. Someone told a story that may not be theologically accurate, but it certainly reflects a point. He said that he had a terminal illness and the doctors gave him only six months to live. He was still living, however, nearly twenty years later. He explained it this way: "For many years I did not tithe. Then I became converted on the stewardship question and began tithing. My wife and I decided to give a little extra each week to catch up on our tithe for the many years that we had failed to give according to God's Word." At this point, he laughed and said, "When I was about to die, God checked my record and found that I had not caught up on my tithe, so he's let me live twenty more years in order to catch up." One may not agree with his theology, but from a practical standpoint, this is the way he felt. We all would be wise to take our stewardship responsibility as seriously.

Haggai told the people that they were to put God first with their material possessions. Dr. George Truett said that if a man is right on the question of his money, he is likely to be right or easily led to be right on other subjects. However, if he is wrong on the question of his money, he is likely to be wrong on all other matters of the Christian faith. Dr. Truett added, "I know that's putting it strongly, but I believe that with all my heart."

III. God will reward his leaders.

A. *The last of Haggai's four messages is about Zerubbabel the governor (2:20–23).* He was the grandson of King Jehoiachin and in the direct line of David. Since he was governor of Judah, he was the civil ruler. This passage has deeper meaning than simply personal reward to Zerubbabel.

Haggai referred back to the theme of the second oracle (2:1–9). A shaking of the heavens and the earth would take place, and the thrones of pagan kingdoms would be overthrown. When this occurred, Zerubbabel would be exalted and given a position of honor. The Lord would make him as a signet, the most treasured of all possessions at that time. This means that Zerubbabel had been chosen by God for special favor, and that God would keep him under his protecting care.

B. *Scholars do not entirely agree regarding the fulfillment of this promise, but one thing is certain.* God has his eye on his own, and in due season he will exalt them and give proper reward for their deeds. God was still alive even during the dark days of the postexilic community and had neither forgotten nor forsaken his people. Every generation needs to be freshly reminded of this truth. Paul said it this way: "Therefore, my dear brothers and sisters, stand firm. Let nothing move you. Always give yourselves fully to the work of the Lord, because you know that your labor in the Lord is not in vain" (1 Cor. 15:58 NIV).

Conclusion

Do you become discouraged amid situations that bring hardship or setback to your life? If so, the book of Haggai has a word for you. It might be summarized in the words of the poet who said:

In the darkest night of the year,
When the stars are all gone out,
The courage is better than fear
And faith is truer than doubt.

And fierce though the fiends may fight,
Long by the sun they hide,
I know that truth and right
Have the universe on their side.

God's work must go on. And it will go on because God stands within the shadow keeping watch and working to bring about his purposes in history.

SUNDAY EVENING, OCTOBER 4

Title: A Beatitude for Simon Peter

Text: "Simon Peter answered and said, Thou art the Christ, the Son of the living God. And Jesus answered and said unto him, Blessed art thou, Simon Bar-jona: for flesh and blood hath not revealed it unto thee, but my Father which is in heaven" (**Matt. 16:16–17**).

Scripture Reading: Matthew 16:13–26 (parallel passages: Mark 8:27–37; Luke 9:18–25)

Introduction

About two years had passed since Jesus chose his apostles. Only a little more than six months remained before his crucifixion. Our Lord needed to intensify his efforts to prepare the apostles for that event. After Jesus refused to become a king, great multitudes of his disciples turned away and opposition against him increased. For the purpose of testing his disciples, Jesus chose to take them north from Galilee into the district of Caesarea Philippi, which was ruled by Herod Philip. This region was on the slope of Mount Hermon near the headwaters of the Jordan River.

I. Simon Peter was blessed because, by the help of God, he confessed faith in Jesus Christ as the Son of God (Matt. 16:13–17).

A. *Jesus asked his disciples, "Who do men say that the Son of man is?"* "Son of man" was a term Jesus often used of himself. The disciples were ready with several answers. Some said John the Baptist had come to life. Herod Antipas held this opinion (Mark 6:14). Others said Elijah, probably because of the prophecy in Malachi 4:5. Yet others named Jeremiah or another one of the prophets. These questions had been introductory to the main question: "But who do you say that I am?" (Matt. 16:15 RSV). Simon Peter replied, "You are the Christ, the Son of the living God" (Matt. 16:16 RSV).

That Jesus is the Messiah was not a new claim. When Andrew first brought Simon to Jesus, he declared, "'We have found the Messiah' (which means Christ)" (John 1:41 RSV). Early in his ministry, Jesus revealed himself to the Samaritan woman as the Messiah (John 4:25–26). Because of growing opposition, Jesus ceased to use the term and referred to himself as "Son of man," which was a veiled messianic term that did not arouse opposition.

A few weeks earlier, when Jesus entered the boat after walking on the sea, the disciples worshiped him and said, "Of a truth thou art the Son of God" (Matt. 14:33). Jesus concurred, for he accepted their worship. When his hour did come, Jesus, on oath before Caiaphas, affirmed that he was "the Christ, the Son of God" (Matt. 26:63–64).

B. *Jesus was pleased with Peter's answer.* At a time when others had turned away, Peter had remained steadfast. He joyfully said to him, "Blessed art thou, Simon Bar-jona: for flesh and blood hath not revealed it unto thee, but my Father which is in heaven" (Matt. 16:17). Simon Peter's confession of faith was an experience wrought by the power of God. This ought to teach us that Christianity is not signing a creed, nor is it thinking out a philosophy of life; it is primarily an experience that comes from God.

II. Simon Peter was blessed because he was acting like a rock (living up to his name) in so confessing Christ.

Jesus added, "And I say also unto thee, That thou art Peter, and upon this rock I will build my church; and the gates of hell shall not prevail against it" (Matt. 16:18).

A. *Christ is the architect and builder of his church.*

B. *Christ's church is composed of all persons who have answered his call to come out of sin into salvation and who, as did Simon Peter, confess him to be the Messiah, the Son of the living God.* The Greek word *ekklesia*, translated "church," means an assembly or congregation. It was used in the Septuagint for the congregation of Israel. In secular Greek, it was used for the assembly of the people in a Greek city-state for the purposes of transacting business. *Ekklesia* means "called out." Christ's church is composed of all the redeemed of all time in heaven and earth, all those who have been called out by him.

C. *Peter had acted like a rock in making this noble confession.* A little later he would act like Satan in suggesting that Jesus not go to the cross. Peter was no more actually a rock than he was actually Satan. In confessing faith in Christ, he was acting like a rock (a play on words). On this rock of a person confessing faith in him, Jesus would keep building his church. He had begun to build with the winning of the first disciples. He will continue to build until the end of time. Saved persons are, as it were, spiritual stones in the temple Christ is building.

III. Simon Peter was blessed by being a member of an indestructible church.

The literal translation, "The gates of Hades shall not overpower it," is correctly explained, "The powers of death shall not prevail against it" (Matt. 16:18 RSV). Christ's church is composed of redeemed people who have eternal life and either live here or with the Lord in paradise. Christ was not guaranteeing the perpetuity of an institution but rather the eternal life of his people. Christ's church would not be destroyed here or hereafter. Christ, the builder and head of the church, has conquered death. He promised, "Because I live, ye shall live also" (John 14:19).

IV. Simon Peter was blessed because he was a member of a church with a mission of eternal consequences.

A. *The keys of the kingdom of heaven are entrusted to all the church.* To Peter, Jesus said, "I will give unto thee the keys of the kingdom of heaven: and whatsoever thou shalt bind on earth shall be bound in heaven: and whatsoever thou shalt loose on earth shall be loosed in heaven" (Matt. 16:19). This promise was not to Peter alone nor restricted to the twelve apostles, for in Matthew 18:15–18, on an occasion when Jesus was speaking to the whole congregation, that is, the church, he used the same words.

B. *The steward kept the keys to his master's building.*

  1. The keys denote stewardship. The steward was responsible for using his master's property in accord with his master's express desire. Christ has committed to his church the stewardship of the gospel. The "keys of the kingdom" mean the gospel, especially the conditions of salvation, namely, repentance and faith.

  2. "Binding and loosing" is a bold figurative expression for allowing or disallowing. This gospel has eternal consequences. What people bind or loose on earth stays bound or loosed in heaven. The "keys of the kingdom" do not operate apart from the response of a person to the gospel. No person is given power to save another nor to keep another from being saved. Surely the Lord did not expect his followers to misconstrue this figure of speech to negate John 3:16.

     God alone has the power to forgive sins, to save, or to refuse to save. He has not delegated this power to any person, group of persons, or institution. It is folly to speak of passing on by apostolic succession a power the apostles never had.

Conclusion

The true apostolic succession is to accept the stewardship of the gospel. We are to witness to Jesus, who is the Son of God, Messiah, Savior, Word of God, Lamb of God, and the Resurrection and Life. As people accept the Christ of the gospel, they enter the kingdom of God. If people reject this Christ, they remain outside. Decisions made here and now have eternal consequences. What is bound here on earth stands bound in heaven. What is loosed here on earth stays loosed in heaven.

WEDNESDAY EVENING, OCTOBER 7

Title: The Results of Your Roots

Text: "It came to pass in those days, when Moses was grown, that he went out unto his brethren, and looked on their burdens: and he spied an Egyptian smiting an Hebrew, one of his brethren" (**Ex. 2:11**).

Scripture Reading: Exodus 2:1–25

Introduction

Alex Haley wrote an intriguing book titled *Roots* that traces the heritage of the black people of America to their beginnings in Africa. He makes a strong case for the fact that a person's heritage greatly affects his or her life.

In studying the life of Moses, one should always be aware of Moses' "roots." He was born in the home of a Hebrew family from the tribe of Levi (Ex. 2:1), but circumstances ordained by God caused him to be reared in the house of Pharaoh.

Let us notice how our heritage affects our lives.

I. Our heritage identifies our loyalty.

The account of Moses killing an Egyptian discloses Moses' loyalty to the Hebrews.

A. *The influences on our lives are great.* No one is unaffected by background. Moses came under the influence of two distinct backgrounds. He was reared in the Egyptian culture. "Moses was instructed in all the wisdom of the Egyptians" (Acts 7:22 RSV). Without a doubt, the Egyptian environment had a strong influence on him, yet Moses was also influenced by his mother's training. She taught him that he was a Hebrew and told him of the faith of his ancestors. This training was a powerful influence on Moses.

B. *The personal choice makes us what we become.* Though Moses was influenced by the Egyptian culture and the Hebrew faith, the responsibility of his life's direction depended on his personal choice. The record of Moses identifying with the Hebrews indicated his loyalty to the Lord.

Irrespective of a person's background, whether good or bad, one must choose. Each person is responsible. Our daily actions will identify our loyalty.

II. Our heritage builds character.

The account of Moses killing an Egyptian discloses another result of his religious roots; it reveals the fiber of his character.

A. *A godly heritage teaches justice.* "He spied an Egyptian smiting an Hebrew, one of his brethren" (Ex. 2:11). When Moses saw an Egyptian taskmaster strike a Hebrew slave, he was moved. He had been trained to be tender and compassionate toward his people. The sight of injustice moved him to desire justice for others.

Christian experiences build into people the idea of justice. Seeing injustices and various needs motivates Christians to respond. Let us be careful to respond wisely and in love.

B. *A godly heritage moves one to act decisively.* Without a doubt, Moses moved in decisive action. His solution was wrong. Surely he could have found some way other than murder to protect the Hebrew people. We cannot correct one injustice with another. Nevertheless, God incorporated Moses' actions into his own larger plan.

The Christian must act decisively. We cannot ignore the immorality of our times. Our heritage teaches us to speak against crimes of injustice, sexual perversion, and racial prejudice. To act on these issues requires courage.

III. Our heritage brings rebuff.

The account of Moses killing an Egyptian reveals another interesting result of his religious heritage: his action brought estrangement.

A. *A stand for God irritates the world.* Moses' action was not without an audience. The next day, Moses tried to mediate an argument between two Hebrews. One of the arguing men disclosed Moses' murder of the Egyptian. "Now when Pharaoh heard this thing, he sought to slay Moses" (Ex. 2:15). Pharaoh was not sympathetic to Moses' religious roots. In fact, he was enraged by Moses' action.

The secular world will never be pleased with the Christian position. Paul said, "All that will live godly in Christ Jesus shall suffer persecution" (2 Tim. 3:12). To confront the world with God's way irritates them.

B. *A stand for God brings human suffering.* Moses' action brought suffering. He became afraid. "And Moses feared, and said, Surely this thing is known" (Ex. 2:14). Furthermore, it caused him to leave Egypt and flee to the land of Midian.

One must not merely see suffering. Through the vicissitudes, God worked in Moses' life. Oftentimes our courageous stand will bring suffering, but God will bring growth and maturity through these experiences.

Conclusion

What is your heritage? Have you committed your life to the Lord? If you have, your background should identify your loyalty. Out of this background you will act on behalf of the Lord.

If you have never committed your life to the Lord, you can begin your "religious roots." It is life's best and most illustrious background.

SUNDAY MORNING, OCTOBER 11

Title: God's Spirit Makes the Difference

Text: "'Not by might nor by power, but by my Spirit,' says the LORD Almighty" (**Zech. 4:6 NIV**).

Scripture Reading: Zechariah 4:1–10

Hymns: "Be Thou My Vision," Byrne, Hull
"Holy Spirit, Faithful Guide," Wells
"Seal Us, O Holy Spirit," Meredith

Offertory Prayer: Our Father, you have given us the ability and the will to make a living for ourselves and our families. We pray that you will give us wisdom to handle our money properly and that you will make us generous givers. May we see the treasure of our hands transformed into the treasures of your eternal kingdom as we invest our money in your work. We have received much from you. May we not only be receptacles of your grace, but channels to bless the lives of others. May your kingdom be advanced because of our gifts today. In Jesus' name we pray. Amen.

Introduction

After Haggai had been preaching two months about the need for rebuilding the temple, a younger man appeared on the scene as a coworker. An optimist, he has been called "one of the brightest, the clearest, the most hopeful to be found in prophetic literature." The general background of his ministry was obviously the same as Haggai's. The small band of returned exiles were seeking, against great odds, to serve the Lord in a land where they were hemmed in with little or no breathing room.

The two prophets varied in personality. Haggai was an activist, bustling with energy and practicality. Zechariah, being a priest, was a student of Scripture and one likely to see visions and dream dreams. One scholar contrasts them: "Haggai will handle the hammer and nails, but Zechariah will supply the blueprints of the Utopia. The spiritual insight of the idealist will be wedded to the practical drive of the realist." Both men, however, had the same consuming passion. The temple had to be rebuilt so Jerusalem could become the center of universal religion.

Reading and interpreting the book of this mysterious man of God is not easy, but a simple outline should help. The book opens with an earnest appeal for the people to return to the Lord (1:1–6). This appeal is followed by a series of eight visions (1:7–6:8) containing words of encouragement for the people as they dwell in the land without a temple, oppressed by hardship. The third section (6:9–15) has been called a historical appendix to the symbolic messages. Zechariah is urged to crown Joshua as high priest and declare him the "Branch" who will rule over the people. A fourth division (7:1–8:23) deals with a question about the days of fasting. These days will be times of celebration when Jerusalem becomes the center of true religion and a source of blessing to all the world. The final part of the book (9:1–14:21) concerns a later situation when the nations are restless and threaten Jerusalem with attack. The small community in the city and the people scattered among many nations are assured of God's help in gaining victory over their enemies. The book closes with a graphic description of the Lord's universal reign, with Jerusalem being the center of holiness.

To cover Zechariah's book in such a brief message is impossible. But we can discover several key teachings that seem to summarize its theme.

I. The priority of repentance.

Before either nations or individuals can be right with God, they must face their sin and forsake it. Zechariah began his ministry with a strong announcement regarding sin. The children were warned against following the paths of their fathers. The previous generation had turned a deaf ear to the words of the prophets and had failed to change their ways. The postexilic community needed to avoid a repetition of this tragic mistake.

    A. *Zechariah's first message was a clarion call to repentance.* He said, "'Return to me,' declares the LORD Almighty, 'and I will return to you'" (1:3 NIV). The result of the previous generation's sin was their captivity. When individuals look back at the blessings a previous generation has missed because of sin, they should determine to follow God in their own lifetime. The disobedient predecessors of Zechariah's generation once worshiped in Solomon's temple, and the song of the Levites rang through the arches of the Lord's house. At one time, the banners of Judah had struck terror into the hearts of their enemies. But those days were gone forever!

    B. *After Zechariah gave a call to repentance, he probably advised the people to rebuild the temple.* Although we do not have a record of these words, he must have mentioned the temple, because the first part of his ministry paralleled Haggai's and preceded the temple's construction. Every person and every nation must repent in order to please God in service. Activism alone is often shallow. Unless accompanied by a spiritual approach to life, no human works can advance God's kingdom.

II. Vision keeps us from perishing.

Zechariah's visions following his call to repentance, though varied, emphasized God's presence with his people. Jonathan Swift said, "Vision is the art of seeing things invisible." Ralph Waldo Emerson wrote:

> Couldst thou in vision see,
> Thyself, the man God meant;
> Thou never more wouldst be
> The self thou art, content.

    A. *God will always be with his people.* He had chosen Israel for a redemptive mission, to bring the Messiah into the world. They were a small people in a large world, but no one should ever despise small things. Although God's work may have a feeble beginning, he will bring it to pass. Dr. Clyde Francisco said, "It is not a question of your strength but of God's strength."

    B. *God has the power to break through evil.* He will do this to bring salvation to his people and dwell with them. But for this to be done, sin must be punished and God's holiness must prevail. Only God can break the deadly grip of sin and remove its contaminating presence. An ideal land is one where sin is banished, but we cannot win the victory in our own strength. God must come into the arena for us. He promised Israel that he would do this in Jesus Christ. The victory is not complete until he returns in glory, but the promise is here.

III. God will win.

The latter part of Zechariah's prophecy is difficult to understand. Scholars have disagreed as to the fulfillment of many things he predicted. But one thing is certain: God will never be defeated. His purposes in history will triumph. In Jesus Christ redemption has come to the world. Those who have received Christ are on God's side and will emerge victoriously when history is consummated. During the dark days of the Civil War, someone asked Abraham Lincoln, "Mr. President, have you prayed for God to be on our side?" He replied, "No, I have not prayed that prayer. But I have prayed another. I have prayed that God will help me to be certain that I am on his side." This is what matters! God is righteous and righteousness will win. The mark of wisdom is to find out where God is going and go with him.

Conclusion

The theme of our text runs throughout the entire book of Zechariah. Human effort will not win the victory. Assyria, Babylon, and Persia were nations that had been built on might and power. The first two had already fallen, and the third would fall soon. Those who followed their actions would likewise rise and fall. But God's kingdom will go on forever because it is a spiritual kingdom. We would be wise to build our lives, not on material things that fade away, but on spiritual things that last forever.

SUNDAY EVENING, OCTOBER 11

Title: Peter on the Mount of Transfiguration

Text: "While he yet spake, behold, a bright cloud overshadowed them: and behold a voice out of the cloud, which said, This is my beloved Son, in whom I am well pleased; hear ye him" (**Matt. 17:5**).

Scripture Reading: Luke 9:28–36 (parallel passages: Matt. 17:1–8; Mark 9:2–8)

Introduction

Jesus' experience with his disciples at Caesarea Philippi marked a distinct turning point in his ministry. He was obviously pleased with Peter's confession of faith in him as the Christ, the Son of the living God (Matt. 16:16). How utterly impossible it was for Peter and the other disciples to consider death and suffering for the miracle-working Messiah. Not being able to take Jesus' prophecy of death literally, they were puzzled rather than helped by his prophecy of resurrection. "Then Peter took him, and began to rebuke him, saying, Be it far from thee, Lord: this shall not be unto thee" (Matt. 16:22).

At Jesus' baptism, he had dedicated himself to a ministry that would culminate in his death and resurrection. (The symbolism of baptism is death and resurrection.) In this the Father was well pleased. The voice from heaven said, "This is my beloved Son, in whom I am well pleased" (Matt. 3:17).

In the temptations in the wilderness, Satan sought to persuade Jesus to take another way (see Matt. 4:1–11; Luke 4:1–13). "And when the devil had ended all the temptation, he departed from him for a season" (Luke 4:13). Peter unwittingly became the devil's mouthpiece to renew the temptation. But Jesus turned and said to Peter, "Get thee behind me, Satan: thou art an offence unto me: for thou savourest not the things that be of God, but those that be of men" (Matt. 16:23). Peter was no more actually Satan than he had earlier been an actual rock.

The disciples must have been further confused by Jesus' paradox about saving life by losing it (Matt. 16:24–25) and by his statement, "The Son of man shall come in the glory of his Father with his angels; and then he shall reward every man according to his works" (Matt. 16:27). How could Jesus talk of his return in glory as the final Judge and of death at the same time?

The transfiguration was God's answer to their confusion. Each of the accounts in the Synoptic Gospels bears its own unique witness.

I. The transfiguration assured the disciples that Jesus was other than they.

"After six days Jesus taketh with him Peter, and James, and John, and leadeth them up into an high mountain apart by themselves: and he was transfigured before them" (Mark 9:2). Luke gave the time as "about eight days after these sayings." He also notes that it was "as he prayed" (9:28–29) that Jesus' countenance was altered and his raiment became white and dazzling.

No one knows enough about the person of Jesus to know what the transfiguration meant to him. As the temptations to avoid the cross were real, surely the assurance of the transfiguration must have meant much to him.

II. The transfiguration affirmed that the death of Jesus fulfilled the Law and the Prophets.

"Behold, two men talked with him, Moses and Elijah, who appeared in glory and spoke of his departure, which he was to accomplish at Jerusalem" (Luke 9:30–31 RSV).

Moses was the representative of the Law. Elijah was the representative of the Prophets. They were speaking with Jesus about his coming death at Jerusalem. Elijah's presence affirmed: "In your death and resurrection you are fulfilling all that the prophets said." Moses' presence likewise attested: "In your death and resurrection you are doing what the law demands."

Paul also witnessed that the Law and the Prophets are fulfilled in Jesus, as for example, Romans 10:4 and Galatians 3:21–29. Peter did not understand it all at this time, but the Holy Spirit would interpret the experience for him. On the day of Pentecost, his sermon would clearly expand this theme, as would his epistles at a later time. For an example, note 1 Peter 1:10–12.

III. The transfiguration assured the disciples concerning life after death.

"So Moses the servant of the LORD died there in the land of Moab, according to the word of the LORD. And he buried him in a valley in the land of Moab, over against Beth-peor: but no man knoweth of his sepulchre unto this day" (Deut. 34:5–6). According to the account in 2 Kings 2, Elijah did not die; he was translated. "It came to pass, as they [Elijah and Elisha] still went on, and talked, that, behold, there appeared a chariot of fire, and horses of fire, and parted them both asunder; and Elijah went up by a whirlwind into heaven" (2 Kings 2:11).

Moses represented all the redeemed who had died or would die, whether the place of their burial is known or not. Elijah represented all who had been or would be translated without seeing death, as the redeemed living on earth when Jesus returns at the end of the age. Both men are with Jesus in glory now; both are talking to him; both are interested in what he is doing.

Peter, James, and John did not need to be introduced to Moses and Elijah. They knew them intuitively. Their bodies probably were fashioned like unto our Lord's glorious body after his resurrection.

IV. Peter's foolish proposal.

"As the men were parting from him, Peter said to Jesus, 'Master, it is well that we are here; let us make three booths, one for you and one for Moses and one for Elijah'—not knowing what he said" (Luke 9:33 RSV). Two objections to Peter's suggestion are evident. First, disciples cannot always be in worship on the mountaintop. There is work to be done in the valley. Second, and more important, Jesus is not to be equated with Moses and Elijah. Jesus is unique. He is the only begotten Son of God. He is not *a* prophet but *the* Prophet. By the same token, Christianity is not to be thought of as one of the world's great religions. It is the true religion by which all others are to be tested.

V. The Father bore testimony to Jesus—his Sonship, his messiahship, his authority.

The presence of God was manifested in the Shekinah cloud of glory, the cloud that had led the children of Israel in the wilderness. The voice from the Father spoke the same words as he had spoken at Jesus' baptism: "This is my beloved Son, in whom I am well pleased; hear ye him" (Matt. 17:5).

Hear Jesus as the fulfiller of the law, the greatest of God's messengers, the Suffering Servant, the Savior of the world, the final Judge, the Way, the Truth, the Life. Hear him as he interprets his death and as he calls to salvation.

Conclusion

The disciples fell on their faces in reverence. They arose at Jesus' touch and heard him say, "Arise, and be not afraid."

"And when they had lifted up their eyes, they saw no man, save Jesus only" (Matt. 17:8). Moses and Elijah were gone, their work fulfilled in Jesus. He alone abides. Let us not be afraid of life nor of death, for Jesus is the Lord of both. Let us hear him, for all truth is fulfilled in him.

WEDNESDAY EVENING, OCTOBER 14

Title: The God Who Introduces Himself

Text: "God said unto Moses, I AM THAT I AM: and he said, Thus shalt thou say unto the children of Israel, I AM hath sent me unto you" **(Ex. 3:14).**

Scripture Reading: Exodus 3:1–22

Introduction

I once attended a conference of twenty-five church leaders from different parts of the United States. The first activity on the agenda was the introduction of ourselves. As I waited for my turn, I thought of how difficult it was to introduce oneself. What do you say about yourself? You do not want to say too much, yet you want to say enough. Introducing yourself can be difficult.

God introduced himself to Moses. "Moses said unto God, Behold, when I come unto the children of Israel, and shall say unto them, The God of your fathers hath sent me unto you; and they shall say to me, What is his name? what shall I say unto them?" (Ex. 3:13). God proceeded to give one of the clearest disclosures of himself. Let us notice some truths that God said about himself.

I. God described himself as a personal God.

A. *The Old Testament disclosures of God are personal.* When God revealed himself to humankind, he disclosed himself in personal terms. He talked with man. "The LORD God called unto Adam, and said unto him, Where art thou?" (Gen. 3:9). God is described as walking with human beings: "And Enoch walked with God" (Gen. 5:24).

God shared feelings in a personal way. "God heard their groaning, and God remembered his covenant with Abraham, with Isaac, and with Jacob" (Ex. 2:24). God is not an impersonal force. He is not an unmoved mover. He is the Lord God Almighty, a personal God.

B. *The New Testament disclosures of God are personal.* "The Word was made flesh, and dwelt among us" (John 1:14). God came in human flesh to give us understandable disclosure of himself. Because Jesus came to earth, he identified with personal problems and situations.

C. *God disclosed himself in a personal Holy Spirit.* God is at work in the world today in a personal way. He works through his Holy Spirit to convince the unsaved of sin, righteousness, and judgment. He seeks entry into human lives. When a person opens his or her life to God, the Holy Spirit lives within that person. The Holy Spirit is not a force or influence. He is a person.

II. God disclosed himself as a powerful God.

A. *The Old Testament discloses God as powerful.* The Old Testament begins with God's ability to create a world out of nothing. It continues with his ability to destroy the world with a flood. When God introduced himself to Moses, he made it clear that he had the power to deliver Israel from the Egyptians. Look through the Old Testament, and the prominent fact of God's power emerges.

B. *The New Testament discloses God as powerful.* One cannot read about the life and ministry of Jesus Christ without seeing God's power. Jesus' miracles dramatically disclose his power. He showed his power over nature by calming a storm. He commanded demons with authority. He healed handicaps and disease. And he even defeated death.

C. *God is still as powerful as he ever was.* He is changing lives. Look around and see the lives he is in the process of changing.

III. God disclosed himself as a preeminent God.

A. *The Old Testament reveals God as one who tolerates no rival.* Pharaoh sought to get the Israelites to compromise. God spoke through Moses about total commitment to him. He would not tolerate partial allegiance to Jehovah and partial allegiance to Egypt. Throughout all of the Old Testament, God demanded allegiance to him and to him alone.

B. *Jesus allowed for no divided loyalty.* He forbade a man to buy a farm before following him. He left a man who wanted to try out some oxen. He stated quite clearly, "No man can serve two masters" (Matt. 6:24). He demanded preeminence in a person's life.

C. *God deserves preeminence.* God can command undivided loyalty because he is the only true God. If people will not allow him preeminence now, he will demand preeminence later (Phil. 2:10–11).

IV. God disclosed himself as a pardoning God.

A. *The Old Testament pictures God as forgiving:* When God introduced himself to Moses, he disclosed many traits about himself. One feature inherent in God's character is his willingness to forgive. When Israel broke the covenant and worshiped a golden calf, God was willing to forgive. Look through the Old Testament, and you will see the God who forgives.

B. *The New Testament dramatically portrays God's nature as one who forgives.* A casual reading of the life and ministry of Jesus discloses God as willing to forgive. Jesus practiced the art of forgiving sinners, and the world of his day could hardly believe the magnanimity of his forgiveness.

C. *God is ready to forgive today.* Many groan in their guilt because they do not know the real nature of God. He is willing to forgive. This means that he restores their relationship with him, and he remits the sin debt. Praise God for One who forgives!

Conclusion

God introduced himself to Moses and told Moses about his character. Moses in turn opened his life to this great God.

The same God introduces himself to you. Open your life to him.

SUNDAY MORNING, OCTOBER 18

Title: Obey God Because You Love Him

Text: "Have we not all one father? hath not one God created us?" **(Mal. 2:10)**.

Scripture Reading: Malachi 1:2–5

Hymns: "Our Best," Kirk
"Serve the Lord with Gladness," McKinney
"More Love to Thee," Prentiss

Offertory Prayer: Our Father, we remember that Jesus was once offered all the material things of the world if he would fall down and worship Satan. We also remember that he refused because he realized that it was a "bad deal." Help us always to keep our priorities straight and to view all the kingdoms in this world from the perspective of him who said, "Lay not up for yourselves treasures upon earth, where moth and rust doth corrupt." Help us not only to recognize that the tithe is holy to God, but to realize also that our motive in bringing our gifts is of equal concern to you. Knowing that God loves a cheerful giver, may we bring our gifts gladly. We pray in Jesus' name and for his sake. Amen.

Introduction

The last prophetic voice to Israel before the coming of John the Baptist and Jesus was Malachi. He actually lived after the golden age of prophecy had waned, but his insights equaled, and in some cases, exceeded anything to be found in messages of his predecessors. He possessed a concept of God's universal kingdom as great as Isaiah. His high and holy view of marriage was worthy of any eighth-century voice of God. His teaching that divine love is holy love rooted in God's majesty ranks with Hosea's. Although he came last, there was nothing inferior or second-rate about this final Old Testament spokesman for God. Malachi stood far above any man of his day and compares favorably with any prophet of any period.

311

What about Malachi's background? One wise man said that "eternal vigilance is the price of liberty," while a contemporary theologian says that when any generation "has been robbed of its familiar gods of material security, progress, human self-sufficiency . . . by the marauding forces of agnosticism, trouble, and despair, then strikes God's hour." That hour had arrived for Judah! Haggai and Zechariah had led the people to build the temple, but now the people's spiritual life was slipping backward. A need existed for a man of God to declare the divine counsel without compromise. Such a man was available: Malachi. Three main themes are found in his book.

I. Dreamers must face reality.

Deep scars were left on Israel because of the postexilic age's bitter frustration. The returning captives came to Jerusalem with tremendous enthusiasm, aspiring to reestablish the glorious days of Israel. They believed that the promises of the prophets who preceded them would come to pass with amazing and literal accuracy in their day. They looked for the land to produce a miraculous abundance and for all nations to serve them. How disappointed they were! Every dreamer must, somewhere down the line, face the cold, hard facts of life. Dreams may motivate us for the future, but dreams never win the game!

Four strong personalities preceded Malachi. Haggai and Zechariah were the prophets of that time. Ezra and Nehemiah likewise played an important part in the history of this period. Ezra led the group from Babylon to Jerusalem and then taught the law to the Israelites. Nehemiah was a layman who left a place of personal prestige in the king's service to come to Jerusalem to lead the people in rebuilding a great wall around the city to replace the one that had been destroyed. Ezra followed him with another great teaching program. But always the people went back to their careless living and superficial commitment. Malachi came on the scene at the close of the work of these great people during a period of discouragement and moral retrogression. He had to remind them again and again that a great nation is not built on dreams but on deeds.

How true this is of life in any generation! Dreams are important, but they alone are not enough. Someone said, "You've built a great castle in the air. That's fine. Now put a foundation under it!" As in everything else, we receive our greatest example in "dreaming and doing" from our Savior, of whom it was written:

> Dear Master, in whose life I see,
> All that I long and fail to be;
> Let Thy clear light forever shine,
> To shape and guide this life of mine.
>
> Though what I dream and what I do
> In my poor ways are always two;

Help me, oppressed by things undone,
Oh, Thou, whose dream and deed were one.

—John Hunter

II. God's presence is purifying.

Precious metal is very rarely found without other substances being present within it. The refiner's work is to free it from these lesser things. He heats the ore mixed with lead in a crucible and blows air on it until the lead is oxidized. The films rise to the surface and are all removed. The refiner watches the process closely and keeps the heat at the proper degree. The color becomes clearer as the impurities disappear. He knows when the process is finished because he sees his own face reflected in the substance. Malachi used this figure of speech (3:2) to convey the fact that God is constantly at work in the lives of his loved ones. Adversity is often the greatest blessing a Christian can encounter. Suffering drives people to knock at the gate of God in prayer. The poet said:

My life is but a field,
Stretched out beneath God's sky
Some harvest rich to yield.

Where grows the golden grain?
Where faith? Where sympathy?
In a furrow cut by pain.

—Maltbie D. Babcock

God had disciplined Israel because he loved them and saw the possibility of using them in his work. Likewise, God must refine us in the furnace of disappointment and tears. But when he sees his image reflected in us, he knows that his work has been successful.

III. The King is coming.

Old Testament prophecy concludes with a clear statement that the "Sun of Righteousness" will "arise with healing in his wings" (4:2), a clear reference to the coming of Jesus Christ. Also, Malachi said that God will send "the prophet Elijah" to "turn the hearts of the parents to their children" (4:5–6 NIV). The New Testament says that this was John the Baptist (Matt. 11:14; Mark 9:11, 13). However dark Israel's history was, God never failed to speak through his prophets a message of hope and deliverance. The great theme of the Old Testament is God's redemptive work both present and future. God chose Abraham as his instrument, promising that in his seed all the nations of the earth would be blessed. For us also the promise is sure. Our King is coming. We don't know when, but we know he is coming. Therefore we should wait, watch, and work!

Conclusion

All is both law and love! God commands us, but we do not obey merely through a sense of obligation. We obey because we have been redeemed. Any other motive for service than that of love will fall short at the crisis time. We may do certain things because we fear God and his wrath, but maturity will not come until we learn that the love of Christ is the constraining force for all of our Christian service. Faith and hope are great, but love is the greatest of all!

SUNDAY EVENING, OCTOBER 18

Title: Peter's Lesson on Humility

Text: "Whosoever therefore shall humble himself as this little child, the same is greatest in the kingdom of heaven" **(Matt. 18:4)**.

Scripture Reading: Matthew 18:1–10; Mark 9:33–37; Luke 9:46–48

Introduction

Jesus' experience with his disciples at Caesarea Philippi was a distinct turning point in his ministry. He was obviously happy about Peter's confession and looked forward to the continued, triumphant growth of his church. He pressed onward in his plan to provide salvation for humankind by preparing his disciples for his approaching death at Jerusalem. His transfiguration one week later was also a step in the disciples' preparation for his death and resurrection.

Following the transfiguration, as the disciples traveled to Capernaum, they argued among themselves as to which of them would be the greatest in the kingdom of heaven. Scripture informs us that Jesus perceived the thought of their hearts. "They came to Capernaum. When he was in the house, he asked them, 'What were you arguing about on the road?' But they kept quiet because on the way they had argued about who was the greatest" (Mark 9:33–34 NIV).

I. "Who is the greatest in the kingdom of heaven?" (Matt. 18:1).

This is the question, after some delay and embarrassment, the disciples finally asked.

    A. *Causes for the question.*
        1. This must be conjecture, but Andrew and John were the first to become disciples. Peter, James, and John formed an inner circle with special nearness to Jesus. Perhaps Judas had a claim as the treasurer. There is no evidence that Jesus' words to Peter at Caesarea Philippi entered into this discussion.
        2. The disciples had a secular, perverted view of the nature of the kingdom of God. They still held this view after Peter was rebuked

for it at Caesarea Philippi and after the transfiguration. They would continue to hold this view until after Pentecost. Just prior to the ascension, the disciples asked Jesus, "Lord, wilt thou at this time restore again the kingdom to Israel?" (Acts 1:6).

B. *If we were not so spiritually sluggish, we might think them stupid.* If we were not so jealous of each other, we might criticize them severely.

II. The answer: An object lesson in humility.

A. *"Jesus called a little child unto him, and set him in the midst of them" (Matt. 18:2).* According to Mark 9:36, Jesus took him in his arms. He was probably Peter's little boy or Andrew's, since Jesus was in their home. There is something peculiarly tender about Jesus holding a little boy on his lap. He cared for children. With the child in his arms, Jesus said, "Verily I say unto you, Except ye be converted, and become as little children, ye shall not enter into the kingdom of heaven. Whosoever therefore shall humble himself as this little child, the same is greatest in the kingdom of heaven" (Matt. 18:3–4).

B. *By this object lesson Jesus rebuked the self-seeking of the disciples and affirmed the essential qualifications of the kingdom person and of true greatness.* He did not say that one must be a child to be saved, and he certainly did not say that one must be childish. He did say that disciples must be childlike in humility. What are the characteristics of a child, as compared to an unregenerate adult, that the Master praises?

   1. Humility. The child usually trusts his parents to care for him. He accepts his parents and is willing to be taught by them. As compared to an adult, a child is not self-seeking. It would be commendable for the disciples to accept their Master and believe that he will do what is best for them. The condition of entering the kingdom is a right heart attitude.

   2. Readiness to forgive is suggested in Matthew 18:6–10. As compared with an adult, a child is slow to take offense and does not hold grudges.

   Other qualities inferred from the nature of the child as compared with an adult might be confiding trust, teachableness, democratic spirit, and loyalty.

III. The difficult lesson had to be repeated.

A. *James and John asked for the first places in the kingdom (Matt. 20:20–28; parallel passage: Mark 10:32–45).* A few weeks after the object lesson of the child, Jesus was leading his disciples through Perea on the way to Jerusalem. He was telling them that he would be crucified there (see Matt. 20:17–19). The thoughts of the disciples were on selfish ambitions. Salome, the mother of James and John, came with them to Jesus and requested, "Grant that these my two sons may sit, the one on thy right hand, and the other on the left, in thy kingdom" (Matt. 20:21). Jesus did not rebuke them. Speaking of his death, he did ask them, however, "Are ye able to drink of the cup that I shall drink of, and to be baptized with the baptism that I am baptized with?" They replied, "We are able" (Matt. 20:22).

James did go to death and John to exile for Jesus. Our Lord explained to them that in the kingdom of heaven there are no favorites. Greatness will be on the basis of faithfulness and service. "Whosoever will be great among you, let him be your servant" (Matt. 20:26). James and John may be first and second in the kingdom of God. However, they will not be there because of favoritism but because of faithfulness and service.

B. *The disciples did not learn the lesson.* The contention continued in the upper room on the night Jesus established the Lord's Supper. Jesus gave them an acted parable by washing their feet (see John 13:1–17).

Conclusion

The door of the kingdom of heaven is closed to those who do not turn and humble themselves. It is open to all who do. Jesus is the example: He is the Servant of God foretold by Isaiah. Jesus bids us to serve in his name, "even as the Son of man came not to be ministered unto, but to minister, and to give his life a ransom for many" (Matt. 20:28). Humility is the willingness to put God first and to serve others in accord with his will. (Reverently read again the way Paul wrote it in Phil. 2:5–11.) "Let this mind be in you, which was also in Christ Jesus" (Phil. 2:5).

WEDNESDAY EVENING, OCTOBER 21

Title: The Possibility of Positive Thinking

Text: "Moses said unto God, Who am I, that I should go unto Pharaoh, and that I should bring forth the children of Israel out of Egypt?" **(Ex. 3:11)**.

Scripture Reading: Exodus 3:11–4:12

Introduction

You may be living life rather pessimistically today. If so, you can transform your negative thinking into positive thinking by looking at some ways God helped Moses to overcome his pessimism.

I. God builds confidence (Ex. 3:11–12).

A. *The lack of confidence.* Moses' first objection to God's call discloses his reticence. "Who am I, that I should go unto Pharaoh, and that I should bring forth the children of Israel out of Egypt?" (Ex. 3:11).

Moses did not feel prepared, either by personal endowment or by previous experience, to undertake such a tremendous task.

Oftentimes our lack of service stems from a lack of confidence. One cannot serve God effectively without having a healthy and realistic self-concept.

B. *The building of confidence.* God built Moses' confidence with a promise: "I will be with thee" (Ex. 3:12). Then the Lord followed his promise with a sign.

God builds confidence with the promise of his presence. Anyone's confidence can be enhanced with the assurance of God's presence and with reliance on the trustworthiness of God's Word.

II. God reveals his name (Ex. 3:13–22).

A. *The lack of knowledge about God's name.* Moses' second negative thought was that he did not know the name of the God who was sending him to Egypt. "Behold, when I come unto the children of Israel, and shall say unto them, The God of your fathers hath sent me unto you; and they shall say to me, What is his name? what shall I say unto them?" (Ex. 3:13). Moses' question was a desire to know what kind of God sent him to Egypt. The name represents a person's attributes or character.

B. *The revelation of God's name.* God helped Moses' negative attitude by disclosing his name: "I AM THAT I AM" (Ex. 3:14). The Hebrew word has a rich background. It is the word *YHWH.* It was used in the Old Testament to describe One who is adequate for every situation.

The more one learns of God the greater will be the positive attitude.

III. God demonstrates his power (Ex. 4:1–9).

A. *The lack of trust in the people's response.* Moses' third negative thought was that Israel would not believe that the Lord had sent him. "But, behold, they will not believe me, nor hearken unto my voice: for they will say, The LORD hath not appeared unto thee" (Ex. 4:1).

Doubts fill the minds of many of God's workers. They fail to place confidence in what might happen when they present God's message.

B. *The demonstration of God's power.* God met Moses' negative mood by giving three signs. A wooden staff was changed to a serpent. Healthy skin was made leprous. Water from the Nile was turned into blood. These signs would have convinced the most skeptical.

You can be a more effective servant by observing God's power. Read about the power of God in the Bible. Observe the power of God in the lives of people today.

IV. God will equip for assigned tasks (Ex. 4:10–12).

A. *The thought of humanism.* Moses knew that his confrontation with Pharaoh would require convincing words. This led to a fourth negative thought. "O my LORD, I am not eloquent" (Ex. 4:10). Moses felt inadequate as an orator.

God's call to service often overwhelms an individual. At first glance one might recoil, thinking that he or she must face a task with human strength and wisdom.

B. *The promise of divine equipping.* God responded to Moses' reluctance with a promise of divine equipping. God reminded Moses that he had equipped man with a voice. If he equipped man with a mouth, God was surely capable of endowing him with the necessary gifts to serve him.

A call to service means a divine endowment. Look through the Bible and you will discover that when God calls a person to a task, he equips for the task.

Conclusion

God could be calling you for a service. Is your attitude negative? Open your life and respond positively to whatever God wants you to do.

SUNDAY MORNING, OCTOBER 25

Title: Doing God's Will, Not Ours

Text: "Jonah rose up to flee unto Tarshish from the presence of the LORD" **(Jonah 1:3).**

Scripture **Reading:** Jonah 1:1–17; 4:7–11

Hymns: "Hark, the Voice of Jesus Calling," March
           "We've a Story to Tell," Nicol
           "O Zion, Haste," Thomson

Offertory Prayer: Our Father, today is a very special day. This is the one day in the week that you have set apart for yourself in a unique way. We call it the "Lord's Day," which means that it is a time for worship and wholesome life-enriching activities. It is also a day to bring our gifts of money to carry on your work. Every one of us has been blessed abundantly. Even the poorest among us is rich when compared with many people throughout the world. Those of us who know Jesus Christ in forgiveness of sin have all the riches of heaven. We bring our gifts so that the message of Christ may be preached to those who do not know him here in our own community, in the larger land in which we live, and even unto the uttermost parts of the earth. Bless our gifts. We pray in Jesus' name. Amen.

Introduction

We know that Jonah lived sometime before or while Jeroboam II ruled in Israel, because he prophesied the conquests of this great king (2 Kings 14:25).

This means he preached about the eighth century before Christ or sometime earlier.

Since Jonah's prophecy was favorable to Jeroboam, he must have been a popular prophet at first. Perhaps he had a large following and thus was reluctant to go to Nineveh with a message of God's judgment. Nineveh was the capital of the great Assyrian Empire, the archenemy of Israel. Four steps predominated the ministry of Jonah as recorded in the book that bears his name.

I. Jonah at first ran from God.

The call to Nineveh was far more significant than appears at first sight. For Jonah to preach to the enemy would have caused a serious loss of popularity among his fellow citizens. The average Israelite of Jonah's day probably did not care whether Assyria lived or died. In fact, he probably preferred the latter. Assyria was competition to Israel commercially and a potential threat militarily. Why should the average Israelite feel any necessity to bring Assyria into favor with God? Perhaps Jonah felt he could hear the people say, "Why waste a good preacher on those pagan people?"

A) *Thus Jonah rebelled against God's call.* When he caught a boat at Joppa to go to Tarshish, he may have been going to Tarsus, the hometown of Saul (Paul). Many, however, feel that he was headed for a city in Spain. The exact destination is not important, but Jonah was going in an opposite direction from Assyria. This happens so often when people rebel against God's will. They travel to a different place, sometimes even morally, and find themselves in a far country of disobedience. God is always present, however, even when we are out of fellowship with him. He forever stands within the shadow and keeps watch over his own. The mighty tempest in the sea was no freak of nature but was planned by God.

B) *Are you in rebellion to God's will?* We will never find peace with God until we are saved by Christ. We will never know, as Christians, the peace that passes all understanding until we are obedient to God's will. God may not call us to a place of service that the world considers significant, but wherever he wills for us to serve is important, and we should delight in prompt obedience.

> There's surely somewhere a lowly place
> In earth's harvest fields so wide,
> Where I may labor thro' life's short day,
> For Jesus the Crucified;
> So, trusting my all unto Thy care,
> I know Thou lovest me,
> I'll do Thy will with a heart sincere,
> I'll be what You want me to be.
>
> —*Charles E. Prior*

II. Jonah next ran to God.

The second chapter is a prayer of Jonah in which he gave thanks. He had already been delivered from the big fish. Part of the chapter is a flashback in which he described his previous condition before his deliverance. We are not told all of the details concerning Jonah's repentance and his eventual willingness to obey God. The last scene we have in chapter 1 is of Jonah being cast into the sea and the men actually turning to worship Jehovah, Jonah's God, when the sea became calm.

To run from God is a traumatic experience, but to surrender to him can be an equally emotional decision. Some Christians must be chastised greatly before they will do the thing God wants them to do. Many ministers and laypersons alike tell stories of how God "whipped them into line" before they would be faithful in service. Others, of course, need only mild corrections. Jonah's experience was, in many ways, as traumatic as that of Saul the persecutor.

III. Jonah did best when he ran with God.

A) *God always gives us another chance.* We cannot be certain where the fish delivered Jonah, but the prophet was ready to listen to the call! This second call must have been briefer, for God merely said that Jonah should do the thing he had told him to do previously.

The city of Nineveh was one of the great metropolitan areas of the ancient world. The "three days" refers to the time that it took to go through the city, not the time it took Jonah to reach it from where he landed on the shore. The message was brief. The Hebrew is quite literal—"Forty more days and Nineveh will be overturned."

When one works with God, great blessings are available. In fact, there is no limit to what can be done in God's kingdom when one is fully committed to God's will. Elisha A. Hoffman penned these lyrics in "Is Your All on the Altar":

> Oh, we never can know what the Lord will bestow
> Of the blessings for which we have prayed,
> Till our body and soul He doth fully control,
> And our all on the altar is laid.

B) *Jonah preached and God did the blessing.* The king repented. Those who treat this story as merely a parable should familiarize themselves with the history of Assyria. There was a period preceding the beginning of the new kingdom under Tiglath-pileser III in 745 BC that seems an ideal time for the repentance of the Assyrian king. Several unexplained changes in policy occurred during this century, and we have every reason to believe that some of these were brought about directly because of Jonah's preaching.

C) *The repentance was complete.* Personal sorrow for sin was evident. To have an effective revival, a community needs an intense feeling of the sinfulness of sin and of the necessity to change its course of action. The people of Nineveh were confronted with their sin and fled to God for mercy.

IV. Sometimes good people run ahead of God.

If most of us were writing the story of Jonah, we would leave out chapter 4. Yet God saw fit to put it in! Why? Because spiritual pride is an ego-fulfilling experience rather than a humble declaration of God's purpose in judgment and his delight in mercy.

The lesson God taught Jonah by means of the gourd should say to all of us that God has ways beyond us and we must never question his judgment. God's purpose includes the world, not merely our small field of existence. He made everyone and loves everyone. Unless we understand this, we run counter to his purposes. Jonah was a great preacher, but even in the midst of a great evangelistic campaign in Assyria, he still had the need to "grow up" in understanding the complete nature of God. So do we!

Conclusion

To know God's will is not always easy. He does not speak audibly, but rather through his Word, the Bible, and through deep impressions that he sends to us by means of the Holy Spirit. At the wedding of Cana of Galilee, Mary, the mother of Jesus, said to the people concerning Jesus, "Whatsoever he saith unto you, do it" (John 2:5). This is good advice for us today.

SUNDAY EVENING, OCTOBER 25

Title: Peter's Lesson on Forgiveness

Text: "Then came Peter to him, and said, Lord, how oft shall my brother sin against me, and I forgive him? till seven times? Jesus saith unto him, I say not unto thee, Until seven times: but, Until seventy times seven" **(Matt. 18:21–22).**

Scripture Reading: Matthew 18:15–35

Introduction

"Then came Peter to him, and said, Lord, how oft shall my brother sin against me, and I forgive him? till seven times?" (Matt. 18:21). Peter's question was important, for Jesus placed great emphasis on right relations with others. The first priority for any person is to be right with God. Second only to that in importance is to be right with other people. In this message, we assume that you are right with God. What is your obligation to be right with others?

I. What to do when you have wronged others.

A. *Ask God's forgiveness.* "Forgive us our debts, as we forgive our debtors" (Matt. 6:12). Our Lord's comment on this petition in the model prayer is, "For if ye forgive men their trespasses, your heavenly Father will also forgive you: But if ye forgive not men their trespasses, neither will your Father forgive your trespasses" (Matt. 6:14–15). Debts are sins of omission. They include obligations unfulfilled. Trespasses are sins of commission, in which one walks where God says not to walk. Sin is any lack of conformity to God's will. If we have sinned against a brother or sister, we first ask God's forgiveness, because all sin is fundamentally against God.

B. *Then go to the person you have wronged, make an honest confession, and in so far as it is possible, make restitution for any wrong you have caused.* The Lord's instructions are clear: "Therefore if thou bring thy gift to the altar, and there rememberest that thy brother hath ought against thee; Leave there thy gift before the altar, and go thy way; first be reconciled to thy brother, and then come and offer thy gift" (Matt. 5:23–24). More important than worship is the reconciliation with a brother or sister against whom one has sinned. Be reconciled if that person is willing to forgive. If not, you have done what you can. "If it be possible, as much as lieth in you, live peaceably with all men" (Rom. 12:18). Paul recognized that it takes two persons to reconcile differences.

II. What to do when someone has wronged you.

A. *Go to that person personally and privately.* Human nature counsels that since another person has wronged you, that person ought to come to you and ask forgiveness. Jesus turns the tables, however: "If thy brother trespass against thee, rebuke him; and if he repent, forgive him" (Luke 17:3). If the other person is a Christian, you will find almost certainly that the differences between you and him have been because of a misunderstanding. Misunderstandings can come because words are misunderstood, because of an ambiguous meaning, or perhaps because either you or the other person did not get all of the facts and jumped to an erroneous conclusion. If you can effect reconciliation, you have gained your brother or sister. If not, you have done all that you can do.

B. *More specific and detailed are the instructions when the person is a member of your church.* The first step is the same: "Moreover if thy brother shall trespass against thee, go and tell him his fault between thee and him alone: if he shall hear thee, thou hast gained thy brother" (Matt. 18:15).

The second step is, "But if he will not hear thee, then take with thee one or two more, that in the mouth of two or three witnesses every word may be established" (Matt. 18:16). If the person will not hear you or the witnesses, Jesus commands that the disagreement be brought before the church. If this person will not hear the church, it is evidence that he or she is not a Christian. In that case, the person is to be treated as a sinner in need of your prayers and witness. He or she should not be treated as one to be kept on the church roll in good and regular standing. (Read how Jesus said it, and the importance of it, in Matt. 18:17–18.)

Even God cannot forgive a person who will not repent. "And be ye kind one to another, tenderhearted, forgiving one another, even as God for Christ's sake hath forgiven you" (Eph. 4:32).

III. Jesus answers Peter's question.

A. *Peter no doubt thought that his offer to forgive a brother who sinned against him as many as seven times was magnanimous.* "Jesus saith unto him, I say not unto thee, Until seven times: but, Until seventy times seven" (Matt. 18:22). Whether Jesus' answer is "seventy times seven" or "seventy-seven" (the texts do not agree) matters little, for Jesus is saying that forgiveness is unlimited. His own spirit was manifested by his prayer from the cross for his enemies, "Father, forgive them; for they know not what they do" (Luke 23:34). Jesus' attitude is further revealed in Matthew 5:43–48. One forgiven by God will have a forgiving spirit.

B. *This truth is enforced by the parable of the unmerciful servant.* (Read Matt. 18:23–35.) This parable is not an allegory. It deals with principles and relationships rather than with persons. If, for example, one erroneously says the king represents God, there are many contradictions:

1. God never forgives unless the sinner repents. God is never fooled. The king in the parable was fooled.

2. God never makes mistakes, so he never revokes a pardon. The king did make a mistake and did revoke the pardon.

3. God never forgives without regeneration. The king did forgive the servant without any renewal taking place within him.

   The kingdom of heaven, that is, the reign of God or the way God rules, will in some way be illustrated by the story.

C. *Exposition of the parable.*

1. The magnitude of the debt (Matt. 18:23–25). Jesus showed humor in making the debt of the servant so great. One talent was six thousand denarii (translated pence). A denarius was the amount of a day's wage in the parables. Ten thousand talents would be sixty million denarii. Josephus, a Jewish historian, wrote that the imperial taxes for Judea, Idumea, and Samaria were only six hundred talents. Ten thousand talents! An impossible sum! The servant was utterly, completely insolvent, yet in his pride and desperation he cried, "Have patience with me, and I will pay thee all" (v. 29).

The application seems valid that our sin debt to God is more than we can pay. The sinner is "dead in trespasses and sins" (Eph. 2:1). A dead man cannot save himself. Human pride says, "I can atone for my sins with good deeds." God's Word says, "For the wages of sin is death" (Rom. 6:23).

2. The forgiveness of the debt. On the basis of the debtor's pitiful plea, the king forgave him his debt and freed his family from bondage. This suggests the greatness of God's mercy in forgiving the sin debts of all those who call on him in sincerity. God's forgiveness is offered to all. His offer is free but costly. (Read John 3:16; Rom. 8:1; Titus 2:14.)

3. The terms of forgiveness. The king was fooled concerning the nature of the servant he forgave. He had expected that on the forgiveness of his debt, the forgiven man would be forgiving. Instead, he found a fellow servant who owed him one hundred denarii (pence). This was only 1/600,000 of what he had been forgiven. The man begged him to delay payment. His servant used the very words that he had used in beseeching the king. He would not forgive his servant and instead cast him into prison. When the king learned what he had done, he called him and said, "O thou wicked servant, I forgave thee all that debt, because thou desiredst me: Shouldest not thou also have had compassion on thy fellow-servant, even as I had pity on thee? And his lord was wroth, and delivered him to the tormentors, till he should pay all that was due unto him" (Matt. 18:32–34).

Happily, God never makes a mistake, but God also never forgives until there is genuine repentance. (Read Matt. 21:32; Luke 24:47; Acts 20:21.) God desires to forgive. He has made provision for forgiveness, but he cannot bestow forgiveness apart from repentance. (Read Rom. 3:23–26.) Whom God forgives he also regenerates. One who has been forgiven of God desires to forgive others.

Conclusion

"If ye forgive not men their trespasses, neither will your Father forgive your trespasses" (Matt. 6:15). "So likewise shall my heavenly Father do also unto you, if ye from your hearts forgive not every one his brother their trespasses" (Matt. 18:35). Unforgiveness in the heart is evidence that one is not saved. When one has been forgiven ten thousand talents, one hundred pence is as nothing.

Never does the Christian pray, "Father, damn them." Instead, we pray, as did Jesus, "Father, forgive them."

WEDNESDAY EVENING, OCTOBER 28

Title: When Discouragement Comes

Text: "Moses returned unto the LORD, and said, Lord, wherefore hast thou so evil entreated this people? why is it that thou hast sent me? For since I came to Pharaoh to speak in thy name, he hath done evil to this people; neither hast thou delivered thy people at all" **(Ex. 5:22–23)**.

Scripture Reading: Exodus 5:1–23

Introduction

Nothing hurts so badly as having excitement suddenly affected by disappointment. I remember the first date with the girl who is now my wife. Over a period of weeks, I had made a careful approach. Finally, I threw caution to the wind and asked her to meet me at a bowling alley. We carefully arranged the time and place. Then the day arrived for the meeting. Excitement filled my day. I arrived early at our meeting place. Time passed. The designated hour passed. Another hour passed. She did not come. My thrill turned to disappointment. Nothing hurts quite that badly. To clear the mistake, I must tell you that I didn't wait long enough. She arrived late because of car trouble.

Moses knew the hurt of disappointment. Soon after he settled the matter of God's call to him and of his negative attitude, he went to Pharaoh. The first attempt was met with a setback. Our text reflects an anguished cry of discouragement (see Ex. 5:22).

Have you ever experienced any type of discouragement? Let us examine the causes of Moses' discouragement and see if we can receive help.

I. We are discouraged when a person rejects our God (Ex. 5:2).

A. *The presentation of the great God.* Moses and Aaron were granted an audience with Pharaoh. They requested that he allow the Hebrews to go and hold a feast in the wilderness (Ex. 5:1). The word for feast comes from a Hebrew word that means "to make a pilgrimage." Moses and Aaron presented the greatness of a God who wanted his people to follow him.

Modern Christians need a boldness akin to that of Moses and Aaron. Without apology or without being ashamed, we need to present the true and living God to a secular society.

B. *The audacious rejection of God.* Pharaoh's answer to Moses and Aaron was one of contempt. "Who is the LORD, that I should obey his voice to let Israel go? I know not the LORD, neither will I let Israel go" (Ex. 5:2). Pharaoh did not know or acknowledge the power of God.

Nothing causes greater disappointment than when people reject our God. Jesus knew this disappointment. Often he presented God as the loving heavenly Father, and people refused to be his children. What a disappointment!

II. We are discouraged when the world retaliates (Ex. 5:10–14).

A. *The world's scorn of God's people.* Because of Pharaoh's disdain of the Lord, he scorned God's people. He assigned impossible quotas for making bricks. When a quota was not met, the Israelite foreman was beaten by the Egyptian taskmaster.

Scorn for God leads to disrespect for God's creation. Rejecting God leads to a persecution of God's people. God is intimately bound with his people. To persecute his people is to hurt him.

B. *The world's injustices to people.* Having to meet an unreasonable quota of bricks discouraged the Hebrews as well as Moses and Aaron. In addition to making the bricks, the Hebrews also had to gather the straw to make them. Pharaoh had no sense of responsibility for reasoning fairly. His cruelties and injustices chilled the fervor and enthusiasm of Moses and Aaron.

Nothing brings more discouragement to a person than seeing God's people treated unjustly. When the world retaliates with ruthless cruelty, we tend to become discouraged.

III. We are discouraged when our own people renounce our leadership (Ex. 5:15–21).

A. *Opposition from without causes grumbling within.* The Israelite foremen complained to Pharaoh, but they could find no relief. Finding no redress there, the foremen met Moses and Aaron and blamed them for their difficulties. "You have made us obnoxious to Pharaoh and his officials and have put a sword in their hand to kill us" (Ex. 5:21 NIV). Oppression from without caused restlessness in the Hebrew camp.

The world's scorn makes a Christian tired. At these times it is easy to have division and complaints within the group.

B. *The lack of unity discourages leaders.* Nothing caused any more discouragement to Moses' mission than the disunity among his people. Because of Pharaoh's opposition and the people's grumbling, Moses accused God. This is the ultimate in discouragement.

When life hands us disappointments, we have a tendency to be discouraged and may find ourselves lashing out at God.

Conclusion

Look at the man Moses. After his enthusiastic confrontation with Pharaoh, he became discouraged. The Lord dealt with him and promised to be with him. That same God can help you with anything that causes you to be discouraged.

NOVEMBER

■ **Sunday Mornings**

"Taking the Stew out of Stewardship" is the suggested theme for Sunday mornings in November. Many people think of stewardship only in terms of offerings for some worthy cause. The principle of stewardship applies to every area of life.

■ **Sunday Evenings**

Continue the series on the life of the apostle Peter, using the theme "Some Personal Portraits of Peter."

■ **Wednesday Evenings**

Continue the messages based on Exodus using the theme "The God Who Reveals Himself in Times of Need."

SUNDAY MORNING, NOVEMBER 1

Title: The Stewardship of Time

Text: "Be very careful, then, how you live—not as unwise but as wise, making the most of every opportunity, because the days are evil" **(Eph. 5:15–16 NIV)**.

Scripture Reading: Ephesians 5:15–21

Hymns: "O Zion, Haste," Thompson
"Jesus Is Calling," Crosby
"Only One Life to Offer," Christiansen

Offertory Prayer: Our Father in heaven, we thank you for the opportunity to think together about the matter before us this morning. We thank you, our Father, that we may have fellowship in thinking about a phase of our stewardship that is so relevant, so applicable to the life of every one of us. We pray that we may realize, whether we are only in the beginning of our lives or whether we are nearing the end, that time is running out, that "Man . . . is of few days, and full of trouble" (Job 14:1). Bless the offering that we bring, for we ask it in the name of our Savior. Amen.

Introduction

A college Latin professor entered a pen shop to buy a fountain pen. He wrote on the pad on the counter, *"Tempus fugit."* The sales girl read what he had written and remarked helpfully, "Perhaps you would like to try this one, Mr. Fugit." However we view it, "time flies," moves on, and like a plot of land, there is just so much of it. God has given each one of us a measure of time. How are we using it? What will happen to us when we are called before the Judge of all the earth to give account of our use of the time we were allotted?

I. Time: Where do we get it?

Who gives time to us? The first principle of stewardship is this: God is the owner, and we are stewards. God owns everything; we are his tenants. We are accountable, therefore, to him for the use of his gifts, and this includes the gift of time. God created time and gave it to us. This is his fundamental gift, for all other gifts are conditioned upon it.

God gives to all equally. Though others may have more talents, we all have the same amount of time. No matter how rich we are, time cannot be bought. No matter how poor, we cannot receive less. The president of our nation or the CEO of the largest corporation has no more time than you. Every person has sixty minutes to the hour, twenty-four hours to the day, and seven days per week.

Jesus was both urgent and careful about the use of God-given time. On one occasion, he said, "As long as it is day, we must do the work of him who sent me. Night is coming, when no one can work" (John 9:4 NIV). Where do we get time? God gives it. It is his gift.

II. Time: How shall we use it?

The use we make of time is our stewardship of it. In this we may be faithful or unfaithful. We may use time in the wrong way; we may use it in the right way.

    A. *On the one hand, we use time in the wrong way.* "Be . . . wise, making the most of every opportunity" (Eph. 5:16 NIV), Paul said. But sometimes we fail to do this.

        1. For one thing, we can just wish away our time for half a lifetime. We grasp at life yet fritter it away.

            Time dragged by when we were children. It seemed that Christmas would never come, and we were wishing the days away until it did. The same held true for our birthdays, or until some party, or until school was out. We were always wanting to grow up. We were wishing the time away.

            But this way of thinking isn't confined to children. Many in their teens are wishing their time away. They fall in love, or they think they do. A few years must pass before they can marry, so they wish the time away instead of having the patience to say, "Let's enjoy what we have now. We'll take on such responsibilities soon enough."

        2. Again, we can be careless with time. Henry David Thoreau said, "You cannot kill time without injuring eternity." Victor Hugo said, "As short as life is, we can make it shorter still by the careless

waste of time." In this regard, three things may take the keenness from the life of the professing Christian: first, carelessness with time; second, carelessness with prayer; and third, carelessness with money. Often these three sorry sisters live together and make for a dismal household.

3. But still again, we can be tyrannized by time. Americans have more time-saving devices and less time than any other people in the world. We need a better perspective on time. We make a fetish of hectic activity. We admire the person who is always dashing off to keep an appointment. We assume that person must be very successful. We are time-conscious people.

When we use time in the wrong way, time passes and with it our expectations and hopes, unfulfilled, just as buds fall from the trees without having become fruit.

B. *On the other hand, we may use time in the right way.* The NIV renders our text: "Be very careful, then, how you live—not as unwise but as wise, making the most of every opportunity, because the days are evil" (Eph. 5:15–16). How can we "make the most" of our time and opportunities? We must do four things.

1. We must determine our priorities. We must decide what we shall do first. We cannot do everything, so we must decide what we will give time to, and then do it.

An old proverb says, "One has to spend money to make money." Likewise, one must spend time to save time. The efficient person who gets the most done in a twenty-four-hour period is the person who has learned to make time work for him or her through careful scheduling, budgeting, and planning. We don't have time to do what we consider most important; we make it.

2. We must change pace in our activities. This is necessary if we are going to avoid high blood pressure, heart disease, and a host of other ills. At least once under great pressure Jesus told his disciples, "Come ye yourselves apart into a desert place, and rest a while" (Mark 6:31).

Have you ever wondered how some people manage to get so much done in the average day, so much more than others? How do they do it? They pause. They take time to think, to meditate, to pray. From these periods of apparent inactivity, they draw rich resources of mind and spirit that give purpose and direction.

Once accused of wasting time, Leonardo da Vinci replied: "When I pause the longest, I make the most telling strokes with my brush." A change of pace is necessary.

3. We must concentrate on the primary things. Life is continually saying to us: "Now hear this!" And we had better listen. Jesus urged us to concentrate on the primary things: "Seek ye first

his kingdom, and his righteousness; and all these things shall be added unto you" (Matt. 6:33 ASV). This is both a command and a promise; and let us not say that it won't work if we have never tried it. When Paul said, "One thing I do, forgetting the things which are behind, and stretching forward to the things which are before, I press on toward the goal unto the prize of the high calling of God in Christ Jesus" (Phil. 3:13–14 ASV), he was saying that he was not going to waste time worrying about the foolish mistakes and sins of the past but, concerned with the main thing, he was going to press on toward the goal ahead.

4. We must dedicate our time to God. With his typically Puritan emphasis, John Milton said that he was to live each minute, "As ever in my great taskmaster's eye." Paul's statement is better: "Whether therefore ye eat, or drink, or whatsoever ye do, do all to the glory of God" (1 Cor. 10:31). We need to offer God everything, not only our abilities, our money, our energies, but also our time. This is what we mean by the stewardship of time.

III. Time: What will result?

What will be the fruit of a truly Christian stewardship of time?

A. *First, we will multiply ourselves in his service.* We will multiply our usefulness both to God and to our fellow humans. The person who is organized, motivated, and dedicated in the use of time can accomplish more than three people who are heedless, careless, and frustrated where time is concerned.

B. *We will advance the work of the kingdom.* A certain businessman was a tither. He had learned tithing from his father. But the conviction grew within him that he should do more than tithe his money, so he made a decision to tithe his time as well as his money. He decided to give each Tuesday afternoon of his busy week to soul winning and to the enlistment for Christ of businessmen with whom he had done business from time to time. The first week he visited three men. He won one of the three to Christ, and the next Sunday he was the happiest man in that city as he went down the aisle with this man and his family as they made a public profession of Christ. But he didn't stop with just winning them to Christ; he won them to his conviction about tithing and giving a tenth of one's time to the Lord. And those he won, won others.

C. *Last of all, we will bring glory to God.* The faithful steward of time is fruitful, and a fruitful Christian life brings glory to God. Jesus said to his disciples the night before he died, "Herein is my Father glorified, that ye bear much fruit; and so shall ye be my disciples" (John 15:8 ASV). In the final analysis it is only by deliberately paying our attention and giving our primary allegiance to eternity that we can prevent time from turning our lives into a pointless foolery. If we do this, all else will fall into place.

Conclusion

This is the stewardship of time, but I would be a poor steward of time if I should close this message and fail to urge upon those unsaved that the time to be saved is now. Paul told the Corinthians, "Behold, now is the acceptable time; behold, now is the day of salvation" (2 Cor. 6:2 ASV).

SUNDAY EVENING, NOVEMBER 1

Title: Peter in the Upper Room

Text: "Very truly I tell you, no servant is greater than his master, nor is a messenger greater than the one who sent him. Now that you know these things, you will be blessed if you do them" **(John 13:16–17 NIV).**

Scripture Reading: John 13:1–17

Introduction

Jesus and his disciples had come to the upper room (probably in the home of Mark's mother) where Jesus would eat the Passover meal with his disciples and ordain the Lord's Supper, the new Passover. It was Thursday after sunset (the beginning of Jewish Friday). Before the night was over, Jesus would be betrayed, and on the morrow he would be crucified.

On the previous Tuesday night, Judas, stung by the rebuke of Jesus at the feast in the home of Simon the leper (John 12:2–8), had bargained with the rulers to betray Jesus (Matt. 26:14–16; Mark 14:10–11; Luke 22:3–6). Jesus was aware of Judas's treachery, but the disciples were not. Jesus arranged for the large upper room and sent Peter and John to make ready the Passover (Luke 22:7–13). This may have been done secretly so that Judas would not suspect that his treachery was known.

I. The state of mind of the disciples and of Jesus.

A. *The contention continued among the disciples as to "which of them should be accounted the greatest" (Luke 22:24).* This contention had surfaced a few months earlier on the way from Caesarea Philippi to Capernaum. They had not learned the lesson that Jesus had tried to teach them by setting a child in their midst as an object lesson of humility (Matt. 18:1–6). Nor had they heeded Jesus' words to James and John, who on the way to Jerusalem had requested the first places in the kingdom (Matt. 20:20–28; Mark 10:35–45). The disciples continued to think of the kingdom as political.

B. *Jesus' state of mind contrasted with that of the disciples.* "Now before [just before rather than a whole day earlier] the feast of the passover, when Jesus knew that his hour was come that he should depart out of this world unto the Father, having loved his own which were in the world, he loved them unto the end" (John 13:1). Jesus was aware that his death was at hand, and his love for his disciples was intensified. "When the hour was come, he sat down, and the twelve apostles with him. And he said unto them, With desire I have desired to eat this passover with you before I suffer: For I say unto you, I will not any more eat thereof, until it be fulfilled in the kingdom of God" (Luke 22:14–16). Jesus was not as a baby prince who does not know that he is destined to rule. He was fully aware of his deity and of his mission to die for the sins of humankind.

II. Jesus washed his disciples' feet.

According to the custom of the day, the host would provide a basin of water for the washing of guests' feet. Since people traveled barefoot or in open sandals, they needed to wash away the dust of their journey. A servant would normally render the service if the host himself did not perform it. None of the disciples had volunteered. They had all apparently taken their places reclining on couches (as was the custom) around the table. "And during supper . . . Jesus . . . rose from supper, laid aside his garments, and girded himself with a towel. Then he poured water into a basin, and began to wash the disciples' feet, and to wipe them with the towel with which he was girded" (John 13:2–5 RSV). This act was a characteristic example of the Master's spirit. It was an acted parable, an object lesson in humility. He effectually rebuked the contention of the disciples.

"Then cometh he to Simon Peter: and Peter saith unto him, Lord, dost thou wash my feet? Jesus answered and said unto him, What I do thou knowest not now; but thou shalt know hereafter" (John 13:6–7). Peter felt that it wasn't right for the Master to wash the disciples' feet and said to Jesus, "'You shall never wash my feet.' Jesus answered him, 'If I do not wash you, you have no part in me.' Simon Peter said to him, 'Lord, not my feet only but also my hands and head!' Jesus said to him, 'He who has bathed does not need to wash, except for his feet, but he is clean all over; and you are clean, but not every one of you.' For he knew who was to betray him; that was why he said, 'You are not all clean'" (John 13:8–11 RSV).

Jesus indicated that there was a hidden meaning. It seems to be this: one who had bathed did not need to bathe again. He needed only to wash off the defilement of his feet. One saved does not need to be saved over again. He needs only the daily cleansing from the sins of his daily walk. They had all been bathed (saved) except Judas. Peter would be an example of this. He was a saved person, but before the night was over, he would deny his Lord. He would not need to be saved again, but he would need to confess and get forgiveness (have his feet washed), which he would do.

III. The significance of Jesus' action.

"Know ye what I have done to you?" (John 13:12).

A. *It was an example, an acted parable (John 13:13–15).*
1. True humility does not disparage one's powers. Jesus is Master and Lord. It is false humility that does not acknowledge that one is a person made in God's image and of infinite worth. What some people call humility is poor posture.
2. The spirit of Jesus in stooping to serve is true humility. The mind of Christ is portrayed in Philippians 2:5–11 and in Mark 10:45. Jesus came from heaven's glory as the incarnate Son of God. He humbled himself to death on the cross. This was necessary for our salvation. We cannot do what he did. We need not. But in the same spirit we can serve others.
3. If Christ served, how much more should we? Jesus concluded the story about the good Samaritan who helped the wounded man by charging us all, "Go, and do thou likewise" (Luke 10:37).
B. *In Jesus' picture of the last judgment, he indicated that the way his disciples serve him is to serve others in his name.* "Inasmuch as ye have done it unto one of the least of these my brethren, ye have done it unto me" (Matt. 25:40). Jesus commanded, "If I then, your Lord and Master, have washed your feet; ye also ought to wash one another's feet. For I have given you an example, that ye should do as I have done to you" (John 13:14–15). Some persons think that in these words Jesus is commanding another ordinance (in addition to baptism and the Lord's Supper) for perpetual observance. There is no evidence that the disciples so understood Jesus. Most Christians understand Jesus to command needful service to others on the basis of his example.

Conclusion

Happiness comes from following Jesus' example. "If ye know these things, happy are ye if ye do them" (John 13:17). Jesus was happy. For the joy of being the Savior, Jesus endured the cross. He fulfilled the words of Isaiah 53:11 about the Messiah, "He shall see of the travail of his soul, and shall be satisfied." The happiest people in the world are Christians. The happiest Christians are those who are serving others in the name of Jesus. Try it.

WEDNESDAY EVENING, NOVEMBER 4

Title: When God Brings Reassurance

Text: "God spake unto Moses, and said unto him, I am the Lord" (Ex. 6:2).

Scripture Reading: Exodus 6:2–13

Introduction

Moses was greatly discouraged over the opposition of Pharaoh, but God came to bring him a great reassurance. He promised that Moses would see God at work against Pharaoh.

Fighting the enemy and standing for God's way often causes God's people to be weary. Paul said it was possible to be "weary in well doing" (Gal. 6:9). When we become weary, we have a tendency to doubt, so we need God's reassurance. Let us look at the great assurance God gives.

I. God assures us of his character (Ex. 6:2–3).

A. *The majesty of God.* God brought to Moses' remembrance his names. The names disclosed God's character. "I appeared unto Abraham, unto Isaac, and unto Jacob, by the name of God Almighty, but by my name Jehovah was I not known to them" (Ex. 6:3). God Almighty (Heb., *El Shaddai*) means "Mountain God." In this name there is the feeling of fear and trembling in the face of God's overwhelming majesty.

Nothing brings greater assurance than a new insight into the majesty of God. We need a new sense of awe about God's greatness.

B. *The God who relates.* The climactic step in God's revelation to Moses came with the disclosure of God's new name as Jehovah or Yahweh. The new name assured Moses that God continued to relate to Israel in a personal way.

II. God assures us by his covenant (Ex. 6:4–5).

A. *God's faithfulness in the past.* God told Moses of his faithful covenant to the patriarchs. "I have also established my covenant with them, to give them the land of Canaan, the land of their pilgrimage, wherein they were strangers" (Ex. 6:4). God told Moses that he had been faithful in the past.

Look at God's work with his people in previous years. He has never renounced one of his promises. When God makes a covenant, he will be faithful.

B. *God's pledge for the future.* After reminding Moses of his past faithfulness, the Lord pledged the trustworthiness of his word to Israel in bondage. "I have also heard the groaning of the children of Israel, whom the Egyptians keep in bondage; and I have remembered my covenant" (Ex. 6:5). God pledges to fulfill his covenant with Israel.

Much of the Christian's assurance is the promise of God. Let us trust the covenant that God has made with us. He will do exactly what he said.

III. God assures us of his challenges (Ex. 6:6–13).

A. *The promise to anticipate.* Seven Hebrew verbs portrayed what God promised to do for Israel: "bring you out," "rid you," "redeem you," "take you," "will be to you a God," "bring you," "give you." All of these promises related to the Lord's redemptive activity of Israel and the gift of a land for their possession. Slaves in Egypt had a wonderful promise to anticipate.

God's people have a great future. God has made bountiful promises of what is ahead for the Christian. God has made marvelous promises about life on earth and even greater promises about life after death.

B. *The charge to obey.* God challenged Moses to proclaim faithfully the Lord's will despite the circumstances. He charged Moses to combat opposition of Pharaoh and to counteract the indifference of the Hebrews. God challenged Moses to obey him despite obstacles and hindrances encountered in the process.

God's reassurance does not come with promises of an easy road. He forecasts obstacles and hindrances, but he gives a challenge to obey him, regardless of anything.

Conclusion

Are you discouraged in your work for God? Has persistent doing good made you tired? Has the lack of response caused you distress? God can encourage you and bring great comfort. Listen to him say, "I am the Lord."

SUNDAY MORNING, NOVEMBER 8

Title: The Stewardship of Talents

Text: "To each according to his ability" (**Matt. 25:15 RSV**).

Scripture Reading: Matthew 25:14–30

Hymns: "Open My Eyes, That I May See," Scott
"Make Me a Channel of Blessing," Smyth
"Give of Your Best to the Master," Grose

Offertory Prayer: Our Father in heaven, we thank you for the opportunity to lay our tithes and offerings on your altar. We thank you for the opportunity to share, by this means, in the ongoing program of our Lord's cause through the only institution he has commissioned to do his work in this world—his church. As we lay our gifts of money on the altar, may we also bring our gifts of time and talents, of service and love. In Jesus' name. Amen.

Introduction

Faithful or unfaithful, all of us are stewards and will be all our lives. We can't help it. We are stewards of the years, the time God has given us to live. We are stewards of our bodies. We must care for them and use them for God's glory. We are stewards of all we possess. Our possessions belong to God and must be used for him. And we also are stewards of our minds and our abilities. It is our responsibility to develop our skills and use them for God's purposes. This is the stewardship of talents.

As our parable illustrates, a talent was an ancient unit of money or weight varying with the time or place. The parable that is our text has largely given us the use of this word to refer to a special, natural ability. This is true because it tells us of the master's delivering his goods, his talents, to his servants, "to every man according to his several ability" (Matt. 25:15).

Let us think of this parable as a drama that Jesus presented to get those who heard and saw it to understand a timeless truth. Consider this parable as a drama in three acts. Each act can be described by a single word. The characters are sharply drawn. Their exits and their entrances are in perfect sequence. The staging is clear.

I. Act I we may call "investiture" (Matt. 25:14–15).

It "is as a man traveling into a far country, who called his own servants, and delivered unto them his goods. And unto one he gave five talents, to another two, and to another one; to every man according to his several ability" (vv. 14–15). We are to understand that all we are and all we have is a gift from God; and therefore we are his stewards.

But we learn here that God does not give to all alike. "And unto one he gave five talents, to another two, and to another one; to every man according to his several ability." This is a clear and sober statement of the inequality of human endowment. The findings of the intelligence testers are not new: they were succinctly expressed long ago in this story. We are genetically different and therefore have various levels of intelligence and potential. God created us that way, and our parable illustrates this fact of life.

A. *First, we have our five-talent man.* "And unto one he gave five talents." We need these five-talent people. Although we have not always been true to it, the genius of American democracy is equality of opportunity. But we must not go beyond this and insist that there shall be no difference in status whatever, regardless of a person's aptitudes, abilities, and energy. We must not fall into the error, on which some insist, that these people of superior ability are more trouble to society than they are worth. The words of the pioneer psychologist William James, spoken on the campus of Stanford University in 1906, were prophetic: "The world . . . is only beginning to see that the wealth of a nation consists more than in anything else in the number of superior men that it harbors" (quoted by John W. Garner in *Excellence* [New York: Harper & Row, 1961], 33). Dr. James was more than half a century ahead of his time.

B. *But we also have our two-talent man.* "And unto one he gave five talents, to another two." The five-talent people are the bright stars in the human firmament, but the vast majority have two talents. They are the hordes of useful, average folks. It is these two-talent people who really bear the burdens of the world—people of good, average ability who use the talents they have to serve God and man. The five-talent people are few and far between, and too often they succumb to the lust for power or the temptation to greed. The one-talent people are too easily manipulated by unscrupulous demagogues for their own ends. But the two-talent people form the working nucleus. They stay hitched. We need these two-talent people.

C. *Still, we have our one-talent man.* "And unto one he gave five talents, to another two, and to another one." Could it be that the parable was told for the benefit of one-talent people?

In the drama the five-talent man and the two-talent man are really minor characters. It is the one-talent man who is the chief actor and the villain of the piece. His portrait is sketched in detail. Nothing in this parable is clearer than the fact that the one-talent man was expected to be as faithful to his master's interests as the five-and two-talent men. We need these one-talent men.

Are you a one-talent person? Don't worry about it. Be faithful to what you have. We must accept those limitations we cannot change as the will of God for us and then go on to serve God the best we can.

The master, after these things had taken place, "straightway took his journey" (v. 15). And the curtain comes down on Act 1.

II. Act 2 we may call "performance" (Matt. 25:16–18).

"Then he that had received the five talents went and traded with the same, and made them other five talents. And likewise he that had received two, he also gained other two. But he that had received one went and digged in the earth, and hid his lord's money" (vv. 16–18). This is the stewardship of talents.

What do we do with the Master's talents? Do we invest them for his glory, or do we hide them in a hole in the ground? Do we use them for the advancement of his kingdom? Do we perform according to the abilities he has given us? Are we true to trust? A man is accountable in accordance with his endowment.

A. *The five-talent man has his hour on the stage.* How did he perform? "Then he that had received the five talents went and traded with the same, and made them other five talents" (v. 16). He performed well. He was true to trust. His shrewd investments proved immensely profitable, even a profit of 100 percent. All people should use their talents for God's glory and the welfare of others.

B. *The drama moves on.* How did the two-talent man perform? He performed well also. "And likewise he that had received two, he also gained other two" (v. 17). We would visualize the two-talent man as the blunt, honest type, a solid man. If he invested in a farm, he would drive his oxen hard and work from sunrise to sunset. By sheer fidelity and hard work, he doubled his invested capital.

Abraham was a five-talent man, and so was his grandson Jacob, but you cannot get from Abraham to Jacob except through Isaac, and Isaac was a two-talent man. If we preach only of Abraham and Jacob and Luther and Wesley, the ordinary person in the pew may get the idea that among Christians is a hierarchy with the giants at the summit, the lesser heroes below, and himself or herself far, far down the line. But not so! In the divine economy what is required is not that a person be spectacular or successful, but that he or she be faithful. Therefore Isaac stands with Abraham and Jacob on equal terms.

C. *Now the main character appears on stage.* How did this one-talent man perform? Not well! "But he that had received one went and digged in the earth, and hid his lord's money" (v. 18). This man neither invested nor squandered the money given to him. He put it in a hole in the ground. He was afraid to risk it. He avoided the responsibility of investing it.

But this need not be true of the one-talent man. Not at all! If only he is willing to be used, God *will* use the one-talent man. Philip Bliss was a one-talent man. He was no poet. He had a single, simple gift of versification, and he put it on the altar of God. God has greatly used his gift as Christians around the world sing with joy the songs he wrote.

The question is, have we been faithful or unfaithful in the use of the talents God gave us? The question is not, did you have five talents or two or one? But what use did you make for the Master's gain of the talents he gave you?

III. Act 3 reaches the climax; it is the "reckoning" (Matt. 25:19–30).

"After a long time the lord of those servants cometh, and reckoneth with them" (v. 19). There will be a reckoning! The central interest of the drama lies in the scene of the reckoning and in particular in the position of the cautious servant, whose faithfulness receives such a stern rebuke.

Every Christian should have the ambition to be a successful servant of God. Success, as God reckons it, has no relation to our being equal to any other individual. Success depends not on equality but on individuality. Success is measured in terms of faithfulness. Carefully constructed to show exactly the lessons Jesus intends, this climactic portion of the drama falls naturally into two scenes.

A. *The first scene we may call "Reckoning and Rewards" (vv. 20–23).*
   1. First, there was the accounting with the five-talent man. He had been faithful to the trust. He was rewarded. He was commended with his lord's "Well done." He was promoted to greater responsibilities, a great reward. The master also said, "Enter thou into the joy of thy lord" (v. 21).

2. Second, there was the accounting with the two-talent man. We must not miss the thrust of our Lord's teaching here. This two-talent man was just as faithful to his trust as was the five-talent man. "I have gained two other talents" (v. 22). Like his more gifted fellow servant, his increase was also 100 percent. That the master's commendation was in exactly the same words for the two-talent man as for the five is not accidental. Jesus deliberately constructed his story to show that though there may be degrees of endowment, every person is required to make the most of his or her gifts.

B. *The second scene we may call "Reckoning and Judgment" (vv. 24–30).* In an emotion-packed scene, Jesus showed us the third servant's report and the master's response: "And he also that had received the one talent came and said, Lord, I knew thee that thou art a hard man, reaping where thou didst not sow, and gathering where thou didst not scatter; and I was afraid, and went away and hid thy talent in the earth: lo, thou hast thine own" (vv. 24–25 ASV). What was the matter with this man?

1. For one thing, he had no character. He blamed his failure on his master. This is why his master called him a "wicked" servant.

2. But then again, he had no courage. "I was afraid," he said, "and hid thy talent in the earth" (v. 25). Being a man of only one talent was something for which he was in no way responsible, but for being afraid he was entirely responsible.

3. And again, he had no imagination. This man missed the point. He did not see that in his master's plans and purposes he was needed as much as the men with two and five talents. That is the thing that many of us fail to see. We also lack imagination.

4. But above all, this man had no motivation. He didn't try. Everyone agrees that motivation is a powerful ingredient in performance. Talent without performance is inert and of little use.

5. What was the master's response? "But his lord answered and said unto him, Thou wicked and slothful servant, thou knewest that I reap where I sowed not, and gather where I did not scatter; thou oughtest therefore to have put my money to the bankers, and at my coming I should have received back mine own with interest. Take ye away therefore the talent from him, and give it unto him that hath the ten talents. For unto every one that hath shall be given, and he shall have abundance: but from him that hath not, even that which he hath shall be taken away. And cast ye out the unprofitable servant into the outer darkness: there shall be the weeping and the gnashing of teeth" (vv. 26–30 ASV).

This was judgment—judgment on the man's failure in stewardship, judgment on the sin of omission.

a. The master judged his character.
b. The master judged his motives.
c. And the master judged him unfit to serve.

The first two men got to go to the big party celebrating the master's return: "Enter thou into the joy of thy lord" (vv. 21, 23). This man didn't even get his foot in the door.

Conclusion

The Master's words cause us to examine ourselves. If the man who kept his talent intact, returning it undamaged and unused, received such heavy judgment, what must they expect who destroy God-given talents by drunkenness and lust, or squander the property they might have used for God's purposes on the vanities of the world? It makes us shudder to think of it. Don't lose your talent by default. It can happen to anybody.

SUNDAY EVENING, NOVEMBER 8

Title: Peter in Gethsemane

Text: "What, could ye not watch with me one hour? Watch and pray, that ye enter not into temptation: the spirit indeed is willing, but the flesh is weak" **(Matt. 26:40–41).**

Scripture Reading: Matthew 26:36–56

Introduction

Some Christians believe in soul sleeping after death. Soul sleeping before death is evident. Jesus' request that the disciples watch with him during his anguish in Gethsemane raises the very interesting question as to why Deity ever needs help from humanity.

I. Jesus desired his disciples to watch with him.

A. *Early in his ministry after a night of prayer, Jesus had chosen twelve from his disciples and called them apostles.* Mark said that one of Jesus' reasons for choosing disciples was "that they should be with him" (Mark 3:14).

B. *The Savior faces a crisis.*

1. Note the intensity of the struggle: "And he took with him Peter and the two sons of Zebedee, and began to be sorrowful and very heavy. Then saith he unto them, My soul is exceeding sorrowful, even unto death: tarry ye here, and watch with me. And he went a little farther, and fell on his face, and prayed, saying, O my Father, if it be possible, let this cup pass from me: nevertheless not as I will, but as thou wilt" (Matt. 26:37–39). Luke indicated the intensity of the struggle with these words: "And being in an

agony he prayed more earnestly: and his sweat was as it were great drops of blood falling down to the ground" (Luke 22:44).

2. What was the cup about which he prayed?
   a. Was it the fear of death? Of bodily pain? Of the shame of crucifixion? If so, the stream has risen higher than its source, for thousands of the followers of Jesus have gone to the rack, to the stake, to death, not even asking that they might be spared, counting it all joy that they might suffer for the sake of his name.
   b. Was the anguish that of a sense of failure? Of futility? Was he as the poor dying scholar who cries, "My book, my book, it will never be finished"? The facts are quite otherwise. The disciples were very sorrowful. They thought the end was at hand, but there was not a word on Jesus' lips suggesting defeat. A reading of the account of Jesus in the upper room in John 13 through 17 will reveal that Jesus interprets his death in terms of victory. Note a few of many examples:
      - *John 13:3.* Jesus did not expect to stay dead. He knew that he came from God and would go to the Father. He had earlier spoken of the voluntary nature of his death as recorded in John 10:17–18. The last words of Jesus from the cross, "Father, into thy hands I commend my spirit" (Luke 23:46), implied voluntary action on Jesus' part, and that he was going to the Father rather than to extinction in the tomb.
      - *John 13:31–32.* Jesus considered that his death would glorify God. This could not have been true if he had feared death as extinction.
      - *John 14:1–3.* How could Jesus so confidently promise eternal life in the Father's house if he were afraid of death?
      - *John 14:26–31; 15:26–27; 16:7–16.* Jesus would depart and send the Holy Spirit. He would fulfill his promise, "Lo, I am with you alway, even unto the end of the world" (Matt. 28:20).

      These examples could be multiplied. The anguish of our Lord in Gethsemane was not fear of death.
3. The cup was filled with the penalty of humankind's sins. It represents all that a holy God must do to forgive sinners. It is the Father's will that Jesus drink the cup. "The cup which my Father hath given me, shall I not drink it?" (John 18:11).

   John the Baptist had identified Jesus as "the Lamb of God, which taketh away the sin of the world" (John 1:29). Jesus' baptism symbolized his ministry that would culminate in death and resurrection. The voice from heaven identified him as the Son of God and the Servant of Jehovah. (Note that Matt. 3:17 is a combination of Ps. 2:7 and Isa. 42:1.) Jesus identified himself to the woman of Samaria as the Messiah (see John 4:25–26) and to the people in the synagogue at Nazareth as the Servant of Jehovah predicted by Isaiah (see Luke 4:16–21). On his authority we can apply to him the passages about the Servant of Jehovah, including Isaiah 52:13–53:12.

The drinking of the cup was necessary for Jesus to be the Savior of the world. His real prayer was not "If it be possible, let this cup pass from me" (Matt. 26:39) but, rather, "Nevertheless not as I will, but as thou wilt" (Matt. 26:39). If the former had been his prayer, the author of Hebrews would have erred in saying that God heard him. Note carefully: "Who in the days of his flesh, when he had offered up prayers and supplications with strong crying and tears unto him that was able to save him from death, and was heard in that he feared; though he were a Son, yet learned he obedience by the things which he suffered; and being made perfect, he became the author of eternal salvation unto all them that obey him" (Heb. 5:7–9; read thoughtfully Heb. 2:9–10 and 12:1–2).

II. The contrast between Jesus and his disciples was great.

A. *They did not understand the issue.* They did not know what was in the cup that the Lord was about to drink. They were asleep to the importance of the hour.

B. *Why Jesus, the Son of God, needed his disciples is a great mystery, but he did.* In his hour of need, they were asleep. When Jesus found them sleeping, he was disappointed, but his reprimand was very gentle and understanding: "What, could ye not watch with me one hour? Watch and pray, that ye enter not into temptation: the spirit indeed is willing, but the flesh is weak" (Matt. 26:40–41).

We do not understand why the Lord needs our witness. Could he not accomplish his purposes without our prayers? Or our participation? The record is clear. God has chosen to use his disciples in accomplishing his purpose. He says, "Watch with me."

Conclusion

Jesus Christ is the same yesterday, today, and forever. His love for lost persons is unabated; his passion for God's kingdom is unchecked; his call for our service, our companionship, and our witness is clear. Do we care? Do we pray, "Thy kingdom come"? Is it any concern of ours that people are lost? Or do we say, "Let me sleep"?

"Awake thou that sleepest, and arise from the dead, and Christ shall give thee light" (Eph. 5:14).

WEDNESDAY EVENING, NOVEMBER 11

Title: The Power to Say No

Text: "Pharaoh called for Moses and for Aaron, and said, Go ye, sacrifice to your God in the land" **(Ex. 8:25)**.

Scripture Reading: Exodus 8:25–28; 10:9–11, 24

Introduction

In the English language one of the hardest words to say is *no*. Of course it is not hard to pronounce, but it is difficult to say no to some entreaties. For example, saying no to an abundance of food is hard for most Americans. When strawberry shortcake loaded with whipped cream is offered to me, I cannot say no. In every case I yield.

God's people have numerous solicitations from Satan to compromise. One of the hardest responses is to say no or to resist the devil. When Moses prepared the people to leave Egypt, Pharaoh made some interesting proposals of compromise. In each case, Moses led the people to say no. Let us notice the compromise.

I. Satan seeks to retain God's people (Ex. 8:25–28).

A. *The solicitation of Pharaoh.* When Moses requested Pharaoh to let the Hebrews leave Egypt, Pharaoh presented a compromise. "Go ye, sacrifice to your God in the land" (Ex. 8:25). He wanted the Hebrew people to remain in Egypt. If he could keep them in the land, they would remain slaves.

B. *The solicitation of Satan.* Satan loses the main battle when a person becomes a Christian. The warfare continues though. The opposer of God seeks to persuade the child of God to "stay in the land." He urges us to be borderline Christians.

II. Satan urges God's people to neglect family care (Ex. 10:9–11).

A. *The solicitation of Pharaoh.* When Moses confronted Pharaoh on another occasion, Pharaoh presented a compromise proposal. "Let the Lord be so with you, as I will let you go, and your little ones: look to it; for evil is before you. Not so: go now ye that are men, and serve the Lord; for that ye did desire" (Ex. 10:10–11). Pharaoh wanted to split the Hebrew family. He knew that if he could divide the household, the nation would soon die.

B. *The solicitation of Satan.* Satan seeks to destroy the family unit in today's society. He opposes God's divine intention, which is one man for one woman until death parts them. The opposer of God seeks to get families to compromise with regard to spiritual care and nurture.

343

III. Satan desires God's people to leave possessions out of their commitment to the Lord (Ex. 10:24).

A. *The solicitation of Pharaoh.* Moses' additional request to Pharaoh for release was again met with another compromise. "Go ye, serve the Lord; only let your flocks and your herds be stayed: let your little ones also go with you" (Ex. 10:24). Pharaoh agreed to let Israel leave and worship God, but he insisted that they leave their flocks and herds behind. Moses refused, for he knew the people needed the flocks and herds to make sacrifices.

B. *The solicitation of Satan.* The devil always desires halfhearted commitment from God's people. He wants professing Christians to compromise regarding the stewardship of possessions. Those who think they can serve the Lord without any responsibility to possessions have yielded to a satanic compromise.

Conclusion

The hardest response for a Christian to make is to say no to a plausible compromise. Moses' ability to refuse Pharaoh came from the Lord. God will give you strength to say no.

SUNDAY MORNING, NOVEMBER 15

Title: The Stewardship of the Body

Text: "Or know ye not that your body is a temple of the Holy Spirit which is in you, which ye have from God? and ye are not your own; for ye were bought with a price: glorify God therefore in your body" (**1 Cor. 6:19–20 ASV**).

Scripture Reading: 1 Corinthians 6:12–20

Hymns: "Take My Life and Let It Be," Havergal
"I Hear the Savior Say," Hall
"Savior, Thy Dying Love," Phelps

Offertory Prayer: Our Father in heaven, we thank you for the opportunity to think together about the matter before us this morning. We pray that as a result of our meditating on what your Word teaches us about our physical bodies, our attitudes may be different and we may in deed and in truth be acceptable stewards of our bodies, which you have so wonderfully designed and so freely given us. Bless us now as we lay our tithes and offerings on your altar, acknowledging your ownership of all we are and all we have. Bless them to the expansion of your kingdom on earth. This we ask in Jesus' name. Amen.

Introduction

Paul took a high view of the body. Its care and discipline were an essential part of his thought. Would Paul have agreed with the proverb "Cleanliness is next to godliness"? No doubt he would have said, "Cleanliness is a part of godliness, especially so if you understand this to include ethical and moral cleanliness." Paul did nothing to impair the functions of his body, to enfeeble its powers, or to prostitute it to base uses.

Concerning the relation of the body to religion, human opinion has oscillated between two extremes. On the one hand, some have considered the body to be the seat of sin and have set themselves to degrade and debase it with every indignity and torture. But sin must be dealt with in the heart and soul, where it has its inception (James 1:14–15). If we overcome bad thoughts and evil suggestions, we will not have so much trouble with the body.

The other extreme was represented in Greek religion. The temples that stand in ruins, the works of art that have survived the ravages of time, the poetry and literature that have survived—all sustain and illustrate the devotion of the Greek mind to beauty. Surely it ought to be evident that our modern society with its cult of "body beautiful," its worship at Aphrodite's shrine of sex appeal, is more inclined to go along with the Greeks than with those who suppressed and debased their bodies.

Both extremes are wrong. There are two ways *not* to be spiritual. Undue and unnatural suppression of the body will make one materialistic, as will also unbridled and uncontrolled indulgence. Both put a disproportionate emphasis on the body. One cannot do that and be a spiritual person.

The Christian position is that the body is the temple of the Holy Spirit, the instrument of the mind, the dwelling place of the inner person. In considering its stewardship, give attention to four questions.

I. The body: Whose is it?

The body is God's. This is why, as far as our bodies are concerned, we have a stewardship.

A. *The body is God's; he designed it.* From ancient times people have studied the heavenly bodies; yet until the modern era, they never dared to investigate the human body. The scientific study of anatomy dates back to the work of the Flemish anatomist Andreas Vesalius and the publication of his book *On the Fabric of the Human Body.* Today what doctor would say, even four hundred years later, that medical science has no need of further knowledge of the body? Centuries ago the psalmist said, "I will give thanks unto thee; for I am fearfully and wonderfully made" (Ps. 139:14 ASV). What would he have said had our modern knowledge of anatomy been available to him? We are "fearfully and wonderfully made."

Think of those giants of the body: the brain, the heart, the lungs. Even primitive humans sensed that these organs played dramatic roles within the body, though their functions long remained clothed in mystery and superstition.

Think of those remarkable sentinels of the body: the eyes, ears, nose, throat, and skin. They keep us in contact with the world around us, introduce us to its delights, and protect us from its dangers. Think of the marvelous teamwork of command and control. Together the muscles, nerves, and bones give us the control we need to carry out the incredibly complex commands of the brain. Think of the laboratories of the body: the stomach, the liver, the colon, the gallbladder, the pancreas, and the kidneys. Think of the chemical wizardry of the blood and glands. God designed the body. Only he could have done it.

B. *The body is God's; he created it.* In the simplest language possible, the creation record tells us the true nature of man. "Jehovah God formed man of the dust of the ground, and breathed into his nostrils the breath of life; and man became a living soul" (Gen. 2:7 ASV). It is the fact that "God breathed" that makes humans different from animals. In this sense, humans are like God, for God's breath is in them. Because they have a body, they are like the animals. Humans, therefore, enjoy the privileges of participating in a good world with the capacities of growth and fellowship with God.

C. *The body is God's; he redeemed it.* Long ago God spoke thus to his people: "Now thus saith Jehovah that created thee, O Jacob, and he that formed thee, O Israel: Fear not, for I have redeemed thee; I have called thee by thy name, thou art mine" (Isa. 43:1 ASV). Just believe this word, and your body, your life, becomes sacred, and daily living a sacrament. You will hear with joy Paul's appeal to the Roman Christians to "present your bodies a living sacrifice, holy, acceptable to God" (Rom. 12:1 ASV).

II. The body: What is it?

In simplest terms, the Bible tells us that the body is a dwelling place, the house of the inner person. Paul tells the Corinthians, "We know that if the earthly house of our tabernacle be dissolved, we have a building from God, a house not made with hands, eternal, in the heavens" (2 Cor. 5:1 ASV).

A. *The body is the dwelling place of our minds, our rational nature.* In the creation records, we are told, "God said, Let us make man in our image, after our likeness" (Gen. 1:26). Created in the image of God could not refer to man's body because "God is a Spirit" (John 4:24) and has no body such as we have. It must be, then, that the rational, moral, and spiritual nature of humans are all included in "the image of God."

B. *The body is also the dwelling place of the human spirit and sold.* We *have* a body; we *are* a soul. It is good to care for the body but only as we would care for a complex and fine piece of machinery made to serve us. For the Christian the body is the dwelling place, the instrument of the soul.

C. *Most important for the Christian, the body is the dwelling place of the Holy Spirit.* Our text tells us this. Of the Holy Spirit, Jesus told his disciples on the night in which he was betrayed: "He abideth with you, and shall be in you" (John 14:17 ASV). This is the full impact of our text: "Or know ye not that your body is a temple . . . ?" Paul admonished the Ephesians: "Be filled with the Spirit" (5:18), but too often we are filled with something else. We are apt to be filled with ourselves instead of him.

III. The body: How should we use it?

Here are two sides of a coin to consider.

A. *On the one hand, there are the wrong uses of the body.* This is to be unfaithful in our stewardship.

    1. Whatever impairs the body's normal functions is wrong. We know that the habitual use of alcohol can cause cirrhosis of the liver and damage certain parts of the brain. Who has the right to treat his body in this way? No faithful steward of the body would do it. Smoking causes lung cancer, emphysema, and other respiratory diseases. How can any pleasure from smoking compensate for such damage to the body? The point is that whatever impairs the body's normal functions is wrong, is sin, is poor stewardship of the body.

    2. Whatever enfeebles the body's power is wrong; whatever makes it old before its time is sin. "Confound these legs of mine," Lord Northampton said as he came tottering out of a long court session. "If I had thought they would one day carry a lord chancellor, I would have taken better care of them in my youth."

    3. Whatever prostitutes the body to base uses is wrong. In the paragraph from which our text comes, fornication, or sexual impurity, is the concern at hand. There is a corporate application in 1 Corinthians 6:15–18. Fornication, as a form of unfaithfulness to God, has no place in the church. Fornication characterized worship in the temple of Aphrodite in Corinth. It has no place in the temple of the Holy Spirit, which is the body. The Holy Spirit, Paul said, cannot be joined to a harlot (v. 16).

    4. Whatever defiles the body is wrong. In the city of Strasbourg on the Rhine in Europe, there is a world-famous cathedral that was more than four centuries in building. When Napoleon captured the city, he stabled his horses in that cathedral. Think of it! He let those beasts live in the light of jeweled windows before the altar that was meant for prayer. He defiled the temple. How often we do the same to the body, the temple of the Holy Spirit.

    5. Whatever permits the body to become a vehicle of uncontrolled passions is wrong. When we study the parable of the prodigal

son, we see that everything the boy had came from his father. His body, which he used for base purposes, came from his father. His body became a vehicle of uncontrolled passions. Make no mistake about it, this prodigal is dramatizing our lives. As we look at him we are compelled to say, "There am I. I am that boy."

B. *But on the other hand, there are the uses of the body that God intended.*

1. God intends that our bodies be used as instruments of his worship and praise. The parts of the body—the eyes, the tongue, the mind, the emotions—have important parts to play in worship.

2. God intends that our bodies be vehicles of righteousness. For the Christian, a twofold process is going on as the years pass. Paul wrote to the Corinthians, "Though our outward man is decaying, yet our inward man is renewed day by day" (2 Cor. 4:16 ASV). The body decays as time destroys it. But while we are wearing out a body, we are growing a soul.

3. God intends that our bodies be instruments of his glory. The resurrection body of Christ bore the print of the nails in his hands and of the sword thrust into his side (John 20:27). Paul's battles for Christ left scars on his body, but he did not consider them a disgrace. They were a badge of honor. He wrote to the Galatians, "Henceforth, let no man trouble me; for I bear branded on my body the marks of Jesus" (Gal. 6:17 ASV). Paul prayed that Christ might be magnified in his body (Phil. 1:20). Oh that his prayer might be ours.

IV. The body: What of it?

To what conclusion are we to come? In ancient Greece there was a thinker named Porphyry who was so devoted to the life of the Spirit that he was ashamed of his body. There could be no greater error. The supreme revelation of God was in his taking on of human flesh in the person of his Son. "The Word became flesh" (John 1:14 ASV). This is why Christians must think of the body as sacred.

Jesus, our Savior, had a human body subject to all the ills and pains that "flesh is heir to." He shared all our sorrows and woes but not our sins. Wherefore, let no one despise his or her body, abuse it, pollute it, defile it, or fail to be a steward of it. God himself once took on a human body.

Conclusion

To speak thus is to put our finger on one of the most precious elements of Christian hope. Paul wrote to the Corinthians: "So also is the resurrection of the dead. It is sown . . . a [physical] body; it is raised a spiritual body. If there is a [physical] body, there is also a spiritual body" (1 Cor. 15:42–44 ASV). What does he mean, "a spiritual body"? We cannot know fully. But we do know this: the body is the carrier of our individuality, and that individuality survives the grave. In speaking of a spiritual body, the New Testament is saying that, by God's grace, we have a means by which we can be known on the other side. Meanwhile, let us wear this physical body well.

SUNDAY EVENING, NOVEMBER 15

Title: Peter Denies His Lord

Text: "Peter then denied again: and immediately the cock crew" **(John 18:27)**.

Scripture Reading: John 18:1–40

Introduction

The Bible is always fair but frank. It records faults as clearly as virtues. Its portrayal is true to life. It presents Peter as the rock on the day of Pentecost, but it does not hesitate to tell that he was Satan's mouthpiece at Caesarea Philippi and to record in detail his denials of Jesus.

No Christian is sinless; every Christian strives to be. No Christian continues willfully in sin, but Satan trips up the best Christians at times. His attack is often sudden and always subtle. In Simon Peter's denials and restoration are warnings we shall do well to heed and assurances of grace in which we can rejoice.

I. Look at the record.

    A. *In the upper room.*

        1. The disciples continued their contention over who would have first place in the kingdom of God (Luke 22:24). How foreign this was to the spirit of Jesus, who washed the feet of the disciples (John 13:1–20).

        2. Jesus knew that Judas had bargained with the rulers to betray him. "Have not I chosen you twelve, and one of you is a devil?" (John 6:70). Jesus is troubled in spirit. He predicted that Judas would betray him, although the disciples did not understand the sign Jesus gave them (John 13:21–30).

        3. Jesus predicted that Peter would deny him three times before daybreak (John 13:36–38).

            a. Peter protested vigorously. "Lord, I am ready to go with thee, both into prison, and to death" (Luke 22:33). "But he spake the more vehemently, If I should die with thee, I will not deny thee in any wise. Likewise also said they all" (Mark 14:31).

            b. The Lord had very graciously prayed for Peter (Luke 22:31–32). Peter seemed offended that Christ should pray for him. "Pride goeth before destruction" (Prov. 16:18). "Wherefore let him that thinketh he standeth take heed lest he fall" (1 Cor. 10:12).

349

B. *In the garden of Gethsemane (Matt. 26:30, 36–46; Mark 14:26, 32–42; Luke 22:39–46).*

    1. Jesus asked Peter, James, and John to watch with him while he prayed. He said, "Pray that ye enter not into temptation" (Luke 22:40). They went to sleep. They had no appreciation of the Lord's anguish nor of their own need to strengthen themselves by prayer against temptation.

    2. At the betrayal and arrest of Jesus, Peter showed that he was not a coward. He rashly pulled out his sword and cut off the right ear of Malchus, the servant of the high priest (see Matt. 26:47–58; John 18:2–12). He probably tried to cut off his head. "Then Jesus said unto him, Put up again thy sword into his place: for all they that take the sword shall perish with the sword. Thinkest thou that I cannot now pray to my Father, and he shall presently give me more than twelve legions of angels? But how then shall the scriptures be fulfilled, that thus it must be?" (Matt. 26:52–54). "Then all the disciples forsook him, and fled" (Matt. 26:56). Fearful, yet drawn by love and curiosity, "Peter followed him afar off" (Matt. 26:58).

II. The denials.

All four of the Gospels carry accounts of Peter's denials. They differ enough to indicate that they are independent accounts. Perhaps in some of the denials more than one person accused Peter. This sermon will primarily follow John's account in John 18. The denials took place Friday before or about dawn.

A. *At the gate of the court of the high priest's residence (John 18:15–17).* Peter and John followed Jesus. John was known to the high priest and was admitted to the courtyard. It is pure speculation, but it may be that he had sold fish there. John returned to request the maid who kept the door to allow Peter to enter. "Then saith the damsel that kept the door unto Peter, Art not thou also one of this man's disciples? He saith, I am not" (John 18:17). How strange that one who had not feared Pilate, nor soldiers, nor the Sanhedrin, would be frightened into a denial by a slave girl!

B. *By the fire in the courtyard (John 18:18–25).* The night was cold. The servants and officers were warming themselves by a fire of coals. Peter joined the group and warmed himself by the enemy's fire. A maid, a man, and others said unto him, "Art not thou also one of his disciples? He denied it, and said, I am not" (John 18:25; cf. Matt. 26:69–72; Mark 14:66–70; Luke 22:55–58).

C. *In the court by the kinsman of Malchus.* "And about the space of one hour after another confidently affirmed, saying, Of a truth this fellow also was with him: for he is a Galilaean. And Peter said, Man, I know not what thou sayest" (Luke 22:59–60). John wrote, "One of the servants of the high priest, being his kinsman whose ear Peter cut off, saith, Did not I see thee in the garden with him? Peter then denied again: and immediately, the cock crew" (John 18:26–27). Luke added, "And immediately, while he yet spake, the cock crew. And the Lord turned, and looked upon Peter. And Peter remembered the word of the Lord, how he had said unto him, Before the cock crow, thou shalt deny me thrice. And Peter went out, and wept bitterly" (Luke 22:60–62).

Jesus' anguished look broke Peter's heart, but it must also have been a look of assurance. Peter had not lost faith, but he had lost face and courage. He would later bitterly confess it all. He was humbled and weak and was now ready for help and strength.

III. Why did Peter backslide?

A. *Self-sufficiency.* "He that trusteth in his own heart is a fool: but whoso walketh wisely, he shall be delivered" (Prov. 28:26). Others may need to be careful, but not I.

B. *Spiritual negligence.*
1. Lack of prayer. Peter was asleep when he should have been praying. There is power in worship, both private and public.
2. He did not rightly apprehend the meaning of the cross nor the nature of Christ's kingdom. His perplexity added to his discouragement. He did believe in Jesus, however, even as he denied him.
3. He warmed himself at the enemy's fire. He followed afar off. He stayed at the gate rather than going on in with John.

C. *He underestimated the power of sin.* Satan is cunning—"As a roaring lion, walketh about, seeking whom he may devour" (1 Peter 5:8).

Conclusion

A. *Profit by Peter's experience.* You have never denied Jesus by oaths and cursing. Be not proud but humble. Watch and pray.

Have you ever been in a group in which some unchristian action was proposed, and by your silence you denied the Lord?

B. *Was Peter lost?* If he had died while cursing and swearing would he have gone to hell? Was he at heart a hypocrite? No! A thousand times, no! He was not another Judas. God does not cast off a Christian when he or she sins any more than a loving parent disowns a disobedient child. If one were lost whenever he or she fell short of God's glory, salvation would be of self. The child of God hears the cock crow and sees the look of Jesus. In bitter tears, the believer repents and confesses to God with the assurance that "if we confess our sins, he is faithful and just to forgive us our sins, and to cleanse us from all unrighteousness" (1 John 1:9).

WEDNESDAY EVENING, NOVEMBER 18

Title: A Night to Be Remembered

Text: "It shall come to pass, when your children shall say unto you, What mean ye by this service? That ye shall say, It is the sacrifice of the Lord's passover, who passed over the houses of the children of Israel in Egypt, when he smote the Egyptians, and delivered our houses. And the people bowed the head and worshipped" **(Ex. 12:26–27)**.

Scripture Reading: Exodus 12:1–27

Introduction

Clarence Macartney, a famous American preacher during the first half of the twentieth century, wrote a book titled *The Great Nights of the Bible*. In the work, he discussed some nights of the Bible in which great events occurred. In Egypt the Hebrews experienced one of the most meaningful nights in their history—the night of the Passover feast, when the death angel destroyed the firstborn of the Egyptians.

The Israelites left Egypt at midnight by the light of a full moon, the full moon of the spring equinox, the night of the fourteenth of Abib, which corresponds to March or April in our calendar. The Passover has been celebrated by Jewish people for more than 3,200 years as a memorial to the Israelites' deliverance out of Egypt. The Passover feast has lessons for us today.

I. It causes us to reflect.

A. *The human tendency to forget.* Human beings possess the unusual tendency to forget. Some of the greatest events of life are soon forgotten. God knew that the further the Israelites moved from the memorial night of the Passover the less they would remember of this great event. Therefore he gave instructions for an annual observance of the Passover: "This day shall be unto you for a memorial; and ye shall keep it a feast to the Lord throughout your generations; ye shall keep it a feast by an ordinance for ever" (Ex. 12:14).

B. *The subject of reflection.* God gave the Passover to reflect on him and his great acts. "It is the LORD's passover" (Ex. 12:11) instituted by him to keep his nature and his action before the people continuously.

Christians observe the Lord's Supper. It causes us to reflect on Jesus Christ and our relationship to him.

II. It causes us to celebrate.

A. *Worship as celebration.* The Israelites engaged in the Passover as a celebration. "And ye shall observe the feast of unleavened bread; for in this selfsame day have I brought your armies out of the land of Egypt" (Ex. 12:17). From the beginning the Passover had a festival atmosphere.

Modern worship should have the atmosphere of a celebration. Weekly worship should not be a dull, meaningless religious routine. It should be festive.

B. *The celebration of victory.* Times of victory call for celebrations. God gave Israel a special night when he defeated the Egyptians and delivered the Israelites from the land. That called for a victory celebration.

Each Lord's Day is a victory celebration. It is a day we celebrate the victory of Jesus over sin and death. It is a day we celebrate his presence.

III. It aids us in instruction.

A. *An effective teaching method.* God instructed Israel to continue the Passover feast. "And it shall come to pass, when ye be come to the land which the LORD will give you, according as he hath promised, that ye shall keep this service" (Ex. 12:25). The observance of the Passover would elicit questions from children in future generations: "What mean ye by this service?" (Ex. 12:26). There is not a greater teaching than to answer according to God's revelation the queries of an inquisitive child.

B. *The subject of instructions.* Questions from Jewish children gave an opportunity to share God's revelation. "It is the sacrifice of the LORD's passover, who passed over the houses of the children of Israel in Egypt, when he smote the Egyptians, and delivered our houses" (Ex. 12:27). The children could be taught the theological significance of Israel's history.

Nothing is more beneficial to children than to instruct them in the ways of the Lord.

Conclusion

The Passover was a memorial night in Israel's history. It tells us about a God who delivered a nation from an enemy and sent the people to a new land. That same God delivers you from sin and gives you a new life.

SUNDAY MORNING, NOVEMBER 22

Title: The Stewardship of Thanksgiving

Text: "O give thanks unto the LORD; for he is good: because his mercy endureth forever" **(Ps. 118:1).**

Scripture Reading: Psalm 118:1–18

Hymns: "Come, Ye Thankful People, Come," Alford
"Now Thank We All Our God," Rinkart
"We Plow the Fields, and Scatter," Claudius

Offertory Prayer: Our Father in heaven, for the year past, so richly blessed, so soon gone, we give you thanks. For your sovereign grace, your boundless love, your constant watching over us, we give you thanks. For the great blessings, the wonderful things, but also for the simple, the familiar, the commonplace, we give you thanks. For the Bible, the privilege of fellowship with our brothers and sisters in Christ in the church, your Holy Spirit abiding in us, but most of all, for your Son, our Savior and Lord, we give you thanks. Bless the offering that we now bring. Help us to remember that "we give thee but thine own." Accept us, Lord, as we give ourselves unto you, and then to your cause according to your will. This we ask in Jesus' name. Amen.

Introduction

If, as someone has said, the giving of thanks is a vaccine, an antitoxin, an antiseptic, what person is there who does not need such protection against spiritual infection? "He who receives a benefit with gratitude," said the Roman philosopher Lucius Seneca, "repays the first installment on his debt."

In our text, the psalmist revealed several things about thanksgiving. First, he pointed out its object: "O give thanks unto the LORD." As James said, "Every good and every perfect gift is from above, coming down from the Father of lights" (1:17 ASV). God owns all things. Second, the psalmist showed its reasonableness: "for he is good." The abundance of his blessings flows naturally out of the graciousness of his character. And third, the psalmist revealed its motivation: "his mercy endureth for ever." This note is sounded throughout this psalm.

What about thanksgiving? Gratitude is a grace, a gift from God. Like all his gifts, we can take it or leave it. We can use it or neglect it. In this, as in all good things, we have a stewardship.

I. Our stewardship of thanksgiving must be constant.

It must be unvarying. We should give thanks at all times and under all circumstances.

At Mandeville Encampment in Louisiana one summer, I was asked to give the message at the "Morning Watch," a thirty-minute service before breakfast. There had been a great deal of griping and groaning, criticizing and complaining. I spoke on 1 Thessalonians 5:18: "In every thing give thanks," urging that for one day, at least, we put Paul's word to the test, demonstrating its power to ourselves. Maybe it was just "for kicks," but those young people actually did it. When a table waiter brought food to a table, everybody at the table said thank you. When a speaker had brought his message, when a teacher had taught a class, when a recreational leader had led in one of these sessions, when any person had done something for another person in the encampment that day, the beneficiary said thank you. For a day this remade the place. By the time of the evening meal, the whole encampment was bubbly. Why should we not be this constant in expressing our thanks to one another every day and always and especially to God?

A) *In times of prosperity we should give thanks.* By and large we are an affluent people. The bounty of our tables on Thursday will demonstrate this. Whether prosperity makes for good or ill depends, in part, on the spirit in which we receive. Are we thankful? God has given us this grace. Are we using it?

B) *In times of adversity we should give thanks.* Some will say that this is the hardest of all, and it is. But this will bless our lives as it helps us grow to be like him. In the Old Testament the prophet Habakkuk is a choice example. In the midst of utter desolation he gave thanks like this:

> Though the fig tree does not bud
> > and there are no grapes on the vines,
> though the olive crop fails
> > and the fields produce no food,
> though there are no sheep in the pen
> > and no cattle in the stalls,
> yet I will rejoice in the LORD,
> > I will be joyful in God my Savior.
>
> —*3:17–18 NIV*

That is thanksgiving!

I have been told that the hymn "Now Thank We All Our God" was written when the news of the end of the Thirty Years' War was announced, even though the population had been decimated by a terrible plague, which left scarcely a household without someone dead. Likewise, when our Pilgrim forefathers celebrated that first Thanksgiving, they were still in dark days, but they were thankful.

C) *In times of doubt we should give thanks.* This is difficult indeed, but by God's help we can do it. No matter how dark the day or how heavy the clouds, there are some things we know for certain.

1. We know that high above the clouds the sun is shining, unhindered and undimmed. We know that God is there for us.
2. We know that there is One who knows the way. In his gospel, John said that before the feeding of the five thousand, Jesus asked Philip where they were to buy bread so all of the people might eat. John added parenthetically, "And this he said to prove him: for he himself knew what he would do" (6:6). Thank God for One in this universe who knows what to do.
3. We know that there is a way that is right and true and that that way will win in the end. Even in the darkest day, if we have ears to hear, we might hear God's voice saying, "This is the way, walk ye in it" (Isa. 30:21).

II. Our stewardship of thanksgiving must be discerning.

When Paul wrote to the Philippians, "Forgetting those things which are behind" (Phil. 3:13), he did not mean that he wanted to forget everything. He was saying that his memory was selective. He did not want to forget such things as his experience with Christ on the Damascus road. In fact, he told that story again and again. He did not forget God's help in hard places nor his guidance when he didn't know which way to turn. Like Paul, our thanksgiving must be discerning.

A. *True thanksgiving remembers the best of the past.* Dr. Alexander Whyte of Edinburgh was listening one day to the long list of ills of a member of his church. He listened to her recital unto the end and then said kindly, "Mind you, 'Forget not all his benefits.'"

B. *True thanksgiving sees the blessings of today, the blessings of the present.* Ours is a day of uncertainty and confusion, of war and strife, of injustice and evil. Instead of bemoaning our lot, we should say, "What a day to be alive!" Search and see. Such turbulent, volcanic times have been the creative ages of history. One of the church fathers, Polycarp, said, "My God! in what a century you have caused me to live." Polycarp was born about AD 70, and he was burned at the stake at the age of eighty-six because he refused to "swear by the fortune of Caesar."

C. *But even more important, true thanksgiving undergirds us for the future.* Perhaps the most remarkable of the recorded prayers of Jesus is his prayer before the tomb of Lazarus, a man dead four days. He prayed to the Father in the past tense, as he thanked God for what God was about to do as though it were already an accomplished fact: "Father, I thank you that you have heard me. I knew that you always hear me, but I said this for the benefit of the people standing here, that they may believe that you sent me" (John 11:41–42 NIV). Our faith can never compare with his, but we do have the promises of God. We can thank God for what we know he will do for us. In the material world, science promises us some wonderful things. The same is true in the realm of general knowledge. If we desire, he will so bless us in the realm of the Spirit.

III. Our stewardship of thanksgiving must be vocal.

"Let the redeemed of the LORD say so" (Ps. 107:2), the psalmist cried. And should we not also testify of his goodness and love?

Returning from an around-the-world trip in 1970, I went through customs in Honolulu, Hawaii. I was asked: "Have you anything to declare?" This meant, "Do you have anything in your baggage purchased abroad for which you should pay customs as you bring it into the United States?" But the question is interesting, spiritually interpreted. "Have you anything to declare?" Well, do you? What is there in your mental and spiritual luggage to declare—to declare with thanksgiving unto God?

Robert Louis Stevenson, in pain much of his life, was sure that the man who had forgotten to be thankful had fallen asleep in life. Thousands today who are not thankful to God are walking around in their sleep.

Conclusion

Let us be thankful for the lavish beauty of the natural world. Let us be thankful that we live in this Heaven-blessed land. Let us be thankful that Christ is our Savior and Lord.

SUNDAY EVENING, NOVEMBER 22

Title: Peter's Restoration

Text: "And the Lord said, Simon, Simon, behold, Satan hath desired to have you, that he may sift you as wheat: But I have prayed for thee, that thy faith fail not: and when thou art converted, strengthen thy brethren" **(Luke 22:31–32)**.

Scripture Reading: John 21:1–19

Introduction

How bitter were the tears of Peter as he wept over his denial of Jesus! Peter was denying with oaths that he knew Jesus. "And immediately, while he yet spake, the cock crew. And the Lord turned, and looked upon Peter. And Peter remembered the word of the Lord, how he had said unto him, Before the cock crow, thou shalt deny me thrice. And Peter went out, and wept bitterly" (Luke 22:60–62). Would he ever have a chance to confess to Jesus and ask forgiveness? Did he remember the Lord's words in the upper room as recorded in Luke 22:31–32? Since apparently none of the disciples expected the resurrection, Peter must have felt perplexed as well as discouraged, thinking that in the death of Jesus all hope had died.

Peter loved Jesus. He was not as Judas, who for a price had bargained to betray him. He was a saved man who had stumbled over Satan's snare; but he stumbled toward Jesus.

The late Dr. W. W. Hamilton asked three questions and answered them as follows: "Do you think sinners will get to heaven? They are the only persons who will. Do Christians sin? Saved sinners are the only kind of Christians. Do you love the Lord? Not nearly as much as I ought, but, better still, he loves me."

The significant factor in Peter's restoration was that Jesus loved him. He loved him enough to convict him of his sin. If God did not love us, he could leave us alone. As a parent who loves his child will discipline him, God loves his children enough to convict them of sin and to discipline them. Hebrews 12:5–13 will reward your careful reading. Jesus loved Peter enough to pray for him. Jesus loved Peter enough to go to him.

I. Jesus prayed for Peter a revealing prayer (Luke 22:31–32).

A. *The place of Satan in temptation is limited.*

    1. By the permissive will of God. "And the Lord said, Simon, Simon, behold, Satan hath desired to have you, that he may sift you as wheat" (Luke 22:31). Satan had to have God's permission to test Peter.

        In the ancient book of Job, Satan had to report to God and get permission to test Job (see Job 1:6–12; 2:1–6). Christianity rejects the idea that in the battle between good and evil the ultimate issue is in doubt. There will be bruises on both sides, but ultimately the Messiah will crush Satan (Gen. 3:15). Jesus will be enthroned and Satan will be cast into the lake of fire.

    2. Satan was permitted to "sift as wheat" but not to burn as chaff. The threshing of wheat by the sifting process will not hurt the wheat. God will overrule so good will come out of what Satan intends for evil. Peter needed his pride, conceit, and self-confidence exploded.

    3. Satan was limited by Jesus' prayer, "that thy faith fail not" (Luke 22:32). Jesus' prayer was answered. Peter's faith did not fail. He lost face; he backslid in conduct; but he did not lose his faith. Jesus promises that he will never give Satan the power to take salvation from a saved person. On the contrary, he pledges eternal life, which would not be eternal if it could be lost. "My sheep hear my voice, and I know them, and they follow me: And I give unto them eternal life; and they shall never perish, neither shall any man pluck them out of my hand. My Father, which gave them me, is greater than all; and no man is able to pluck them out of my Father's hand. I and my Father are one" (John 10:27–30). "Wherefore he is able also to save them to the uttermost that come unto God by him, seeing he ever liveth to make intercession for them" (Heb. 7:25). Because Jesus intercedes for his people, pleading the merit of his atoning blood, Peter was safe, as are all other believers.

B. *Jesus expressed confidence that Peter's backsliding would turn from sin to service.* Then he would entrust him again with work to do. "And when thou art converted, strengthen thy brethren" (Luke 22:32). Simon would become Peter; the backslider would be restored; he would preach and souls would be saved.

II. Jesus sought Peter.

A. *"But go your way, tell his disciples and Peter that he goeth before you into Galilee: there shall ye see him, as he said unto you" (Mark 16:7).* These are the words of the angel to the women at the tomb. How gracious of our Lord to send a special message to Peter, who needed it most.

Sometime during that first Resurrection Day, the Lord appeared to Peter. The disciples in the upper room greeted Cleopas and his companion with the astonishing news: "The Lord is risen indeed, and hath appeared to Simon" (Luke 24:34).

B. *There is no record of that meeting of our Lord and Peter.* It was too personal, too precious to record. We can imagine the hot tears of repentance, the full confession, and the kisses of reconciliation.

III. The restoration of Peter (John 21:1–19).

Since Peter had denied publicly, he must be restored publicly.

A. *The situation (John 21:1–14).* It is not too difficult to persuade a fisherman to go fishing. As soon as Peter announced that he was going fishing, he was promptly joined by Thomas, Nathanael, James, John, and two unnamed disciples. The miracle of the great catch of fish at the time Peter and Andrew, James and John had been called to follow Jesus as full-time ministers (see Luke 5:1–11) was reenacted. John was the first to perceive that the stranger on the shore was Jesus. Peter impulsively jumped into the sea to go to him. All of the seven recognized him. "None of the disciples dared ask him, 'Who are you?' They knew it was the Lord" (John 21:12 NIV). John preserved the memory of an eyewitness as he remembered the exact number of large fish that were caught.

B. *Jesus probed Peter's love.* "So when they had dined, Jesus saith to Simon Peter, Simon, son of Jonas, lovest thou me more than these?" (John 21:15). In the context, "these" could refer either to the disciples or to the fish.

Peter had affirmed in the upper room, "Though all men shall be offended because of thee, yet will I never be offended" (Matt. 26:33). Peter had left the fishing business to fish for men. Did his return to a night of fishing signal a retreat from full discipleship? In his reply, "Yea, Lord; thou knowest that I love thee," Peter did not use the same strong word for love that Jesus used in his question. Jesus said, "Feed my lambs." The question was repeated the second time with the response, "Feed my sheep." Again Jesus asked the question, but he dropped his strong word for love and used Peter's word.

Peter had denied Jesus three times, yet he was grieved that Jesus repeated his question three times. He said, "Lord, thou knowest all things; thou knowest that I love thee." He seemed to be saying, "Lord, I know I haven't acted like it. I've caused others to doubt my love to you, but, Lord, you can look down into my heart. You know that in spite of all appearances, I love you." Peter would not even then come up to Jesus' word for love. He was thoroughly humbled, but he had been forgiven and restored publicly as an apostle. He would shepherd the Lord's sheep.

C. *A tender word for Peter (John 21:18–19).* Jesus predicted that Peter would be loyal even to the point of dying a martyr's death. He would be crucified in loyalty to his Lord. Jesus said, "Keep on following me."

Conclusion

"Do you love me?" Jesus asks. Do you love Jesus? He is not asking, "Do you like me?" but rather, "Do you love me?" Love in this sense is almost synonymous with loyalty or obedience. "If you love me, you will obey my commandments" (John 14:15 GNT). "Those who accept my commandments and obey them are the ones who loves me. My Father will love those who love me; I too will love them and reveal myself to them" (John 14:21 GNT). The proof of love is obedience. "Follow me." "Feed my sheep."

If as Peter we backslide, we shall find Jesus ready to forgive. In fact, he loves us so much that, rather than let us go on in sin, he will convict us of sin. Because of this, we shall ask forgiveness.

WEDNESDAY EVENING, NOVEMBER 25

Title: He Leadeth Me—O Blessed Thought!

Text: "God led the people around by the desert road toward the Red Sea. The Israelites went up out of Egypt ready for battle. . . . By day the LORD went ahead of them in a pillar of cloud to guide them on their way and by night in a pillar of fire to give them light, so that they could travel by day or night" (**Ex. 13:18, 21 NIV**).

Scripture Reading: Exodus 13:17–14:31

Introduction

We often think of the deliverance of Israel from the Egyptians as the only theme in the book of Exodus. To be sure, the exodus motif is strong, but there are other important ideas, for example, the leadership of the Lord.

Exodus records a great account of God's leadership in 13:17–14:31. It relates the journey of the Israelites from Egypt to the other side of the Red Sea. To move so many people this distance required leadership. The author of Exodus attributed this accomplishment to the Lord.

God still leads his people today. Without a doubt, God delivers initially from sin, but he also leads us in the Christian pilgrimage. Let us notice how God leads his people.

I. The Lord leads by his wisdom.

A. *God knows his people.* "And it came to pass, when Pharaoh had let the people go, that God led them not through the way of the land of the Philistines, although that was near" (Ex. 13:17). God had been intimately acquainted with his people during the plight of their bondage.

He heard their groanings and knew their sufferings. When he set the people free from bondage, he continued to know them. God knew that people so recently set free from years of bondage were not physically or psychologically ready to fight an enemy. He knew that they might turn back to Egypt.

God knows us. He knows the exact nature of our lives. In his great wisdom, he knows what is best for us.

B. *God has a better perspective.* The Israelites could only see the traditional, shorter route. They ignored the danger of the Philistines. God had a greater perspective. He could see both the danger and the shorter route.

He knew that the longer route was not the easiest way but the best and only way for Israel to travel.

God has a better perspective on life than we do. The best route of life may not be the easiest, but God will give us grace for our journey.

II. God leads by his presence.

A. *God goes with his people.* "By day the LORD went ahead of them in a pillar of cloud to guide them on their way and by night in a pillar of fire to give them light, so that they could travel by day or night" (Ex. 13:21 NIV). The cloud and fire suggested the continual presence of the Lord. God did not leave the Israelites alone to figure out how to move to Sinai; he went with them.

God is with his people. The Holy Spirit abides in every believer. With him we can be led in every life situation.

B. *People can be assured by God's presence.* The presence of the Lord never departed from the traveling Israelites. The Lord was with them by day in a pillar of cloud. He symbolized his presence with them by night with a pillar of fire. With the knowledge of God's presence the people could attempt any venture of their pilgrimage.

God's presence gives comfort as well as guidance. The child of God does not travel through life by guesswork but by the guidance of God.

III. God leads by his power.

A. *Human power fails.* The Israelites traveled from Egypt until they came to the Red Sea. The barrier presented a dilemma. Behind them the Hebrews heard the pursuing Egyptians. Before them they saw the formidable body of water. These two barriers caused the Israelites to come to the end of their power. They could neither defeat the Egyptians nor cross the sea.

Life often brings us to barriers where human strength fails. These experiences teach us that we are the creatures and that God is our powerful Creator.

B. *Divine power avails.* "The LORD caused the sea to go back by a strong east wind all that night, and made the sea dry land, and the waters were divided" (Ex. 14:21). The parting of the sea was a miraculous intervention of God for the Israelites. God's power made a way through the sea.

God's power is available to us. As we face insurmountable obstacles, we need God's power. Only he can help us.

Conclusion

You need leadership through the journey of life. No one is capable of leading you but the Lord. You cannot make the journey by yourself. Allow the Lord to lead you.

SUNDAY MORNING, NOVEMBER 29

Title: The Stewardship of Money

Text: "The love of money is a root of all kinds of evil: which some reaching after have been led astray from the faith, and have pierced themselves through with many sorrows" (**1 Tim. 6:10 ASV**).

Scripture Reading: 1 Timothy 6:3–19

Hymns: "We Give Thee but Thine Own," How
"All Things Are Thine," Whittier
"Trust, Try, and Prove Me," Leech

Offertory Prayer: Our Father in heaven, we pray your blessings on the message for this hour. Bless us now as we return unto the support of your kingdom's cause a portion of what you have entrusted to us as your stewards. Bless these tithes and offerings as we lay them on your altar. This we ask in our Savior's name. Amen.

Introduction

What is money? One says, "Money is life transmuted into currency." Another tell us, "Money . . . is a naturalized citizen of all lands and . . . speaks all languages, and can be at work wherever the sun shines" (Harry Emerson Fosdick, *The Meaning of Service* [New York: Association Press, 1944], 162). Another contends that money is "dirty stuff." This is confirmed by at least one Scripture that describes money as "filthy lucre" (1 Tim. 3:8). Money comes close to ruling the world. This, no doubt, is why Jesus revealed it as the other god, over against the real God: "Ye cannot serve God and mammon" (Matt. 6:24). Another calls money "the sign and symbol of our material possessions." A well-known psychiatrist contended that "to be normal is nothing to brag about." Continuing in this same vein, he said, "Money, pure and simple, is the god of the average normal. Lesser gods are bluff, show, and fake, all members of the same club. *Get the money!* is the slogan. Make good in *that,* never mind how!" (Louis E. Bisch, *Be Glad You're Neurotic* [New York: McGraw Hill, 1946], 29).

When we think about it, what in life is more intimate than the money we handle? It represents our labor, our investment of time, talent, and skill, our choice of life's purposes. The way we spend money represents the real desires of our hearts, the secret motives by which our lives are guided.

The stewardship of money is a Christian concern. In 1 Timothy 6 Paul dealt with this matter most pointedly. In verses 6–10 he showed the peril for God's saints in the desire to be rich and said that "godliness with contentment is great gain" (v. 6). In verses 11–16 he warned Timothy against this same peril and pointed him to faith in God as the way out. In verses 17–19 he gave Timothy a charge to pass on to those who were already rich. Let us look at the truths about money that are implied by our text.

I. Money in itself is amoral.

Money in itself is neither good nor bad. Our text does not say that money is "a root of all kinds of evil," but that "the love of money" is (ASV). It is our attitude toward and use of money that tip the scales one way or the other, toward good or evil. Money is one of God's gifts to us, but it is hard to possess it without considering it as our own instead of realizing that we are only stewards.

In no realm is the best work ever done for the love of money, but rather for the joy of achievement and the love of God and others.

> One may write hack music for money, but when Handel in a passion of tears and prayer wrote the "Hallelujah Chorus," money was forgotten. Caiaphas might well have been high priest for pay, but the Master's saviorhood had no such motive. How much money do we think would buy Luther to go to Worms; or buy John Knox to brave the wrath of Mary, Queen of Scots; or buy Washington to endure the winter at Valley Forge? Money can do some things; for the sake of it men have sometimes done good work, often devilish work, but for the sake of it no man ever did his best work (Fosdick, *Meaning of Service*, 181).

William Carey was reproached by friends for giving so much time to studying and preaching, to what they felt was the neglect of his little business as a shoe cobbler. Carey's reply was simple: "The gospel is my business. I only cobble shoes to pay expenses."

In a poem titled "I Am Money," an unknown poet stated this point exactly.

> Dug from the mountainside, washed in the glen,
> Servant am I, or the Master of men,
>   Steal me, I curse you,
>   Earn me, I bless you,

Grasp me and hoard me, a fiend shall possess you.
    Lie for me, die for me,
    Covet me, take me,
Angel or devil, I am what you make me.

II. The wrong attitude toward money is immoral.

The "love of money" is self-destructive, self-condemning, and harmful. To covet it, to be greedy and ruthless in pursuit of it, to let our lust for money become the overpowering passion of our lives is morally wrong and self-destructive. In our text and its context, Paul showed us four things.

A. *For one thing, to let the passion for money come first in our lives will lead us astray from the faith.* "The love of money is a root of all kinds of evil: which some reaching after have been led astray from the faith" (1 Tim. 6:10 ASV). Nothing can be more depressing or heartbreaking for a pastor than to see some person or some family who were once faithful to Christ and his church become affluent and prosperous and lose all interest. Every pastor has seen this, and how tragic it is! Perhaps it would not be wrong if the pastor asked some consecrated people to join him in the prayer that the income of these people might be reduced to the point that they would return to their faith.

B. *To let the passion for money come first in our lives will be the means of bringing grief and sorrow on ourselves and on others.* Paul warned that as well as being led astray from the faith, those who chase after money will also pierce "themselves through with many sorrows" (1 Tim. 6:10 ASV).

An Associated Press story told of a seventy-seven-year-old man being found dead, a suicide, in a bedroom of the eighteen-room mansion that had been his family's home for eighty-seven years. This would not be so remarkable were it not for the fact that his father, a sister, and a brother had preceded him in death in exactly the same way—four members of the same family in the same house. What was the matter with this family? This was an old and famous brewery family in a midwestern city whose "love for money" had led them to traffic in the health and misery of their fellow humans. They had indeed pierced "themselves through with many sorrows."

Emerson once said, "The worst thing about money is that its costs so much." In many instances, people have paid for their fortunes with every good thing in their lives. They ended up with money, but they had not one thing besides.

C. *The possession of money may lead to worldly pride.* In 1 Timothy 6:17 Paul gave Timothy a warning to pass on to those who are already "rich in this present world." He said, "Charge them that are rich in this present world, that they be not high-minded, nor have their hope set on the uncertainty of riches" (ASV). Paul was not condemning the possession of wealth as such. The great moral questions are how one makes money, how one uses it, and to whom that person considers himself or herself accountable. Paul warned against being "high-minded." This is false pride. We somehow have the idea that money has the power to buy anything, that everything has its price. But this is not true. Money will buy a bed but not sleep, food but not appetite, finery but not beauty, a house but not a home, medicine but not health, luxuries but not culture, amusements but not a Savior, a church building but not heaven.

D. *Faith in the power of the money we possess will prove to be a false faith.* Paul's warning was not only against worldly pride but that the believers also not "have their hope set on the uncertainty of riches, but on God, who giveth us richly all things to enjoy" (1 Tim. 6:17 ASV). The reign of material things is only temporary at best, and at worst it can be taken from us in a night.

A pastor was a Sunday luncheon guest in the lovely home of a successful farmer. As the farmer's wife was finishing preparations, the farmer was showing his pastor about the farm—the bulging barns; the filled silos; the beautiful cattle, horses, and sheep. He taunted the minister about his morning sermon on God's ownership of all things. "Look at all these buildings and land, these cattle and livestock," the farmer said; "they are mine, not God's. I planned and worked for them. Do you still think God owns them?" After a long pause, the preacher asked quietly: "Whose will they be one hundred years from now?" Yes, whose?

To reach old age, possessed only of money and the desire to increase it, is not success, but a sad and terrible failure. It is better to die impoverished in purse than impoverished in soul.

III. The right attitude toward and use of money is moral.

A. *This will please God and bless the world and everybody in it.* The right attitude toward money is not to love it, nor covet it, nor push and shove and cheat and kill in the effort to accumulate large sums of it. It is right to regard money as a means, an instrument. We should use it as a servant of God, who is the owner, and as a servant of our fellow humans.

B. *The right attitude toward and use of money will bless us here and now.* In his farewell address to the Ephesian elders, Paul preserved a beatitude of our Lord's, which otherwise would have been forgotten: "It is more blessed to give than to receive" (Acts 20:35). The whole history of revelation demonstrates this truth. Giving, if rightly motivated, becomes an investment in eternal securities. Not getting but giving enlarges life. When we give that others may be blessed, we recover life.

C. *The right attitude toward and use of money will bless us in our posterity, in our children after us.* Years ago one of the favorite stories of Dr. Prince E. Burroughs was about a widow everyone called "Mrs. Mac." The neighbors thought she was foolish because she tried to raise five children, send them to college, and give the Lord the first and best of her earnings. But time revealed who was foolish. Seventeen preachers came out of the little country church she supported so bravely. Three of her own sons became ministers, one a Christian businessman, and her daughter a minister's wife.

D. *The right attitude toward and use of money will bless us in heaven.* The New Testament is very clear on this. Jesus said, "Lay not up for yourselves treasures upon the earth, where moth and rust consume, and where thieves break through and steal: but lay up for yourselves treasures in heaven, where neither moth nor rust doth consume, and where thieves do not break through nor steal" (Matt. 6:19–20 ASV). In Florence, Italy, an epitaph on a tombstone reads, "Here lies Estrella, who has gone to heaven to enjoy a fortune of fifty thousand florins, which she sent on ahead."

In Jesus' parable of the unrighteous steward (Luke 16:1–12), the steward, who was to be fired, quickly ingratiated himself with his master's debtors so they would take him into their homes when he became unemployed. The punch line is this: "I say unto you, Make to yourselves friends by means of the mammon of unrighteousness; that, when it shall fail, they may receive you into the eternal tabernacles" (Luke 16:9 ASV). Jesus was saying, "Think of arriving at the 'pearly gates' and being greeted by someone with a shining face saying, 'Welcome, I've been looking for you to come. I wanted to greet the one whose investment of money in God's work changed my life and opened heaven for me.'"

E. *The right attitude toward and use of money will bless the work of the kingdom of God.* John Wesley had a famous sermon on stewardship that had three points: (1) get all you can, (2) save all you can, and (3) give all you can. Wesley practiced what he preached in the matter of the stewardship of money. He began, when he was young and his income was only £30 per year, to give £2 to the church. When his salary rose to £60, he was still living on £28 and giving £32 to the church. When his salary rose to £120, he gave £92 away. In the course of his life, his recorded benefactions exceeded £30,000.

Conclusion

What is your attitude toward money? How do you get money? How do you use it? The answer to these questions makes all the difference in the world.

Years ago Horace Bushnell said, "One more revival, only one, is needed, the revival of Christian stewardship, the consecration of money power to God.

When that revival comes, the kingdom of God will come in a day" (quoted by Ralph S. Cushman in *Practicing the Presence* [Nashville: Abingdon-Cokesbury, 1936], 172). Horace Bushnell died in 1876, and this last great revival has not yet come. God grant that it may come now, and that it may begin in your heart and mine.

SUNDAY EVENING, NOVEMBER 29

Title: Misplaced Concern

Text: "Peter turned and saw that the disciple whom Jesus loved was following them. (This was the one who had leaned back against Jesus at the supper and had said, 'Lord, who is going to betray you?') When Peter saw him, he asked, 'Lord, what about him?'

"Jesus answered, 'If I want him to remain alive until I return, what is that to you? You must follow me'" **(John 21:20–22 NIV).**

Scripture Reading: John 21:20–22

Introduction

Have you ever been embarrassed by asking a question to which the proper reply should have been, "None of your business"?

Our Scripture presents us with such a case from the irrepressible Simon Peter. Jesus had forgiven Peter for his denials and had restored him, commanding, "Feed my sheep" and "Follow me." He had told Peter that Peter would die a martyr's death by crucifixion. Then Peter, turning around, had seen John and had asked Jesus, "Lord, what about him?" Jesus answered, "If I want him to remain alive until I return, what is that to you? You must follow me" (John 21:21–22 NIV).

I. This question is characteristic of Peter.

Peter was impulsive and impetuous. He often tried the patience of others by rash and bold utterances. As the popular saying goes, he had foot-in-mouth disease. Illustrations are abundant. For example, at Caesarea Philippi after confessing Jesus to be the Christ, Peter had allowed Satan to use him as a mouthpiece to suggest that Jesus not go to the cross. On the Mount of Transfiguration, Peter had said to Jesus, "Master, it is good for us to be here. Let us put up three shelters—one for you, one for Moses and one for Elijah." Luke added in parentheses, "He did not know what he was saying" (Luke 9:33 NIV).

II. The answer is characteristic of Jesus.

    A. *He answered in love.*

        1. Jesus answered questions. Christianity is the gospel of an open mind. When Andrew and John first sought an audience with

Jesus, he replied, "Come and see" (John 1:39). When Nicodemus sought the answer to problems he didn't know how to ask about, Jesus spoke with him of the birth from above.

The disciples seemed to have a speculative rather than a personal interest in the man born blind. They asked, "Master, who did sin, this man, or his parents, that he was born blind?" (John 9:2). Jesus corrected their theology and then gave their question a practical answer by his reply, "We must work the works of him who sent me, while it is day; night comes, when no one can work" (John 9:4 RSV).

    2. Even when persons asked questions to test him and trap him rather than out of a desire for the truth, as in Matthew 22:15 and 35, Jesus answered in love.

B. *He gave a practical turn to speculative questions.* "Then said one unto him, Lord, are there few that be saved? And he said unto them, Strive to enter in at the strait gate: for many, I say unto you, will seek to enter in, and shall not be able" (Luke 13:23–24).

When Peter inquired about John, "Lord, what about him?" Jesus answered, "If I want him to remain alive until I return, what is that to you? You must follow me" (John 21:21–22 NIV). John's future was between him and the Lord. Peter's responsibility would not be changed by what happened to John. His practical responsibility was to follow Jesus.

III. Follow Christ's example.

A. *Answer in love.* Even if one should ask a question just to provoke a discussion, it is possible that one can use the occasion as a witness to the truth.

B. *Welcome questions.* A thinking person will never be able to answer all questions that he or she or others ask. It is not surprising that finite people cannot understand nor explain God and his purposes. Do not be afraid to say, "I don't know." After diligent search for the truth, you may be able to add, "I don't think any person living knows." Jesus does not demand that his disciples comprehend him, but that they believe on him and follow him.

C. *Follow Jesus even if you lack answers to the big questions.* Problems do not begin with Christianity. They begin to end there. Unbelief has even graver problems than belief.

    1. Some speculative problems that lie outside revelation are:

        a. The problem of evil. Revelation did not create this problem; it found it existing. It is not our business to solve the problem of evil but to escape the ravages of sin. Jesus did not argue about the problem of evil; he gave himself to the practical task of providing salvation. When the building is burning, try to put out the fire. The inquest can be held later.

   b. The anomalies of God's providence—the seeming prosperity of the wicked and the adversity of the righteous. Job and his friends wrestled with this question and left it right where they found it: in God's hands. Faith believes that when God finally balances his books, we will see that he has worked all things for good to them that love him.

2. Some mysteries spring out of revelation, such as:
   a. The nature of the Trinity.
   b. The person of Christ.
   c. The problem of God's sovereignty and man's free will.
   d. The nature of the future life. Will we recognize people in heaven? Due to our human limitations, God cannot give a full answer to this question. As an adult cannot explain some things to a child because the child does not have the capacity to receive it, so our finiteness limits us.

3. There are other problems that we cannot settle because of lack of knowledge. One's understanding of Christ's return is a case in point. Intelligent people may take the premillennial, postmillennial, or amillennial view or may just admit ignorance. If the Lord had wanted us to know, he would have made it plain. Christians arguing over speculative problems are like cooks arguing about whether there will be six or eight guests when preparation has not been made for any.

Conclusion

We know in part, but we know enough. The way to be saved and the obedience that our Lord desires are plain enough.

Some matters the heavenly Father has kept to himself. Peter did not need to know whether John would live until Jesus comes again. What folly if he should fail to follow Jesus because of his lack of knowledge on that point. What God does with John is God's problem. What John does with Jesus is John's problem. Neither should keep Peter from following Jesus.

The essence of faith is to act on the light one has. Obedience to one's own light will bring added light. "If any man will do his will, he shall know of the doctrine, whether it be of God, or whether I speak of myself" (John 7:17).

Simon Peter's brother, Andrew, set a good example when he brought the Greeks to Jesus (John 12:20–22). He acted on the good principle that whatever the problem or difficulty, take it to Jesus, rather than allow the problem to drive one away from Jesus.

DECEMBER

■ **Sunday Mornings**

The message theme through Christmas is "The Great Words of Christ," a series that will help people relate to Christ during the holiday season. The last message of the year focuses on thanking God for the year's blessings.

■ **Sunday Evenings**

Much of our studying is concerned with what God says to us through the Bible. But on Sunday evenings this month, let's emphasize what we have to say back to God in a series called "Our Response to God."

■ **Wednesday Evenings**

Complete the studies on Moses and the exodus. On the last Wednesday evening of the month, incorporate a message that looks forward to the new year.

WEDNESDAY EVENING, DECEMBER 2

Title: The Helper for Human Situations

Text: "If thou wilt diligently hearken to the voice of the LORD thy God, and wilt do that which is right in his sight, and wilt give ear to his commandments, and keep all his statutes, I will put none of these diseases upon thee, which I have brought upon the Egyptians: for I am the LORD that healeth thee" **(Ex. 15:26)**.

Scripture Reading: Exodus 15:22–18:27

Introduction

Think with me for a moment. Try to imagine any situation in life that you might face: marriage, vocational choice, education, loss of health, rearing children, inward struggles, or countless others. As you think of these situations, ask yourself, "How can I face these situations?" Let me challenge you to bring God into every circumstance of your life.

Exodus 15:22–18:27 tells about the Israelites' journey from the Red Sea to Sinai, including their pilgrimage in the wilderness. The author of Exodus intended to tell more than the narration of a journey. He wanted the Israelites to know that God could help them in various situations in life. Let us notice some of these situations.

I. God helps with our daily necessities.

A. *God helped Israel with some necessities of life.* Three stories in Exodus 15:22–18:27 have to do with the practical necessities of food and drink (15:22–27; 16:1–36; 17:1–7). God came to meet these daily situations of the Israelites time and time again. He sweetened the bitter waters of Marah (Ex. 15:22–25). He spread a table in the desert and supplied it with bread from heaven (Ex. 16:1–36). He brought water from a rock at Meribah (Ex. 17:1–7).

These episodes tell us that God is interested in the daily necessities of life.

B. *God helps people with the necessities of life.* The psalmist said, "The LORD is my shepherd; I shall not want" (Ps. 23:1). This last sentence could be translated, "I shall not want for anything that I really need." The psalmist expressed confidence that God would help us with our needs.

Jesus taught us to pray, "Give us this day our daily bread" (Matt. 6:11). The Lord wanted his followers to seek the daily provisions of life.

Notice that God helps with our needs, not our wants. The Lord might listen to our wants, but he basically seeks to provide what we need. Whenever a need arises, ask God for help.

II. God helps with our aggravating enemies.

A. *God helped Israel win over their enemies (Ex. 17:8–16).* As the Israelites traveled toward Sinai, they encountered the Amalekites, who attacked them.

This was the first conflict of the Israelites. With Moses on the mountain and Joshua in the valley, God helped Israel win over the Amalekites. After the battle ended, the Israelites raised a victory altar and named it Jehovah-nissi, which means "The LORD is my banner" (Ex. 17:15–16). This story of the defeat of the Amalekites showed how the Lord saved his people from the enemy.

B. *God will deliver his people today.* God has not changed. Furthermore, God's people still encounter enemies. God will be our "banner," our inspiration to defeat our enemies, including Satan. The devil seeks to thwart God's purpose in our lives. If we depend on the Lord and look to him, we can win over Satan. James said, "Resist the devil, and he will flee from you" (James 4:7).

God has also provided victory over our final enemy, death, by Jesus' crucifixion and resurrection. To the enemy of death, the Christian may say: "O death, where is thy sting? O grave, where is thy victory? The sting of death is sin; and the strength of sin is the law. But thanks be to God, which giveth us the victory through our Lord Jesus Christ" (1 Cor. 15:55–57).

III. God helps with our godly service.

A. *God used Jethro to help Moses with the administration of justice.* Jethro's visit to the camp of the Israelites was more than a mere meeting. God used Jethro to help Moses with his godly service. Jethro spent a day watching Moses judge the people and observed that the responsibility was too great for Moses alone. Thus he counseled Moses to share the responsibility with others. Moses took Jethro's advice and selected others to help.

    The story reflects three prominent traits of Moses: his devotion to the people, his readiness to take advice, and his willingness to delegate authority. Moses evidently wanted to be a more effective servant of the Lord.

B. *God helps us with our godly service.* God uses other people to help us with our service and also to reprimand and counsel us. No service we render for God to others is ever perfect. Let us listen and heed advice so that we might be equipped for more effective ministry.

Conclusion

God can help you in every human situation. The only reason that God will not help you is if you refuse to let him. Open your life to the Lord; he will help you.

SUNDAY MORNING, DECEMBER 6

Title: Glory to God in the Highest

Text: "An angel of the Lord appeared to them, and the glory of the Lord shone around them, and they were filled with fear. . . . And suddenly there was with the angel a multitude of the heavenly host praising God and saying, 'Glory to God in the highest, and on earth peace among men with whom he is pleased!'" **(Luke 2:9, 13 RSV).**

Scripture Reading: Luke 2:8–14

Hymns: "Joyful, Joyful, We Adore Thee," Van Dyke
           "He Is Coming," Crosby
           "Holy Spirit, Faithful Guide," Wells

Offertory Prayer: God of grace and God of glory, thank you for revealing your love and compassion and power in the gift of your Son, Jesus Christ. Thank you for the new insights and assurances you give us in and through his life, teachings, death, victorious resurrection, and continuing presence with us. Thank you for the deep inward disposition that you have given to us that causes us to hunger for you and that causes us to rejoice in the privilege of worshiping you. Today we bring tithes and offerings to express our love for you and our desire that others come to know the joy of forgiveness and the gladness of new life. Bless these gifts to the advancement of your kingdom, and help us to give ourselves in loving service day by day. In Jesus' name. Amen.

Introduction

During this month in which we face the Christmas holidays, we will look at some of the great words associated with Christmas. Today we look at the word *glory*. The Scriptures declare that "the glory of the Lord shone around them" and that the angels sang, "Glory to God in the highest." John said, "We have beheld his glory, glory as of the only Son from the Father" (John 1:14 RSV). By his first miracle in Cana of Galilee, John records that Jesus "manifested his glory; and his disciples believed in him" (John 2:11 RSV).

Dr. William E. Hull has said, "Glory is one of the richest terms in the theological vocabulary of the Bible, referring primarily to the visible manifestations of God in power. The life of Jesus was radiant with the focused presence of the divine majesty. Throughout his earthly ministry, God made a weighty impact upon men which summoned them to a new awareness of His purpose and prestige" (*The Broadman Bible Commentary*, ed. Clifton Allen, 12 vols. [Nashville: Broadman, 1969], 9:218).

I. The glory of God and human fear.

"They were filled with fear."

A. *The glory of God was a visible manifestation of the invisible but powerful God.* The glory of God was revealed in Old Testament days, indicating God's presence, power, and authority.
B. *In the exodus experience, the glory of the Lord appeared to the people in a cloud.* "In a pillar of cloud to lead them along the way, and by night in a pillar of fire to give them light, that they might travel by day and by night" (Ex. 13:21 RSV). By means of this brilliant and shining manifestation of his presence, God revealed himself to Israel in both grace and judgment.

The glory of God in the form of a cloud and a pillar of fire also came in judgment on the Egyptians. "And in the morning watch the LORD in the pillar of fire and of cloud looked down upon the host of the Egyptians, and discomfited the host of the Egyptians, clogging their chariot wheels so that they drove heavily; and the Egyptians said, 'Let us flee from before Israel; for the LORD fights for them against the Egyptians'" (Ex. 14:24–25 RSV).

When God instructed Moses concerning the building of the tabernacle and the services that were to be conducted there, he declared, "There I will meet with the people of Israel, and it shall be sanctified by my glory" (Ex. 29:43 RSV).

Isaiah was to experience an awareness of the universal glory of God in his call experience (Isa. 6).

The glory of God was a visible manifestation of his burning presence in Old Testament days. It created an attitude of dread and fear and anxiety in the hearts of men and women because they felt unworthy to come into the presence of this holy God.

II. Christ came to manifest the glory of God and to bring glory to God.

John said, "We have beheld his glory, glory as of the only Son from the Father" (John 1:14 RSV). Jesus, in his great High Priestly Prayer recorded in John 17, said to the Father, "I glorified thee on earth, having accomplished the work which thou gavest me to do; and now, Father, glorify thou me in thy own presence with the glory which I had with thee before the world was made. I have manifested thy name to the men whom thou gavest me out of the world; thine they were, and thou gavest them to me, and they have kept thy word" (John 17:4–6 RSV).

    A. *Jesus revealed the grace and truth about God in what he said.*
    B. *Jesus revealed the grace and truth about God in the works of mercy, kindness, and helpfulness that he did.*
    C. *Jesus revealed the grace of God supremely in his sacrificial death on the cross.* Jesus went to the cross because of the command of the Father and because he wanted to demonstrate to an unbelieving world the greatness of his love for the Father (John 14:31). Jesus went to the cross for the joy of the benefit that would accrue to people as a result of this new revelation of the glory of God (Heb. 12:2).

III. The followers of Christ are encouraged to glorify God.

The heavenly hosts praised God and sang, "Glory to God in the highest." If we would glorify God in the highest, we must also glorify God here in the present. If we would glorify God, we must be visible manifestations of his presence in the world today. We must let him live within us in such a way that others can see his grace and goodness.

There are at least three different ways in which we can glorify God.

    A. *We are to glorify God in our bodies.* "So glorify God in your body" (1 Cor. 6:20 RSV). The New International Version translates this verse, "Therefore honor God with your body." The *Good News* translation translates this phrase, "So use your bodies for God's glory."

        It is possible for us to glorify God in our bodies because Jesus Christ has come to dwell within us through faith (Eph. 3:17). We have become the dwelling place of the Holy Spirit.

        It is with our bodies that we are to glorify God. Annie Johnson Flint expressed it well in her poem "The World's Bible":

        Christ has no hands but our hands
        To do His work today;

He has no feet but our feet
To lead men in His way;
He has no tongue but our tongues
To tell men how He died;
He has no help but our help
To bring men to His side.

We are not to use our bodies for immoral purposes, for they have been made for the Lord (1 Cor. 6:13–14).

B. *We are to glorify God by bearing much fruit (John 15:8).* Our Lord declared, "By this my Father is glorified, that you bear much fruit, and so prove to be my disciples" (RSV). There are at least two kinds of fruit that we can experience and by which we can glorify God.

  i. We can cultivate the fruit of the Spirit (Gal. 5:22–23). The Holy Spirit has been given to us in order that he might reproduce within us the character and the very nature of Jesus Christ. As we let the Holy Spirit produce the fruit of love, joy, peace, patience, kindness, goodness, faithfulness, gentleness, and self-control, we will become living exhibitions of what God can do when he is permitted to come and live in the hearts of human beings.

  ii. We can experience the fruit of the seed sower and, by so doing, bring glory to God (Matt. 13:1–9). As we sow the seed of the Word of God in the hearts and lives of those about us, some will hear and respond. Some will believe and be saved. Some will reflect God's grace and glory, and we will experience the joy of the harvester who comes with rejoicing, bringing his sheaves with him (Ps. 126:6).

C. *We are to glorify God by good works (Matt. 5:16).* Our Lord, in the Sermon on the Mount, said that we are to live as an example of what God can do in the hearts of those who obey Jesus Christ.

The believers in the Thessalonian church were glorifying God with their good works. They demonstrated works of faith, labors of love, and great patience of hope. By so working, they were glorifying God.

Conclusion

Paul said, "Christ in you, the hope of glory" (Col. 1:27 RSV). The indwelling Christ is the hope that God has for us to manifest his presence in the world. The presence of Christ in each of us is the only hope that the world has today for beholding God's glory and experiencing his loving presence.

The Christ of Christmas came long ago, but he comes today to live in our hearts. The indwelling Christ is God's hope for revealing his presence through you. Christ in you is the basis for your hope for a home in God's final glory.

SUNDAY EVENING, DECEMBER 6

Title: Reverence for God

Text: "When the LORD saw that he turned aside to see, God called unto him out of the midst of the bush, and said, Moses, Moses. And he said, Here am I. And he said, Draw not nigh hither: put off thy shoes from off thy feet, for the place whereon thou standest is holy ground" **(Ex. 3:4–5)**.

Scripture Reading: Exodus 2:11–3:12

Introduction

Moses, whose name means "drawn out," was born of Israelite parents in the land of Egypt. His father's name was Amram (Ex. 6:18, 20; Num. 26:59; 1 Chron. 6:3). His mother's name was Jochebed (Ex. 6:20; Num. 26:59).

Times were difficult and perilous when Moses was born. The Israelites were enslaved, and a royal edict ordered the execution of all Israelite male children at birth. When Moses was born, he was hidden among the reeds near the bank of the Nile River. Pharaoh's daughter came to bathe in the river and discovered Moses in the reeds. She took the child and secured a Hebrew woman to nurse him. Unknown to her, the Hebrew woman chosen was Moses' real mother, Jochebed. Moses spent the first forty years of his life in Pharaoh's court.

When Moses was grown, he went out to look on the burdens of his real people, the Israelites. While there he observed an Egyptian smiting a Hebrew. He slew the Egyptian and hid him in the sand. While trying to settle a dispute the next day between two Hebrews, they reminded him that he had killed the Egyptian. Fearing the revengeful hand of Pharaoh, he fled to Midian, where he spent forty years in seclusion. In Midian he found favor in the home of a priest named Jethro. He gained the hand of Jethro's daughter Zipporah in marriage.

Moses served as a shepherd in Midian. It was a great day for Moses and his people when at the back side of the desert at the foot of Mount Horeb he saw the miracle of the burning bush that was not consumed.

In the miracle we find three things necessary for the service of the Lord.

I. Revelation from God is necessary for service.

Someone has said that "revelations are for the observant." Moses turned aside to observe the burning bush, a thorny shrub, a species of acacia. He was eager to investigate. What revelations came to Moses as a result of his investigation?

    A. *God reveals his person.* The bush represented Israel, and the fire was a symbol of God. At the burning bush, the angel of the Lord appeared to Moses in a flame of fire out of the midst of the bush.

In the Bible, God often revealed himself as fire. He did so at the burning bush, the pillar of fire by night (Ex. 13:21), at Sinai (Ex. 19:18; 24:17), to Solomon (2 Chron. 7:1–3), to Ezekiel (Ezek. 1:4–28), and to Daniel (Dan. 7:9–10). He is also referred to as a consuming fire in Hebrews 12:29.

B. *God reveals his holiness (Ex. 3:5).* The words "holy ground" literally mean "ground of holiness." It was rendered holy by God's presence.

C. *God reveals his grace and love (Ex. 3:7–8).*

D. *God reveals his eternity of being.*
   1. He is the God of the past (Ex. 3:6).
   2. He is the God of the present (Ex. 3:7).
   3. He is the God of the future (Ex. 3:10).

We need a revelation from God if we are to serve him effectively.

II. Reverence for God is necessary for service.

God said to Moses, "Moses, Moses. And he said, Here am I. And he said, Draw not nigh hither; put off thy shoes from off thy feet, for the place whereon thou standest is holy ground" (Ex. 3:4–5). God was there at the burning bush, and his presence made the ground holy. When Moses heard his name called twice, he knew the message was urgent. "Moses hid his face; for he was afraid to look upon God" (Ex. 3:6). He who comes to God and serves him must come with bowed head, with reverence. He who serves God must do so with much reverence.

III. Readiness to obey God is necessary for service (Ex. 3:10–12).

The call of Moses was clear and distinct, the will of God was known, and the way of action clearly and plainly indicated. Even though these things were clear to Moses, he was reluctant to begin the task. He started looking at himself and began making excuses: personal unworthiness (Ex. 3:11–14), the unbelief of the people (Ex. 4:1), and physical infirmity (Ex. 4:10). Moses' basic problem is found in the personal pronoun *I . . . I . . . I.*

The lack of readiness on Moses' part did not turn God aside from his purpose. Eventually Moses became God's mouthpiece and Aaron became God's spokesman.

Conclusion

So often we shrink back from the commands of our Lord to serve him. We seek every reason for evading his will. He calls today just as sure as he called Moses. He will not only call us and convince us, but he also will equip us for service.

Talleyrand, a leader of the French Revolution, said he had a speaking acquaintance with God. A Christian leader must have more than a speaking acquaintance with God. That is not enough. God's claims on our lives for service cannot be ignored. We must serve him because he has revealed himself to us. Let us reverence him and obey his commands.

WEDNESDAY EVENING, DECEMBER 9

Title: Sign Your Contract with God

Text: "Now therefore, if ye will obey my voice indeed, and keep my covenant, then ye shall be a peculiar treasure unto me above all people: for all the earth is mine: And ye shall be unto me a kingdom of priests, and an holy nation. These are the words which thou shalt speak unto the children of Israel" **(Ex. 19:5–6)**.

Scripture Reading: Exodus 19:1–24:18

Introduction

Contracts are important documents. School teachers know the importance of signing a contract. Professional athletes also know the importance of a contract. Technically speaking, a contract is an agreement between two parties.

Strangely enough, we come to a section in Exodus (19:1–24:18) that deals with God making a covenant, or contract, with Israel. God led the people from Egypt to Sinai, where he made them an offer. He wanted to negotiate a covenant. If Israel accepted the covenant and its terms, they were bound to execute it. To fail was to forfeit the covenant's promises.

God desires a unique relationship with people. Signing a contract with God is no small thing, for it means that we are entering into a covenant relationship with him.

I. The covenant God discloses his character (Ex. 19:1–25).

Before one enters into an agreement with another party, it is wise to know the character of the other person or persons. God wanted Israel to know the kind of God he was; therefore he disclosed himself.

    A. *God is good and kind.* The writer of Exodus gives an account of God as being good and kind. Reflecting on the previous months in Israel's life, the writer attributed goodness to God. "Ye have seen what I did unto the Egyptians, and how I bare you on eagles' wings, and brought you unto myself" (Ex. 19:4). The writer described God's goodness in terms of the tenderness of a mother eagle toward her young.

    B. *God is holy.* God also taught Israel about his holiness. He had taught them about his goodness. Now he appeared on Mount Sinai and taught about his holiness. Jehovah announced that he would come in a thick cloud on the mountain. The mountain was to be sealed off from the people. To touch the mountain would be fatal. When God descended, thunders and lightning appeared.

When one enters into a covenant with God, the parties are not equals, as in a covenant between a king and his subjects. God is different from us. He is holy. Human beings are to be subject to him; they are not to bargain with him.

II. The covenant God stipulates his demands (Ex. 20:1–17; 20:22–23:33).

Before you sign a contract, you should read all the demands. Likewise, God wants us to know what he expects of us. In Exodus 20:1–17 and 20:22–23:33, he stipulates his demands. Read them carefully before you decide.

A. *God demands total allegiance toward him.* In Exodus 20:1–17 we find the Ten Commandments. In Exodus 20:22–23:33 we find a section of Scripture commonly called the Book of the Covenant. These two sections give intimate details of God's demands within the covenant. The first and foremost truth in both sections is that God demands total allegiance to him. God demands priority—"No other gods." God demands sovereignty—"No graven images." God demands sincerity when we enter into covenant with him—"Do not take the name of the LORD in vain." God also demands sanctity—"Keep the Sabbath day holy."

B. *God demands that we have respect for others.* The last six commandments deal with human relationships that issue from a right relationship with God. These demands call for honor of the home, reverence for another's life, fidelity within marriage, freedom from theft, integrity of word, and freedom from envy.

The Book of the Covenant (Ex. 20:22–23:33) expands on God's demand for the respect of others. It deals with the humanitarian spirit, justice in human affairs, and the prevention of crime.

Before you sign your contract, notice that God's demands are twofold: total allegiance to him and love for your neighbor as you love yourself.

III. The covenant God ratifies a relationship (Ex. 24:1–14).

When both parties agree on a contract, there is a signing. Often this is quite ceremonial, as, for example, when a ball player signs with a professional team. God wanted a celebration when Israel agreed to obey him and to be faithful to him.

A. *God assures that he is a friend to people.* In the ancient Near East, covenants were sealed by eating a meal together. In Exodus 24:9–11 there is a record of the eating of the communal meal. God assured Israel that he was solemnly bound to them. He would be their Friend. God loves people and wants to be their Friend.

B. *God pledges that his covenant is irrevocable.* In Exodus 24:3–8 there is a record of the covenant sealed with blood. Through this symbolic act, God assured Israel that as long as he lived he would fulfill his side of the covenant.

Others may renounce their commitment, but God assures us that he will be constant. When he makes a covenant, it is in blood. He will remain forever true to his agreement.

Conclusion

God wants a unique relationship with you. He makes his demands yet promises enormous dividends. Sign your contract with him.

SUNDAY MORNING, DECEMBER 13

Title: And on Earth Peace

Text: "Suddenly there was with the angel a multitude of the heavenly host praising God and saying, 'Glory to God in the highest, and on earth peace among men with whom he is pleased!'" **(Luke 2:13–14 RSV)**.

Scripture Reading: Luke 2:4–14

Hymns: "Glorious Is Thy Name," McKinney
"Joy to the World! The Lord Is Come," Watts
"Majestic Sweetness Sits Enthroned," Stennett

Offertory Prayer: God of grace and God of glory, God and Father of our Lord Jesus Christ, to you we come today in worship and humility that we might acknowledge you as the Lord of Lords and King of Kings. We acknowledge you as our Creator and as the giver of our life. We come today offering the love of our heart, the praise of our lips, and the service of our hands. We come bringing tithes and offerings that we might, with your help, minister to others and publish abroad to the ends of the earth the good news of your love revealed in and through Jesus Christ our Lord and Savior. We pray in Jesus' name. Amen.

Introduction

The great prophet Isaiah looked forward by the help of the Holy Spirit and gave gracious descriptive titles to the Messiah, who would be born in the distant future. We hear him say, "For to us a child is born, to us a son is given; and the government will be upon his shoulder, and his name will be called 'Wonderful Counselor, Mighty God, Everlasting Father, Prince of Peace'" (Isa. 9:6 RSV).

One of the very significant words of Christmas is *peace*. The hearts of people everywhere hunger for peace. Many pray for peace. Some have wondered when Jesus Christ will bring peace. They have surmised that this peace will come only at the end of the age when he comes back as Lord of Lords and King of Kings. Some have surmised that Jesus Christ is a failure as a peace-bringer. To take this position is to misunderstand the nature of true peace and the character of the peace that he brings to the human heart. Jesus had much to say about peace: "Peace I leave with you; my peace I give to you; not as the world gives do I give to you. Let not your hearts be troubled, neither let them be afraid" (John 14:27 RSV). Following his resurrection from the dead, our Lord greeted his apostles on three different occasions with "Peace be with you" (John 20:19, 21, 26 RSV).

Douglas J. Harris, in his splendid book, *The Biblical Concept of Peace* (Grand Rapids: Baker, 1970), made a study of the Hebrew word *shalom*. He provided great insight into the rich meaning, connotation, and application of what Isaiah was talking about and what Jesus referred to in this word translated "peace." "People of Semitic background in the Near East greet those they regard as true brethren with *Shalom*. Where there is any barrier, the greeting is impossible" (p. 13). The root meaning of the word *shalom* means to be whole, sound, safe. Dr. Harris continued, "The fundamental idea is totality. God is the source and ground for *shalom*. Anything that contributes to this wholeness makes for *shalom*. Anything that stands in the way disrupts *shalom*" (p. 14). A study of the Old Testament's use of this word reveals that the presence of *shalom* makes for wonderful community relationships in which people participate in the blessings of God. The absence of *shalom* makes for war and turmoil and unhappiness.

The word *shalom* is used to describe the health and well-being of individuals and true prosperity. It is used to describe the harmony that exists when there is an absence of war. Peace is the condition that prevails when everything is sound and solid and stable and dependable and reliable. The term *shalom* is used to describe the experience of salvation, particularly when the fruits of salvation are health, prosperity, well-being, and long life. The result is joy and blessing that come from doing God's will (p. 23). When there is an absence of this soundness and integrity in personal character and in personal relationships, the result is defeat, disunity, distrust, alienation, poverty, and misery.

God is the giver of *shalom*. In the Old Testament, this concept included material prosperity as well as spiritual well-bring. Peace could not be enjoyed by those who walked away from God in stubbornness and rebellion and in self-destructiveness. "There is no peace, says my God, for the wicked" (Isa. 57:21 RSV). Even God cannot give peace to one who is unwilling to live a life of faith and faithfulness.

Jesus Christ, as the Prince of Peace, came into the world to help people enter into a relationship with God and with self and with one another so that they can enjoy this precious gift of *shalom*.

What did Jesus mean when he said, "Peace I leave with you; my peace I give to you; not as the world gives do I give to you" (John 14:27 RSV)? To enjoy peace is to be in harmony with God and self and others and things.

I. Christ gives us the peace of a clean heart.

A. *Christ came as the Lamb of God to take away our sin (John 1:29).* Jesus Christ died on the cross under the penalty of our sin that he might save us from the condemnation of sin and return us to God.

B. *As the Lord of life, Jesus offers us forgiveness of sin that is full, free, and forever.* By his sacrificial death on the cross, he has made it possible for us to be cleansed from all sin (1 John 1:7).

II. Christ gives us the peace of a right relationship with God.

Until people enter into a faith relationship with the Father God, they experience a rupture or a shattered relationship. In many respects, this is like a broken bone or a dislocated joint. People stand in desperate need of entering back into a relationship with God that will bring inward peace.

To receive Jesus Christ as Savior and Lord into the heart is to be introduced into a child-Father relationship with God (John 1:12).

A. *We need to enter into a faith relationship with God so that we might be declared acceptable by God.* This happens through faith in Christ, and we receive the peace of God (Rom. 5:1).

B. *In this new relationship with God, we love him because we know that he first loved us (1 John 4:19).*

III. Christ gives us the peace of a Spirit-controlled life.

A. *The Lamb of God who came to take away the guilt of our sin comes in the Spirit to be the Lord of our life.* He will deliver us from the power of sin.

B. *Until we are controlled by the Holy Spirit, we can have no peace.* It is only when we let the controlling authority of the Lord of love become real in our hearts that we begin to experience the true peace God has for us. This is in the background of Paul's warning against seeking to cope with the pressures of life by means of some artificial stimulant or depressant. He said, "Do not get drunk with wine, for that is debauchery; but be filled with the Spirit" (Eph. 5:18 RSV). To seek help through alcohol is to worship a false god that will always disappoint. Only through the control of the Spirit of God rather than under the influence of an alcoholic spirit can we experience true control over our lives. In describing the end result of the fruit of the indwelling Spirit, we find that the individual experiences both peace and self-control (Gal. 5:22–23).

IV. Christ gives to us the peace of a proper attitude toward others.

This new attitude is implied and is to be implemented by a commandment: "A new command I give you: Love one another. As I have loved you, so you must love one another. By this everyone will know that you are my disciples, if you love one another" (John 13:34–35 NIV). Oh, the great inward peace that comes to the individual who relates to others in terms of unconditional love.

V. Christ gives us the peace of a worthy purpose for living.

Many people are anxious about their reason for being. Jesus encourages us to so let God do his good works within us that others cannot help but recognize the presence of God in our lives (Matt. 5:16). They will come to know God through our attitudes, actions, ambitions, and all that we seek to do. This kind of a purpose for being will bring God's peace into your life.

VI. Christ gives us the peace of adequate reserves for all situations.

A pastor in Oklahoma City describes the financial peace he enjoys because of a habit he formed of always carrying a hundred-dollar bill in his wallet. It gives him a sense of well-being and security. The security that a hundred-dollar bill brings is nothing compared to the assurance of divine resources made available to us through Jesus Christ, God's Son and our Savior. Paul spoke of this sense of adequacy that came to him as a result of his relationship with Jesus Christ (Phil. 4:13).

Conclusion

Jesus Christ offers you the peace of forgiveness that is full and free forever. Jesus offers the peace of belonging to the Father God and to the family of God. Jesus offers the peace of partnership and fellowship in his great work of bringing love, mercy, grace, power, and wisdom into the hearts and lives of people. Jesus offers the peace of his perfect provisions, not only in the present but in the future (John 14:1–3). When Jesus Christ is in the heart, we do not have to worry about a home at the end of the way.

Jesus Christ is the peace-bringer to the individual heart. He will work to bring about harmony and peace within the relationships of the home and help you establish harmonious relationships with those about you. He came that there might be peace on earth among people of goodwill.

SUNDAY EVENING, DECEMBER 13

Title: A Hymn of Praise

Text: "The LORD is my strength and song, and he is become my salvation: he is my God, and I will prepare him an habitation; my father's God, and I will exalt him" (**Ex. 15:2**).

Scripture Reading: Exodus 15:1–21

Introduction

One of the greatest oratorios in musical composition is Felix Mendelssohn's *Hymn of Praise.* It is a work of praise to the Lord based on various Scripture passages from Psalm 40.

The proper response of human beings to the mighty acts of God is praise.

The Israelites sang hymns of praise about God's mighty deliverance through the sea. Israel broke out in praise to God.

Our worship experiences need more praise to the Lord. Let us notice the directions of our praise to God.

I. Praise God for his marvelous character (Ex. 15:1–3).

The opening hymn of praise in verses 1–3 contains Israel's earliest theology in a concise summary. Its theme is not the people of the exodus but the God of the exodus.

   A. *The divine names.* Go through the first three verses and discover the divine names: "LORD" my father's God," "man of war." These divine names give us a disclosure of God's nature. When we learn his nature, the response will be praise to the Lord.
   B. *The divine titles.* The divine names have parallel descriptive titles with them. The titles are "my strength," "[my] song," "my salvation." Faced with such a God as this, the writers used verbs of praise: "I will sing," "I will prepare him an habitation," "I will exalt him."

II. Praise God for his mighty deeds (Ex. 15:4–12).

The song at the sea continues to praise the Lord. In Exodus 15:4–12 the Israelites praise God's mighty deeds in the victory at the sea.

   A. *The mighty strength of God.* To describe the mighty victory, Moses referred to the Lord as "a man of war" (Ex. 15:3). He uses a series of war images to describe God's mighty strength over his enemies.
   B. *The incomparable God.* In response to the act of God's deliverance at the sea, the song declares the incomparable nature of the Lord. "Who is like unto thee, O LORD, among the gods? who is like thee, glorious in holiness, fearful in praises, doing wonders?" (Ex. 15:11). God is without a peer. He is to be praised for his marvelous strength.

III. Praise God for his ultimate purpose (Ex. 15:13–17).

The last stanza of the Israelites' "Hymn of Praise" ends with an acknowledgment of God's ultimate purpose. Exodus 15:13–17 makes clear that the goal of Israel was not the other side of the sea but the land of Canaan.

   A. *The manner of God's purpose.* The manner in which God accomplished his purpose is fittingly described. "Thou in thy mercy hast led forth the people which thou hast redeemed: thou hast guided them in thy strength unto thy holy habitation" (Ex. 15:13). God guided them as a shepherd. He led them in love and with his strength.
   B. *The ultimate purpose of God.* The Lord redeemed Israel from bondage for a specific purpose. He intended them to be his own possession. Various terms were used to designate the place of the Lord's abode

with his people in 15:17: "mountain of thine inheritance," "the place," "Sanctuary." These words promise that God will secure Israel's true destiny.

Let us praise the Lord as we see him accomplishing his ultimate purpose. God is working in our day. His ultimate purpose is the reign of righteousness.

Conclusion

Do you have anything to praise the Lord about? You can praise him. Allow him to deliver you from sin. The subsequent response will be, "Praise ye the Lord!"

WEDNESDAY EVENING, DECEMBER 16

Title: God of Grace and God of Glory

Text: "He said, I beseech thee, shew me thy glory" (**Ex. 33:18**).

Scripture Reading: Exodus 33:1–23

Introduction

Often a child feels a parent does not love him anymore. When he disobeys a parent's command, he fears that the parent's love no longer exists.

Then the child is overwhelmed when the parent continues to love, despite the disobedience.

Israel faced a similar situation. They defiantly disobeyed one of God's clear commands. Like a rebellious child, the nation diverted its attention away from God to an idol. After their rebellion, the people thought that God had withdrawn himself from them. Moses, their leader, knew that Israel needed a fresh vision of God. On behalf of the people, he prayed to God, "Shew me thy glory" (Ex. 33:18). Moses wanted the people to understand God's nature. He wanted them to see that God's anger had abated and that Israel's sin had been forgiven.

I. God shows his goodness.

In answering the quest of Moses, God showed his goodness. "He said, I will make all my goodness pass before thee, and I will proclaim the name of the Lord before thee" (Ex. 33:19).

A. *Look at God's previous actions.* How does one understand and comprehend the goodness of God? Present circumstances might cause one to think that God is not good. For example, God's stern rebuke of Israel's idolatry distorted Israel's concept of God. They conceived of him as angry. The best way to think about God amid our sin is to look at the past. The disclosures of God have always been pictures of a good God. Israel had only to look a few months prior to see God's

385

goodness. He had redeemed them from Egyptian slavery and had provided for them during the wilderness wanderings. Israel needed to let God's goodness "pass before them."

B. *Look at God's present actions.* Israel needed to see that God's present action of judgment and rebuke was a disclosure of his goodness. One could not respect a parent who refused to discipline a wayward child. The parent's goodness is at stake if he tolerates rebellion. God disciplined Israel for rebellion. It was not in their best interest to worship the golden calf.

II. God shows his graciousness.

God wanted Moses to understand his true nature. Rebellious people often get the idea that God is angry with them rather than ready to forgive them. Notice what God said about himself: "I . . . will be gracious, and will shew mercy on whom I will shew mercy" (Ex. 33:19).

A. *Look at God's previous acts of graciousness.* The quality of God's grace can be seen since the beginning of human rebellion. What was the predominant feeling of God when Adam and Eve rebelled? God was hurt deeply, and he sought desperately to heal the broken relationship. God's grace was displayed throughout the deliverance of Israel and the wilderness wanderings. When Moses presented excuses, God dealt with him graciously.

B. *Look at God's present magnanimous act of grace.* Israel stood at a magnificent opportunity after the tragedy of their idolatry. Instead of eliminating Israel, God gave them another chance. God disclosed himself to be the God of grace and mercy to a rebellious people.

III. God shows his greatness.

When God showed himself to Moses, he let him know the limitations on revelation. Because human beings are limited, God cannot show his full greatness. "And he said, Thou canst not see my face: for there shall no man see me, and live" (Ex. 33:20). To behold God face-to-face is to know him absolutely, to exhaust the depth of his being, to remove the vestige of mystery from the being of God.

A. *People have known God's greatness but not all of his greatness.* God taught Moses that he is always the God of the beyond. God directed Moses to a cleft in the rock on Mount Sinai. Here he covered Moses with his hand until he passed by. When he had passed, he removed his hand so that Moses was permitted to see his back but not his face (see Ex. 33:22–23). This teaches us that no person has ever seen God face-to-face, which means that no person has ever apprehended God fully.

B. *People have more to learn about God.* Although we shall never fully understand God, the more we relate to him the more we learn about him.

This should challenge us to see ever greater visions of God. More experiences will continue to teach us the greatness of God.

Conclusion

You can learn about God. God reveals himself as the God of goodness, graciousness, and greatness. You need not fear that you will run out of things to learn about him. But you will learn all you need to know to worship and serve him.

SUNDAY MORNING, DECEMBER 20

Title: Good News of Great Joy

Text: "The angel said to them, 'Be not afraid; for behold, I bring you good news of a great joy which will come to all the people'" **(Luke 2:10 RSV)**.

Scripture Reading: Luke 2:8–14

Hymns: "Rejoice—The Lord Is King!" Wesley
"Great Redeemer, We Adore Thee," Conte
"I Love Thee," Anonymous

Offertory Prayer: Loving Father, we thank you for the rich fellowship we enjoy as a part of your family. We thank you for work to do in and through your church. Bless our efforts to the end that we might be your people in this community, and that we might be the means of bringing light to those who live in darkness. Accept our monetary gifts today that we might share in the work of the church and in the missionary enterprise to the ends of the earth. In Jesus' name we pray. Amen.

Introduction

On this Lord's Day morning immediately before Christmas, many of us are experiencing the joy, peace, and happiness that come during this festive season. On the other hand, many others are experiencing the agony of what is known as the "Christmas blues."

Why is it that some people feel blue at Christmas? There are a number of contributing factors.

1. Some experience depression at Christmastime because they have exaggerated expectations of themselves and others. They hope that Christmas will solve their problems, and when it doesn't, they go into despondency.
2. Christmas brings out our need for dependence on others. At times others fail us, and this can be very depressing.
3. In the United States, Christmas is a family-oriented experience that often causes memories to come to the fore. Some of these blight rather than bless, hurt rather than help.

387

It is highly possible that each of us will come into contact with someone during these next couple of weeks who is experiencing depression. Depression can be detected in one who experiences a serious loss of sleep or appetite. Only those who are alert will recognize this as depression.

It has been suggested that each of us can give psychological first aid to depressed people if we can engage them in meaningful activity, such as volunteering to help someone else. In some instances, we will need to help them alter their goals and their expectations for life. They may need to break down their tasks into little pieces so they can get a firm grip on them. In these ways, we can help those who are depressed feel more hopeful and optimistic.

Alcohol consumption increases during the holiday season. Those who use alcohol as a means of coping with stress and depression find that it does relieve tension temporarily, but it ultimately worsens depression.

Does the message of Christmas, which is supposed to produce great joy, have anything relevant to say to people who are depressed? Christianity, which begins with the promise of good news that will bring great joy, should be more than just a strategy that enables us to cope with the pressures of life. Through the Christ who came at the first Christmas, God provides us with the ability to cope with life in a manner that will bring joy to us and will reflect his glory. The gospel, which is not good advice but good news, can produce great joy in living every day.

The angels who announced the birth of the Christ to the shepherds were bringing good news that continues to be good news for all who will listen and respond.

I. There is good news about God in the gospel.

   A. *The message of Christmas is that the God behind and above it all is a living God.* The Bible does not seek to tell us *when* and *how* our universe came into being. Its major concern is with the *who* and the *why*. The writer of the book of Hebrews declared, "By faith we understand that the world was created by the word of God" (Heb. 11:3 RSV). The message of Christmas speaks to us of a living God who is above and behind the world. He is the God who comes into this world. He wants to dissipate our fears and encourage us to live a life of faith.

   B. *The message of Christmas proclaims the good news about the living God who loves.* In Jesus Christ, the living God declares to us that he cares and that he wants to help us. In Jesus Christ, God came into this world bringing great and precious gifts to humankind.

II. The good news of Christmas is for all people.

The good news of Christmas is universal in its application, for it meets the deepest needs of people of all colors, cultures, and countries.

A. *God in Jesus Christ comes with good news regarding the forgiveness of sin.* Forgiveness does not appear in the glossary of a psychiatric dictionary. The psychiatrist does not have a basis for offering the gift of forgiveness to those who are experiencing depression because they have broken God's law or violated their own conscience. Jesus Christ came that he might bear the penalty of our sin and offer to us the priceless gift of forgiveness.

B. *Jesus Christ brings good news regarding life.* Around the world in every age people have stood in terror before the grim specter of death. Christ came to bring life to those who were in spiritual death because of sin (cf. John 1:4; 10:10; Rom. 6:23). The assurance of a life that endures beyond the curtain that people call death can do much to dispel the gloom that threatens the souls of humans.

C. *Jesus Christ brings good news about belonging to God and to the family of God.* The church is spoken of as the family of God and the household of faith. A warm, wonderful Sunday school class can provide tremendous support for one who is experiencing stress. A genuine Christian friend can be of tremendous value in a time of crisis. In this Christmas season, let us extend hands of Christian love and fellowship to those who are experiencing loneliness and discouragement.

D. *Jesus Christ brings good news regarding help.* Every one of us will stand in need of the help of God and others as time goes by. Paul said, "I can do all things in him who strengthens me" (Phil. 4:13 RSV). The psalmists bore testimony, saying, "My help comes from the LORD, who made heaven and earth" (Ps. 121:2 RSV), and "God is our refuge and strength, a very present help in trouble" (Ps. 46:1 RSV).

E. *The Christ brings to us the good news concerning a precious home at the end of the road (John 14:1–3).* Many home owners consider their home to be their best investment. But there are others who never have the joy of owning a house they can call their own. Through the grace of God and the provisions of his Son, Jesus Christ, all believers can look forward to having a house not made with hands, eternal in the heavens, when this life is over.

Conclusion

In a world in which much bad news is delivered to us each day by the internet, newspapers, radio, and television, let us listen to the good news that comes from God in and through Jesus Christ. Let us individually respond to the full implications of the good news the angels sang about on that first Christmas. Let us trust in Jesus Christ as the promised Messiah who came to meet the deepest needs of our lives. Let us trust in his death for the forgiveness of our sin and in his resurrected and living presence for the gift of eternal life. Let us face life with the resources he promises.

Sunday Evening, December 20

Title: The Ten Commandments for Today

Text: "He was there with the Lord forty days and forty nights; he did neither eat bread, nor drink water. And he wrote upon the tables the words of the covenant, the ten commandments" **(Ex. 34:28).**

Scripture Reading: Exodus 20:1–17

Introduction

Many of today's popular psychologists assert that the Decalogue is just as relevant to people today as when Moses first received it. They support the thesis that a lifestyle based on the Ten Commandments reduces the vulnerability of an individual to mental illness. The Decalogue offers a basis of prevention and a means of cure. These findings should not surprise us. God gave the Ten Commandments to Israel to promote their well-being. Let us notice why the Ten Commandments are needed for today's world.

I. The Ten Commandments reveal a great God (Ex. 20:1–11).

The Ten Commandments are divided into two parts. The first four deal with humankind's relationship with God. Exodus 20:2 serves as a preamble to all of the commandments and shows the kind of God who makes demands. He introduces himself as the Redeemer who brought Israel out of Egypt. We are to recognize the Lord as the following:

A. *An exclusive God.* "Thou shalt have no other gods before me" (Ex. 20:3). The ancient world was full of gods. In Egypt, where the Israelites had lived, the Egyptians worshiped a variety of gods. This commandment discloses the exclusiveness of God; he will not tolerate second place.

B. *A jealous god.* "Thou shalt not make unto thee any graven image, or any likeness of any thing that is in heaven above, or that is in the earth beneath, or that is in the water under the earth: Thou shalt not bow down thyself to them, nor serve them: for I the Lord thy God am a jealous God, visiting the iniquity of the fathers upon the children unto the third and fourth generation of them that hate me; And shewing mercy unto thousands of them that love me, and keep my commandments" (Ex. 20:4–6). The purpose of this commandment is to forbid Israel to make or worship any image of God. It emphasizes God's separateness from all created things. Bringing an image into worship leads to the image taking God's place. The Lord is a jealous God; our allegiance belongs to him.

C. *A guarding God.* "Thou shalt not take the name of the LORD thy God in vain; for the LORD will not hold him guiltless that taketh his name in vain" (Ex. 20:7). This command protects the divine name (Jehovah) from profane use. Whenever one uses the name of God, it should be with thought and reverence. God guards the use of his name against empty and vain purposes.

D. *A God worthy of worship.* "Remember the sabbath day, to keep it holy" (Ex. 20:8). Worshiping God on a special day acknowledges divine ownership. All of time belongs to God. All of the created order belongs to God. Observing one day in seven symbolizes the consecration of all of time. Because God created the world and ordered time, he is a God worthy of our worship.

II. The Ten Commandments have reasonable regulations of human behavior (Ex. 20:12–17).

The first four commandments deal with a person's relationship with a great God. Having a strong relationship with God results in a healthy self-concept and in good relationships with others. The next six commandments give regulations of human behavior.

A. *The protection of the home.* "Honor thy father and thy mother: that thy days may be long upon the land which the LORD thy God giveth thee" (Ex. 20:12). The first duty in the social sphere is the duty toward parents. When this is ignored or abused, the social structure collapses. The family is the foundation of human society.

B. *The sacredness of life.* "Thou shalt not kill" (Ex. 20:13). The Bible teaches a reverence for life. Therefore, taking the life of another by murder is forbidden. Every human life is sacred, and we should honor it.

C. *The sanctity of marriage.* "Thou shalt not commit adultery" (Ex. 20:14). The Bible maintains monogamy as the norm for marriage. That means one man and one woman living together for a lifetime. To violate this intention undermines God's plan and brings injury, grief, guilt, and shame. God urges his people to protect the sanctity of marriage.

D. *The respect for ownership.* "Thou shalt not steal" (Ex. 20:15). The Bible recognizes the right of a person to accumulate material things. Working for personal property is never condemned in Scripture. God ordained a society where people would respect the property of others.

E. *The regard for truth.* "Thou shalt not bear false witness against thy neighbor" (Ex. 20:16). To live together in a happy relationship, society must have truthful people. Others have the right to expect the truth. Nothing so threatens the fabric of society as the disregard of the truth.

F. *The control of inward thoughts.* "Thou shalt not covet thy neighbour's house, thou shalt not covet thy neighbour's wife, nor his manservant, nor his maidservant, nor his ox, nor his ass, nor any thing that is thy neighbour's" (Ex. 20:17). The other commandments have dealt with outward actions. The final commandment deals with inward thoughts. It commands one to control thoughts that would be injurious to another person's life.

Conclusion

The Ten Commandments were handed down to Moses almost 3,500 years ago, yet these ten precepts apply to life in the twenty-first century. If these commandments are applied to life today, they will guarantee self-respect, an obedience to God, and a healthy relationship with other human beings.

WEDNESDAY EVENING, DECEMBER 23

Title: A Significant Symbol—The Tabernacle

Text: "There I will meet with the children of Israel, and the tabernacle shall be sanctified by my glory. And I will sanctify the tabernacle of the congregation, and the altar: I will sanctify also both Aaron and his sons, to minister to me in the priest's office. And I will dwell among the children of Israel, and will be their God. And they shall know that I am the LORD their God, that brought them forth out of the land of Egypt, that I may dwell among them: I am the LORD their God" (**Ex. 29:43–46**).

Scripture Reading: Exodus 35:1–40:38

Introduction

A vital part of a pilot's war training is survival. Pilots face the possibility of being shot by the enemy and having to eject from their airplane. In many cases, pilots have had to land in a deserted area where they needed to know how to survive in a hostile environment. A survival kit is part of a pilot's basic equipment.

God gave Israel a means of survival. The Israelites were destined to wander in the desert from Mount Sinai to the land of Canaan for forty years. They never would have survived the years of wilderness living had not God accompanied them and watched over them day and night. The tabernacle symbolized survival.

Worship is the survival kit for people in the twentieth-first century. It helps us cope with the stresses of our time. Let us notice some important truths the tabernacle teaches.

I. The tabernacle symbolizes God's presence.

The word *tabernacle* means "dwelling place." In Hebrew the word came from a verb that meant "to encamp." The general view of the Old Testament is that the Lord's permanent dwelling place is in heaven, but he "tabernacles" with people. The portable desert tent known as the tabernacle symbolized God's presence.

    A. *God's continual presence.* Two defective ideas about God are common among us today. One sees God as the creator of the universe who walked away from his creation. The second view sees God only as an occasional visitor. He intervenes from time to time in the world's affairs and then withdraws again.

The presence of God in the tabernacle suggested God's continued presence. The Israelites looked at the tabernacle and were assured that God was eternally present with them. Wherever they went, God went with them.

B. *God's comforting presence.* Human beings in today's world have the idea that they can survive life by their own strength. Israel knew that they could not cope with the dangers of the wilderness without divine help. Each time they looked at the tabernacle, they were comforted to know that God lived with them.

Try as we might, we cannot survive in today's world without God's help. We need the Lord who is beyond ourselves.

II. The tabernacle teaches the precepts of God.

The construction of the tabernacle involved intensive preparation: the construction (36:8–38), the making of the ark and the mercy seat (37:1–9), the making of the table for the shewbread (37:10–16), the making of the golden lampstand (37:17–24), the making of the altar of incense (37:25–28), the preparation of incense (37:29), the building of the altar (38:1–7), the making of the laver (38:8), the erection of the court (38:9–20), the sewing of the priestly garments (39:1–31), the blessings of the people for their work (39:32–43), the location of furnishings in their places (40:1–33), and the filling of the tabernacle with God's glory (40:34–38).

A. *The instructions of the Lord.* Another important truth that emerges about the tabernacle is that God gave detailed directions and specifications for its construction. This was because the Lord would use the tabernacle to teach his precepts. We, too, must listen carefully to the instructions of the Lord.

B. *Obedience to the Lord.* One of the aspects of the tabernacle construction is the obedience of the people. Moses said, "This is the thing which the LORD commanded" (Ex. 35:4). From that point onward until the end of Exodus, the reader is amazed to discover the verbs that depict the obedience of the people to the precepts of God.

The only way to survive in today's world is to discover God's will and determine to obey him.

III. The tabernacle utilizes the priests of God.

Attention is given in Exodus to the priests who were to minister at the tabernacle. Chapter 29 is devoted to their ordination. Chapter 39 is devoted to the priestly dress.

A. *The inward cleansing.* The elaborate consecration of the priests recorded in Exodus might cause us to think this does not apply to us. But it does. Before the priests could be involved in service for God, ceremonial washing, robing, and anointing were necessary, which suggests that before one could minister, one must first have in one's own life the experience through which he sought to lead others.

B. *The outward service.* Priests had a variety of functions. They offered sacrifices, made various offerings for the people, burned incense, and related God's word. Regardless of what they did, they did it to glorify God and to help people.

Every Christian is a priest before God. "Unto him that loved us, and washed us from our sins in his own blood, and hath made us kings and priests unto God and his Father" (Rev. 1:5–6). God uses Christians to minister to others.

Survival in today's world depends on Christians being priests. We need to help others, and we need the help given to us from others.

Conclusion

We face survival in an alien world. Like Israel of old, we need to discover the worship of God. When we walk with him, we discover his presence, his will for our lives, and his task for us.

SUNDAY MORNING, DECEMBER 27

Title: Let Us Thank God and Take Courage

Text: "On seeing them Paul thanked God and took courage" (**Acts 28:15 RSV**).

Scripture Reading: Acts 28:11–16

Hymns: "God, Our Father, We Adore Thee," Frazer
"Have Faith in God," McKinney
"Lead On, O King Eternal," Shurtleff

Offertory Prayer: Holy Father, as we come to the last Lord's Day in this year, it is with humility and gratitude that we look back and thank you for the abundance of your blessings on us. We come trusting in your forgiving grace to cleanse us of all our faults and mistakes and sins against you and against others. We come thanking you for letting us walk through this year with you. We thank you for the hope that we have a meaningful and productive life as we face the coming year. Bless these gifts to that end. We pray in Jesus' saving name. Amen.

Introduction

Approaching the end of an era in life is always a solemn occasion. This is true of a student who approaches the completion of a course of study, of an employee who comes to the end of a relationship with an employer, of a professional who finds it necessary to move to a new location to carry on his or her work, and of each of us as we say goodbye to someone or something. And it is also true concerning us as we approach the end of the year.

As we come to the end of this year, let us look back and thank God with gratitude for what he has done. Then let us look forward with faith and hope for what he will continue to be and to do.

Our Scripture reading portrays a significant moment in the life of the apostle Paul. His had been a life of impactful service, with a combination of both successes and failures. His was not a life of perfect performance and total success along the way. There were periods and experiences in his life that could have caused him to go into deep discouragement and depression. Paul had been imprisoned in Caesarea for perhaps two years and had endured a difficult journey from Caesarea to Rome, where he was to face Caesar's court.

We can be certain that Paul was exhausted in body and, at least at times, troubled in mind. We find that in those moments of uncertainty when Paul faced a new era in his life, God provided for him. We read how, when the believers in Rome heard of Paul's approach, they immediately went to meet him. Some of them traveled as far as forty-three miles, and others traveled thirty-three miles. "At the sight of these people Paul thanked God and was encouraged" (Acts 28:15 NIV). The pattern of Paul's actions at this point provides us with a program for facing the coming year.

I. Let us thank God and take courage because God remains the same.

Through Malachi, God spoke to the people and said, "For I the LORD do not change" (Mal. 3:6 RSV). The author of the book of Hebrews spoke of the unchanging Christ as being "the same yesterday and today and for ever" (13:8 RSV).

As we face the uncertain and uncharted road of 2021, we can be certain that God has not changed his character or his purpose nor his promises or provisions. He is the solid Rock in whom we can trust and on whom we can place our feet for safety and security when the storms of life beat down on us. The psalmist declared, "God is our refuge and strength, a very present help in trouble" (Ps. 46:1 RSV).

Individual human beings change. Families change. Businesses change. Nations change. Constant changes always present a threat. In the midst of whatever may threaten us, we can take courage and be strong in the faith that our God who has revealed himself in Jesus Christ will remain the same.

II. Let us thank God and take courage because the Bible continues to nourish us.

Psalm 119 is a hymn of praise to the benefits that come to those who delight themselves in the Word of God, who let God speak to their deepest needs through his law, his teachings, and his promises.

The apostle Peter encouraged all believers to "long for the pure spiritual milk, that by it you may grow up to salvation; for you have tasted the kindness of the Lord" (1 Peter 2:2–3 RSV).

During the past year and in every past year, God has spoken words of guidance and comfort and help to his people as they have feasted on the words of his inspired book, the Bible.

Through studying the Bible, we have found guidance for our feet in times of uncertainty and have found strength for our times of weakness. By meditating on the Word of God, we have received divine warnings in times of danger. By listening to the words of the Bible, we have received divine directions concerning decisions that we were to make. In times of grief and sorrow, we have found the encouragement and the comfort that God has to offer. Let us thank God, as we come to the end of this year, for the benefits that have come to us through Bible study. Let us take courage as we face the future, because the Word of God will continue to speak to us according to our individual needs and on the basis of God's great generosity.

III. Let us thank God and take courage because the Holy Spirit continues the good work of God within us.

One of the most precious promises that our Lord made concerned the permanence of the presence of the Holy Spirit in the hearts of believers. "I will pray the Father, and he will give you another Counselor, to be with you for ever, even the Spirit of truth, whom the world cannot receive, because it neither sees him nor knows him; you know him, for he dwells with you, and will be in you" (John 14:16–17 RSV). Our Lord was contrasting the length of time the Holy Spirit would be present in the hearts of believers with the brevity of his own time with them. He was to depart, but the Holy Spirit was to come as an abiding companion and counselor, to be to them on a permanent basis what Jesus had been for a brief three years.

Let us thank God and take courage as we face the future, because God the Holy Spirit will be at work in us to help us know what God would have us do (Phil. 2:13).

IV. Let us thank God and take courage because the gospel continues to save those who trust Jesus.

As Paul faced the challenge of visiting the capital city of the Roman Empire, he did so with full confidence in the power of the gospel to save any individual who would put faith in Jesus Christ as Lord and Savior (Rom. 1:16). Let us not fear any decrease in the divine energy that is at work in the preaching of the gospel from the pulpit. Let us trust God to help us witness on a one-to-one basis concerning what God has done and what he is seeking to do through Christ.

God is still in the business of saving people from the waste, ruin, and disappointment of life without faith. Let us thank God and take courage as we respond to the truth that people can still be saved.

V. Let us thank God and take courage that God's invitations are still open.

Many people see the Bible only in terms of restrictions and prohibitions. Others see the Bible in terms of orders and commandments. Let us look into the Bible for the thousands of invitations that God extends to us. For example, he invites us to come into the throne room for prayer, he invites us to be a part of his family, and he invites us to be in partnership with him in his redemptive program. Let us discover and respond to the great invitations that he continues to offer.

VI. Let us thank God and take courage because the future belongs to believers in Christ.

We follow a victorious leader who has defeated Satan, sin, death, and the grave. Paul closed his great resurrection chapter of 1 Corinthians 15 with the shout, "Thanks be to God, who gives us the victory through our Lord Jesus Christ" (15:57 RSV). There are times when it seems as if the devil is on the throne and that wickedness rules the universe. In such times, we need with the eyes of faith to see that the decisive battle of history has already been fought and won on a cross and in an empty tomb. Because Christ Jesus lives again, we also shall live with him beyond the curtain of death (John 14:19; Rev. 1:17–18; 14:13).

Conclusion

Paul wrote to the church in Thessalonica, "Give thanks in all circumstances; for this is the will of God in Christ Jesus for you" (1 Thess. 5:18 RSV). If we have thanksgiving for the past, we will have courage to face the future as we enter 2021.

SUNDAY EVENING, DECEMBER 27

Title: The Joy of Restored Relationships

Text: "He said, Behold, I make a covenant: before all thy people I will do marvels, such as have not been done in all the earth, nor in any nation: and all the people among which thou art shall see the work of the LORD: for it is a terrible thing that I will do with thee" **(Ex. 34:10).**

Scripture Reading: Exodus 34:1–35

Introduction

A couple in my church started their marriage with happiness. But with the passing of years, a division came within their relationship. For years they lived in matrimonial misery. Eventually the marriage ended with a divorce. Their miseries did not cease, however. They continued to be as miserable apart from each other as they were together. Both of them came to me.

Over a period of months, I counseled with both of them individually and then together in numerous sessions. Gradually I could see them facing their faults. They admitted personal responsibilities and then later agreed to marry again. Nothing brought me greater joy than to see them begin again and to live together with a greater degree of happiness.

Nothing brought Moses greater sorrow than to see the divorce of Israel and God. The fault was clear: Israel had gone after other lovers. But nothing gave Moses greater joy than discovering that God was willing to restore his relationship with Israel. Restored relationships bring great joys. Let us notice these joys.

I. Restored relationships bring new appreciations (Ex. 34:5–9).

A. *The estrangement.* The Israelites' rebellion brought alienation. God had not changed in his feelings, but Israel's sin had separated them from God. The estranged party felt alone and isolated.

Sin brings estrangement and alienation. One of the horrible results of sin is that it separates us from God.

B. *The appreciation.* To an estranged people, God showed himself. "The LORD, the LORD God, merciful and gracious, longsuffering, and abundant in goodness and truth, Keeping mercy for thousands, forgiving iniquity and transgression and sin" (Ex. 34:6–7). The Israelites came to a new appreciation of God. They discovered that he was gracious and willing to forgive.

Restored relationships bring a new appreciation for the person who forgives. God is to be praised, for he has absorbed the hurt of our rebellion. He has canceled the debt that was against him.

II. Restored relationships bring new obligations (Ex. 34:10–28).

A. *The obligation of exclusiveness.* After God restored relationships with Israel, he reminded them of some obligations. The Lord banned covenant relationships with other religions. They were to maintain a single-minded obedience to the Lord.

Just as marriage relationships are broken when a third party enters, so relationships with God are hindered when a third party enters. "For thou shalt worship no other god: for the LORD, whose name is jealous, is a jealous God" (Ex. 34:14). The Lord demands worship of him alone.

B. *The obligations of obedience.* Having been restored to relationship with his people, the Lord placed the obligation of obedience on Israel. Disobedience had caused their problem. Now the Lord makes the case strong that Israel should obey his will. Included in the Lord's commands are expansions of the first (34:11–16), the second (34:17), and the fourth (34:21) commandments.

Restored relationships bring a new sense of obligation, which causes one to see the reason for the breaking of a relationship. One can assess the situation, make amends, and learn from the experience. Beginning again causes one to be more aware of the obligations within the restored relationship.

III. Restored relationships bring personal transformation (Ex.34:29–35).

A. *Evidence of transformation.* When Moses returned from the mountain, the relationship with God had been restored. Moses' face radiated light, a reflection of the divine glory he had seen on the mountain (34:29–35). To describe the light, the Hebrew text employs a word that means "to send forth horns." Obviously "horns" means "rays." Moses had lived in such communion with God that he had come to reflect God's glory.

Restored relationships bring transformation. When a person experiences communion with God, that person's life is transformed.

B. *Sharing God's glory.* The cause of Moses' shining face was the reflective glory of God in his life. Moses lived in God's presence, and he became like God.

We can live in God's presence and share his glory. Having communion with God will cause us to become like God. We begin to resemble the object of our communion and contemplation.

Conclusion

How is your relationship with God? If it is broken, it can be restored. If it is restored, it can be strengthened.

WEDNESDAY EVENING, DECEMBER 30

Title: Looking Backward and Forward

Text: "Grace and peace be multiplied unto you through the knowledge of God, and of Jesus our Lord" (**2 Peter 1:2**).

Scripture Reading: 2 Peter 1:1–11

Introduction

As we come to the end of one year and approach the beginning of a new year, it would be profitable to take a look backward and count our blessings and then take a look forward and make our plans to cooperate with the Lord,

The first few verses of Peter's second epistle provide us with an opportunity to look at some of the blessings God has bestowed on us in the past. It also provides us with some words of instruction and encouragement to live a life in which we are growing spiritually and serving significantly.

Peter addressed his message "to them that have obtained like precious faith with us through the righteousness of God and our Saviour Jesus Christ" (v. 1:1). He wrote from the perspective of an aged pastor who was living on the edge of eternity. He spoke of his body as a tabernacle, or tent, from which he would soon depart. He referred to his approaching death as his "exodus," or departure—the word used for the departure of the children of Israel from Egypt.

I. The blessings of the past (2 Peter 1:3–4).

The apostle called to the attention of his readers the exceeding great and precious gifts from God to them through Jesus Christ. These two verses are a spiritual treasure chest that reveal the blessings that God has bestowed on believers through Jesus Christ. The generosity of God's provisions for his children is magnified and emphasized.

A. *"All things that pertain unto life and godliness."* In Christ Jesus, believers have received everything necessary for experiencing the abundant life. It is unnecessary for them to turn to any other teacher or discipline to be all God would have them to be.

B. *"Through the knowledge of him that hath called us to glory and virtue."* Through the beauty and the glory of the life and character of Jesus Christ, God calls all people to himself. The initiative belongs with God. Salvation is of the Lord. The human response to the gospel is a voluntary commitment of faith that makes possible the bestowal of these divine gifts.

C. *"The exceeding great and precious promises."* The Bible is a record of God's promises to his people. The Old Testament contains a continuing series of promises concerning the Messiah who was to come. Peter had witnessed the fulfillment of these exceeding great and precious promises in the person and life of Jesus Christ.

Jesus made many promises to his disciples. We will greatly enrich our spiritual life and deepen our faith if we will discover these promises, claim them for our own, and move forward depending on the Lord to keep his promises as people of faith have done in the past.

D. *"That by these ye might be partakers of the divine nature."* Faith in the promises of God makes possible the new birth. The new birth does not produce a divinity in people, but it does mean that the divine character, the divine nature, has been imparted in embryonic form. This new nature provides the believer with the possibility of experiencing and demonstrating the holiness, the tenderness, the gentleness, and the power of God.

By every means at our command, we should cooperate with the Holy Spirit as he seeks to develop the new nature we received in the miracle of the new birth.

E. *"Having escaped the corruption that is in the world through lust."* Through
    their experience with Jesus Christ, believers receive the potential for
    complete deliverance from the powerful evil forces that work in the
    world. Christ has granted forgiveness from sin. He provides spiritual
    power to overcome the contaminating presence of evil in the world.
    Through faith in him and through obedience to him, we can be vic-
    torious over the assaults of the devil.

II. The opportunity of the future (2 Peter 1:5–7).

The gift of new life has been given to those who had put faith in the
promises of God. This new life is like a divine seed that needs to be developed
by earnest care. Spiritual growth will not take place automatically or acciden-
tally. Peter encouraged his readers to hasten with all diligence to cooperate
with the Spirit of God in developing the beautiful graces that are associated
with spiritual maturity.

As we enter a new year, we should give careful consideration to these
words of encouragement from the apostle Peter.

A. *"Giving all diligence, add to your faith."* Faith is the human response to
    God's grace that makes possible the gift of new life. Faith is the basic
    foundation for all spiritual growth and service.

    Peter challenged his readers to supplement their faith with the
    Christian graces that are needed for fruitful Christian living. Seem-
    ingly, each of the graces mentioned grows out of the preceding grace.
    The word translated "add" probably would be more correctly translated
    by the word "supply." This word was used by the Greeks to describe the
    actions of those who provided financial resources for the production of
    the great plays and dramas. It was also used for the action of furnishing
    the provisions and supplies for an army. Peter declared that Christians
    are to supplement their faith with these virtues, which are actually the
    pieces of equipment needed for the living of a genuine Christian life.

    The apostle gave us a blueprint for spiritual progress.

B. *In your faith supply virtue.* Faith makes possible the power by which
    virtue is to be developed. The word *virtue* means courage, moral
    excellence, noble character. It is not tame and passive; it is active,
    aggressive, and on the march.

C. *To virtue supply knowledge.* In the practice of virtue an effort is put
    forth to gain knowledge, which is practical skill in choosing the right
    and refusing the wrong. To secure this knowledge, one must make a
    diligent study of God's Word.

D. *To knowledge supply temperance or self-control.* Self-restraint enables a
    person to curb his evil impulses and resist the lures of sin in the
    world that surrounds him. Each person must be in command of his
    own moods and impulses, or his life will end in ruin.

E. *To temperance supply patience.* The grace needed is endurance, steadfastness, fortitude, perseverance. Patience is that attitude of determination that enables a person to stay under the load until the victory is won.

F. *And to patience add godliness.* Godliness is that trait that characterizes the life of a person who lives continually "as seeing him who is invisible." Perhaps this grace refers to the growth of the divine nature received in the new birth.

G. *To godliness supply brotherly kindness.* The life of reverence for God is issued in brotherly kindness. The genuine worship of God will affect one's attitude toward fellow human beings (1 John 4:20).

H. *To brotherly kindness supply love.* The crown of Christian graces is love. Paul affirmed that love is the chief gift of the Holy Spirit (1 Cor. 13:13). It was concerning Peter's love that the Lord had inquired (John 21:15–17). Peter recognized and commended the believer's love for Christ (1 Peter 1:8) and encouraged love within the Christian brotherhood (1 Peter 1:22).

Conclusion

The apostle Peter was concerned that his readers experience the benefits that flow from spiritual maturity. He was eager that they escape the tragic results of persistent immaturity (1 Peter 2:8–9).

MISCELLANEOUS HELPS

MESSAGES ON THE LORD'S SUPPER

Title: The Savior, Our Daily Bread

Text: "Then Jesus said unto them, Verily, verily, I say unto you, Moses gave you not that bread from heaven; but my Father giveth you the true bread from heaven. For the bread of God is he which cometh down from heaven, and giveth life unto the world. Then said they unto him, Lord, evermore give us this bread. And Jesus said unto them, I am the bread of life: he that cometh to me shall never hunger; and he that believeth on me shall never thirst" **(John 6:32–35)**.

Introduction

In his book *Christ in Your Shoes*, Buckner Fanning told the story of Mrs. Kamilia Michowski of Warsaw, Poland. When he first met her in 1969 in the Baptist church in Warsaw, she was ninety years old. During the World War II German occupation of Poland, Hitler had pushed a half million Jews into a ghetto in which forty thousand people had lived. Fifty thousand died the first month. Mrs. Michowski, a Christian, jeopardized her life by putting on a star of David armband and going into the Jewish ghetto. Thus identifying herself with the people, she would smuggle bread and Bibles into the ghetto, always the two—bread and Bibles. She would distribute a loaf of bread and the Living Bread. Over a hundred people were introduced to faith in Christ because of the bread and the Bibles. She was giving the Bread of Life.

Jesus proclaimed that he was the Bread of Life. John's gospel contains eight great "I am" claims of Jesus. This is the first "I am," and the time when it was made is significant. It was the day after Jesus fed the five thousand. The people wanted to make him king, for if he were king, he would meet all their needs. So the next day they looked for him. After going to where the miracle had been performed, they went back across the Sea of Galilee to Capernaum. There they found him. And there this discussion took place.

Jesus claimed to be the Bread of Life. Bread sustains life.

Jesus taught us in the model prayer to pray for God to give us each day our daily bread. In a real sense, the Savior is our Daily Bread. He sustains our life. As we gather around the Lord's Table to eat this bread, symbolic of his life that was given to us, consider Christ our Savior as our Daily Bread.

403

I. As our Daily Bread, the Savior demands belief.

These people were impressed by what Jesus had done *for* them. Jesus asked them instead to consider what he could do *in* them. They were to believe on him, not just in his power to work miracles.

J. Wallace Hamilton observed that the history of religion has been divided between people who consider religion magical and others who consider it moral. Magical: What it can *do for you*. Moral: What it can do *in* and *through* you. The difference is in the prayer, "God, give me something," or "God, make something of me."

The people wanted a sign. We always want a sign. But Jesus brings us back to himself. We have no sign but him. Belief in Christ is what makes life real and meaningful. For, as Jesus reminded the Tempter, man does not live by bread alone.

II. As our Daily Bread, the Savior is concerned with behavior.

Jesus urged those who followed him not to work for bread that would perish and spoil. He echoed the cry of the prophet in Isaiah 55:2. He challenged them to work for the imperishable food God gives.

How? How can we do right? This is the question of John 6:28: "What shall we do, that we might work the works of God?" They thought in terms of *do*. Jesus again emphasized the need for faith: "This is the work of God, that ye believe on him whom he hath sent" (v. 29). What you do is believe.

They challenged Jesus with the manna Moses gathered. He reminded them that God had sent the manna. Consider the manna a moment: it was something that had to be gathered fresh every morning. This is also true of our Christian life: we start every day fresh with faith.

III. As our Daily Bread, the Savior gives us benefits.

Bread sustains life. And this is what Jesus does for us. Our problem is that we have interpreted life materially while God interprets it spiritually. The prodigal son went off in search of life, but he found the things he wanted in his father's house.

We must see life spiritually. Once Napoleon and an acquaintance were talking about life. It was dark, and they walked to the window and looked out. In the sky were distant stars, little more than pinpoints of light. Napoleon, who had sharp eyes while his friend was dim-sighted, pointed to the sky: "Do you see these stars?" he asked. "No," his friend answered. "I can't see them." "That," said Napoleon, "is the difference between you and me." The man who is earthbound is living half a life. It is the man with the vision, who looks at the horizon and sees the stars, who is truly alive.

Conclusion

At this Lord's Supper service, we realize anew that Jesus is our Daily Bread. This gives sustenance and meaning to life.

Title: The Tableau of the Table

Text: "When Jesus had thus said, he was troubled in spirit, and testified, and said, Verily, verily, I say unto you, that one of you shall betray me" **(John 13:21)**.

Scripture Reading: John 13:21–30

Introduction

Without a doubt, the best-known representation of the Last Supper is Leonardo da Vinci's painting *The Last Supper.* It represents the precise moment that Jesus said, "One of you will betray me." It shows the effect of that word "betray" on the twelve men most closely associated with Jesus during his life and ministry.

The scene is the night of the Passover supper. In a small upper room in Jerusalem, Jesus, surrounded by his disciples, is breaking the bread of their farewell meal. Love, terror, grief, and amazement find expression in the question, "Lord, is it I?" The disciples sit in four groups of three each. In their bewilderment, the disciples have drawn away for the moment, so that Christ sits alone. Each disciple is expressing his feeling in his own way.

The picture was painted on the wall of a monastery dining room in Milan, Italy. Seated at their meal, the brothers of the monastery could look upon the table of Christ as if he were their guest. It is said to be an exact copy of the table, linen, and dishes used by the monks.

The original of da Vinci's *The Last Supper* is nearly lost to us. Its history is a sad one. Being painted in oil, it suffered serious injury from the dampness of the plastered walls. Not many generations had passed before it began to fade. In the seventeenth century, a door was cut into it. During Napoleon's invasion, the hall was used as a military camp and the soldiers amused themselves by throwing bricks at the painting. At one time, the French king Francis I was so impressed with this painting that he bargained for its removal to France. An attempt was made, but the plaster began to crumble and the work of removal was abandoned. Fortunately, Leonardo da Vinci's pupils made many copies of the masterpiece in the earlier years of its history, so there is a complete knowledge of it. It is a well-known tableau of the table at the Last Supper.

Now let's read the passage of Scripture on which it is based: John 13:21–30.

Gathered around the table with the Savior were twelve men. Each had his particular need, his personal character, and his own thoughts.

Gathered around this table today are all of us. Each of us has our particular need, our personal character, and our own thoughts. The tableau of this table would likely reflect some of the same things seen at that first one. With whom would you identify?

I. Those to whom it means nothing.

Judas Iscariot has to be at the bottom of the scale. To him the Last Supper with the Lord meant nothing. He had decided to betray him.

405

But notice this. As Jesus made appeal after appeal to Judas, the other disciples were apparently not aware of what was going on. To them Judas had given the appearance of loyalty and love. Only Jesus knew exactly how he felt.

Some may gather at the table of the Lord on this day, and it means nothing to them. Only you and the Lord know how you feel about it.

II. Those for whom it means examination.

It has always interested me that the disciples were so unsure of their own commitment that they had to ask, "Lord, is it I?"

Simon Peter, impulsive person that he was, tried to find out who would betray the Savior. For him it was a time to examine his own loyalty. Peter was able to channel his energy into effective service.

Paul said that each person ought to examine himself before partaking of the meal (1 Cor. 11:28). It is a time for examination.

III. Those to whom it means love.

The Gospel of John identifies one disciple as "the disciple whom Jesus loved." Usually this is understood to be a cryptic reference to John himself.

Obviously, Jesus loved all the disciples. But there was some special bond of love between Jesus and this disciple. John may have been the person whose love was so strong, so sure, and so certain that he gave Jesus support and affirmation when he needed it. There was no question of his love. He did not have to ask, "Lord, is it I?"

This kind of total commitment in love is necessary for Christ and his church. In the Napoleonic wars, a certain Russian officer was branded with an *N* on his hand after capture. When told this meant that he belonged to Napoleon, he grabbed a hatchet, cut off his hand, and said, "Take what belongs to Napoleon. I belong to the Czar."

IV. Those to whom it means loyalty.

Three disciples are mentioned by name. There were nine others. What of them? They were persons who served with loyalty, faithfulness, and obedience. For the most part, after their choice by Jesus, their names drop out of the gospel record.

Does this mean they dropped out? No, indeed! In every advance for Christianity, they were there. Unsung heroes perhaps, but they were there.

In football, for instance, people know the names of the quarterback and the running backs, but what about those linemen who man the trenches? They are essential to any team and to any victory. The church must have these kind of people.

V. Those to whom it means forgiveness.

Any meditation on the Lord's Supper has to center on Jesus Christ.

For Jesus the supper meant forgiveness. He gave his life so that we can be forgiven of our sins and receive new life. The elements are visual reminders of this. So we have come here today with our sins. What we need is forgiveness. What we need is empathy, someone who can feel with us.

Earnest Campbell told of a friend of his who killed a German soldier in World War II. In some ways, as he tells it, it was an unnecessary killing; at least it was to him. The fact that the victim was an exceedingly youthful man burdened his conscience all the more. Presently he was given a Silver Star for his "achievement." But the star hung heavy on his uniform, and he sought counsel of three different chaplains. Admittedly distraught and beside himself, he walked into the office of the first chaplain, flung the star down on the desk, and said, "Here, justify this!" The chaplain's answer was simply, "Render unto Caesar the things that are Caesar's." My friend grabbed the star and said, "To hell with Caesar!" He went into the quarters of the second chaplain, and the answer there was, "Onward Christian Soldiers." He took the star and went off to the third. "Justify this," said the soldier. The chaplain broke down and cried. Then they wept together. Finally, they prayed. The soldier's question called not for clarity but for empathy.

Conclusion

So we have before us the tableau of the table, the grouping of the people who shared that table with Jesus Christ on that day. And to this day we share this table with Jesus Christ. With which people do you identify: those to whom it means nothing, those to whom it means examination, those to whom it means love, those to whom it means loyalty, or those to whom it means forgiveness?

Title: A Time for Beginning

Text: "And he took the cup, and gave thanks, and said, Take this, and divide it among yourselves: For I say unto you, I will not drink of the fruit of the vine, until the kingdom of God shall come. And he took bread, and gave thanks, and brake it, and gave unto them, saying, This is my body which is given for you: this do in remembrance of me. Likewise also the cup after supper, saying, This cup is the new testament in my blood, which is shed for you" **(Luke 22:17–20)**.

Scripture Reading: Luke 22:14–23

Introduction

We all like new things: the smell of a new car, the feel of a new suit, the thrill of a new challenge, the promise of a new year. And we are so geared to the new that advertisers are convinced the best way to get us to buy something is to show us that it is new. We must believe that new is best.

But today we are gathered here for a very old rite. The observance of the

Lord's Supper is as old as the Christian faith itself. For two thousand years now, Christians have been gathering at the table of the Lord in remembrance of Christ through this memorial meal.

Even though it is old, there is also something eternally new about the Lord's Supper. In Luke's account, Jesus used the word "new" twice. First, he said that this was a last supper for him. No more would he share these elements with them until he drank the wine new in God's eternal kingdom. Then Jesus said that he was making a new covenant with his followers. Jesus' sharing of the bread and wine was the seal of a new promise that God had made with his people through him.

I. A new remembrance of Jesus.

   A. *How would the disciples remember Jesus?* Doubtlessly in many ways: teaching on the mountain, walking by the seashore, healing in the streets, teaching. But this is a new way to remember him. And each time it is repeated it strikes the memory again: Jesus died for me.

   We can't look at this service without the new memory of the Savior. All other things dim except this one remembrance of his love.

William L. Stidger told about a young lad he had baptized as a baby.

> The boy grew up, and when World War II began, he joined the navy. One night his ship came into Boston, and the young man visited the former pastor and friend. During their visit together, Dr. Stidger said, "Bill, tell me the most exciting experience you have had thus far." The boy seemed to hesitate. It wasn't that he had difficulty in selecting the most exciting experience. Rather, the experience he had in mind was so wonderful and sacred that he had difficulty in putting it into words.
>
> He was the captain of a large transport and, along with a convoy, was making his way across the Atlantic. One day an enemy submarine rose in the sea close by. He saw the white mark of the torpedo coming directly toward his transport, which was loaded with hundreds of young men. He had no time to change course. Through the loudspeaker, he shouted, "Boys, this is it!"
>
> Nearby was a little escorting destroyer. The captain of that destroyer also saw the submarine and the torpedo. Without a moment's hesitation, he gave the order, "Full speed ahead." Into the path of the torpedo, the tiny destroyer went and took the full impact of the deadly missile midship. The destroyer was blown apart, quickly it sank, and every crew member was lost.
>
> For a long time, the boy remained silent. Then he looked at his beloved pastor and said, "Dr. Stidger, the skipper of that destroyer was my best friend." Again he was quiet for a while, then slowly he said, "You know there is a verse in the Bible that has

special meaning for me now. It is, 'Greater love hath no man than this, that a man lay down his life for his friends' (John 15:13)."

II. A new responsibility.

A. *We have a new responsibility for Jesus.* If he were no longer to be present on the earth, then his work and his witness would have to be entrusted into the hands of his followers. He could not continue it alone. Someone else would have that responsibility: us.

We have the responsibility to carry on Christ's work.

Dr. S. D. Gordon's imaginary story illustrates our problem perfectly.

He dreamed of the excitement among the hosts of heaven when Christ was preparing to leave the courts of heaven to become the Babe of Bethlehem in an effort to win the world. During the course of the dream, thirty-three years passed quickly and Christ was greeted by the angel Gabriel as he returned to heaven from his earthly mission. Gabriel seemed shocked that Christ had been gone such a short time to have accomplished such a monumental task. Gabriel asked in amazement, "Have you already converted everyone on earth to your heavenly Father?"

Christ responded, "No, Gabriel, in fact, there are only a few of my followers on the earth, but they are going to tell everyone else the good news about me."

"But what if they don't?" Gabriel asked.

Bowing his head, Christ replied, "I have no other plan."

III. A new relationship.

Salvation hinges on the new relationship we have with Christ. That is why he called it a new covenant. It is a relationship of faith. Before, people were related to Christ by law, now by love. We enter this relationship when we give ourselves to him in faith.

Conclusion

Each time we participate in the Lord's Supper, it is as though we begin again. He who makes all things new makes it a new experience with each observance.

MESSAGES FOR CHILDREN AND YOUNG PEOPLE

Title: Growing What You Plant

Text: "Ye shall know them by their fruits. Do men gather grapes of thorns, or figs of thistles? Even so every good tree bringeth forth good fruit; but a corrupt tree bringeth forth evil fruit. A good tree cannot bring forth evil fruit, neither can a corrupt tree bring forth good fruit" (**Matt. 7:16–18**).

Scripture Reading: Matthew 7:15–20

Object: Vegetable seeds

Objective: To show that we grow in our lives those things we cultivate.

Have you ever grown a garden? If you have, there is one thing you know for sure: you grow only what you plant. If you plant corn, you won't grow beans. And if you plant peas, you won't grow tomatoes.

One spring when I was young, about the same size as some of you, the little neighbor girl and I decided that we would grow a garden. So we got out a shovel and hoe and rake and prepared a garden. We dug up a space in the backyard about six feet long and three or four feet wide, pulled all of the grass out of it, and prepared it for planting.

Then we gathered up everything that we could find for seeds. As I recall, we had various kinds of beans, some peas, and some corn. When we planted these seeds, we just stuck them around in the dirt rather than planting them in rows. We did not have all the beans at one place or all the peas at another place. They were all mixed in together in our garden plot.

Some of that garden came up. And it was the biggest mess you have ever seen. There was no order to it. It was almost like harvesting corn. That is a law of nature: you grow what you plant.

That is also a law of life: you grow in your life only those things that you plant in your life. If you put into your life hate, darkness, and bad things, there is no way in this world that you can develop a life with love, light, and good things. What you sow in your life you will reap in your life.

Jesus mentioned that in the Sermon on the Mount. He said, "Ye shall know them by their fruits. Do men gather grapes of thorns, or figs of thistles? Even so every good tree bringeth forth good fruit; but a corrupt tree bringeth forth evil fruit. A good tree cannot bring forth evil fruit, neither can a corrupt tree bring forth good fruit. Every tree that bringeth not forth good fruit is hewn down, and cast into the fire. Wherefore by their fruits ye shall know them" (Matt. 7:16–20).

So you need to be very, very careful about what you plant in your life. What you put into your life is what you will get out of your life in personality and character. Plant a good garden. Cultivate Christian graces and virtues. Your life will be much better because of it.

Title: Why a Cross?

Text: "God forbid that I should glory, save in the cross of our Lord Jesus Christ, by whom the world is crucified unto me, and I unto the world" (**Gal. 6:14**).

Object: Cuff links shaped like a cross; a cross

Objective: To show the meaning of the cross to our lives.

I have a set of silver cuff links that I often wear. This particular set of cuff links has a Crusader's cross, or what is sometimes called the Jerusalem cross, on them. This is a cross whose arms are the same length. The Crusader's cross, or Jerusalem cross, is the symbol of the city of Jerusalem.

This set, made of Israeli silver, was given to me by some friends in Jerusalem. Whenever I wear these cuff links, I think of my friends, of the interesting city of Jerusalem, and of Jesus who died on a cross in Jerusalem many years ago.

A cross is a common sight. Many churches have a cross in front or on a steeple above. We have a cross in the stained-glass window on each side of the baptistery in our church. Some of you probably have a cross on a chain around your neck as a necklace.

Why do we pay so much attention to a cross? Why do we have crosses all around us like this? What is so important about the cross anyway?

I gave you a hint for the answer to this question when I said that every time I wear my cross cuff links I think of a cross in Jerusalem many years ago. Jesus died on a cross, and his death on the cross has a very special meaning. When Jesus died on the cross, it was not just that someone had died. That is always sad. But it was that a special someone—Jesus Christ, the Son of God—had died for a very special reason—to take the blame for our sins.

All of us have sinned. That means that we have done some things that aren't right. And there are some things that we should have done that we have not done.

It was for payment of our sins, for our forgiveness, that Jesus died. When Jesus died on the cross, it was not because of the wrong he had done but because of the wrong we have done. Our sins are forgiven and we are made clean from our wrongs by Jesus' death on the cross.

The apostle Paul once said, "May I never boast except in the cross of our Lord Jesus Christ, through which the world has been crucified to me, and I to the world" (Gal. 6:14 NIV). The cross shows a lot to us about God's love and God's action for us through Christ.

Title: The Lord Is My Shepherd

Text: "The Lord is my shepherd; I shall not want" (**Ps. 23:1**).

"I am the good shepherd: the good shepherd giveth his life for the sheep" (**John 10:11**).

Object: Carved figurine of a shepherd

Objective: To show how God cares for us as a shepherd cares for his sheep.

I keep on my office desk a little hand-carved figurine of a shepherd. Made of olive wood and carved in Bethlehem, the city of the Savior's birth, it is about six inches high. It shows a shepherd with a look of tenderness on his face and a lamb across his shoulders. He is a good shepherd.

The Bible says a lot about sheep and shepherds. In the land where the Bible was written, a lot of people kept sheep. Shepherds took care of these sheep.

King David was a shepherd before he was the king of Israel. He also wrote songs and poems. His best-known and best-loved poem is Psalm 23. It begins by saying, "The Lord is my shepherd" (Ps. 23:1).

Jesus also told his disciples, "I am the good shepherd" (John 10:11).

Now let's think just a minute about why the Old Testament and the New Testament tell us that the Lord is our Shepherd. I think it must be because God is good. God is good, and God loves us. In the Middle East, the flocks of sheep were often small. The shepherd would give each sheep a name. The shepherd then knew each one of his sheep by name. He loved the sheep and was good to them.

God loves us too. The Bible tells us that God knows each one of us. Each of us is precious to God. God shows his goodness to us in many ways. He lets us live. He gives us a world in which to live. He sends rain and sunshine to our world. God is like a shepherd to us because he is good to us.

And we can say that the Lord is our Shepherd because he guides us. When you deal with animals, you can either lead them or drive them. The Judean shepherd would lead his sheep to water or to good grass. God guides us through the Holy Spirit. He guides us to the good things for us. He guides us to do the good things we ought to do.

The Lord is also our Shepherd because God guards us. Shepherds have to protect their sheep from harm because wild animals try to kill them. Through his love and care, God guards us from the things that would harm us.

We can say that the Lord is our Shepherd. And we can know that Jesus is the Good Shepherd. In doing this, we do not actually mean that we are sheep and God is a shepherd. It is a way of saying that God loves and cares for us like a shepherd cares for his sheep.

FUNERAL MEDITATIONS

Title: Christ's Commendation (Funeral Service for a Minister)*

Text: "His lord said unto him, Well done, thou good and faithful servant: thou hast been faithful over a few things, I will make thee ruler over many things: enter thou into the joy of thy lord" **(Matt. 25:21, 23)**.

Introduction

After service on a denominational board or committee, or as an officer of an organization, a minister often receives a plaque as a commendation from the denomination or organization.

---

* This order of service uses the masculine gender for convenience, but the pronouns can easily be changed if the service is for a woman.

Someone may remark about a particularly strong aspect of one's ministry. That may be a commendation by a Christian.

Many times during a man's ministry someone may say to him, following a sermon or a visit, "That was a good message," "That helped me," or "Thanks for being here." That is a commendation from the congregation.

But I think today of the commendation from Christ: "Well done, thou good and faithful servant" (Matt. 25:21, 23).

This brother has completed both his life and his ministry. And we think of many things at this time. But most of all, we think of Christ's commendation: "Well done, thou good and faithful servant."

The end of a Christian minister's life is marked by the same faith that sustained it. The context in which Jesus spoke the words "Well done, thou good and faithful servant" was a parable concerning his return. It is one of the parables that teaches faithfulness. The lord had given to each of three servants varying talents to use while he was gone. On his unannounced return, he called each of them to account for his use of the talents.

A talent was a sum of money. Two had used what had been entrusted to them and had returned dividends on the investment. To them the master said, "Well done, thou good and faithful servant."

Our brother has invested his life in the ministry for Jesus Christ. There have been dividends through the years. His ministry was not a talent that was buried in the ground. His talent was put to use in the marketplace of human needs and spiritual demands. His investment has brought eternal dividends. For this our Master says, "Well done, thou good and faithful servant."

What is involved in Christ's commendation?

I. Christ's commendation involves communication.

To the servants, the master communicated a commendation: "Well done." This commendation communicates to us at least two things.

A. *God's promises.* We know well the promise of the Savior. These promises ring true to us today. "Come unto me, all ye that labour and are heavy laden, and I will give you rest" (Matt. 11:28).

"Let not your heart be troubled: ye believe in God, believe also in me. In my Father's house are many mansions: if it were not so, I would have told you. I go to prepare a place for you" (John 14:1–2).

"Peace I leave with you, my peace I give unto you: not as the world giveth, give I unto you. Let not your heart be troubled, neither let it be afraid" (John 14:27).

B. *God's presence.* But even more meaningful than God's promises is God's presence. This day we are very much aware of God's presence with us, giving strength, grace, help, and hope. Jesus himself said, "Lo, I am with you alway, even unto the end" (Matt. 28:20).

II. Christ's commendation indicates completion.

When the master commended the servants, they had completed their tasks. Knowing that they had completed their tasks, the master opened to them even greater responsibilities.

Our friend completed many things. He completed his formal education but continued his study. He completed a pastorate in a particular church but continued in the pastorate at other places. Perhaps he was never given the opportunity to serve God in the big places, the prestigious pulpits, or the spotlight of public attention, but he always faithfully served in that corner of God's vineyard where he was placed. His service and his faithfulness are worthy of note.

He completed his time as an active minister and retired in ministry. And now he has completed life. But even though life, as we know it, is completed here on earth, this is not the end. Death is *an* end but not *the* end. Opened up for this faithful brother are even more opportunities for service, for praise, for the enjoyment of Christ's presence.

Life and ministry have been completed, and the Master says, "Well done."

III. Christ's commendation includes comfort.

After saying, "Well done, thou good and faithful servant," the master said, "Enter thou into the joy of thy lord." This is the word of comfort we have now. We can know the fullness of the joy of the Lord.

We are confident that our brother is in the presence of Christ. He can know the joy of the Lord without the impediments of a weakened body or a sickened system. This is the comfort of Christ. Joy is a part of the Christian life. Greater joy is known in unfettered fellowship.

Comfort is one of the by-products of faith. Great comfort is found in God's presence and is experienced by those who are left here. The God of all comfort will surely comfort us in this hour as well as in the days ahead.

Conclusion

Christ's commendation rings in our ears this day: "Well done, thou good and faithful servant . . . enter thou into the joy of thy lord." It gives to us both assurance in our time of sorrow and awareness of the dimensions of God's grace. This commendation points us to our Savior, to whom we would look for power and strength in this hour.

Title: Easter Assurances

Text: "Now if Christ be preached that he rose from the dead, how say some among you that there is no resurrection of the dead? But if there be no resurrection of the dead, then is Christ not risen: And if Christ be not risen, then is our preaching vain, and your faith is also vain" (**1 Cor. 15:12–14**).

Scripture Reading: 1 Corinthians 15:12–19

Introduction

Something about a funeral service right after Easter seems out of place. Easter is the time when we think of new life, of renewal. Easter is the time when we focus on resurrection. And now we are gathered here for a funeral service. It seems to negate the promises of Easter.

But look again. The Easter season is the time when we think of the meaning of death and the reality of the resurrected life. Life is what is on our minds at Easter as we focus on the resurrection of Jesus Christ and its assurance that we shall be raised from the dead also.

When we consider the Easter promises, we are able to face this time of sorrow and loss with the strength of God's grace. We are reminded by Easter that love is stronger than hate, that life is stronger than death, and that hope is stronger than sorrow. We have some definite assurances at Easter.

We come to this funeral service as Christians. We can witness to the grace and strength of the God whom we trust and serve. First Corinthians 15:19 expresses something of the Easter hope for us: "If in this life only we have hope in Christ, we are of all men most miserable." We usually interpret this to mean that we have hope, not only in this life but also in a life to come. And that is right.

But I recently read another interpretation. It was that if we *only* had hope, we were of all men most miserable. But it is not just *hope* that we have; we have *assurance*. And this assurance is because of the resurrection of Christ.

What are the Easter assurances?

I. The reality of the resurrection.

We celebrate Easter because Jesus was raised from the dead. We have the Easter assurance of the reality of the resurrection. What we have celebrated at this time is real.

God has power over death. Paul once described death as the final foe we face in life. But the resurrection of Jesus Christ assures us that we can defeat that final foe. We will be raised from the dead to defeat death and to live eternally with God.

II. The strength of love.

Another Easter assurance is the strength of love. Love is stronger than death. God's love sustains us now. Without the sustaining, strengthening love of God, we could hardly face this hour. But the resurrection that we have just celebrated assures us of this love, both in this hour and in the days of adjustment that will come.

III. The hope of heaven.

The hope of heaven is another of the Easter assurances that we claim on this day. Jesus said that he would go and prepare a place for us. That place is heaven. The resurrection gives witness to the fact that he will carry out that promise. Jesus also said that he would take every Christian there to share eternity with him. Heaven is described as a place of rest, peace, and no pain. Each of these features appeals to one who has faced many problems and painful situations in life yet has faced them with strength and hope in this same Savior. Above all, heaven is where we will be in God's presence.

Conclusion

The Easter assurances are real assurances. In this time of sorrow, grief, and loss, we turn to them for comfort, strength, help, and hope. But beyond them we look to the God who gave them to us. It is to him that I point you at this time.

Title: Our Adequate and Abiding Shelter

Text: "For thou hast been a shelter for me, and a strong tower from the enemy" (**Ps. 61:3**).

Scripture Reading: Psalm 61:1–8

Introduction

The storms of life blow over us unceasingly. They may be storms of difficulty, trouble, sickness, loneliness, or death. We seek to find a shelter, a refuge, from these storms. As they blow over us, we turn to One who can give us help and hope. Our adequate and abiding shelter is God. The psalmist once said of God, "For thou hast been a shelter for me, and a strong tower from the enemy" (Ps. 61:3). The psalmist called to God in his time of need. He expressed his desire and need for shelter. Physical shelters do not always give us refuge. Our spiritual shelter does. In your need now of a shelter, look to God, who is our adequate and abiding shelter.

I. Petition (Ps. 61:1–2).

The psalmist called out for God to hear his prayer.

There are two reasons for our petition to God. First: we are at "the end of the earth," at our spiritual, not geographical, extremity. When we go as far as we can alone, then we go to God. Second: our "heart is overwhelmed." At a time of uncertainty, insecurity, need, we call to God. Our request is "Lead me to the rock that is higher than I." We need God's protection. This is our petition to God this day.

II. Promise (Psalm 61:3–7).

God has given his promise that he will hear our prayer and deliver us. God has done this so many times in the past. Knowing this, we are assured that he will continue to be with us. Throughout all of life, we know that we have shelter and strength in God. Jesus invited the weak and heavy laden to come to him. In our present need, this is our promise.

God gives us two things to uphold us: mercy and truth. The Revised Standard Version translates these as "steadfast love" and "faithfulness." Whatever we need, God stands by us with mercy and truth. This is his promise.

III. Praise (Psalm 61:8).

Our response is praise and promise. We will praise God for what he has done. We will keep our promises to him who kept his promises to us.

Conclusion

In this time of need, we turn to God and draw strength from him. As he shares his love to give strength, comfort, hope, and help, he will prove to us in every way that he is our adequate and abiding shelter.

WEDDINGS

Title: A Christian Wedding Gives God First Place

The presentation

God saw that it was not good for man to live alone. He created woman so that life could be shared. _____ and _____ have come at this time to pledge their lives to one another that life and love may be shared together. Who now gives this woman to be wed?

Father: Her mother and I.

The body

At the time of his marriage to Eve, Adam said, "This is now bone of my bones, and flesh of my flesh" (Gen. 2:23). God's Word says, "Therefore shall a man leave his father and his mother, and shall cleave unto his wife: and they shall be one flesh" (Gen. 2:24). This same expression is found at two other places in the Scripture, quoted by both Jesus and the apostle Paul.

In establishing your home, you are indeed forsaking all others to pledge your love and your devotion to one another. Life lived together can be richer, happier, and more fulfilling than life lived alone. To each other you will express the fullness of your love.

As Christians in a Christian wedding, you are aware of the place of God in your lives and in your new home. Well does the psalmist say, "Except the LORD build the house, they labour in vain that build it" (Ps. 127:1). Make God a part of your lives, and give him a dominant place in your home.

Your love for one another should be a reflection of God's love for you. Love indeed "beareth all things, believeth all things, hopeth all things, endureth all things" (1 Cor. 13:7).

So if you are assured that there are no legal, moral, or religious barriers hindering this proper union, and you are now willing to enter this holy commitment of Christian marriage, will you please join your right hands.

The vows

Groom: I, _____, take thee, _____, as my lawful wedded wife; to have and to hold from this day forward. I promise to love and cherish you, to honor and sustain you, in the bad that may darken our days, in the good that may light our ways, in sickness as in health, in poverty as in wealth, for better or for worse, and forsaking all others, to be true to you in all things until death alone shall part us.

Bride: I, _____, take thee, _____, as my lawful wedded husband; to have and to hold from this day forward. I promise to love and cherish you, to honor and sustain you, in the bad that may darken our days, in the good that may light our ways, in sickness as in health, in poverty as in wealth, for better or for worse, and forsaking all others, to be true to you in all things until death alone shall part us.

The ring ceremony

_____, do you bring a gift as a token of your love for _____?

Groom: Yes.

The ring is a simple band that is unending. Made of gold, it is precious. As you give these rings to one another, you are reminded that your love, too, should be unending and precious. As you place the ring on the ring finger of the left hand, please hold it for the following questions:

Do you, _____, give this ring to _____ as a token of your love for her?

Groom: I do.

Will you, _____, accept this ring as a token of _____'s love for you, and will you wear it as an expression of your love for him?

Bride: I will.

And now, _____, what gift do you bring as a token of your love for _____?

Bride: A ring.

Do you, _____, give this ring to _____ as a token of your love for him?

Bride: I do.

Will you, _____, accept this ring as a token of _____'s love for you, and will you wear it as an expression of your love for her?

Groom: I will.

The pronouncement

_____ and _____ have pledged their love to each other. They have expressed their faith in each other. They have vowed to spend their lives together in Christian marriage. They have exchanged the rings as a token of their mutual love.

Therefore, by the authority vested in me as a minister of the gospel, I now pronounce _____ and _____ husband and wife.

Let us pray that they will ever keep these vows sacred, and let us remember that "what God hath joined together, let no man put asunder."

Prayer

Title: The Basis of a Christian Marriage Is Love

Message

The oldest of all human institutions is the home. Before the church, before the school, before parliaments and government, God established the home.

The first marriage ceremony was performed in the beautiful garden of Eden, where golden-throated birds provided the music and angels were the witnesses of the wonderful scene. There Jehovah God brought the woman, whom he had made, to the man, whom he had made, to be the man's wife. _____, do you now bring your daughter, _____, to give her in marriage to this man?

Father: I do.

The occasion of a marriage is one of the happiest occasions known to humankind. At this time, two people are brought together to pledge before their heavenly Father and all the assembled witnesses their desire for fellowship, companionship, love, and mutual endeavor. The marriage relationship is much more beautiful when the young people both come with a firm belief in God and a trust in God to guide their way. This should then be expressed in a desire to serve God.

The nature of marriage was expressed at the time of Adam's marriage to Eve in the garden of Eden: "Therefore shall a man leave his father and his mother, and shall cleave unto his wife: and they shall be one flesh" (Gen. 2:24). This so well expresses the unique nature of marriage that both Jesus and the apostle Paul quote it. When two people marry, they become one flesh. This is a physical union. But it is much more than that. It is a spiritual union. Becoming a spiritual union means that when two become one flesh, they also become one in thought, in intent, in purpose, and in all the concerns of this present life.

But this union is also an exclusive union. As you become one in marriage, your prime concern is now for your loved mate and your family.

The basis of marriage is love. This is to be the type of love that doesn't think of itself, but rather expresses itself in concern, consideration, dedication, and devotion. This is a love so strong that it can overcome all obstacles. In joys and victories, in defeats and frustrations, in adjustments and routine, this is the love that undergirds it all and ties it all together. This love, as expressed in marriage, completes personalities and lives. For both partners, it should bring a new fullness, a new satisfaction, a new contentment into life.

Marriage, then, is the oldest of all institutions and the most honored of all institutions. It is a divine institution. And so, today, you found your home. The very basis of our entire way of life is built on the home. Children come to bless it and to grow up according to the beliefs and practices of their parents. Jesus visited in homes and honored them. Paul tells the husband to love his wife as Christ loved the church and gave himself for it, and the wife to be faithful to her husband even as the church is obedient to Christ in everything. You will want to make Christ a dominant figure in your home. Prayer and family worship will help to give the strength, peace, and power to make your home a home where Christian values and virtues are ever held uppermost.

So if you, _____ and _____, having chosen each other as partners in this holy estate, being assured that no legal, moral, or religious barrier hinders this proper union, are now ready to enter this holy union, will you please join your right hands.

Vows

Groom: I, _____, take you, _____, as my lawful wedded wife; to have and to hold from this day forward. I promise to love and cherish you, to honor and sustain you, in the bad that may darken our days, in the good that may light our ways, in sickness as in health, in poverty as in wealth, for better or for worse, and forsaking all others, to be true to you in all things until death alone shall part us.

Bride: I, _____, take you, _____, as my lawful wedded husband; to have and to hold from this day forward. I promise to love and cherish you, to honor and sustain you, in the bad that may darken our days, in the good that may light our ways, in sickness as in health, in poverty as in wealth, for better or for worse, and forsaking all others, to be true to you in all things until death alone shall part us.

Ring ceremony

_____, what gift do you bring as a token of your love for _____?

Groom: A ring.

Pastor: Then place it on her ring finger.

From the earliest of times, the ring has been used to seal important covenants. Kings at one time wore rings upon which were fixed the seal of state, and its stamp was the sole sign of imperial authority. Friends often exchanged simple bands of gold as a token of friendship and goodwill. The wedding ring is made of gold, that metal which is purest and least tarnishable. The ring forms an unbroken circle, which means that it is measureless. We trust that your love shall be as the ring: pure, untarnishable, unbroken, measureless.

Do you, _____, give this ring to _____ as a token of your love for her?

Groom: I do.

Will you, _____, take this ring as an expression of _____'s love for you, and will you wear it as a token of your love for him?

Bride: I will.

_____, what gift do you bring as a token of your love for _____?

Bride: A ring.

Pastor: Then place it on his ring finger.

Do you, _____, give this ring to _____ as a token of your love for him?

Bride: I do.

Will you, _____, take this ring as an expression of _____'s love for you, and will you wear it as a token of your love for her?

Groom: I will.

And now as you rejoin your right hands, I would remind you of your responsibilities to each other as husband and wife. The life that lies ahead of you can be made much more meaningful if you approach it in harmony and mutual love. Surely you will each support the other in sacrifice, reverence, and love.

You have pledged your faith in, and your love to, each other. You have sealed your vows by giving and receiving the rings. Now I, by the authority vested in me as a minister of the gospel by the laws of the state of _____, and by the Word of God, and looking to heaven for divine sanction, do pronounce you husband and wife in the presence of God and all of these witnesses. Let us all take care that this holy covenant shall ever remain sacred, for "what God hath joined together, let no man put asunder."

Prayer

Sentence Sermonettes

TRUSTING IN GOD

Faith will not make the sun rise sooner, but it will make the night seem shorter.

I am not too small for God's attention.

"Trust in the Lord with all our heart" means taking God at his word without any back talk.

The beginning of faith is the end of anxiety.

God's people never meet for the last time.

God delights to disappoint man's fears.

When we look within us, we are depressed. When we look around us, we are impressed. But when we look at Jesus Christ, we are blessed.

Because Christ lives, we have no reason to fear the future.

The valley of the shadow of death holds no darkness for the child of God.

When you are in the furnace, remember God knows how much heat to turn on.

The only thing in the world that is more powerful than fear is faith.

Life with Jesus is an endless hope, but without Jesus life is a hopeless end.

When you cannot sleep, instead of counting sheep, talk to the Shepherd.

No problem is too big for God's power, and no person is too small for God's love.

Nothing lies beyond the reach of prayer except that which lies outside the will of God.

By a Carpenter humankind was made, and only by that Carpenter can humankind be remade.

Worry is a tool used by Satan to separate us from the peace of God.

GETTING ALONG WITH OTHERS

The man who rows the boat usually does not have time to rock it.

Cutting comments create hostility.

No act of kindness, no matter how small, is ever wasted.

The Golden Rule never tarnishes.

If you were another person, would you like to be a friend of yours?

A house is made of brick, but a home is made of love.

A smile is the light in your face that tells everyone your heart is at home.

There is no exercise better for the heart than reaching down and lifting people up.

He who cannot forgive others destroys the bridge over which he himself must pass.

A true follower of Jesus will use a map that includes the whole world and all the people in it.

God gave us two hands: one with which to receive and the other with which to give.

Your love for humankind has a broken wing if it cannot fly across the sea. An act of kindness is the shortest distance between two hearts.

Does your walk match your talk as a Christian?

Blessed are those who can give without remembering and receive without forgetting.

DEVELOPING CHARACTER

The start is important, but it is the finish that counts.

Our failure to speak out is often a sign of giving in.

Our attitude determines our altitude.

One courageous thought will put to flight a host of troubles.

It is the spirit of old age that determines whether it be a nightmare or a golden sunset.

No sin is small.

To go bravely forward is to invite a miracle.

There is no sunset to a Christian's life.

In the straight and narrow way, the traffic is all one way.

Do you possess or are you possessed by your possessions?

You can be too big for God to use, but you cannot be too small.

Each day is a little life; fill it with hours of gladness if your can—with courage if you cannot.

Today is yours; use it kindly.

Prevent truth decay; read your Bible every day.

Life is like a ladder—every step we take is either up or down.

Subject Index

administration, 127–129, 372
advice, 13–14, 54, 165, 321, 372, 388
apostleship, 82–83, 163, 243

Beatitudes, the, 23–27, 31–34, 47–49, 54–57, 61–64, 68–71, 298–301
belief, 14, 149, 164, 169–170, 184, 213, 216, 368, 404, 419
body, the, 24, 72–73, 96, 122, 135, 238, 344–348, 417; of Christ, 52, 81, 92, 135, 138–141, 150, 153, 164, 238
born again, 151, 159, 160–163, 226, 251, 258, 265, 271, 279

Christ. *See* Jesus
Christians, 14, 24, 43, 44, 52, 56, 58, 63, 69, 74–75, 105, 115, 121, 132, 146, 148, 170–171, 182–184, 277–278, 283–284, 408; living as, 13, 31, 55, 71, 95–96, 104, 115, 128–129, 130, 134, 137, 140–141, 148–150, 154, 228, 230, 245, 270–272, 290–292; new birth of, 43, 55, 58, 73, 79–80, 93, 97, 99, 101, 127, 149, 160–163, 168, 217, 242, 255, 400, 402
Christmas, 192, 328, 370–402
church, the, 30–31, 129–133, 138–141, 147–150, 185–188, 196, 197, 300–301, 276–278; salvation and, 79–82
consecration, 270–272
counterfeit Christianity, 230–231, 237–239, 244–245
covenant, 201–203, 208–209, 257, 294–296, 334, 378–380, 397–399, 409

cross, the, 104–107, 116–118, 410–411

death, 412–414; of Christ, 28–29, 111–116
discernment, 175–177
discipleship, 81, 87, 104–108
discouragement, 181, 325–326, 351, 395
doubt, 135, 216, 285, 287–290, 298, 333–335, 355

encouragement, 20, 36, 89, 122, 136–138, 179–182
evangelism, 38, 154, 159–160
exhortations to Christians, 95, 164, 177, 215–217, 221-223, 228–229

faith, 19, 29, 33, 36, 45, 60, 65, 93–94, 101, 103, 106, 108, 112, 176
family of God, the, 36, 72, 102, 129–133, 150, 161, 168, 252, 278, 293, 383, 389
fatherhood, 36, 124, 162, 191–194, 204–287
fellowship, 26 ,28, 40 ,62, 66, 82, 84, 92, 100–101, 124, 150, 161–162, 167–169, 217–219, 223–225
forgiveness, 26, 29, 47, 49, 54, 66, 69, 80, 85–86, 89, 92, 132, 134, 174, 218, 244, 247, 321–325

gifts of the Spirit, 52–53, 66–67, 82–83, 87–89, 95–97, 103–104, 111–113, 119–120, 127–129, 136–138, 144–146, 153–154, 159–160, 165–167, 171–172, 178–179, 190–191, 196–197

giving, 37–39, 144–146, 362–367
God, 267–270, 309–311, 334, 380;
  glory of,372–375, 112; grace of,
  209–210, 280–283, 385–387;
  as helper, 44–46, 394–397;
  as leader,131–132, 292–294;
  providence of, 45, 292–294;
  reassurance of, 209, 242–244, 282,
  333–335; Spirit of, 60, 78, 100,
  148, 303–306, 382; as tabernacle,
  202, 311–314, 373, 392–394; will
  of, 249–251, 273–276; work of,
  295–298, 318–321
grace, 86–87, 126, 229, 246–249,
  280–283, 372–375

happiness, 39–42, 41–42, 54–57,
  61–64, 68–71
healing, 111–113
heaven, 29, 51–52, 168, 212–215,
  315–316
helping, 119–120
heritage, 73, 189, 301–303
Holy Spirit, the,16, 35–36, 43, 60–61,
  75; community and, 147–150
hope, 141, 154, 216–217, 242–244,
  415–416
household, 36, 186, 389
humility, 15-17, 66, 83, 158, 314–316,
  331, 333
hunger and thirst, 39–42

Jesus, 83–86; Apostle and High
  Priest, 163–165, 175–177, 188–190,
  194–494; challenge from, 164,
  182–184, 222–223; death of,
  111–116; Divine Stranger, 173–175;
  God's messenger, 150–152;
  humiliation of, 157–159; as leader,
  360–362; as light, 210–212; the
  living God, 164, 208–210, 300,
  388; as Lord, 37, 43, 60–61, 78–79;
  the Mediator, 123, 135, 194–196;
  promises of, 219–221; rest and,

169–171; resurrection of, 120–123,
  141–144; the Rock, 183, 395; as
  temple, 89–93; as testator, 201–203
Joseph (husband of Mary), 191–194

knowledge, 178–179

Lamb of God, the, 76–79, 90, 190, 382
living for today, 14
Lord's Supper, the, 403–409
love, 206–208, 272–273, 311–314,
  419–421

Mary (mother of Jesus), 154–156, 321
meekness, 31–34
mercy, 47–49, 153–154
miracles, 103–104, 184, 310
mission, 77, 123–147
money, 362–367
motherhood, 154–156

neutrality, dangers of, 259–262

obedience, 44, 74, 164, 224, 284,
  311–314, 335, 377, 398–399
optimism, 242–244, 303–306. *See
  also* hope.

Passover, the, 77, 91, 98, 114,
  331–333, 352–353, 405–407
peace, 380–383
peacemaking, 14, 49, 75, 221, 61–64
perfection, 182–184, 259
persecution, 68–71, 227, 236–237,
  274, 294, 303, 326
Peter, 235–237, 298–301, 306–309,
  314–316, 321–324, 331–333,
  340–342, 349–351, 357–360
power of God, the, 103, 182, 249–251,
  294, 299, 301, 317, 400
praise, 13, 75, 169, 188, 223, 343,
  383–385, 417
prayer, 20, 36, 59, 64–66, 80, 112,
  188, 226, 229, 322, 340

Index of Scripture Texts